After Putin's Russia

After Putin's Russia

Past Imperfect, Future Uncertain

Fourth Edition

Edited by Stephen K. Wegren and
Dale R. Herspring

ROWMAN & LITTLEFIELD PUBLISHERS, INC.
Lanham • Boulder • New York • Toronto • Plymouth, UK

ROWMAN & LITTLEFIELD PUBLISHERS, INC.

Published in the United States of America
by Rowman & Littlefield Publishers, Inc.
A wholly owned subsidary of The Rowman & Littlefield Publishing Group, Inc.
4501 Forbes Boulevard, Suite 200, Lanham, Maryland 20706
www.rowmanlittlefield.com

Estover Road, Plymouth PL6 7PY, United Kingdom

British Library Cataloguing in Publication Information Available

Library of Congress Cataloging-in-Publication Data

After Putin's Russia : past imperfect, future uncertain / edited by Stephen K.
   Wegren and Dale R. Herspring. — 4th ed.
      p. cm.
   Includes bibliographical references and index.
   ISBN 978-0-7425-5784-0 (cloth : alk. paper) — ISBN 978-0-7425-5785-7
(pbk. : alk. paper) — ISBN 978-0-7425-5786-4 (electronic)
      1. Russia (Federation)—Politics and government—1991– 2. Putin, Vladimir
   Vladimirovich, 1952– I. Wegren, Stephen K., 1956– II. Herspring, Dale R.
   (Dale Roy)
   DK510.763.P88 2010
   947.086'3—dc22

                                                                  2009006771

Printed in the United States of America

♾ ™ The paper used in this publication meets the minimum requirements of
American National Standard for Information Sciences—Permanence of Paper for
Printed Library Materials, ANSI/NISO Z39.48-1992.

To James R. Millar, for his lifetime of service to Slavic studies and for being a wonderful friend, scholar, and inspiration to so many.

Contents

Preface to the Fourth Edition

Since the publication of the third edition of this book, Russia has experienced significant change in many ways. In politics, for the first time in Russia's history, a "normal" transfer of power occurred, as Vladimir Putin handed power to Dmitri Medvedev after the March 2008 election without incident and without the changes or challenges to Russia's constitution that many had suspected or feared might occur.

In the economy, Russia experienced significant increases in oil revenues, as the price per barrel climbed steadily upward after 2003, reaching a peak of $147 per barrel in July 2008 before declining later that year to less than $50 and even dipping below $40 in early 2009, which in turn led to projections of budget deficits and lower economic growth extending to 2012 according to some forecasts. During 2003–2007, the increase in revenue to government coffers allowed the government to build the third largest hard currency reserves in the world. When the global credit and financial crises hit in latter 2008, Russia did not escape the fallout, but it was in a position to offer financial relief to banks and other institutions without destabilizing the entire economy. Even as the ruble declined against other currencies and oil revenues plummeted, Russia was in a much better financial condition than in 1998. In other words, the economic achievements since 1998 made the entire financial system and the economy much better able to withstand external shocks than previously.

In foreign policy, Russia remained assertive on the international scene and especially toward nations on its borders. Simmering disagreements with Georgia exploded into war in August 2008. Tensions remained high between the United States and Russia, and between Russia and the European Union. Many observers feared that Russia intended to re-create its former empire and would act to undermine democratic regimes around its border. As Russia's foreign relations unfolded in ways that were sometimes uncomfortable to the West—witness renewed military ties to Cuba, a developing relationship with Chavez in Venezuela and Ortega in Nicaragua, and recognition of the break-away republics of South Ossetia and Abkhazia—Russia continued to position itself to be an important and influential player for years to come, for instance through long-delayed military reform.

Understanding change in Russia is not as straightforward as it might appear. Putin's two terms suggested that he was not a leader who moved quickly. Instead, he was a "gradualist," a person who introduced change in a piecemeal fashion and moved cautiously. Gone were the days of Yeltsin's impetuous actions and radical change. But before long, the "small" and seemingly unrelated modifications added up to major changes. As a result, Russia is a very different country today than it was in 2000 when Putin first became president. Whether the trajectories and trends begun under Putin will continue under Medvedev is a crucial question that affects not only how Russia will be ruled but also Russia's relations with the outside world. Because Medvedev is not only Putin's successor but also has been his long-time colleague, there are compelling reasons to believe that he will build on the foundations that Putin created. This is especially so since Putin has not entirely left the political scene—the day after Putin nominated Medvedev as president, Medvedev nominated Putin as prime minister, and Putin was subsequently confirmed to the position. Many indicators suggest that Putin remains the real power in Russian politics, such as the events during the Georgian crisis in August 2008. But Russian politics rarely is predictable or follows conventional wisdom. Consequently, it is critical for interested observers to understand not only where Putin took Russia since the third edition of this book was published, but also where Russia is headed in the post-Putin presidency.

Accurately documenting and analyzing change across different policy spectrums require the combined efforts of an excellent group of scholars. Because these trends are difficult for nonspecialists to discern, the editors have endeavored to recruit some of "the best and brightest" to help the reader understand Russia's ongoing evolution. Updating chapters or writing new ones is not an easy task. Most of the authors who wrote chapters for the second or third edition were able to update their work. Building on the success of previous editions, the fourth edition adds a new editor to this collective effort. A decision was made to recruit some new authors of the same high quality as in previous editions and to widen the scope of topics and coverage. We believe the reader will agree that this edition contains many of the top scholars in Russian studies. We are deeply grateful for their contributions to this fourth edition.

In addition to our colleagues, the editors thank Susan McEachern of Rowman and Littlefield for her excellent editorial skills and patience in producing this book. We also thank Christine Carberry, who expertly prepared the index. Finally, this book is dedicated to James R. Millar, who passed away in November 2008 after a battle with cancer. Jim, a giant in the field of Slavic studies, was recognized for his lifetime of service with the highest award that the American Slavic Association can bestow. He was also a generous and kind friend. His scholarship has stood the test of time, and several of his books remain classics. There are few people so admired and liked by all. Jim had originally agreed to update his chapter on the economy that appeared in the first three editions. Tragically, he was unable to do so due to his illness and subsequent death. The profession, his family, his friends, and his colleagues will sorely miss him. The editors in particular express their sympathy to his family, and their sadness for the loss of such an outstanding man.

Introduction

Stephen K. Wegren and Dale R. Herspring

With this fourth edition, *Putin's Russia* becomes *After Putin's Russia*, reflecting the 2008 change in Russia's leadership. Despite the change in title, the book remains as timely and appropriate as ever. The years of Putin's presidency were, by many standards, highly successful and marked by significant achievements. At the same time, notable causes for concern continued to confront Russia as Putin left that office. Russia's recent past has been imperfect, and its future is uncertain as it faces challenges on several fronts.

When Putin ascended to power in 1999–2000, he was virtually unknown both in Russia and abroad. A former KGB officer, he had returned to his native Leningrad (St. Petersburg) from a KGB assignment in East Germany less than ten years earlier. Although relatively short in the context of Russian history, Putin's eight years as president were critical in Russia's development. Just as Russia was at a crossroads when Boris Yeltsin vacated the presidency, so too is the nation at a critical juncture now that the office has passed from Putin to Dmitri Medvedev. Although Putin is no longer president, with his transfer to the position of prime minister, it is apparent that he will continue to exert considerable power and authority in Russia. Indeed, many questions continue to circulate regarding Putin's position vis-à-vis his longtime colleague and protégé, President Dmitri Medvedev.

When Vladimir Putin became interim president of Russia on January 1, 2000, he was confronted with a staggering array of daunting problems. As he put it, "Russia is in the midst of one of the most difficult periods in its history. For the first time in the past 200–300 years, it is facing a real threat of sliding into the second, and possibly even third echelon of world states."[1] The country's economy was in shambles, its political system was in chaos, and its social and moral structure was in an advanced state of decay.

During Putin's two terms as president, the political system was stabilized as executive-legislative relations became less acrimonious, and restive governors

1

were reined in as the center reestablished political control. In the economic sphere, economic growth revived a moribund economy. As real incomes increased, life became "normal" for most Russians. Based on rising energy prices, Russia became an important economic player in Europe and Asia, exporting not only energy but also grain and other raw materials. At times, Russia appeared to misuse its energy power, as in 2006 when it cut off gas supplies to Ukraine over disputes concerning prices, payment of debt, and theft.[2] Whether or not Russia was "right" in this and other energy disputes, the effect was to raise concern in Europe over Russia's reliability as an energy supplier, and in the United States over Russia's perceived use of energy as a tool of foreign policy.[3]

Although Russia is in much better shape today than it was in 2000, President Medvedev is confronted with an array of problems and challenges, several of which appear particularly intractable. On many fronts, the future is uncertain. To what extent will Medvedev continue the political system of "managed democracy"? Will political power be decentralized or continue to gravitate toward the center at the expense of the regions? Does Putin's assumption of the post of prime minister represent a shift in power relations without formal constitutional change? Will Medvedev be able to eradicate corruption? Will he be able to eradicate "legal nihilism" so that Russia may become governed by the rule of law? What will be the economic and political effects of the global financial crisis and how will the leadership respond? After several years of prosperity, will a sudden drop in standards of living lead to mass protests? Will falling energy prices in 2008 have the same effect on Russia that falling oil prices had on the Soviet Union in 1986? Will Russia continue its demographic decline, with its implications for economic growth, the labor force, the military, and Russia's power projection? Will Russia ever be able to feed itself? Will military reform be successful? What effect will falling energy prices and reduced revenues have on foreign policy—will Russia remain assertive? What does the future hold for relations between Russia and Central Asia?

With Russia's future so uncertain, the chapters in this book focus on three central questions. First, to what extent was Putin and his regime successful in addressing the problems that were inherited from the Yeltsin era? In this respect, the chapters update the political, socioeconomic, foreign policy, and security trends during Putin's second term. The second question concerns the legacy that Putin passed on to Medvedev, which to a large extent shapes the present policy agenda. Will Medvedev be able to maintain the political system—to consolidate the status quo—that he inherited from Putin while also dealing with both old and new socioeconomic and other problems? The third question is perhaps the most important. Where is Medvedev leading the country, and to what extent does he represent a departure from Putin (and Putinism)?

RUSSIA'S LEADERSHIP

Vladimir Putin and Dmitri Medvedev have starkly different biographies, yet as the discussion below shows, their paths have crossed for many years and they have worked as colleagues since the early 1990s. The published facts about Putin's career are sketchy, but several major events influenced his life.[4] Putin was born in 1952 in what was then Leningrad, now St. Petersburg. Coming from "a humble background with few advantages," he nevertheless "advanced through a mixture of his own qualities and the strengths of the Soviet system. . . . Neither money, contacts, nor ideology seemed to play a significant role in his early progress."[5] In school, he was a "good, normal, ordinary student, not distinguished from the others."[6] While in school, he trained in judo and in 1974 became the Leningrad city champion. In his autobiography, he credits judo as the turning point in his life. "If I hadn't gotten involved in sports, I'm not sure how my life would have turned out. It was sports that dragged me off the streets."[7] His lifelong dream was to become a member of the secret police, the KGB (Committee for State Security). Indeed, he recalls going to the local KGB office while still in high school and telling a somewhat startled officer, "I want to get a job with you."[8] He was advised instead to attend the university and study law, although there is speculation that he may have been an informer at law school, a claim that a former KGB official supports. Putin denies this in his autobiography but did reveal that 90 percent of information came from ordinary citizens—informers—an assertion that was left out of the Russian version so as not to inflame popular opinion.[9]

After graduating from Leningrad State University in 1975 with a degree in law, Putin applied again to the KGB, this time successfully. He was sent to Moscow for initial training and was then assigned to foreign intelligence in Leningrad, where he spent the majority of his time spying on foreigners and Russians who had contacts with them. He studied German and was eventually posted to Dresden in the German Democratic Republic, where he and his wife spent five years and their two daughters were born. This was also where he perfected his German. Putin was no "natural" in the world of espionage, but he learned the craft quickly and effectively, according to one German agent he controlled.[10]

In 1989, Putin returned to Russia and became head of the Foreign Section at Leningrad State University. In that capacity he served as an assistant for international affairs to his former law professor, Anatoli Sobchak, who was the university's rector. In 1990, Putin made what he described as "the hardest decision of my life" when he resigned from the KGB.[11] Sobchak, who had emerged as one of the leading advocates of democratic reform in Russia and a major force in Leningrad politics, asked Putin to move to city hall as his advisor on international affairs. In 1991, Sobchak became Leningrad's mayor and appointed Putin chairman of the city's foreign relations committee. In reality, Putin's first request to resign from the KGB was ignored, and he remained on the payroll until he submitted a second resignation after the failed coup in August 1991. In working for Sobchak, Putin had responsibility for a number of reform programs, including foreign investments, where Putin impressed those who dealt with him as a man who could get things done.[12] Indeed, it was during his time in St. Petersburg that he made his reputation as an outstanding administrator.

In 1996, Sobchak failed in his bid for reelection amid charges of corruption, and it appeared that Putin's post-KGB career was at an end. Having heard of Putin's reputation as a "doer," however, Anatoli Chubais, a well-connected advisor to Yeltsin, got him a job working with Pavel Borodin, who was head of a staff closely associated with Yeltsin. Yeltsin took notice of Putin's "will and resolve" and admired Putin's "decisive nature and toughness," which had Yeltsin thinking about Putin's political future.[13] In the tumultuous administrative upheavals of the Russian executive in 1998, Putin was appointed first deputy head of the presidential administration in charge of relations with the regions. Later that year, he became head of the Federal Security Service (FSB, the successor to the KGB), a move he claimed made him unhappy because of the secretive life it would entail. "It put you in a constant state of tension. All the papers are secret. This isn't allowed, that isn't allowed."[14] Shortly thereafter, Putin was put in control of the body that coordinated all of Russia's security and intelligence ministries.

On August 9, 1999, the ailing Yeltsin surprised the world by appointing Putin as his prime minister and designated successor. Few people inside or outside of Russia had heard of Vladimir Putin, who had never held an elected office in his life. On December 31, 1999, Yeltsin again astonished everyone by suddenly resigning his post even though his term was not over, thereby making Putin Russia's acting president. Yeltsin explained that he wanted to catch the opposition off guard and ensure his protégé had the best possible chance to win the forthcoming presidential election.[15] After an interim period, on March 26, 2000, Putin stood for election and won over 52 percent of the vote in the first round—enough to avoid a runoff, as Yeltsin had endured in 1996. Putin became Russia's second elected president. In 2004, he stood for reelection and won overwhelmingly—receiving more than 71 percent of the vote. His popularity ratings remained high during his second term, as the Russian economy became a success story life became better for the vast majority of Russians, and the dark days of the Yeltsin era faded into a distant memory. With overwhelming popular appeal, there was swirling speculation that Putin would amend the constitution to allow himself to run for a third term in 2008—he easily could have done so, since the pro-Kremlin party United Russia controlled more than two-thirds of the seats in the Duma. Instead, Putin opted to respect the constitution and stand down at the end of his second term.

However, the story does not end there. A few days after Putin nominated Medvedev to be his successor—thereby all but guaranteeing Medvedev's electoral victory beforehand—Medvedev in turn indicated that he would ask Putin to be his prime minister should he become president. Subsequently, Putin not only became prime minister but also was chosen to head the pro-Kremlin political party United Russia, thereby ensuring legislative compliance for the executive branch. As this book goes to press, political events continue to evolve. In his November 5, 2008, state of the nation speech, Medvedev suggested several important constitutional amendments. Among the most important was that the presidential term be extended to six years from its present four, starting in 2012. Medvedev argued that the present presidential term was too short to successfully tackle the challenges that Russia faced. In his speech, he stated: "Today, when long-term development plans are being implemented and, essentially, tasks of switching over to a new type economy are being resolved, a multitude of very difficult issues will have to be dealt with simultaneously—to counter the global crisis and difficulties of competition, to modernize the army, to govern the gigantic country of the most complicated ethnic and cultural composition, and, in these conditions, to strengthen democratic institutions and maintain stability."[16]

The change in the presidential term passed in both houses of the Russian parliament with extreme speed—a matter of weeks—thereby showing the strength of the Kremlin to get what it wanted. From there it went to the regions, where a two-thirds approval was needed, but with United Russia having governors in 83 of 85 regions, that hurdle was easily overcome. The change in the presidential term was signed into force at the end of 2008, setting off speculation that Medvedev would step down early, allowing Putin to return to the presidency and rule for many more years. Whether or not that scenario comes to be, the Medvedev-Putin team, which is something akin to the odd couple, would seem to have all the cards stacked in its favor.

Who is Dmitri Medvedev? Born in 1965, also in Leningrad, Medvedev is twelve years younger than Putin.[17] His personal demeanor is much less intimidating and milder. He has been described as studious and soft spoken, unlike Putin, who frequently uses coarse language and likes off-color jokes. Medvedev is also rumored to be more "liberal" and "with it" than Putin, based on his like of Western rock and roll (Deep Purple and Led Zeppelin) and an extensive record collection. Medvedev uses the Internet daily and has his own blog site. His knowledge of English makes him appear more refined and cultured. Medvedev grew up in an intellectual atmosphere (his parents were university professors), and therefore he is more reasoned and analytical than emotional, and he never was a member of the security apparatus during the Soviet period or after.

Despite some differences in personality and background, Medvedev is considered "Putin's man" with good reason, as Putin has been instrumental in his career. The two have worked together for nearly half of Medvedev's life. Similar to Putin, he graduated from law school at Leningrad State University in 1987 and completed his postgraduate work in 1990 with a Ph.D. in law and a title of associate professor. During the 1990s, he taught at Leningrad State University and also was an advisor to the Leningrad City Council, where it is reported that Medvedev was responsible for drafting many of the bills that would turn into post-Soviet law. In the first half of the 1990s, when Anatoli Sobchak was still mayor, Medvedev served as a legal consultant for Putin, who was working in the St. Petersburg administration.

After Putin became prime minister under Yeltsin, he invited Medvedev to come to Moscow in 1999. Initially, Medvedev was deputy chief of staff for Yeltsin. In 2000, he ran Putin's presidential campaign, and after Putin's victory Medvedev was named first deputy chief of the presidential administration. Also in 2000, Medvedev was named chairman of Gazprom, the largest natural gas company in the world and responsible for the bulk of Russia's foreign trade earnings. Medvedev remained the head of Gazprom during the takeover of Vladimir Gusinsky's Media-Most, the shutting down of the independent TV station NTV, and the gas-withholding conflicts with Ukraine in 2005 and 2006. Putin's trust in Medvedev was further indicated by the appointment of Medvedev as chief of staff of the presidential administration in October 2003. In November 2005, Medvedev was named first deputy prime minister in charge of the national projects—the areas of the economy that were targeted for special attention and financial assistance, including agriculture, housing, education, and health care. These projects oversaw the expenditure of tens of billions of rubles and were considered central to improving society and making the Russian economy more competitive. From late 2005, Medvedev served as first deputy prime minister until the end of Putin's second term. In December 2007, Putin nominated Medvedev as his successor, and Medvedev easily won the presidential election in March 2008 with more than 70 percent of the vote, handily defeating the communist opponent Gennadi Ziuganov.

From this brief biological sketch, two central elements stand out about Medvedev. First, it is clear that Putin has enormous trust in Medvedev. Putin would not have promoted him up the ladder and given him more and more responsibility if he believed that Medvedev were not responsible, capable, and most of all, loyal. Clearly, the two men have established a good working relationship over many years, and it is likely that this relationship is due in no small part to the fact that they share similar views and values. This was suggested, for example, by Medvedev's statement that those who expected a "softer" Russian foreign policy will be surprised. Medvedev repeated on several occasions that his presentation and demeanor may be different, but in terms of policy and goals he would not differ from his predecessor.[18] Indeed, published accounts suggest that Medvedev conducted himself very differently at the G8 meeting in July 2008 than had Putin in years past, and Medvedev was reported to be jovial, collegial, and had a good sense of humor.[19]

But beyond superficialities, Medvedev shows a tough inner strength and a less compromising side. His language during and after the Georgian crisis of August 2008 was only slightly less harsh than Putin's, and Medvedev made clear that compromise on the recognition of South Ossetia and Abkhazia was not in the cards. Likewise, his threat to station missiles in Kaliningrad (in response to U.S. missile defense in Europe) the day after Barack Obama won the presidency sent a message that Medvedev could be expected to take a hard line in American-Russian relations. Thus, Putin trusts Medvedev for a reason, and that is that the two share common values, perceptions, and worldviews. The first year of Medvedev's presidency suggests that Western analysts who expected to see a falling out between the two leaders over policy or philosophical differences were likely to be disappointed.[20]

The second main element that emerges from Medvedev's biography is that even if Medvedev developed the desire to separate himself politically or in policy from Putin, he is not in a position to do so and instead is likely to remain dependent upon Putin. This statement has multiple subtexts. Even though Medvedev formally is in the more powerful position, Russia appears to still be Putin's—as reflected by the fact that Putin took charge and was the national spokesman during the Georgian crisis. The traditional "reserved domain" of presidents does not appear to exist in Russia, as Putin has shown an ability and willingness to comment on any aspect of economic policy, any political issue, or any foreign policy problem that he pleases. This was also seen in early December 2008 when Putin conducted a live, call-in radio program in which citizens asked questions and expressed concerns on a wide range of topics. Putin traditionally did this once a year when he was president. The fact that Putin continued to hold such a forum as prime minister acted as a symbol that Putin was still in charge.

Moreover, Medvedev does not have independent sources of power or support, although developing one or the other is not excluded. There was, for example, speculation that the naming of Medvedev's "cadre reserve" list in February 2009 may be a precursor to replacing officials who had been placed in power by Putin. For the present, however, Medvedev's men are Putin's men. Further, because Medvedev is not a member of the *siloviki*, he has no natural constituency from which to recruit members of his administration. Thus, leadership personnel continue to bear the heavy stamp of Putin, and many top ministerial posts have carried over from the Putin years. All of this portends an extended "Putinism" for the foreseeable future, even if Putin now occupies only the second most powerful position in Russia.[21]

THE STRUCTURE OF THE BOOK

After Putin's Russia is divided into three sections. The first examines several dimensions of domestic politics. Richard Sakwa begins by exploring the relationship between the nature of political leadership in Russia and the requisites for democratic development and societal modernity. He argues that a contradiction exists in Russia, indicated by the clear tension between liberal democratic aspirations and the state's inability to act as a coherent vessel in which these aspirations can be fulfilled. In particular, Sakwa examines the political characteristics and proclivities of Putin as president and shows that while Putin's administration certainly remained within the letter of the constitution, in fact it undermined the motivating spirit of democracy, political pluralism, and judicial impartiality. Moreover, a characteristic feature of modernity is the emergence of autonomous civic actors. As the state under Putin attempted to manage various transformative actors, the larger contradictions within Russia's modernity were exposed. This is perhaps Medvedev's greatest challenge, and one he has spoken to directly in his early speeches.

Thomas Remington tackles the question of political development from a different angle, focusing on the Duma (the lower house of Russia's parliament) and the party system. Remington concentrates on two closely related developments: the subjugation of parliament and the creation of a party system in which United Russia dominates regional and federal elections and opposition parties are sidelined. Between the Yeltsin and Putin eras, Russia's political system evolved from one in which "super-presidentialism" tended to undermine incentives for politicians to form competing programmatic parties to one in which politicians have a strong incentive to join the dominant pro-Kremlin party, United Russia.

Another critical area where recentralization has taken place has been in center-periphery relations. Nikolai Petrov and Darrell Slider argue that rebalancing the relationship between the center and the periphery in favor of the center was one of Putin's goals. The chaotic nature of Moscow's relations with the rest of the country could not be sustained because the regions were far too strong. Putin's goal was to establish a unitary, centralized state under the guise of "restoring effective vertical power in the country." The problem, they note, is that under Putin federalism was eroded. Going forward, whether Putin will let Medvedev take over the reins of power is a major question, considering the effort that Putin expended on changing the "game" of regional politics. Increasingly, Putin as prime minister has taken on regional oversight functions, and his new role as leader of the dominant party United Russia gives him additional leverage to influence regional politics.

A central aspect of a healthy democracy is a state governed by the rule of law and a court system that is both objective and honest (not corrupted). Kathryn Hendley provides a broad overview of Russian law and how it has developed since the end of the USSR. She argues that under both Putin and Medvedev, the Kremlin's legislative agenda was pushed through with a heavy hand and often with the result of curtailing human rights. In particular, Putin's willingness to use the courts as a weapon for punishing his political opponents quite rightly calls their independence into question. Moreover, the courts represent a central aspect of corruption and the distribution of resources (broadly defined) to individuals and their companies that are loyal and favored by the Kremlin.[22] Such policies would be troubling in any context but are particularly disquieting in post-Soviet Russia. They are disturbingly reminiscent of problem-solving tactics employed by Soviet leaders that would seem to have been renounced as part of the transition to a rule-of-law-based state (*pravovoe gosudarstvo*).

Observers agree that media freedom is one of the most critical areas for democratic development, but under Putin it has been one most affected by Putin's crackdown. Maria Lipman and Michael McFaul argue that Russia has a combination of tightly controlled mass-audience media (this applies first and foremost to national television networks) and smaller-audience outlets that pursue reasonably independent editorial lines (these are found among print dailies and weeklies, radio, the Web, and occasionally smaller-audience TV channels). To the extent that media freedom is interpreted as the availability of outlets that serve to convey uncensored messages, report news, or voice opinions, Russia has this freedom. It appears to be more appropriate, however, to describe the media in Russia as *freedom of expression* as opposed to *the freedom of the press.*

The second part of the book examines the economy and society. Many observers share the view that there is a link between a stable, healthy economy and long-term democratic development. According to this line of reasoning, economic growth will spur the growth of classes that will demand less intrusion, more rights and freedoms, and less restriction by the state. On the other hand, a different school of thought argues that "petro-dollars" allow governments with authoritarian proclivities to remain strong and in power, and undercut any democratizing tendencies. What is undisputed is the fact that economic growth was robust under Putin, averaging nearly 7 percent a year during 2000–2007. The economic future under Medvedev in 2008 and beyond is more problematic.

One of the greatest challenges to the economy is the demographic situation in Russia. In fact, in his 2006 state of the nation address, Putin identified the demographic decline as the country's largest problem. Timothy Heleniak presents a broad and comprehensive overview of demographics in Russia. His chapter examines population change, fertility, mortality, and migration, and the spatial distribution and composition of the population. The chapter concludes with a section that discusses population projections and population policy in Russia. He argues that Medvedev is likely to continue the demographic policy agenda laid out by Putin, although there is only so much a government can do to affect fertility, mortality, and migration trends.

Peter Rutland takes up the question of oligarchs and their role in Russia's economic development. Rutland argues that perceptions about Russia's economic development are now entering their third paradigm shift. The first shift, which took place in 1992, was the conviction that Russia had shed its communist legacy and was building a normal, market economy. The first paradigm collapsed with the August 1998 crash, although it still has some adherents. The second paradigm developed from the appearance of Vladimir Putin, who brought stability and order to Russian politics. According to this second view, while Putin pursued tough, Machiavellian policies toward Chechen separatists, regional leaders, and his political opponents, he wanted to press ahead with market reforms in order to turn Russia into a modern, efficient economy. The second paradigm collapsed with the Yukos affair of 2003–2004, raising profound doubts about the viability of Putin as "market autocrat." The third shift is characterized by a lack of consensus as to what Russia's economic path will be. Some suggest that Putin never intended to coexist with the oligarchs, that he was always bent on establishing a vertical hierarchy of power. In this view, the state will predominate and intervene, with economics the playground for politics. Others argue that Yukos was an exception and Putin never intended reprivatization, and that for most oligarchs business remained as usual. Dmitri Medvedev thus enters the political scene at an interesting juncture in Russia's economic development.

Louise Shelley examines the important topic of crime and corruption. Whereas the Soviet regime hid these unpleasant realities, postcommunist Russia revealed a huge upsurge. The Putin years brought greater stability, but Russia has not been able to eliminate the high rates of violent crime, endemic corruption, or pervasive organized crime. High levels of money laundering and export of capital have continued to deprive Russia of the capital it needs for investment, although the record profits obtained during the boom years of oil revenues masked the impact. The crime problems have evolved in the years since the collapse of the Soviet Union but have remained an important element of the structure of the Russian economy, society, and political system. The homicides associated with organized crime have declined, but overall homicide rates remain high. Conflicts over property are no longer decided by shootings but often instead by expensive litigation in the West, where many of Russia's richest citizens have placed their assets. Property rights are still not secure. The property acquired by force, deception, and coercion in the early days of the post-Soviet period is now often being redistributed by corporate raiding. Over 70,000 cases in 2007 testify to the force often used to wrest property from its current owners. Struggles over property can be as small as one residential building or as large as the stakes of British Petroleum.

One of the main areas of economic success under Putin was the agricultural sector. Stephen Wegren argues that "Putin's quiet revolution" in agriculture has provided Russia with a more stable foundation for future development of the agricultural sector. Since 2000, two main stages of governmental agrarian policy may be discerned. The first stage was the creation of an institutional and policy base that would stabilize the agricultural sector and pave the way for economic growth. The second stage has witnessed the introduction of significant financial assistance that is intended to increase domestic production, make Russian agriculture internationally competitive, and reduce dependence on foreign imports. The chapter traces the government's strategy and policies toward agriculture through these two stages, culminating with the extension of agriculture as a national priority through Medvedev's presidency, to 2012.

The third and final section of the book analyzes foreign policy and military reform. One of Putin's goals, besides rebuilding the Russian state, was to regain the respect and influence Russia had in the heyday of the Soviet period. In foreign policy, this goal has largely been accomplished, due in no small part to both renewed assertiveness and economic growth on the back of high energy prices. In the past few years, Russia has been a major participant in nuclear talks with North Korea and Iran; it held the G8 presidency in 2006 and hosted the meeting in St. Petersburg; and Medvedev has proposed hosting an EU summit to discuss a European-wide security regime.

Andrei Tsygankov provides a broad overview of Russia's foreign policy. In particular, he presents a compelling argument that Russian foreign policy has become more assertive since 2005. He asserts that contrary to some common views that attribute Russia's assertive behavior to its traditionally imperialist and anti-Western political culture, the primary drivers in the Kremlin's foreign policy are contemporary and domestic. They include new opportunities for economic growth and stability, as well as the need to address increasing security threats. Initially the country's leadership was hoping to develop a grand strategy by engaging Western nations, in particular the United States, into projects of common significance, such as counterterrorism and energy security. However, as the West turned its attention elsewhere and as Russia grew stronger, the Kremlin made important adjustments to its policy. The upshot is that Russia is a major player today on the international scene and its importance is not likely to diminish anytime soon. Whether the relationship with the West is cordial and cooperative, or confrontational, remains to be seen.

Gregory Gleason argues that relations between Russia and the all-important Central Asian nations may be understood as a "multivector policy." A multivector policy is a complex stratagem. In practice, multivector foreign policies are essentially risk-avoidant lines of action, emphasizing multiple partners, multiple dimensions, and multiple issues, and relying largely on diplomatic hedging against unreliability, threat, and hard-to-calculate advantage. Multivector foreign policies assign low importance to ideological considerations and high importance to instrumental alliances and calculated advantage. The multivector policy means that any of the Central Asian states will have a policy of one vector toward Russia, one vector toward China, one vector toward Europe, and so on. There is logic to the "balancing symmetry" inherent in the calculation of interests in Central Asia. Russia is a factor in every balance. Russia is too big and too close to ignore, too aggressive to contest. At the same time, Russia is not easy to interact with simply as an equal partner. Central Asian policy officials use the concept of "multivector foreign policy" to explain and justify their diplomatic and security relationships with other countries within the Central Asian region and with other countries outside the region and with international organizations.

Dale Herspring analyzes a topic often overlooked in the post–Cold War period, but one that has increasing importance as Russia reemerges on the international scene: military reform. Late in his second term, President Vladimir Putin came to the conclusion that the Russian military had to be shaken up—that it was so corrupt, only an outsider could do the job. As a result, heads have begun to roll and major changes are under way. If fully implemented, by 2020 the Russian military will have undergone "a revolution in military affairs." In particular, Herspring traces the rise of Anatoli Serdiukov and the policies he has introduced to make the Russian military more efficient and cost effective, but also smaller.

Finally, in the Conclusion, the editors take up the question, where is Medvedev taking Russia? The analysis begins with a summary of Putin's legacy in politics, economics, and foreign policy/security. The trajectory of each of those factors is then analyzed, laying out the challenges that confront President Medvedev. Finally, a series of factors that will affect Russia going forward are examined. The big question organizing the analysis is how much of a departure from Putinism may be expected.

NOTES

1. Vladimir Putin, "Russia at the Turn of the Millennium," www.government.gov.ru/english/statVP_engl_1.html.

2. Ukraine was not the only country that experienced gas cutoffs—nor was 2006 the only time. At the end of December 2008, Russia again cut off gas supplies to Ukraine over disagreements regarding price. The standoff was finally resolved in January 2009 after more than two weeks of wrangling and high tension between the two governments.

3. See Heiko Pleines, "The Natural Gas Conflict between Russia and Ukraine," *Russian Analytical Digest*, no. 41 (May 2008): 8–15.

4. Much of the following biographical information is taken from Dale R. Herspring and Jacob W. Kipp, "Understanding the Elusive Mr. Putin," *Problems of Post-Communism* 48, no. 5 (2001): 3–17.

5. Andrew Jack, *Inside Putin's Russia* (Oxford: Oxford University Press, 2006), 51.

6. Jack, *Inside Putin's Russia*, 51.

7. Vladimir Putin, *First Person* (New York: Public Affairs, 2000), 19.

8. Putin, *First Person*, 23.

9. Jack, *Inside Putin's Russia*, 58–59.

10. Mark Franchetti, "Spy Tells How Putin Blew It as KGB Rookie," *New York Times*, March 11, 2001.

11. Jack, *Inside Putin's Russia*, 67.

12. See Graham Hume's discussion of Putin's role and effectiveness at this time in "Vladimir Vladimirovich Putin in 1994: A Personal Reflection," *E-Notes*, Foreign Policy Research Institute, January 14, 2001.

13. Boris Yeltsin, *Midnight Diaries* (New York: Public Affairs, 2000), 284–87, quotes on 284, 286; and see Timothy J. Colton, *Yeltsin: A Life* (New York: Basic Books, 2008), 430–37.

14. Putin, *First Person*, 131.

15. Yeltsin, *Midnight Diaries*, 286.

16. *Johnson's Russia List*, no. 202 (November 6, 2008).

17. The biographical information for Medvedev is taken from www.kremlin.ru; various articles from *Johnson's Russia List*; and Kathryn Stoner-Weiss, "It Is Still Putin's Russia," *Current History* 107, no. 711 (2008): 317–18. The actual age difference is twelve years, eleven months.

18. For example, prior to his visit to India in December 2008, Medvedev stated: "The tasks do not change. The methods change, the tactical means change, and the style sometimes changes, but the tasks remain the same." ITAR-TASS, cited in *Johnson's Russia List*, no. 220 (December 5, 2008).

19. *Johnson's Russia List*, no. 128 (July 8, 2008).

20. In early December 2008, Medvedev continued to play down differences. "The work of any president and any national leader always differs from the activities of his predecessor. Although I have good comrade-like relations, specific relations with my colleague, former President and now Prime Minister Vladimir Putin, it is absolutely clear that his activities are his job, while my job is my job," Medvedev said. *Johnson's Russia List*, no. 220 (December 5, 2008).

21. For an overview of the leadership style of Putinism, see the Introduction in the third edition of this book.

22. For a concrete example concerning the renovation of Domodedovo airport, see Vladim Solov'ev, *Putin: putevoditel' dlia neravnodushnykh*, 2nd ed. (Moscow: Eksmo, 2008), 394–413.

Part One

DOMESTIC POLITICS

Chapter One

Political Leadership

Richard Sakwa

[I]t is clearly too early to assert that, this time, Russia will complete her real convergence with the West. But it is not too early to assert that, in the normal course, she hardly has anywhere else to go. . . . As has ever been the case since Peter, if Russia wants to be strong, she will have to Westernize. With her Communist identity gone, and with no other ideological identity possible, she has little choice but to become, as before 1917, just another "normal" European power, with an equally normal internal order.

—Martin Malia[1]

The Putin phenomenon remains an enigma. A man with legal training, he spent a large part of his formative adult years in the security apparatus; following the fall of the communist system in 1991, he threw in his lot with the democratic leader of St. Petersburg, Anatoli Sobchak. Elected president for the first time in March 2000, Putin presided over the development of a market economy and endlessly reiterated his commitment to democracy, yet following reelection for his second and constitutionally defined last term in 2004, the system veered ever closer toward some form of state capitalism. *Dirigisme* in the economy was accompanied by ever more suffocating restrictions on the free play of political pluralism and democratic competition. Putin came to power committed to the "normalization" of Russia, in the sense of aligning its internal order to the norms practiced elsewhere and establishing Russia's foreign policy presence as just another "normal great power," yet there remained something "extraordinary" about the country. Putin left the presidency as prescribed by Russia's constitution, and in May 2008 power was transferred to his nominee, Dmitri Medvedev, but Putin then took up the duties of prime minister and was thus able to ensure that "Putinism after Putin" would continue.

It is almost impossible to reconcile the contradiction between the avowed commitment to the development of a modern capitalist democracy and the emergence of a power-hungry monocratic power system that absorbed all independent political life and suffocated the autonomy of civil society. However, this reconciliation is something that we have to do, otherwise we are left with one-dimensional and tendentious accounts of contemporary Russia that fail to capture the complexity and multifaceted nature of developments. The contradictions bequeathed by Putin continue into the Medvedev era, and the task of this chapter is to indicate some of the dimensions of Russia's continuing engagement with the problem of "becoming modern."

RECONCILING CONTRADICTION

Russia under Putin emerged as a dual state. Elements of this were already evident under Yeltsin, but the divergence between the formal constitutional order, the rule of law, and autonomous expression of political and media freedoms, on the one hand, and the instrumental use of law and attempts to manage political processes, on the other hand, became ever wider. Putin's administration was careful not to overstep the bounds of the letter of the constitution, but the system of "managed democracy" conducted itself with relative impunity and lack of effective accountability. It was firmly located in the gray area of para-constitutionalism, a style of governance that remains true to the formal institutional rules but devises various strategies based on technocratic (rather than democratic) rationality to achieve desired political goals. Putin's para-constitutionalism did not repudiate the legitimacy of the constitution but in practice undermined the spirit of constitutionalism. The interaction of real constitutionalism and nominal para-constitutionalism in Russia can be compared to the development of the dual state in Germany in the 1930s. Ernest Fraenkel described how the prerogative state acted as a separate law system of its own, although the formal constitutional state was not dismantled. Two parallel systems of law operated: the "normative state" operated according to sanctioned principles of rationality and impartial legal norms, while the "prerogative state" exercised power arbitrarily and without constraints, unrestrained by law.[2]

The contrast between a prerogative and a constitutional state (I shall use this term for clarity in place of "normative" state) provides a useful key to interpreting development in postcommunist Russia. In Russia, the fundamental legitimacy of the regime is derived from its location in a constitutional order which it is sworn to defend. However, in certain cases—as in the Yukos affair, when the head of the oil company, Mikhail Khodorkovsky, was imprisoned and the company dismembered—elements of the prerogative state have emerged. The interaction between the constitutional and prerogative states in Russia became the defining feature of the regime. Although the rule of law in Russia remains fragile and, as the Yukos affair amply demonstrated, was susceptible to manipulation by the political authorities, no fully fledged prerogative state emerged. Neither, however, has a fully fledged rule of law state, and thus Russia remains trapped in the gray area between a prerogative and a genuine constitutional state. The regime is able to rule *by* law when that suits its purposes, but the struggle for the rule *of* law, even by prominent members of the administration itself, is far from over.

Two political systems operate in parallel. On the one hand, there is the system of open public politics, with all of the relevant institutions described in the constitution and conducted with pedantic regulation in formal terms. At this level, parties are formed, elections fought, and parliamentary politics conducted. However, at another level, a second para-political world exists based on informal groups, factions, and operating within the framework of the inner court of the presidency. This Byzantine level never openly challenged the leader but sought to influence the decisions of the supreme ruler. This second level is more than simply "virtual" politics, the attempt to manipulate public opinion and shape electoral outcomes through the pure exercise of manipulative techniques.[3] However, by seeking to reduce the inevitable contradictions that accompany public politics into a matter of technocratic management, Putin inevitably exacerbated the contradictions between the groups within the regime. Putin placed a high value on civil peace, and thus opposed a return to the antagonistic politics typical of the 1990s, but this reinforced the pseudo-politics typical of court systems. The suffocation of public politics intensified factional processes within the regime.

Medvedev, as we shall see, came to power committed to strengthening the constitutional state vis-à-vis the prerogative state, above all by strengthening the rule of law and tackling corruption. That this was his top priority reinforces the argument that the interaction between the two levels is the key to understanding contemporary Russian politics. Medvedev, moreover, was not so burdened by the concerns of Putin's presidency. He was less scarred by the bitter disappointments of the Yeltsin and Putin years, when it appeared that "strategic partnership" with the West could only be achieved at the cost of Russia's perceived interests as a great power and as a distinct civilization. The origin of the dual state lies in the nature of the modernization program pursued by Putin's leadership. It was genuinely committed to the development of Russia as a modern state and society comfortable with itself and the world. At the same time, it sought to overcome the failings of what it considered the excesses of the 1990s under the leadership of president Boris Yeltsin, notably the pell-mell privatization, the liberalism that gave rise to inequality epitomized by the enormous wealth of a handful of "oligarchs," and the "anarcho-democracy" characterized by the hijacking of the electoral process by business-dominated media concerns and regional elites.

Three main themes emerge from this. The first is the remedial element. Putin's policy agenda emerged not only out of the legacy of seventy-four years of communism and the way that it was overcome, notably the disintegration of the Soviet Union in 1991, but also the need to overcome the perceived excesses of the 1990s, above all the development of inequality, mass poverty, oligarch domination of the media, and the excessive ambitions of the new business elite. The second feature is the type of developmental program that Putin ultimately favored, with a strong role of the state to ensure that the business of business remained business, not politics, and for the state to remain firmly in control of economic policy making, accompanied by support for national champions in the energy, military defense, and manufacturing sectors. The third feature is the political managerialism designed to counter what was perceived as the irresponsibility engendered by an untutored democratic process, a theme that provoked an obsession with security by the *siloviki* (representatives of the security and military) in Putin's team. These three elements combined to create a profoundly tutelary regime that was in some ways reminiscent of the "trustee" democracy practiced in Singapore.[4] While there is much talk of a hegemonic presidency, and undoubtedly the presidency is the core of Russia's political system, hegemonic processes are far deeper than that. The administrative regime exerted a distinctive type of political guardianship over society.

There is a profound historical reality behind the emergence of the guardianship system. As in so many other "third wave" countries that have embarked on the path toward greater political openness since 1974,[5] democracy in Russia was forced to create the conditions for its own existence. This is a type of giant boot-strapping operation described by Ernest Gellner in his work on the development of civil society in Russia and other postcommunist countries.[6] The social subjects of capitalist democracy were being created in the process of the establishment of capitalist democracy, a circular process that engendered numerous contradictions. The relationship between the various subsystems of a dynamic democracy has still to be devised. However, the tutelary role of the regime tended to become an end in itself, and its necessary developmental functions came to substitute for and impede the development of autonomous structures in society. Thus there was a profound ambivalence about Putin's leadership and the nature of his developmental agenda, an ambivalence that is characteristic of Russia's long-term modernization in which adaptation to the technological and economic standards of the West has been accompanied by resistance to political Westernization.

Medvedev was well aware of these dilemmas, and while committed to continue the broad outlines of "Putin's plan" (the term used in the 2007–2008 electoral cycle to describe Putin's policy agenda, later called "Plan 2020")[7]— economic modernization and the creation of a more competitive diversified economy, international integration, social modernization, and efficacious political institutions—Medvedev changed the emphasis from "manual" management toward greater trust in the self-managing potential of the system. In his Civic Forum speech on January 22, 2008, he called for the struggle against corruption to become a "national program," noting that "legal nihilism" took the form of "corruption in the power bodies." Medvedev returned to this idea on January 29 in his speech to the Association of Russian Lawyers, calling on his fellow lawyers to take a higher profile in society and to battle "legal nihilism."[8] He clearly had two evils in mind: corruption in the traditional venal sense, characterized by the abuse of public office for private gain, and meta-corruption, where the judicial process is undermined by political interference, known in Russia as "telephone law," and which had been most prominently in evidence during the Yukos case, which itself had given rise to the term "Basmanny justice."

In a keynote speech to the Fifth Krasnoyarsk Economic Forum on February 15, 2008, Medvedev outlined not only his economic program but also his broad view of the challenges facing Russia. He focused on an unwieldy bureaucracy, corruption, and lack of respect for the law as the main challenges facing the country. He insisted that "freedom is better than lack of freedom—this principle should be at the core of our politics. I mean freedom in all of its manifestations—personal freedom, economic freedom and, finally, freedom of expression." He repeated earlier promises to ensure personal freedoms and an independent and free press. He repeatedly returned to the theme of "the need to ensure the independence of the legal system from the executive and legislative branches of power," and once again condemned the country's "legal nihilism" and stressed the need to "humanize" the country's judicial system.[9] Renewed confrontation with the United States (but not, it should be stressed, to the same extent with the European Union), especially evident during the Five-Day War of August 2008 with Georgia, however, threatened to derail Medvedev's aspirations as the country once again, as in Soviet times, appeared faced with a choice between modernization and militarization.

THE CHARACTER OF LEADERSHIP

More than a decade and a half after the fall of the Soviet regime, there is no consensus about the nature of the system emerging in the country. A whole arsenal of terms has been devised in an attempt to capture the hybrid nature of Russian reality, including "managed democracy," "managed pluralism," "liberal authoritarianism," and many more.[10] Following the Orange Revolution in Ukraine in late 2004, the presidential administration launched the term "sovereign democracy" to indicate that Russia would find its own path to democracy, and that democracy in the country would have Russian characteristics. This was a theme Putin stressed in his state of the federation speech on April 25, 2005. He took issue with those who suggested that Russia was somehow not suited to democratic government, the rule of law, and the basic values of civil society: "I would like to bring those who think like that back to political reality. . . . Without liberty and democracy there can be no order, no stability and no sustainable economic policies." Responding to Western criticism, however, Putin stressed that the "special feature" of Russia's democracy was that it would be pursued in its own way and not at the price of law and order or social stability: "Russia . . . will decide for itself the pace, terms and conditions of moving towards democracy."[11] In other words, while the content of policy would be democracy, its forms and the tempo of development would be a directed and managed process, a division that helped sustain the dual state in Russia.

The continuing debate about the character and direction of Putin's leadership reflects a broader debate about the nature of the new system. Is Russia in "transition" to an arguably more democratic system, despite numerous detours and reverses, a perspective that can be dubbed the "democratic evolutionist" view? Or is Russia stuck in some postcommunist syndrome where democratic accoutrements adorn a society and polity that mimic the authority patterns of the earlier order, although aware that there can be no return to the previous system, the "failed democratization" approach?[12] In the latter camp, Steven Fish is unequivocal: "By the time of Vladimir Putin's re-election as president of Russia in 2004, Russia's experiment with open politics was over."[13] One of the main reasons in his view for the re-creation of a monocratic system is the failure to free the economy from the grip of the bureaucracy. This has inhibited the development of a vibrant economy, notably in the small and medium business sector. Contrary to what critics of the privatization of the 1990s argue,[14] Fish insists that more liberalization was required. The stunted development of an independent business sector deprived political life and the media of the sources of independent support, accompanied by widespread corruption and a corrosive venality in public life. The Yukos affair was a clear manifestation of the attempt to achieve economic goals (their validity is not our concern here) by administrative means. While Putin's administration was clearly in favor of the creation of a capitalist market integrated into the world economy, it feared the free operation of market *forces*. In his 1997 doctoral dissertation, Putin had argued for the creation of national champions, and this long-standing policy goal was reinforced by the concerns of the *siloviki* in Putin's team.[15]

The institutional choices embedded in the 1993 constitution, above all the establishment of a "super-presidential" system, are considered by many to have driven Russia toward monocracy. On the basis of his Parliamentary Powers Index, Fish finds that Russia is considered semi-presidential on rather weak grounds, and that in fact it is super-presidential. Only the right of the lower house to approve the president's nominee as prime minister gives it a tenuous claim to be semi-presidential, but the costs of rejecting the nomination three times are so high, namely dissolution and all the risks associated with a new election, that parliament would have to be suicidal to exercise its formal powers. However, defenders of the constitution, such as one of its authors, Viktor Sheinis, counter by arguing that the letter of the constitution has little to do with the issue; the key problem is that the spirit of constitutionalism is lacking. Democratic evolutionists see plenty of potential for the development of a more robust adherence to the spirit of legality, despite present setbacks.

The tutelary role of the regime may well have helped stabilize the state, but the quality of democracy was bound to suffer. The system in formal institutional terms is undoubtedly a liberal democracy, but practice often falls short of declared principles. The constitution of 1993 is a liberal document enshrining fundamental human rights, the rule of law, separation of powers, federalism, and accountable governance, but the powers of the executive are enormous and allow the emergence of a relatively autonomous power center unconstrained either vertically or horizontally. Elsewhere we have called this a regime system, to a degree unlimited by the constitutional constraints of the formal state order from above, and relatively unaccountable to the representative system from below.[16] The Constitutional Court remains a serious and authoritative body, and there have been sustained attempts to give muscle to the independence of the judicial system, including the widespread introduction of jury trials. However, in practice, Putin's administration, while certainly remaining within the letter of the constitution, undermined the motivating spirit of democracy, political pluralism, and judicial impartiality. There is thus rich ground for disagreement, since partisans of both the democratic evolutionist and failed democratization camps can always find evidence to support their case.

A number of countries can be described as "para-democracies," where real power lies not with the constitutionally vested authorities but with groups outside the formal power system. This was the case, for example, in Greece following the end of the civil war in 1949 up to the military coup of 1967, with the formal democratic procedures vulnerable to interference by forces not subservient to the democratic process. Local bosses were able to carve out fiefdoms, and central government was prey to endless crises, with more than thirty governments between the end of the German occupation and 1967, and at all levels patronage relations prevailed. As in Russia, this system of controlled democracy was characterized by weak political parties, which were based on personalities rather than coherent programs. However, a fundamental difference with Russia is that in the latter there is no equivalent to repeated interventions by the military and the monarchy. Instead, in Russia the interventions come from within the system itself, and this endows the formal institutions of the state with a fungibility that inhibits their hardening into more or less autonomous structures. Instead, they are permanently susceptible to pressure from the administrative regime. A controlled democracy, therefore, is not only a low-quality democracy but is also accompanied by the degradation of the state.

The geopolitical dilemmas facing Putin and Medvedev have a strong historical resonance. Frustrated by the failure to achieve a viable framework for political relations between the post-Soviet states in Eurasia, the resolute geopolitical struggle with external great powers (America, the European Union, China) in the region, and his exasperation with domestic liberal and democratic forces, Putin became ever more a legitimist of the type that Aleksandr I turned into in his final years.[17] Putin's innate antirevolutionism was alarmed by the emergence of social movement "network" revolutions, which adopted a number of colors (rose, orange, and tulip) but which in all cases threatened his sense of the proper order of things. As befitting a person from the security apparatus, he had a deeply conservative view of how political change should take place. At the same time, Putin was unable to understand why Russia was not treated as just another of the great powers; since in his view there was no longer anything to fear from Russia, he assumed that the West would have "the serenity of spirit to understand her more."[18] Putin believed, with justice, that Russia was developing according to the same universal laws as the West, but later and more slowly. The decline in ideological hostility of the communist sort made possible a qualitatively better relationship with the West, but the Cold War spirit on both sides intruded.

Part of the reason for the remaining "extraordinary" elements in Russian politics is the nature of adaptation to contemporary modernity. We can briefly characterize this as a process of partial and dual adaptation.[19] Political adaptation is necessarily a partial process, since only in postcolonial and postwar contexts can one country try to copy wholesale the institutions of another. The nature and parameters of this *difference* need to be explored. Traditionalists insist that the gulf separating Russia from the West is enormous, and therefore favor yet another *Sonderweg* that would affirm Russia's distinctive native traditions (*samobytnost'*). The security-focused part of the elite points to the danger to national security and national interests from full adaptation to external models. For economic liberals, the elements of difference are precisely those that are dysfunctional, and hence in their view Russia should adapt fully and unreservedly to the global economic order. The essence of Putin's leadership was the attempt to negotiate a new balance between adaptation and affirmation. A system of "partial adaptation" emerged, appealing to Russian political culture and shaped by security concerns while at the same time integrating into the international economy. The partial nature of Putin's adaptation strategy was derived in part from the traditional imbalance between economic and political facets of modernization, but also from the belief that excessive adaptation could be as dangerous as too little. While committed to a certain type of democratization, the Putin leadership insisted that democracy needs to be rooted in, and congruent with, national conditions.

The strategy of partial adaptation is therefore a balancing act torn by its inherent dualism. On the one hand, it looks to the norms and standards prevalent in the countries of advanced modernity; on the other, it seeks to root the adaptive process in a native discourse (managed and interpreted, of course, by the regime) while refusing to succumb to nationalist insularism. This dualism characterizes most democratic institutions and processes in Russia and provides the conceptual basis for the dual state. The Putin strategy for political and economic modernization could not depend on the strata or institutions traditionally relied on by modernizing regimes, such as the army or Western-educated elites, and while forced in part to adapt to the social milieu in which it finds itself, it feared above all being absorbed by that milieu, in particular the social forces unleashed by the transition process itself. Thus even the practice of dual adaptation (to external modernity and domestic reality) is partial. Putin's modernizing technocratic regime became increasingly isolated, and bereft of substantive support from abroad and unable to rely on the new sociopolitical forces in the land (big business and regional elites), it became increasingly reliant on epigones of the security apparatus and the bureaucracy, both of which were oriented to the power system itself. The existence of this bureaucratic mass provided scope for innovation, since it furnished critical support to the modernizing leadership, but at the same time it subverted the development of the autonomous agents of a genuinely modern society, while the striving for regulation and control by the *securitistas* threatened liberty itself.

PROBLEMS OF POWER CONCENTRATION

Democracy in Russia is faced with the task of creating the conditions for its own existence; to which postulate Putin has implicitly added that this cannot be done by following the logic of democracy itself. Therein lies a further level of duality—between the stated goals of the regime and its practices—which permanently subverts the principles which it proclaims. Putin's team dismantled the network of business and regional relationships that had developed under Yeltsin, and although in policy terms there was significant continuity between the two periods, where power relations were concerned a sharp gulf separates the two leaderships. Putin recruited former associates from St. Petersburg and the security forces, and on this he built a team focused on the presidential administration in the Kremlin that drove through the new agenda.[20] The power of the most egregiously political oligarchs was reduced, and from their exile in London and Tel Aviv they plotted their revenge, further stoking the paranoia of the *siloviki*. With the fear of the oligarchical Jacobites abroad, instability spreading across the North Caucasus, and the specter of color revolutions, it is not surprising that the regime exhibited all the symptoms of a siege mentality, and its legitimism took an ever more conservative hue.

The Putin administration initially drew on staff from the Yeltsin team, notably Aleksandr Voloshin at the head of the presidential administration and Mikhail Kasianov as prime minister. At the same time, a parallel administration was built up in the Kremlin, and gradually it dispensed with the services of Yeltsin's old guard. This was accompanied by a shift in policy priorities in the middle period of Putin's leadership. The "over-mighty subjects" had been tamed and now the Kremlin went on the offensive, not only to ensure its own prerogatives in economic policy and political life, but also to forge a new model of political economy where the state's preferences predominated. The Yukos affair represented a major disciplinary act, not only ensuring that business leaders stayed out of politics, but also bringing the state back into the heart of business life.[21] This was achieved not so much by renationalization as through "deprivatization." Economic policy was no longer a matter for autonomous economic agents but had to be coordinated with the state, while the state itself became a major player in the economic arena (in particular in the energy sector) through its "national champions," above all Gazprom and Rosneft.

The equivalent of deprivatization in the political sphere was "de-autonomization." The ability of political actors to act as independent agents was reduced through a not-so-subtle and at times brutal system of rewards and punishments, while the economic bases of independent political activity were systematically dismantled. The "imposed consensus" of Russia's elite, as Gel'man notes, was achieved through the Kremlin's use of "selective punishment of some elite sections and selective cooptation of others."[22] As long as the Kremlin had adequate resources in material, political capital, and authority terms to rein in potentially fractious elites, the system could continue, but there was an ever present threat of defection. An unprecedented decade-long economic boom, accompanied by windfall energy rents, reinforced the position of the power elite. This allowed a new type of "neo-Stalinist compromise" to be imposed: the government promised rising standards of living in exchange for restrictions on independent popular political participation, a pact that could only be sustained, as Mikhail Gorbachev discovered to his cost in the late 1980s, as long as the economy could deliver the goods. A decline in primary commodity prices could threaten the support basis of the regime.

The fundamental problem of a concentrated power system is to ensure adequate renewal to avoid rendering itself so inward looking as to become dysfunctional. The reliance on a small coterie of trusted followers and the resulting weakness of competent personnel leads to reduced governmental capacity and poor policy performance. The chief mechanism used by the Putin administration to avoid this fate was to undertake periodic personnel reshuffles. There were four major episodes of these. The first on March 28, 2001, saw some of the most egregiously corrupt of the Yeltsin cohort purged, notably Nikolai Aksënenko from his post at the railways ministry, and the elevation of Putin's allies, notably Sergei Ivanov, who was appointed defense minister. Coming exactly a year after his election, Putin asserted his authority over personnel, hitherto possibly limited by the terms of the transitional deal with Yeltsin. The second reshuffling, on February 24, 2004, saw the appointment of Mikhail Fradkov as prime minister to replace Kasianov. The third, on November 14, 2005, signaled the beginning of an elite realignment in preparation for the succession in 2008. The former head of the presidential administration, Dmitri Medvedev, became first deputy prime minister, and the defense minister, Sergei Ivanov, became a deputy prime minister. Thus the two primary candidates for the succession were in place. They joined the liberal economist Alexander Zhukov, who had earlier been the only deputy prime minister. He also now brought in talented outsiders, including the governor of the energy-producing region of Tyumen, Sergei Sobyanin, as the new chief of staff. The fourth change, on September 12, 2007, saw Fradkov replaced as prime minister by Viktor Zubkov, accompanied by a limited cabinet reshuffle.

The way Putin undertook these periodic personnel reshuffles was typical of his political style: a sudden and dramatic announcement, typically coming like a bolt from a blue sky. At the same time, they revealed the constraints he worked under. Even as president his word was far from law. Some 1,800 policy-relevant decrees issued by Putin during his eight years as president remained unimplemented, and to overcome resistance to his proposals he had to ensure that resistance within his administration was outflanked. These reshuffles created a system that ensured the succession and endured beyond the parliamentary elections of December 2007 and the presidential elections of March 2008.

The reshuffles were accompanied by the strengthening of the "party of power," United Russia (UR), which increasingly became the core of a "dominant-party" system. The establishment of UR represented a significant development, since it did not simply represent the existing power system but sought to set up an alternative structure in whose name a government could be formed.[23] Fear of the autonomous development of an independent political force in the past ensured that no party of power managed to make a credible showing in a second election, but United Russia's triumph in the December 2003 elections indicated that a new pattern of politics was emerging. This was confirmed by its even more convincing victory in the December 2007 Duma election. The party emerged as an instrument in Putin's struggle to bring regional executives to heel, but it began to take on a life of its own. The creation of a system of autonomous political actors came into contradiction with the attempt to subordinate it to the regime-state.

THE PARADOXES OF PUTIN'S LEADERSHIP

A paradox is defined as a self-contradiction that conflicts with preconceived notions of what is reasonable, possible, or true, but which is essentially well founded. Putin's leadership is thus paradoxical in two senses: its self-contradictory internal characteristics, but also in the way that it is received and interpreted. The quality of ambiguity is thus inherent in Putin's leadership, in domestic affairs as much as in foreign policy.

The polymorphous nature of Putin's leadership is striking, and this was reflected in his ability to garner a broad and in some respects incompatible electorate in 2000. As Colton and McFaul put it, "So far as Putin's electorate is concerned, the fascinating thing is how he tapped into the desire of so many Russians to avoid having to make these wrenching choices, as opposed to opting unreservedly for democracy (which very few were willing to do) or choosing autocracy (which most [Gennadi] Ziuganov [the head of the Communist Party of the Russian Federation] voters did not flinch at). Sixty-one percent of Putin voters in 2000 believed Russia could combine democracy and a strong state and 69 percent believed it could experience both democracy and economic growth."[24] Putin's approval rating throughout his presidency rarely dipped below 70 percent, and there was an extraordinary consistency over the years in popular views. Putin reflected the policy preferences of the population, with just under half supporting the continuation of reforms but with a stronger state role and ensuring popular welfare, while only 10 percent called for the continuation of reforms with a decreased role for the state, while another 11 percent supported the swift and decisive implementation of reform. Only 22 percent favored a return to the Soviet system.[25]

Putin's approach to politics was characterized by a number of features. Antirevolutionism was a theme stressed from the very first days of his leadership, and he remained consistent in upholding the principle of constitutionally endowed legitimacy and the ordered transfer of power. In his state of the nation speech to the Federal Assembly on April 3, 2001, Putin noted, "The past decade was a stormy time for Russia. It is no exaggeration to describe that time as revolutionary." Against that background, the early years of the new century appeared calm in comparison. Although he insisted that the country should not be afraid of change, this should be justified by the situation.

People's fears, he noted, were based on the logical chain: revolution was followed by counterrevolution, and "reforms are followed by counterreforms," accompanied typically by a witch-hunt against alleged "culprits of a revolution carried too far." Russia's historical experience was rich in such examples. But then Putin unexpectedly concluded: "This cycle is over. There will be no more revolutions or counterrevolutions."[26] This perhaps was an unconscious echo of the cry of Thermidorians throughout the ages, who seek to repudiate the excesses of the revolution while enjoying the fruits of its achievements. Russia's revolution of the 1990s, of course, was of a distinctive type: seeking not to devise a new model but to graft an already functioning type of democratic capitalist system devised in the West onto Russia. It was, moreover, carried out largely "from above," with the elements of popular mobilization of the late 1980s soon drying up and with a minimum of violence, the events of 1991 and 1993 excepted.[27]

A second key principle of Putin's leadership, following from the first, is his emphasis on legitimism, a feature we have touched on earlier. From the very first, he stressed that he would not change the constitution and would abide by its stipulations. In technical terms, he did just this, and his departure from the presidency in 2008 confirmed Putin as someone who ruled according to the letter of the law. Putin also appealed to the principle of legitimism in his relations with leaders in the Commonwealth of Independent States (CIS). This led him to support what in any lexicon are authoritarian leaders, such as Islam Karimov in Uzbekistan and Aleksandr Lukashenko in Belarus. Of course, legitimism here was reinforced by issues of geostrategic advantage, but the principle was also applied in cases where Russia's national interests were less clear-cut. Putin's overemphatic support for the succession of power from Leonid Kuchma to Viktor Yanukovych in Ukraine in late 2004 ignored the fact that the final winner, Viktor Yushchenko, had forged strong economic and political ties with Russia when he had been prime minister earlier. It may be noted that at this time Putin stuck his neck out in an unusually undiplomatic manner in support of George W. Bush's reelection as U.S. president. It is very much part of his character to take a decision and then stick to it through thick and thin. Putin's legitimist approach is therefore reinforced by his aversion to revolutionary changes of power.[28] In relations with the former Soviet states, however, this did not made him a neo-Brezhnevian, and Russia's lack of intervention in support of Askar Akaev at the time of the Tulip Revolution in March 2005 makes it clear that no updated version of the Brezhnev doctrine was in the offing. Opposition to the expansion of NATO to Ukraine and Georgia was considered resistance to an existential threat to Russia's fundamental security interests and not an attempt to limit the sovereignty of these countries. Equally, intervention in South Ossetia and Abkhazia in August 2008 from the Russian perspective was considered a defensive reaction to the Georgian attack.

The third feature of Putin's leadership is the one referred to above: Thermidor. If we consider Putin's attempts to consolidate the state as a type of Thermidor, then it is indeed of a peculiar "soft" sort, if anything a counter-reform rather than a counterrevolution. Rather than explicitly repudiating the revolutionary regime of the 1990s, Putin in fact was hand-picked as that regime's chosen instrument of succession. His aim was certainly not to undo the work of the 1990s but to give it a firmer legal and economic basis. He sought to perpetuate and consolidate the institutions of the earlier period, with the 1993 constitution at its center. Yet there are Thermidorian elements in Putin's rule, reflected in the rejection of the polarized politics of the earlier period and attempts to build a genuine policy consensus. Above all, Thermidor signals the end of societal predominance and the attempt to insulate the state from direct social power. The nature of Putinite state restoration is certainly capable of contrasting interpretations, but there is a clear tension between a strong state, which in the contemporary world entails the development of a ramified constitutional order, and the strengthening of the power system associated with a particular elite configuration in a regime interposed between the state and society. This would be compatible with an appeal to the constitution in the form of a *Rechtssaat.* Zakaria terms this an "illiberal democracy."[29] Russian idiom at first called this "managed democracy" and later "sovereign democracy," while in the Singapore of Lee Kuan Yew and his successors, it is known as "trustee" democracy. The consolidation of the "vertical" of regime power has been accompanied by the loss of independence of the Duma, the Federation Council, and the judiciary, and the undermining of the federal system, all of which contributed to a weakening of the division of powers and the establishment of a new system of patronage politics. Oligarchic capitalism gave way to neopatrimonial bureaucratic capitalism with corporatist overtones.

The fourth of Putin's paradoxes is his relationship to politics: a consummate politician, he was nevertheless antipolitical. He neutralized the irresponsible utopianism of the communist left while constraining the dangerous ambitions of the nationalist right. He retained the support of a large part of the population, the respect of important sections of the international community, and the loyalty of the bulk of the elite within the country. He drove through a reform agenda designed to turn Russia into a functioning market society. He also had a social agenda that raised living standards, ensured that wages were paid on time, and began to reorient welfare services toward more targeted needs, although as president he failed to push through pension reform, something that he was faced with as prime minister. When faced with mass public protest against the monetization of social benefits in early 2005, he acted like any good politician: he made a concession here, found a scapegoat there, and in general emerged relatively unscathed from the whole episode. The "Teflon" character of his leadership was particularly visible following dramatic and catastrophic episodes such as the *Kursk* disaster in August 2000, the Du- brovka theater siege in October 2002, and the Beslan school hostage crisis in September 2004, accompanied by a growing wave of insurgency throughout the North Caucasus. Although he managed to resolve the Chechen conflict, the price was a radical "Chechenization" that transferred power to native elites, allowing Ramzan Kadyrov from 2007 to consolidate an extraordinary sultanist form of personal power. Putin's popularity endured through care- ful political management, political dexterity, and the ability to evoke trust by resonating with the people's aspirations and self-image.[30]

In international affairs, Putin gained much political mileage in the wake of the September 11, 2001, terrorist attacks in the United States, and he cleverly avoided the pitfalls attending the Iraq War launched by the United States in 2003. However, U.S. plans to place elements of missile defense in Poland and the Czech Republic, announced in January 2007, represented a major threat to his vision of international relations, and his general sense that Russia's views were being discounted provoked his robust speech asserting Russia's interests in Munich in February 2007.[31] International tensions once again threatened to derail domestic development.

Putin's leadership was goal oriented, focusing above all on state rehabilita- tion, while the quality of the political process was a secondary concern. The stress on outcomes fostered a negligent attitude to the finer arts of public debate, winning popular support for policies, and engaging in the cut and thrust of election campaigns. The niceties of democratic politics were not his forte. On several occasions, he noted his distaste for what he considered the populist politicking that accompanies electoral campaigns. His personal distaste for public politics encouraged him to focus on set-piece, staged public events, notably the annual state of the nation speech, question and answer sessions with the people, and speeches at public events. The "malaise of antipolitics," to use Ghia Nodia's expression, is prevalent across the post- communist world, and Putin certainly shares this characteristic with Yeltsin. As Nodia puts it, "The Communist regime parodied and discredited things political, such as political parties, ideologies, institutions, and the notion of a 'public good' as such. The label of 'falsity' firmly stuck to the public sphere, and politics was a priori considered a 'dirty business,' with the values of goodness and truth sought only in the private domain."[32] Antipolitics in the post-Soviet world promoted the anarchic disintegration of the state by delegitimizing its functions and role, and in certain Latin American countries it spawned various types of populism. However, Putin's antipolitics are of a distinctive sort: Putin is resolutely a state builder and certainly not a populist. He did not flinch from adopting policies that threatened to damage his pop- ularity, such as allying himself with American hegemonic power after 9/11, or pushing through the monetization of social benefits in early 2005. He was a conviction politician, fearless in pursuing policies that he believed to be right and in Russia's national interests. This was the case, as he saw it, in deciding to launch the second Chechen war in September 1999, and his decision to endorse an American military presence in Central Asia, traditionally Russia's "back yard." The demarcation of the long border with China was not something designed to win popularity at home, yet it was undoubtedly in Russia's interests finally to put an end to the tensions that in the 1960s nearly led to war between the two "fraternal" socialist states.

The fifth feature, following from the above, is Putin's instrumental view of politics. Putin sponsored the development of the institutions of representative democracy, above all the creation of a viable party system and livelier regional legislatures, but these measures were vitiated by heavy-handed interventions. His antipolitics was of a distinctive sort, lacking an ideological basis but operating strictly at the level of technocratic functionality. While Putin was rhetorically committed to the development of democracy, he retained an instrumental view of its operation. He had a strong sense of the "public good," but the definition of the public weal remained outside the political process. His administration did not hesitate to use whatever administrative measures necessary to achieve the desired outcome. This was notably the case in Chechen policy: from the referendum on the new republican constitution on March 23, 2003; the election of Akhmad Kadyrov on October 5 of that year, when a number of less accommodating candidates were prevented from standing, through to the election of his successor, Alu Alkhanov, on August 29, 2004; the elections to the republic's parliament on November 27, 2005, when turnout figures were greatly inflated; and ending with the confirmation of Ramzan Kadyrov as president on March 2, 2007. As with so many of his policies, Putin's plans to restore normality to Chechnya were vitiated by the means chosen to implement them. Guardianship over the electoral process here and in Russia as a whole could not but weaken the legitimacy of the political system as a whole. Putin's administration in general, despite much Western commentary to this effect, was not bent toward the establishment of an authoritarian system, and neither was it simply interested in hanging onto power at all costs. It had a clear modernizing agenda, and thus it can be seen as a developmental regime. But like so many earlier programs of modernization from above, the means undermined the ends. Both democracy and modernization as a whole require the engagement of free actors and individuals to make the whole process self-sustaining and autonomous.

Putin's instrumental view of politics gave rise to a sixth feature, discussed above: para-constitutionalism. Putin's commitment to legitimism did not prevent him from developing a range of para-constitutional instruments. A number of institutions were created that, while formally not subverting the constitution, are not based on the constitution. These include the presidential plenipotentiary in the seven federal districts, the State Council duplicating some of the work of the Federation Council, and the Public Chamber taking up aspects of the work properly the preserve of the State Duma. Para-constitutional institutions are accompanied by a range of para-constitutional procedures, notably through the use of "administrative resources" in elections, frequent changes in the legislation regulating elections, changes to the way that the Federation Council is formed, and the abolition of competitive elections for regional governors. None of these actions may technically have contravened the letter of the constitution, but they all eroded the spirit of constitutionalism.

The seventh feature is Putin's emphasis on the leading role of the state in Russia's postcommunist modernization. In the postcommunist transitional period, the "dictatorship of the proletariat"—envisaged by Marx as the period of extralegal class dominance of the makers of the socialist revolution—in the 1990s gave way to the dictatorship of the executive designed to push through a modernization process that would ultimately render that dictatorship, as it would for Marx, redundant. But as with Marx, there was no time period suggested, and in any case, the "proletariat" and the "executive" are to a degree abstractions, and the real subject of the dictatorship in both the Soviet Union and postcommunist Russia was the bureaucracy. It was Putin's achievement not only to reconstitute the state but also to endow it with a renewed legitimacy drawn from its developmental agenda. Modernization is complemented by the idea that Russia has to act as an effective "competition state," locked in struggle with other powers for economic and geopolitical advantage.[33] While the state's capacity to enforce rules remains limited, and the gulf between its claims to represent the universal interest of the public good and the empirical reality of self-seeking elites at the national and regional levels mired in corruption remains stark, the regeneration of the legitimacy of state interests is a major achievement. Indeed, the stick may well have been bent too far, and the legitimacy of pluralism, competing interest groups, partisan politics, and open-ended debate has been undermined. Putin's emphasis on modernizing Russia was filtered through partial and dual adaptation, and thus he is wary of political Westernization, and certainly of the influence of Western agencies, and this lingering insularity of the Soviet type has in turn fostered a residual spirit of the Cold War.

The Putin elite embodied a colonial image of state authority. Paternalism was deeply embedded in the operating code of the Soviet system, and the tendency to keep the population in a condition of political infantilism has been perpetuated. Just as colonial regimes typically act *in loco parentis* over their subject populations, so, too, the tutelary nature of the Putin regime failed to foster the spirit of citizenship and political responsibility among the Russian population. Putin's state building was reminiscent of Jacobin holistic or integrative republicanism, deeply opposed to anything that could fragment the unity of the single people. By the same token, vital republicanism, based on the lively interplay of political forces and a distinct concept of "the political," was eroded. The perpetuation, indeed intensification, of patrimonial features of governance exposed the failure of the Putin regime to embrace a more complex model of modernization, when changes from above are rooted in engagement from below. Ironically, the fragmentation that Putin's administration so abhorred in society reemerged at the level of the regime. A system of bureaucratic pluralism and fragmented elite structures at the state level, each with its system of patron-client relations, indicated that Russia had failed to establish an autonomous political sphere, and instead politics was riddled with factional conflicts rooted in the socioeconomic order.[34] The patrimonial party-building endeavor associated with the development of United Russia is a case in point, where the absence of political autonomy rendered the party lifeless and a subaltern agency to the regime.

CONCLUSION

Putin appealed to the principles of stability, consolidation, and reassertion of the prerogatives of the state. However, the concepts of consensus, centrism, and the appeal to "normal" politics were beset by a number of fundamental contradictions. These contradictions are reflected in the central problem facing any analysis of Putin's leadership: the nature of his statism. It is not difficult to identify tensions in the "project" espoused by Putin, but these tensions became the source of much of his power. The issue is not simply that he was able to appeal to a variety of constituencies, many of which would be exclusive if his ideas were enunciated more clearly, but that the very nature of Putin's centrism was a mechanism to reconcile antagonistic and contradictory social programs. He transcended narrow party politics and affiliation with either left or right not by evasion, but by a distinct type of political praxis that was transcendent of the classic political cleavages of the age of modernity. It would be hard to label Putin's policies as president or prime minister as either "left" or "right," and the same applies to Medvedev. The label of "liberal conservative" has been used to describe Putin's leadership, an oxymoron that typifies the contradictory nature of his leadership. In an age when politics is based less on interests or ideologies than on identities and values, Putin reconciled policies and groups that in an earlier period would have been in conflict. Putin's style is antipolitical, although as a leader confronted by the need to reconcile conflicting interests and views, he proved a highly adept politician. Democracy in Russia was forced to create the conditions for its own existence, and this self-constitutive characteristic imbued political processes in the country with a contradictory dynamic.

Putin's new statism carried both a positive and a negative charge. The normative resources of the constitutional state were balanced against the arbitrariness of the prerogative state managed by a security-minded regime.

Putin emphasized "the dictatorship of law," and thus encouraged the development of a genuine rule-of-law state, but it did not subordinate itself to the pluralistic political process enshrined in the constitution. Once again traditions of the "revolution from above" were perpetuated, and patterns of lawlessness and arbitrariness were replicated. Putin insisted that the 1993 constitution established a viable framework for the development of a new governmental order, but his leadership was characterized by the absence of the spirit of constitutionalism, and this in turn undermined faith in the evolutionary potential of the constitution. There were few restraints on presidential power, and parliament and society were unable to call the authorities to account. Medvedev's key challenge was to overcome the gulf between the prerogative and the normative (constitutional) state and finally to achieve not rule by law but the rule of law.

The characteristic feature of modernity is the emergence of autonomous civic actors accompanied by attempts of the state to manage various transformative projects that entail the management and reordering of society. In this respect, Putin reflected the larger contradiction within modernity. It is a contradiction exacerbated in Russia by the clear tension between liberal democratic aspirations and the state's inability to act as a coherent vessel in which these aspirations can be fulfilled. For this reason, many have argued that a strong state is an essential precondition for the development of liberalism,[35] while others see it as the greatest threat to those liberties. This is a contradiction that lies at the heart of Putin's liberal statism, and one that poses the greatest challenge for Medvedev.

SUGGESTED READINGS

Fish, M. Steven. *Democracy Derailed in Russia: The Failure of Open Politics.* Cambridge: Cambridge University Press, 2005.

McFaul, Michael, Nikolai Petrov, and Andrei Ryabov. *Between Dictatorship and Democracy: Russian Post-Communist Political Reform.* Washington, D.C.: Carnegie Endowment for International Peace, 2004.

Remington, Thomas. *Politics in Russia.* 4th ed. London: Pearson Longman, 2006.

Ross, Cameron, ed. *Russian Politics under Putin.* Manchester: Manchester University Press, 2004.

Sakwa, Richard. *Putin: Russia's Choice.* 2nd ed. London: Routledge, 2008.

———. *Russian Politics and Society.* 4th ed. London: Routledge, 2008.

NOTES

1. Martin Malia, *Russia under Western Eyes: From the Bronze Horseman to the Lenin Mausoleum* (Cambridge, Mass.: Belknap, 2000), 411–12.

2. Ernst Fraenkel, *The Dual State: A Contribution to the Theory of Dictatorship*, trans. E. A. Shils in collaboration with Edith Lowenstein and Klaus Knorr (New York: Oxford University Press, 1941; reprinted by Lawbook Exchange, 2006).

3. Andrew Wilson, *Virtual Politics: Faking Democracy in the Post-Soviet World* (New Haven: Yale University Press, 2005).

4. See, for example, Mark R. Thompson, "Whatever Happened to 'Asian Values'?" *Journal of Democracy* 12, no. 4 (2001): 154–63.

5. Samuel P. Huntington, "Democracy's Third Wave," *Journal of Democracy* 1, no. 2 (1991): 12–34. The argument was developed at length in Samuel P. Huntington, *The Third Wave: Democratization in the Late Twentieth Century* (Norman: University of Oklahoma Press, 1991).

6. Ernest Gellner, *Conditions of Liberty: Civil Society and Its Rivals* (New York: Viking, 1994).

7. The "Plan" encompassed all eight of Putin's state of the nation addresses as well as his "Russia at the Turn of the Millennium" article of December 30, 1999; his February 10, 2007, speech to the Munich security conference; and some other key speeches. See *Plan prezidenta Putina: Rukovodstvo dlia budushchikh prezidentov Rossii* (Moscow: Evropa, 2007).

8. "Vystuplenie na vneocherednom s'ezde Assotsiatsii iuristov Rossii," January 29, 2008, www.medvedev2008.ru/live_press_01_29_law.htm.

9. "Vystuplenie na V Krasnoyarskom ekonomicheskom forume 'Rossiia 2008–2020: Upravlenie rostom,'" www.medvedev2008.ru/live_press_15_02.htm.

10. For an overview, see Harley Balzer, "Managed Pluralism: Vladimir Putin's Emerging Regime," *Post-Soviet Affairs* 19, no. 3 (2003): 189–227.

11. See www.kremlin.ru/text/appears/2005/04/87049.shtml; *Rossiiskaia gazeta*, April 25, 2005.

12. See Richard Sakwa, "Two Camps? The Struggle to Understand Contemporary Russia," *Comparative Politics* 40, no. 4 (2008): 481–99.

13. M. Steven Fish, *Democracy Derailed in Russia: The Failure of Open Politics* (New York: Cambridge University Press, 2005), 1.

14. For example, Peter Reddaway and Dmitri Glinski, *The Tragedy of Russia's Reforms: Market Bolshevism against Democracy* (Washington, D.C.: U.S. Institute of Peace Press, 2001).

15. See Harley Balzer, "Vladimir Putin's Academic Writings and Russian Natural Resource Policy," *Problems of Post-Communism* 53, no. 1 (2006): 48–54, with Putin's article "Mineral Natural Resources in the Strategy for Development of the Russian Economy," at 49–54.

16. Richard Sakwa, "The Regime System in Russia," *Contemporary Politics* 3, no. 1 (1997): 7–25; Richard Sakwa, *Russian Politics and Society*, 3rd ed. (London: Routledge, 2002), 454–58; Richard Sakwa, *Putin: Russia's Choice* (London: Routledge, 2004), 86–88.

17. Malia explains Aleksandr I's position as follows: "Hemmed in by his position as one of the chief architects and guarantors of the Vienna system, and increasingly frustrated by his failures to effect reform at home, [Aleksandr] became ever more preoccupied with preserving 'legitimacy' and the established order throughout Europe." Malia, *Russia under Western Eyes*, 91.

18. Malia, *Russia under Western Eyes*, 167.

19. The theme of partial adaptation is explored in Richard Sakwa, "Partial Adaptation and Political Culture," in *Political Culture and Post-Communism*, ed. Stephen Whitefield (Basingstoke: Palgrave Macmillan, 2005), 42–53, from which this paragraph draws.

20. On the size and role of the *siloviki* in Putin's administration, see Olga Kryshtanovkaya and Stephen White, "Putin's Militocracy," *Post-Soviet Affairs* 19, no. 4 (2003): 289–306; for updated figures, see Olga Kryshtanovkaya and Stephen White, "Inside the Putin Court: A Research Note," *Europe-Asia Studies* 57, no. 7 (2005): 1065–75.

21. See William Tompson, "Putin and the 'Oligarchs': A Two-sided Commitment Problem," in *Leading Russia: Putin in Perspective*, ed. Alex Pravda (Oxford: Oxford University Press, 2005), 179–202; also William Tompson, "Putting Yukos in Perspective," *Post-Soviet Affairs* 21, no. 2 (2005).

22. Vladimir Gel'man, "Political Opposition in Russia: A Dying Species?" *Post-Soviet Affairs* 21, no. 3 (2005): 242.

23. Pavel Isaev, "Ob'edinennaia partiia vlasti vystraivaet svoiu regional'nuiu vertikal' so skandalom," *Rossiiskii regional'byi biulleten'* 4, no. 6 (2002).

24. Timothy J. Colton and Michael McFaul, *Popular Choice and Managed Democracy: The Russian Elections of 1999 and 2000* (Washington, D.C.: Brookings Institution Press, 2003), 222–3.

25. Levada Center poll of December 2005, www.levada.ru/press/2005122901 .html.

26. Russian Information Agency Novosti, April 4, 2001, http://en.rian.ru/rian/poslanie.cfm.

27. Gordon M. Hahn, *Russia's Revolution from Above, 1985–2000: Reform, Transition, and Revolution in the Fall of the Soviet Communist Regime* (New Brunswick, N.J.: Transaction, 2002); see also Michael McFaul, *Russia's Unfinished Revolution: Political Change from Gorbachev to Putin* (Ithaca, N.Y.: Cornell University Press, 2001).

28. As Putin put it, "As far as all post-Soviet space is concerned, I am concerned above all about attempts to resolve legal issues by illegal means. That is the most dangerous thing. It is most dangerous to think up a system of permanent revolutions—now the Rose Revolution, or the Blue Revolution. You should get used to living according to the law, rather than according to political expediency defined elsewhere for some or other nation—that is what worries me most. Certain rules and procedures should mature within society. Of course, we should pay attention to, support and help democracies but, if we embark on the road of permanent revolutions, nothing good will come from this for these countries, and for these peoples. We will plunge all the post-Soviet space into a series of never-ending conflicts, which will have extremely serious consequences." Vladimir Putin, "This Year Was Not an Easy One," *International Affairs* (Moscow) 51, no. 1 (2005): 2.

29. Fareed Zakaria, "The Rise of Illiberal Democracy," *Foreign Affairs* 76, no. 6 (1997): 22–43.

30. E. B. Shestopal, *Obrazy vlasti v post-sovetskoi Rossii* (Moscow: Aleteia, 2004), esp. chap. 15.

31. See http://president.kremlin.ru/text/appears/2007/02/118109.shtml.

32. Ghia Nodia, "Putting the State Back Together in Post-Soviet Georgia," in *Beyond State Crisis? Postcolonial Africa and Post-Soviet Eurasia in Comparative Perspective*, ed. Mark R. Beissinger and Crawford Young (Washington, D.C.: Woodrow Wilson Center Press, 2002), 435.

33. This theme has been given public form by Vladislav Surkov, deputy head of the presidential administration, in a number of interviews, including in *Komsomolskaia Pravda*, September 29, 2004; *Der Spiegel*, June 20, 2005; and in comments delivered to a closed meeting of the general council of the journal *Delovaia Rossiia* on May 16, 2005, publicized by Radio Liberty on July 11, 2005. In the first, he talked of Russia's enemies trying "to destroy Russia and fill its enormous expanses with numerous nonviable quasi-state formations. . . . The main aim of the interventionists is the destruction of Russian statehood." In his speech to *Delovaia Rossiia*, he argued that the regime's aim was "sovereign democracy": "I often hear that democracy is more important than sovereignty. We do not agree with that. We think that both are needed. An independent state is worth fighting for."

34. A feature identified already in the mid-1990s by Thomas Graham, "Novyi rossiiskii rezhim," *Nezavisimaia gazeta*, November 23, 1995.

35. For example, Marcia A. Weigle, *Russia's Liberal Project: State-Society Relations in the Transition from Communism* (University Park, Pa.: Penn State University Press, 2000), 458, where she talks of the need for a "state-dominated liberalism."

Chapter Two

Parliament and the Dominant Party Regime

Thomas F. Remington

One of the most important constitutional reforms in Russia after the end of the communist regime was the establishment of the principle of separation of powers. Article 10 of the 1993 constitution stipulates: "State power in the Russian Federation shall be exercised on the basis of the separation of the legislative, executive and judiciary branches. The bodies of legislative, executive and judiciary powers shall be independent." The reason this provision is so significant is that under the Soviet system, constitutional theory held that state power was "fused" in the soviets and that there could be no separation between the branches of state power: "all power to the soviets" meant that state power was unitary. All state power, though exercised through multiple instruments, derived from a single source and served a common purpose. In reality, state power did not flow from the soviets, of course; it was exercised by the Communist Party in the name of the soviets. But the party and state officials nonetheless adhered to the doctrine of the unity of state power, itself a legacy of tsarist absolutism. For this reason, the doctrine of constitutional separation of power represented a revolutionary break from the traditional model of Russian state power.[1]

In the Yeltsin period, there was some separation of powers in fact. To a large degree this was due to the weakness of the executive and the fact that the opposition forces were well represented in the legislature. The president's inability to impose control over all parts of the executive and to enforce his will throughout the regions (in part because of the sharp divisions within the political elite) permitted opposition forces to exert influence over policy through parliament. It also allowed the Constitutional Court a degree of independence in adjudicating disputes arising between the other branches.[2] At one point in 1998, in fact, President Yeltsin backed down in the face of adamant opposition from the Duma to his proposed candidate for prime minister and chose a figure (Evgeni Primakov) more acceptable to the

Duma. Therefore there is no starker contrast between the Putin and Yeltsin presidencies than in the steady aggrandizement of presidential power at the expense of legislative and judicial autonomy under Putin.

Under the constitution, Russia's parliament, the Federal Assembly, has two chambers. The lower chamber is the State Duma and the upper is the Federation Council. In the State Duma, President Putin has achieved total dominance on the basis of a two-thirds majority of seats controlled by the loyal United Russia (UR) faction. In the Federation Council, the Kremlin's managers have seen to it that only individuals loyal to the president are selected as members of the chamber and potential opponents are coopted or intimidated. Similarly, the independence of the judiciary has been sharply restricted by the overwhelming concentration of administrative power in the hands of the presidential administration, so that no significant measure of the president is blocked by the courts. Like the parliament, the courts have become instruments for the endorsement of presidential prerogatives and the suppression of political opposition.

This chapter will concentrate on two closely related developments: the subjugation of parliament, and the creation of a party system in which United Russia dominates regional and federal elections while opposition parties are sidelined. Between the Yeltsin and Putin eras, Russia's political system evolved from one in which "super-presidentialism" tended to undermine incentives for politicians to form competing programmatic parties to one in which politicians have a strong incentive to join the dominant pro-Kremlin party, United Russia.[3] The model resembles that of Mexico's political system in the 1950s and 1960s, when the dominant party, PRI, was intertwined with all institutions of government, which it used to maintain its dominance.[4] The PRI's organizational strength and large majority in the legislature ensured that any laws submitted by the president were rubber-stamped; opposition parties faced a variety of legal and extralegal forms of repression but were allowed to win minor electoral victories for the sake of preserving the façade of democracy; and the country's president headed a system of patron-client networks through which he dispensed rewards and punishments intended to keep him and his supporters in power.[5] Such a system, the Mexican example suggests, can be stable for decades. Since Putin left the presidency to become prime minister, the dominant party regime model is becoming still more entrenched. The regime appears intent on consolidating United Russia's position as the premier political institution linking executive and legislative branches, and central government with government in the regions.

Putin's team created this configuration of power through a succession of skillful institutional maneuvers. Moreover, Putin benefited from a spike in world oil prices that began almost at the same time he became president and continued through mid-2008; like the oil prices, his domestic popularity reached extremely high levels (especially impressive in view of Russians' generally cynical view of their leaders).[6] His strategy for taming parliament and building a dominant "party of power" had four elements.

First, beginning in January 2000, when he became acting president, Putin worked to create a loyal majority in the Duma that would ensure passage of any legislation he proposed. He was relatively successful in the Third Duma (2000–2003), when the pro-Putin parliamentary faction Unity formed an alliance with three other factions, and gained control over the agenda. He was spectacularly successful with the Fourth Duma, which convened following the December 2003 parliamentary election. The Fifth Duma elected in December 2007 continued the same pattern.

Second, Putin established direct control over the upper chamber of parliament, the Federation Council, through a reform of the way its members were chosen. The reform, enacted in summer 2000, removed the regional governors from the chamber and replaced them with permanent representatives appointed by the regional governors and legislators. The Kremlin oversaw the appointments process, ensuring that the new members would be faithful to the president's wishes. Since then, the Federation Council has voted by overwhelming margins for all of the president's initiatives.

Third, Putin moved to make United Russia the dominant party throughout the political system, controlling not only the State Duma in Moscow but regional parliaments as well. He did this through a series of legislative acts making it more difficult for other quasi-party structures (such as governors' or oligarchs' machines) to enter the political arena, by pressuring officials at all levels to affiliate with United Russia, and by dividing and diverting the followings of rival parties, such as the communists. These moves gave United Russia a resounding victory in the 2003 and 2007 Duma elections; both elections awarded United Russia a two-thirds majority in the Duma. Now Putin's followers did not need to ally with any other forces in the Duma but had complete control over the agenda and the outcome of all voting.

Finally, Putin created a series of extra-constitutional "parallel parliaments," that is, pseudo-parliamentary deliberative bodies that divert policy-making expertise and debate from the parliament to alternative arenas, which the president can consult at his pleasure. To the extent that the president grants these "parallel parliaments" the right to advise him on a particular policy matter, the Federal Assembly loses its constitutional monopoly on lawmaking and executive oversight and simply becomes one more consultative body lending the president the appearance of political support. Among these parallel structures are the State Council (formed in 2000 as part of the reform of the Federation Council) and the Public Chamber (formed in 2005 as one of the reforms Putin proposed following the Beslan incident). In addition, Putin sometimes also relied on the Security Council, a constitutional body which advises the president on national security matters but can be used to develop policy in a wide range of areas.

Taken together, these measures reflect a coherent strategy to ensure that the president can exercise power unchecked by parliament or by opposition forces. Let us review this record in more detail, examine what Putin has done with the power he accumulated so successfully, and see whether the same arrangements are likely to continue under President Dmitri Medvedev.

PUTIN AND THE DUMA

Although the Russian constitution gives the president far-reaching political prerogatives, he must nonetheless obtain the consent of parliament if he seeks to pass legislation. In all cases, the Duma must approve draft legislation before it can be signed into law. There are certain categories of legislation that the Federation Council must consider, and it can consider any bill if it takes it up within two weeks of passage by the Duma. The Federation Council's vetoes of legislation, however, can be overridden by the Duma. The two chambers can also override a presidential veto by a concurrent two-thirds vote. Therefore, if the president wants to enact a law, he must obtain the consent of a majority of the Duma members. The president can enact measures by edict if a law is not already in force, but even then, experience has shown that a law is more stable and therefore more authoritative than a decree, which can be more easily reversed. Putin has preferred to operate by the normal legislative process, in contrast to President Yeltsin, who often relied on presidential decrees (*ukazy*) to enact important policy changes, particularly in 1992–1994. Under Putin, the number and importance of presidential decrees continued to decline. Most presidential decrees concerned not policy matters but appointments, or classified issues such as military procurement.[7]

Thanks to a reliable base of support in the Federal Assembly, Putin's administration and government have enacted a comprehensive body of legislation, some of it aimed at stimulating economic growth and some at restricting the political rights of potential opposition. His success was owed not only to his control over lawmaking in parliament but also to his ability to place the policy development process under central control.

One of Putin's first steps as acting president was to institute a more orderly process for developing policy than had been the case under Yeltsin. The loose and fragmented nature of policy making in the Yeltsin regime meant that many interests, both inside the state's official bodies and outside them, initiated policy. For instance, well-connected business tycoons occasionally pushed through presidential decrees or pieces of legislation, and often presidential initiatives were successfully blocked by powerful but anonymous resistance from within the government bureaucracy.[8]

Putin demanded a much more centralized approach to policy development, and in his first term, he used it to advance a far-reaching agenda of economic and institutional reform. In his first message to parliament in July 2000, Putin listed several ambitious policy measures that he wanted to enact into law. These included a flat income-tax rate, lower taxes on profits, a lower social tax, firm protections on property rights, less intrusive regulation of business, banking reform, property rights in land, labor relations, reform of the customs regime, and a new law on political parties. In his April 3, 2001, message he called for new legislation on federal relations and criminal and civil procedure, administrative reform, reducing the regulatory burden on business, further tax cuts, reform of the pension system, a system of mandatory federal health insurance, a new labor code, and intellectual property rights protection.

His 2002 message was still more ambitious. Here he called for legislation demarcating the jurisdictions of the federal government and federal territorial subjects, reform of local government, a series of judicial reforms (including delineation of the jurisdictions of general and arbitration courts, reform of the criminal code, new codes of civil and arbitration court procedure, a law on arbitration tribunals [*treteiskie sudy*], amendments to the law on the procuracy, and penal reform), reform of the structure of the state bureaucracy and the rules governing state employment, reform of banking, reform of bankruptcy law, a law allowing the sale of agricultural land, and legislation harmonizing Russian trade law with WTO standards. Moreover, he called for breaking up the large natural monopolies (the gas industry, electric power, and railroads) and for reform of the housing and utilities sector. This was the most ambitious program of his first term.

The spring and summer of 2003 witnessed a marked slowdown in the pace of economic reform. The president's 2003 message made very little mention of new legislative priorities, calling only for the acceleration of the development of reforms of the state administration and development of a new law on citizenship. A few months later, in summer 2003, the campaign to destroy Yukos began. Putin's 2004 and 2005 messages likewise touched only lightly on economic and institutional reform and emphasized instead the need to improve state services in health, education, and other spheres of social policy. Thus even as his control over the legislative process grew, his interest in using it to advance a radical reform agenda decreased. The "liberal" phase of Putin's presidency thus ended even before his first term was over.

Still, in his first term, Putin won some significant victories in enactment of the liberal agenda. The first several bills of his package of tax reform passed by the end of the spring 2000 term. In the spring 2001 term alone, the Duma enacted the land code (in second reading; the third reading occurred as soon as the Duma reconvened in September); the first bill in a package of pension reform bills (first reading); a new labor code (first reading); comprehensive tax reform, including a low flat income-tax rate, a unified tax for all social assistance funds, a lower excise tax, a lower profits tax, a lower rate on transactions in hard currency, a new sales tax, and a lower tax on production-sharing agreements (all in second reading); the first bill in a package of judicial reform legislation (first reading); part 3 of the civil code, liberalizing inheritance rights (first reading); a set of reforms lowering the regulatory burden for business, including laws on the registration of businesses, licensing of businesses, regulation of stock companies, money laundering, and three laws on banking reform (all passed through third reading); and a law on the regulation of political parties (through third reading). The spring 2002 term was similarly productive from the standpoint of the government. The Duma passed legislation on standards and on bankruptcy, elimination of the last remaining turnover tax, reduced taxes on small businesses, a new code of procedure for arbitration courts, and a law on sales of agricultural land. All of this legislation would have been difficult if not impossible to pass in the Yeltsin-era Duma. Putin's success reflected both the changed balance of political forces in the parliament and the Kremlin's skillful management of its relations with parliament in building majorities for its policy program.

On the other hand, Putin's early reform efforts were not always successful. Resistance came not from the parliament, however, but from the state bureaucracy, which has long experienced quietly torpedoing initiatives aimed at increasing its efficiency and accountability. For example, reform of the state bureaucracy was a theme emphasized in Putin's 2002 message, but eventually the impetus for a major overhaul of the organizational structure of the state bureaucracy died completely. A presidential commission worked for two years to come up with an ambitious plan to restructure the federal executive, eventually dusting off an old reform scheme originally developed under Yeltsin. This plan, called "administrative reform," was implemented in March 2004. Rather than the sweeping overhaul of procedures for recruiting, training, and promoting federal civil servants, enforcing discipline and accountability within the bureaucracy, and rationalizing the organizational structure of the executive branch by eliminating redundancies, the new plan simply reshuffled responsibilities of officials at the top. Observers noted that although the ostensible purpose of the reform was to make the executive branch more streamlined and efficient, it instead increased the number of federal-level executive bodies from fifty-seven to seventy-two. This reorganization plan is widely recognized to have caused little but confusion to the participants and embarrassment to its sponsors. Since then, Putin has quietly shelved the project of administrative reform.

While Putin has not always been able to control the state bureaucracy, he quickly won full control of the parliament. Within days of the convening of the Third Duma in January 2000, the president's chief political advisor, Vladislav Surkov, demonstrated his mastery of parliamentary tactics. Deftly forging an alliance between Unity, which commanded only 18 percent of the Duma's seats, and the communists, Surkov was able to block the election of an opposition figure (former Prime Minister Primakov) to the post of speaker, and he put Unity into the position where it was indispensable to every winning coalition.

The alliance between Unity and the communists was joined by a group of single-member district independents called People's Deputy. Together, these three factions controlled a bare minimum majority in the Duma and succeeded in electing communist Gennadi Seleznev to the speakership and in allocating the committee chairmanships among themselves. Factions excluded from the arrangement—the Fatherland/All-Russia coalition (OVR), Yabloko, and the liberal SPS—walked out in protest and refused to return to the Duma for three weeks.

As Surkov had no doubt foreseen, the communists' triumph was ephemeral. Quickly it became apparent that they had very little power within the Duma. Their committee chairmanships did not include any of the committees with jurisdiction over the main policy issues that were politically important to them or to Putin: they did not control the defense, security, foreign relations, budget, legislation, property, or banking committees. Nor could they determine the majority, as they had done in the two previous Dumas. In 1994–1995 and 1996–1999, the communists were the dominant faction by virtue of the interaction of two crucial advantages: their size and their cohesiveness. In the first two Dumas, it became extremely difficult to form a majority that did not include the communists. As the pivotal faction, they could usually dictate the terms on which they would join a majority coalition. Now, in the Third Duma, they were marginalized, despite holding the speakership and ten committee chairmanships. Their role as the pivotal faction was taken over by Unity. Unity had nearly as many members as the communists (eighty-nine initially for the communists, eighty-one for Unity), and a level of voting discipline that rivaled the communists, but they also had one additional crucial advantage: direct access to the Kremlin. Unity became the Kremlin's majority maker in the Duma and the Duma's major intermediary with the Kremlin. Given the asymmetry in constitutional powers between president and parliament, it became clear that Unity's strength and cohesiveness gave the Kremlin the ability to form majorities around nearly any bill it wanted to pass.[9]

REMAKING THE FEDERATION COUNCIL

At the same time that Putin was maneuvering to win control of the Duma, he took steps to take control of the Federation Council. Although Putin's strategy for the Federation Council was quite different from that used in the Duma, it was equally effective in suppressing independent power and political opposition. The law that he succeeded in getting passed in both chambers in the summer of 2000 that overhauled the method by which the members of the Federation Council are chosen had the result of giving him a secure base of support in the upper house.[10] Under the new procedure, the Federation Council comprises members chosen by the chief executives and the legislatures of the territorial subjects of the federation.[11] Previously, the chamber's members were the chief executives and chief legislative officials of the regions, who held their seats ex officio.

Studies show that the new members generally lack independent resources and tend to follow the lead of the presidential administration. Close coordination between the Kremlin and the chamber is achieved through the weekly meetings between the chamber's first deputy chair and the committee chairs. At these meetings, the Kremlin's position on pending legislation is communicated, and the chamber's position is worked out. As a result, the chamber votes with remarkable efficiency to back the Kremlin on almost every issue: the chamber meets only one day every two weeks, speeding through dozens of bills each time and providing large lopsided majorities on almost every bill. Moreover, even on matters where many governors have registered their dissatisfaction or overt opposition, the Kremlin's influence is sufficient to ensure that members faithfully follow the president's line. Although members can be and sometimes are recalled and replaced, most governors appear to accept the political expediency of allowing their representatives to vote the president's line in the Federation Council as the price for giving them policy influence through lobbying on more particularistic issues. This system has succeeded in guaranteeing overwhelming majorities for almost every piece of legislation that the Kremlin supports.[12]

Thus, in both chambers, President Putin helped to engineer the formation of standing majorities through which the presidential administration and government could obtain support for their major legislative priorities, trading off privileged access to the Kremlin in return for reliable voting support.

BUILDING A PARTY OF POWER

In the 2000–2003 Duma, Unity was the pivotal member of nearly every winning coalition. It delivered the president and government a string of victories, but at a price. The government had to make concessions on a number of policy fronts in order to win passage of its highest-priority legislation, such as the modifications to the annual budget, and tax reform. On land reform, for example, the government simply dropped the provisions which would have legalized the buying and selling of agricultural land as a condition for winning passage of this landmark law. The separate bill dealing specifically with agricultural land then passed the following year, in 2002. The convergence of interests of the government and the key pro-government factions in the Duma led to their efforts to create a more durable alliance structure that would lower the bargaining costs of building a majority.

Putin's team moved methodically to create a permanent coalition supporting Putin and the government in the Third Duma. Called "the coalition of the four," this coalition consisted of Unity and three allied factions: People's Deputy, Russia's Regions, and OVR. In spring 2001, this coalition formed an organizational structure for coordinating positions on major legislation, although they faced continuing difficulty in imposing voting discipline. Unity, which boasted a high level of voting discipline even in comparison with other party factions, sometimes had a difficult time holding its coalition partners in line on divisive votes.[13] Forming majorities for individual pieces of legislation required ad hoc bargaining and concessions—a costly and inefficient procedure from the president's standpoint. Putin's parliamentary managers looked for more direct methods to give Unity a political monopoly. The next step therefore was for Unity to swallow the Fatherland/All-Russia party and become, under the new name United Russia, the dominant party in Russia.

From the Kremlin's point of view, there were three main benefits from using a dominant party as an instrument of rule. First, it would ensure solid, consistent, reliable majorities in legislative voting, both in the Duma and in regional legislatures. Instead of having to cobble together piecemeal majorities for each bill, the Kremlin could instruct its party followers in the legislature how to vote and could let the party deploy the necessary sticks and carrots to enforce party unity on the floor. Second, the party would be the Kremlin's face to the country at election time, advertising the party as a team of politicians faithful to the popular President Putin and devoted to the country's well-being. Success in mobilizing the electorate would discourage the party's opponents, symbolize the party's popularity, and reveal which local officials were not performing up to expected standards. Finally, the party helped to manage the careers and ambitions of politicians. It would decide which politician would get which spot on the party list, who would run for governor, mayor, or local legislator, and who would not be given a party endorsement. Research by political scientists has shown that a dominant party in an authoritarian regime can be a useful device for the rulers, although they have to give up some of their power in order to attract sufficient commitment from other interests.[14]

In order to make United Russia into a dominant party, the Kremlin sponsored a series of legislative measures that made it difficult for governors' machines or big business to sponsor candidates and further squeezed small parties to the margins of the system.[15] Putin put through legislation raising the requirements for registration of parties, so that a party must have 50,000 members and branches in at least half the regions of the country to be legally registered. Moreover, only registered parties (and not other kinds of public organizations) were given the right to run candidates in elections. All these provisions made it still harder for small parties to compete. The tough registration requirements also give federal and local authorities more legal grounds for denying parties access to the ballot. Parties supportive of the authorities are routinely registered in regional and local elections; parties that take an opposition stance find signatures on their petitions disqualified or their candidates removed from the ballot for various alleged administrative violations. The new rules resulted in a massive drop in the number of parties. There were over forty registered parties in 2003, but by January 2006, only thirty-three parties remained. As of January 1, 2007, when the new legislation took force, sixteen more parties were disqualified. By September 2008, only fourteen parties remained. The number continued to fall as minor parties either lost their registration or merged with others to remain viable.

In addition, legislation passed in 2005 eliminated single-member district seats from the Duma, so that all 450 seats in the 2007 election were filled by party lists. Parties had to collect large numbers of signatures or put down sizable deposits to qualify to run, and they had to win at least 7 percent of the vote to win seats. As a result, in the December 2007 election, only four parties cleared the threshold to representation; seven parties (including all the democratic parties) fell below it.

Administrative restrictions pressuring small parties to dissolve or merge into bigger ones are not the only methods by which the regime works to ensure a dominant position for United Russia. Recent elections have seen large-scale manipulation of elections as well, including highly unequal access to the media for parties, court decisions that disqualify particular candidates from running, pressure on business to support United Russia materially, administrative pressure on various groups of the population (such as military service members, government employees, students, farmers, and others) to vote the right way, and in a growing number of regions, outright falsification of results.[16] The election process is thus a mixture of electoral mobilization techniques plus coercion and fraud, all to ensure that United Russia wins by large margins in national and regional races.

The ascendancy of United Russia has transformed the way the Duma is run. Previously, factions had shared power in steering the Duma and setting its agenda roughly proportionally to their voting strength on the floor. Starting in 2004, United Russia took full control of the governance of the Duma. It named UR members to all of the committee chairmanships and cut staff positions for committees but increased the staff for factions and the central staff, greatly expanding its control over the flow of legislation. It gave committees greater power to kill bills to reduce members' agenda rights.

Yet for all United Russia's power in the Duma, it has virtually no influence over the president; the presidential-parliamentary relationship is entirely asymmetric. United Russia contributed almost no members to the new government in 2004 and again in 2008.[17] The oddity of the situation is made even more piquant by the fact that Vladimir Putin declared he would head the party's list in the December 2007 election—thus contributing his own popularity to the party (as soon as Putin made this announcement in October 2007, the party's approval rating rose 6 percent).[18] He publicly stated on several occasions that he wanted United Russia to win a large victory so that the parliament would be capable of working effectively to pass the laws the country needed. As prime minister, he said he needed a solid majority of support in parliament. Finally, in April 2008, as he was preparing to step down from the presidency, Putin agreed to become party chair—although without formally joining the party!—and thus attached his prestige and stature to the party in the eyes of the political elite and electorate.

How did Putin use his two-thirds majority in the Duma in his second term? Surprisingly, his legislative agenda was much more ambitious in his first term than in the second. In contrast to the 2000–2003 period, when Putin enacted a sweeping agenda of generally pro-market reforms, in the 2004–2007 period he tended to concentrate on two other areas of policy. One was to centralize power further by weakening the independence of other centers of power, of civil society, and of rival political parties. The second was the passage of a number of distributive laws that increased spending on social needs of the country and that created a number of new state corporations headed by high-ranking state officials in Putin's entourage. These measures gave politicians in United Russia many ways to champion the interests of business and other interest groups that sponsored their candidacies and allowed United Russia to claim credit for improving the lives of pensioners, teachers, doctors, farmers, and other groups.

Among the measures Putin and the government sponsored and the parliament passed were increased subsidies to mothers for having children, a higher minimum wage, ceilings on rate increases for power and heating utilities for homes, higher pensions, new special economic zones, higher spending on the "national projects,"[19] increased spending on highway construction and maintenance, and creation of new state corporations in aviation, shipbuilding, nuclear power, nanotechnologies, and other fields, as well as the establishment of large new state investment funds to direct public funds into promising new fields. The steady, large increases in federal budget revenues—which owed to soaring world oil and gas prices—allowed the Putin regime to raise spending in a number of politically beneficial ways. Parliament, and United Russia, shared in the general glow of public good feeling.[20] Putin's own approval ratings rose steadily.

In effect, Putin and the Duma entered into an implicit exchange: the Duma approved a range of initiatives expanding executive power at the expense of the legislature, the media, parties, governors, and opposition forces, in return for lucrative patronage opportunities to spread state resources around to their own client groups.[21]

President Putin took the occasion of the Beslan incident in September 2004[22] to propose several pieces of legislation further centralizing power in the state and in the executive branch; the Duma duly enacted all of it, some of it virtually without debate. Among these were a proposal to eliminate direct popular election of regional governors in favor of a system whereby the president would nominate candidates who would be confirmed by the regional legislatures. Second, he proposed changing the law on elections of Duma deputies by eliminating all single-member district seats, another measure intended to strengthen the role of political parties in elections, and United Russia in particular. Finally, he proposed forming a new body, the Public Chamber, to serve as a forum for public discussion of policy and oversight of the bureaucracy.

All three of these measures had the direct or indirect effect of weakening parliament's role in the political system. The new system of appointed governors eliminated regional executive elections, which gave national parties some opportunity to participate in regional politics. The end of the mixed electoral system for the State Duma meant that no deputies in the Duma would represent single-member districts. This reduced the representation of local interests in the parliament and therefore much of the autonomy that Duma had had vis-à-vis the executive branch by virtue of their local bases of support. Finally, the creation of a Public Chamber as a forum for the representation of state-sanctioned nongovernmental organizations (NGOs) effectively weakened parliament's role in deliberating on matters of national policy. None of these specifically addressed the challenge of Islamic terrorism or Chechen separatism. Moreover, they had been discussed before the Beslan incident and were consistent with Putin's policy of strengthening presidential power, imposing strict regulation on party competition, weakening the autonomy of governors, and coopting civil society. For that reason, it is clear that Beslan provided a politically opportune moment to advance them but that political centralization rather than fighting terrorism was their actual goal.

Beslan also spurred other legislation aimed at fighting terrorism. Security legislation was at the top of the priority list when United Russia drew up the legislative agenda for the fall session. The heads of four Duma committees (security, defense, legislation, and state organization) agreed to propose new legislation to strengthen security at sites where large numbers of people congregated and to tighten rules on immigration, residency registration in cities, and registration of automobiles.[23] United Russia introduced a comprehensive new counterterrorism bill, prepared by the Federal Security Service (FSB), giving the police wider powers to prevent acts of terrorism.[24] If they believed that an act of terrorism was about to be committed, the FSB could declare a "regime of terrorist threat" and place the media and society under control, using wiretapping and mail intercepts, limiting travel, and prohibiting meetings and strikes.[25]

The counterterrorism law took a long time to work its way through the Duma. It passed in first reading on December 17, 2004, but did not pass in second reading until February 22, 2006. Four days later, the bill passed in third and final reading. President Putin signed it on March 6. Press reports suggested that the delay had been caused by an interagency jurisdictional squabble over the right to exercise command of antiterrorism operations. Ultimately the FSB won the fight and gained the right to command military, police, and other law-enforcement agency units in the event of a terrorist incident. One week before the bill passed in second reading, Putin issued a presidential decree on fighting terrorism, which called for the creation of a "national antiterrorist committee" to be headed by the director of the FSB. The decree resolved the conflict over whether the FSB would be given operational command over the armed forces in the event of a terrorist crisis and cleared the way for final passage of the law.

Putin also used Beslan and the terrorist threat as a rationale for other bills that limited political freedom and expanded the discretionary rights of the security services. For instance, in December 2005 Putin defended a bill sharply limiting the autonomy of NGOs as being necessary "to secure our political system from interference from outside, as well as our society and citizens from the spread of terrorist ideology."[26] Still another law (in fact, a law amending the counterterrorism law) authorized the president to send armed agents abroad to fight terrorism on foreign soil; this legislation was used as the basis for an operation to find and kill those responsible for killing four members of the Russian embassy staff in Iraq.[27] Before this law passed, President Putin had parliament pass a binding resolution (*postanovlenie*; equivalent to a legislative decree) giving him the authority to send special forces overseas to interdict terrorist activity. What is interesting about this procedural detail is that Putin could well have used his decree power to grant himself the authority to use the special services to use force to deal with terrorism abroad. President Yeltsin, for instance, had used presidential decree authority to launch the federal ground operation in Chechnya in 1994, and was upheld by the Constitutional Court in use of decree power for this purpose. By having parliament enact this power as legislation, President Putin was not so much seeking legal authority for his use of his power as commander in chief of the armed forces as he was seeking to share the *political* responsibility for this grave extension of presidential authority outside Russian borders.[28]

During the Fourth Convocation (2003–2007), the Duma passed all the legislation proposed by the president, and Putin continued to sign nearly everything the Duma passed (over 90 percent of the bills passed by the Duma in third reading were signed by the president in both the Third and Fourth convocations). Substantively, the record of legislative enactments in the Fourth Duma reflected Putin's interest in centralizing power and at the same time gave the dominant party enormous opportunities to meet its funding needs. Thus, although much of the legislation the Duma passed consisted of measures centralizing executive power and expanding the powers of the FSB, the Duma also, at the president's behest, created a number of new state corporations, social spending programs, and state investment funds. These initiatives generated substantial opportunities to provide jobs and income streams for state officials, Duma deputies, and United Russia party function-aries.[29] In effect, parliament entered into a tacit bargain with the president, delegating sweeping unilateral power to the president, the security services, and other arms of the executive branch in return for a plethora of patronage opportunities. The urgency of the terrorist threat *reinforced* Putin's position in this exchange, but it was not the impetus for it.

PARALLEL PARLIAMENTS

Both Yeltsin and Putin used their powers as president to create ad hoc bod-ies for tactical purposes, such as coopting opponents into a consultative structure that gave them honorific status but no real influence, or to avoid becoming dependent on any one source of policy advice and expertise. In most presidential regimes, presidents attempt to escape accountability to po-litical parties, legislatures, and bureaucracies and to retain their influence and freedom of action. This is certainly the case in Russia, where both Yeltsin and Putin worked to make the presidency the central institution of the political system and the president the "patron of patrons." Many observers consider the super-presidential nature of Russia's political system to be the source of many problems, such as low accountability of officials, a weak party system, and disengagement of citizens from the state.[30] In some respects, Putin's ef-fort to restore centralized power has meant rebuilding the old institutional mechanisms of the Soviet system, including a revival of elements of the old nomenklatura system;[31] redundancy between the presidential administration and the executive branch; personalization of state power through a cult of the leader; reliance for political support on personal networks of associates with whom the leader served in the past; balancing across institutional and factional bases of support; and recruitment of top officials from among military and security branches.[32] In addition to these, presidentialism also encourages an impulse to establish ad hoc institutions for tactical purposes. An example is Putin's practice of creating appointive bodies to serve as alter-natives to the parliament. To the extent that Putin relies on them for policy advice, they therefore weaken parliament's role as the principal national arena for political representation and policy deliberation. The two such parallel parliaments that will be briefly described here are the State Council and the Public Chamber.

The State Council was created by a stroke of Putin's decree pen on September 1, 2000. It was clearly intended to compensate the country's regional governors for the painful loss of status that they suffered when Putin deprived them of their seats in the Federation Council. With the loss of their seats, they lost also the immunity from criminal prosecution that members of parliament automatically enjoy, the ability to cast votes on legislation, the additional access to the executive branch that their status as parliamentarians entitled them, and the honor and prestige that came with sitting as members of parliament. To ease the blow, the president created an alternative body, with purely consultative powers, that, in his words, "could be a springboard for preparing and formulating decisions important for the fate of the entire state" and "a political body of strategic importance."[33] To underline its honorific status, President Putin decreed that the president himself would be the chair of the body. Its members would be all the country's governors, but it would form a presidium of seven members, rotated every six months, to be named by the president. Putin thus gave himself maximum opportunity to ensure that the State Council could either play a significant role in shaping national policy, or none at all, because its agenda and leadership would be entirely dependent on his choices. By naming a favored governor to the presidium, the president could provide a small symbolic prize, or likewise punish one who fell out of favor by dropping him from the presidium. This model of organization, reminiscent of the patrimonial system of rule familiar under the tsars, also precluded any possibility that the State Council could enable a smaller group of influential governors to coordinate their efforts in opposition to the president.

A second such body created by President Putin—by legislation in this instance, rather than by decree—is the Public Chamber. If the State Council was intended to parallel the Federation Council, the Public Chamber parallels the Duma. First proposed by Putin in September 2004 as one of the package of reforms that he put on the table following the Beslan incident, it seemed a peculiar response to an act of terrorism. Putin's vision for it was vague. He conceived it as a "forum for broad dialogue, where civic initiatives can be presented and discussed, and public expertise brought to bear on decisions and legislation." It would also exercise "civic oversight" over the state bureaucracy. Thus it was broadly intended to be both a deliberative body and a means for monitoring the state bureaucracy, a "filter" for legislative initiatives and a mechanism for promoting consultation between civil society and the state. The proposal had evidently not been fleshed out in the presidential administration before the president announced it, because a bill was not drafted and debated in the Duma until December.

Gradually the outlines of the body were defined. The chamber would comprise 126 members, to be chosen in three waves. The president would name forty-two members, who in turn would name another forty-two. Then jointly, these eighty-four members would name the final forty-two. The process of forming the chamber took some time; the final forty-two members were chosen only in December 2005, a year after the bill was first considered by the Duma. In practice, the presidential administration chose all the members, sometimes over the opposition of the organizations they came from; the members were not elected as delegates to the chamber.[34]

The Public Chamber's membership is diverse. The chamber includes figures from the worlds of sports, law, medicine, journalism, science, the arts, youth groups, political movements, business, and other sectors. Gradually its role in public life has become clarified. Depending on the interests of its members, and the organizations they represent, it focuses public attention on issues of significant public concern. Members of the Public Chamber sometimes call for investigations into cases where the rights of an individual were violated. They have issued several reports on issues such as freedom of the press in the regions and the state of health of draft-age youth. The Public Chamber is careful never to oppose the president and government directly, but it does serve to some extent as a conduit for communication between civil society and the state. Recently it has sought to become more closely involved in law-making. In view of the United Russia's party control over the Duma, and predominant influence in the upper house, the Public Chamber serves as an alternative forum for public debate on some policy issues. Its close ties to the presidential administration give it what influence it possesses but also limit its capacity to serve as a check on the executive and legislative branches.

CONCLUSION

President Putin undoubtedly sought to expand his freedom of action by creating these deliberative bodies that lack a specific constitutional foundation and that answer only to the president. Such improvised structures have both advantages and disadvantages for the regime. New advisory bodies can give legitimacy to interests and ideas closed off by regular institutional channels. At the same time, if a president refuses to commit himself to working through established mechanisms for decision making, his freedom of maneuver comes at a high price, because other political actors are unlikely to commit themselves to using those channels to solve collective problems. Both the constitutional and extra-constitutional bodies are left in a weakened state, their political legitimacy undercut and their capacity to facilitate deliberation and decision atrophied. Such bodies neither lend a president political support nor provide him with useful policy advice. A president who creates one such quasi-official consultative body after another finds it impossible to exercise any power because all the legitimate channels of representation and policy making have been bypassed and undermined.

This was certainly the case with President Gorbachev. Mikhail Gorbachev took the first steps by opening up the country to competitive elections in 1989 and creating a new, improvised parliamentary structure that allowed the plethora of informal political movements that had arisen under glasnost to channel their energies into electoral contests. Once these groups were organized as parliamentary caucuses, he allowed them formal rights within the parliament and often called on them for information and support. Gorbachev also experimented with a number of ad hoc appointive bodies for the representation of interests from the union republics, including an ill-fated semi-official negotiating forum known as the "9 + 1" talks aimed at salvaging the union on a new constitutional footing. Ultimately, none of the new structures that he devised proved to command sufficient loyalty from any significant forces in state or society to withstand the rapid disintegration of the Soviet state following the August 1991 coup.

This danger faces Putin and Medvedev as well. As successful as the Putin regime was in marginalizing any constitutionally legitimate forms of political representation and aggregation (elections, parties, and parliament), it has been unsuccessful in building any political institutions that are not dependent on personal power. Even United Russia has little political support in the country apart from the resources it enjoys by virtue of its close relation to Putin and the Kremlin, particularly Putin's popularity and the vast administrative carrots and sticks that the presidential administration can wield. If Putin were to lose either his power or his popularity, it is not at all clear that United Russia could survive. Thus super-presidentialism in Russia undercuts the effectiveness of the very structures that sustain it.

SUGGESTED READINGS

Fish, M. Steven. *Democracy Derailed in Russia: The Failure of Open Politics.* New York: Cambridge University Press, 2005.

Gel'man, Vladimir. "From 'Feckless Pluralism' to 'Dominant Power Politics'? The Transformation of Russia's Party System." *Democratization* 13, no. 4 (2006): 545–61.

Hale, Henry. *Why Not Parties in Russia? Democracy, Federalism, and the State.* Cambridge: Cambridge University Press, 2006.

Haspel, Moshe, Thomas F. Remington, and Steven S. Smith. "Lawmaking and Decree Making in the Russian Federation: Time, Space, and Rules in Russian National Policymaking." *Post-Soviet Affairs* 22, no. 3 (2006): 249–75.

McFaul, Michael. *Russia's Unfinished Revolution: Political Change from Gorbachev to Putin.* Ithaca, N.Y.: Cornell University Press, 2001.

Remington, Thomas F. "Majorities without Mandates: The Federation Council since 2000." *Europe-Asia Studies* 55, no. 5 (2003): 667–91.

———. "Patronage and the Party of Power: President-Parliament Relations under Vladimir Putin." *Europe-Asia Studies* 60, no. 6 (2008): 965–93.

———. *The Russian Parliament: Institutional Evolution in a Transitional Regime, 1989–1999.* New Haven, Conn.: Yale University Press, 2001.

NOTES

1. As U.S. Supreme Court Justice Robert Jackson wrote in his opinion in the important case of *Youngstown Sheet & Tube Co. v. Sawyer* (1952), the separation of powers principle in the U.S. Constitution "enjoins upon its branches separateness but interdependence, autonomy but reciprocity."

2. Michael McFaul, *Russia's Unfinished Revolution: Political Change from Gorbachev to Putin* (Ithaca, N.Y.: Cornell University Press, 2001); Michael McFaul, "The Fourth Wave of Democracy and Dictatorship: Noncooperative Transitions in the Postcommunist World," *World Politics* 54, no. 2 (2002): 212–44; Alexei Trochev, *Judging Russia: Constitutional Court in Russian Politics, 1990–2006* (Cambridge: Cambridge University Press, 2008); Lucan A. Way, "Authoritarian State Building and the Sources of Regime Competitiveness in the Fourth Wave: The Cases of Belarus, Moldova, Russia, and Ukraine," *World Politics* 57, no. 2 (2005): 231–61. For a comprehensive account of the weakness of the state in the 1990s, see Kathryn Stoner-Weiss, *Resisting the State: Reform and Retrenchment in Post-Soviet Russia* (Cambridge: Cambridge University Press, 2006).

3. Henry Hale, *Why Not Parties in Russia? Democracy, Federalism, and the State* (Cambridge: Cambridge University Press, 2006); M. Steven Fish, *Democracy Derailed in Russia: The Failure of Open Politics* (New York: Cambridge University Press, 2005).

4. Regina Smyth, *Candidate Strategies and Electoral Competition in the Russian Federation: Democracy without Foundation* (Cambridge: Cambridge University Press, 2006), 201; Vadim Gel'man, "From 'Feckless Pluralism' to 'Dominant Power Politics'? The Transformation of Russia's Party System," *Democratization* 13, no. 4 (2006): 545–61; Ora John Reuter and Thomas F. Remington, "Dominant Party Regimes and the Commitment Problem: The Case of United Russia," *Comparative Political Studies* (forthcoming).

5. On the link between the dominant presidency and the dominant ruling party in Mexico, see Jeffrey Weldon, "The Political Sources of Presidencialismo in Mexico," in *Presidentialism and Democracy in Latin America*, ed. Scott Mainwaring and Matthew Soberg Shugart (Cambridge: Cambridge University Press, 1997), 225–58.

6. Marshall I. Goldman, *Petrostate: Putin, Power, and the New Russia* (New York: Oxford University Press, 2008).

7. Moshe Haspel, Thomas F. Remington, and Steven S. Smith, "Lawmaking and Decree Making in the Russian Federation: Time, Space, and Rules in Russian National Policymaking," *Post-Soviet Affairs* 22, no. 3 (2006): 249–75; Oleh Protsyk, "Regime Type Effects on Presidential Use of Decree Making Authority in Post-Soviet States," paper delivered at American Political Science Association, Boston, Mass., August 28–31, 2008.

8. For a valuable insiders' account of the way the presidency operated under Yeltsin, see Georgii Satarov et al., *Epokha Yel'tsina: Ocherki politicheskoi istorii* (Moscow: Vagrius, 2001). This book is a collective memoir by a team of Yeltsin's political advisors.

9. On the relations between the Kremlin and Duma under Putin, see Paul Chaisty, "Majority Control and Executive Dominance: Parliament-President Relations in Putin's Russia," in *Leading Russia: Putin in Perspective. Essays in Honour of Archie Brown*, ed. Alex Pravda (Oxford: Oxford University Press 2005), 119–38; Paul Chaisty, "Party Cohesion and Policy-Making in Russia," *Party Politics* 11, no. 3 (2005): 299–318; Thomas F. Remington, "Putin and the Duma," *Post-Soviet Affairs* 17, no. 4 (2001): 285–308; Remington, "Taming Vlast': Institutional Development in Post-Communist Russia," in *A Decade of Post-Communism: The Fate of Democracy in the Former Soviet Union and Eastern Europe*, ed. Donald Kelley (Fayetteville: University of Arkansas Press, 2003); Remington, "Coalition Politics in the New Duma," in *Elections, Parties, and the Future of Russia: The 1999–2000 Elections*, ed. Vicki Hesli and William Reisinger (Cambridge: Cambridge University Press, 2003); Remington, "The Evolution of Executive-Legislative Relations in Russia since 1993," *Slavic Review* 59, no. 3 (2000): 499–520.

10. The bill reforming the method for selecting Federation Council members was initially rejected by the Federation Council on June 28, 2000. The chamber passed a slightly modified version on July 26, 2000, after an agreement commission made up of members of the two houses found a mutually acceptable compromise version of the plan.

11. There were eighty-nine such territorial units at the point that Russia adopted the new constitution in 1993. As of fall 2008, a series of mergers of smaller units into larger ones reduced the total to eighty-three.

12. On the manner in which majorities are formed in support of the Kremlin's positions, see Thomas F. Remington, "Majorities without Mandates: The Federation Council since 2000," *Europe-Asia Studies* 55, no. 5 (2003): 667–91; also see L. V. Smirnyagin, ed., *Sovet Federatsii: Evoliutsiia statusa i funktsii* (Moscow: Institut prava i publichnoi politiki, 2003), esp. 443–53.

13. Thomas F. Remington, "Presidential Support in the Russian State Duma," *Legislative Studies Quarterly* 31, no. 1 (2006): 5–32.

14. Reuter and Remington, "Dominant Party Regimes"; Jason Brownlee, *Authoritarianism in an Age of Democratization* (Cambridge: Cambridge University Press, 2007); Jennifer Gandhi and Adam Przeworski, "Authoritarian Institutions and the Survival of Autocrats," *Comparative Political Studies* 40, no. 11 (2007): 1279–1301; Jennifer Gandhi, *Political Institutions under Dictatorship* (Cambridge: Cambridge University Press, 2008); Beatriz Magaloni, *Voting for Autocracy: Hegemonic Party Survival and Its Demise in Mexico* (Cambridge: Cambridge University Press, 2006).

15. Cf. Hale, *Why Not Parties in Russia?* 231–33.

16. Mikhail Myagkov, Peter C. Ordeshook, and Dimitri Shakin, *The Forensics of Election Fraud: Russia and Ukraine* (Cambridge: Cambridge University Press, 2009).

17. Polit.ru, March 3, 2004. According to the deputy chair of the Duma, Viacheslav Volodin, a number of figures from UR were being considered for work in the government, and he expressed certainty that the government would be formed on the basis of a parliamentary majority.

18. *RFE/RL Newsline*, October 10, 2008.

19. The national projects were spending programs initiated by President Putin to improve the state of health care, education, housing, and agriculture. By 2008, they were rolled into regular budget spending.

20. Public opinion polls showed that positive outlooks increased substantially among the public during the Putin years. For example, a survey in May 2008 found that the

number of people calling themselves happy rose from 60 to 77 percent over the past ten years; the number of those considering themselves unhappy fell from 25 to 15 percent. "Po dannym oprosa, v Rossii vozroslo chislo schastlivykh liudei," Kommersant.ru, May 22, 2008.

21. Thomas F. Remington, "Patronage and the Party of Power: President-Parliament Relations under Vladimir Putin," *Europe-Asia Studies* 60, no. 6 (2008): 965–93.

22. The Beslan crisis occurred in September 2004 when a band of Islamist terrorists held hostage an entire school with schoolchildren and teachers inside. On the third day of the crisis, Russian security forces stormed the school, resulting in massive loss of life on the part of the hostages. Nearly all the terrorists were killed. The incident had an impact on public consciousness in Russia comparable to that of September 11, 2001, in the United States.

23. *Izvestiia*, September 7, 2004.

24. The FSB (Federal Security Service) is a successor agency to the Soviet KGB (Committee on State Security).

25. Polit.ru, December 17, 2004; February 27, 2006.

26. Polit.ru, November 30, 2005.

27. *RFE/RL Newsline*, July 7, 2006; Polit.ru, July 14, 2006.

28. On the relationship between presidential decree power and lawmaking under the Russian constitution, see Thomas F. Remington, Steven S. Smith, and Moshe Haspel, "Decrees, Laws, and Inter-Branch Relations in the Russian Federation," *Post-Soviet Affairs* 14, no. 4 (1998): 287–322; and Haspel, Remington, and Smith, "Lawmaking and Decree Making in the Russian Federation."

29. A widely discussed interview with Oleg Shvartsman, head of the Finansgrupp investment fund, published in *Kommersant*, November 30, 2007, sheds light on how the state corporations tie Kremlin factions with the commercial activity of state corporations. He stated that the financial group which he heads (and which won a tender from the Russian Venture Company) handles investments on behalf of families and friends of the "silovik" patron-client network headed by Igor Sechin (deputy head of the presidential administration, chair of Rosneft, and a former KGB officer). Shvartsman revealed that his firm carries out hostile takeovers of potentially profitable companies, sometimes reselling them at a handsome profit, with the assistance of a network of retired MVD and security police personnel who identify promising targets. In this way, Shvartsman observed, his firm was helping to carry out a "velvet reprivatization" of assets on behalf of the silovik clan. Maksim Kvashe, "Partiiu dlia nas olitsetvoriaet silovoi blok, kotoryi vozglavliaet Igor' Ivanovich Sechin," *Kommersant*, November 20, 2007, 20.

30. See Fish, *Democracy Derailed*, 193–245; Hale, *Why Not Parties in Russia?*; and Eugene Huskey, *Presidential Power in Russia* (Armonk, N.Y.: M. E. Sharpe, 1999).

31. Eugene Huskey, "Putin as Patron: Cadres Policy in the Russian Transition," in Pravda, *Leading Russia*, 161–78.

32. Olga Kryshtanovskaya and Stephen White, "Putin's Militocracy," *Post-Soviet Affairs* 19, no. 4 (2003): 289–306; and see Bettina Renz, "Siloviki in Russian Politics," *Russian Analytical Digest*, no. 17 (March 20, 2007).

33. *RFE/RL Newsline*, November 27, 2000.

34. *RFE/RL Newsline*, November 1, 2005.

Chapter Three

The Regions under Putin and After

Nikolai Petrov and Darrell Slider

Dmitri Medvedev's election to the post of Russian president could have important implications for regional policy, given the power that a president normally gains over time as he consolidates control. Whether Vladimir Putin will let him take over the reins of power is a major question, though, considering the effort that Putin expended on changing the "game" of regional politics. Increasingly, Putin as prime minister has taken on regional oversight functions, and his new role as leader of the dominant party United Russia gives him additional leverage to influence regional politics.

When Vladimir Putin became president, one of the first areas he identified for transformation was the relationship between Russia's regions and the federal (national) government. The weakness of the Yeltsin government, both politically and financially, forced Yeltsin to make considerable concessions to the regions. Regional leaders increasingly took on responsibilities that would normally be carried out by federal agencies, and they used these opportunities to entrench themselves in power while often willfully flouting federal laws and presidential decrees.

Putin witnessed the extent of the problem when he supervised Russia's regions for Yeltsin from March 1997 to July 1998. Putin was head of the department within the presidential administration (called the Main Oversight Department, or *glavnoe kontrol'noe upravleniie*) that gathered evidence on violations of federal laws and policies in the regions. Interestingly enough, Putin's predecessor as head of the department was Alexei Kudrin, who was elevated to minister of finance and deputy prime minister, and his successor was Nikolai Patrushev, who became head of the FSB (which had replaced the KGB) until his departure in 2008. Both men were key figures in implementing elements of Putin's policy toward the regions. All three, not coincidentally, were from Russia's second city, St. Petersburg.

This chapter examines the steps Putin took to deal with regional leaders. Most prominent was the creation of a new level of administration between the center and the regions in the form of seven federal administrative districts (*federal'nye okruga*) headed by specially appointed presidential representatives. Announced in May 2000, this initiative was one of Putin's first acts as president, and it reshaped in a fundamental way the nature of the Russian political system. Center-region relations continued to be a key area of concern in Putin's second term, particularly in the aftermath of the Beslan tragedy of September 2004, when rebels seized a school and the poorly coordinated effort to save the hostages resulted in over 300 deaths. One of Putin's responses to Beslan was to eliminate the popular election of governors, in effect taking on the power to appoint and dismiss regional leaders.

Instead of attempting to develop or refine federalism in the Russian context, Putin aggressively pursued an antifederal policy designed to take away or circumscribe many powers exercised by regional leaders. His goal was to establish a unitary, centralized state under the guise of "restoring effective vertical power in the country," to use Putin's own description of his intentions. In keeping with Putin's background in the KGB, the main emphasis is on discipline and order. These institutional and personnel choices, however, were not capable of achieving the desired result. As early as 2005, some Russian officials began to propose what might be described as "redecentralization" in order to correct some of the deficiencies in a centralized model. As of late 2008, these discussions produced nothing concrete, and centralization continued unabated.

ORIGINS OF THE PROBLEM

Even after the other fourteen former Soviet republics became independent, Russia remained the world's largest country; thus, it is perhaps inevitable that there would be serious problems in administering its far-flung territories. This was true both before and after the Soviet state was established. The usual set of solutions involved efforts to tighten control from the center. Despite some outward trappings of federalism (the Russian republic, for example, was called the RSFSR—Russian Soviet Federative Socialist Republic), the Soviet Union was in essence a unitary state supplemented by a parallel hierarchy—the Communist Party of the Soviet Union (CPSU). Even under Stalin, however, "family circles" or cliques based on personal relations and patronage ties arose in the regions, insulating local politics from Moscow and allowing regional elites a free hand in many matters.[1]

In many of the former communist states of Eastern Europe—particularly those whose leaders set a reformist agenda—a comprehensive redrawing of subnational administrative boundaries took place. In Poland, the Czech

Republic, the former German Democratic Republic, Hungary, and Croatia, communist-era regional entities were eliminated or replaced with new ones. In part this was done to meet European Union (EU) entry requirements, but often another important motivation was to break up political and economic power at the regional level that had emerged under communist rule.[2] No such redrawing of the political boundaries took place in Russia, with the consequence that political-economic elites of the communist era remained intact at the regional level. Russia's administrative structure closely mirrored that of the Russian republic under communism. Republics within Russia, designated "autonomous republics" in the Soviet period, received elevated status because they were home to a non-Russian ethnic group. Most often, though, Russians were the largest ethnic group even in republics; the exceptions were Dagestan, Chuvashia, Chechen-Ingushetia, Tuva, Kabardino-Balkaria, North Ossetia, Tatarstan, and Kalmykia. The most numerous administrative entities were *oblasts* (provinces) and *krais* (territories). Autonomous *okrugs* (districts) located within the territory of other entities began to be merged with larger entities in the late Putin period. The cities of Moscow and St. Petersburg also had the status of "subjects of the federation."

Russian and Soviet history had never seen an attempt to apply a federal model as the basis for organizing the relationship between national and regional authorities. In this regard, Yeltsin's policies represented a revolutionary break from past methods of rule. The Yeltsin constitution of 1993 made federalism a core component of the Russian political system. Article 71 of the constitution defines the areas of federal jurisdiction, article 72 defines joint jurisdiction, and article 73 grants all other functions to the regions. Many of these relationships remained to be defined by legislation, however, and Yeltsin did not take the goal of developing federal principles seriously. By the time Yeltsin resigned from office, Russia's federal system remained very much a work in progress, the result of an improvised series of steps and compromises. Yeltsin's "federalism" was the product of a series of crises and struggles that characterized his term as president.

First, there was the battle that took place in 1990–1991 over the fate of the Soviet Union. Both Gorbachev and Yeltsin sought the support of regional elites, particularly those in the ethnically based autonomous republics within the fifteen union republics that became independent in late 1991. It was in the context of the struggle with Gorbachev for the loyalty of republic leaders that Yeltsin in 1990 famously encouraged them to "take as much sovereignty as you can swallow." In most of the republics, local leaders followed Yeltsin's lead and created the popularly elected post of president, thus giving them a status and legitimacy lacked by heads of Russia's other regions at that time.

Almost immediately after the collapse of the Soviet Union, Yeltsin faced a new and lengthy conflict—this time with the Russian legislature. Their disputes covered a wide range of issues but centered on the relative powers of the parliament versus the president and on the strategy of economic reform that the country should pursue. In this struggle, Yeltsin sought the support of regional executives—the governors whom he had the right to appoint and dismiss—and the republic presidents. Ruslan Khasbulatov, the speaker of the Russian parliament who became Yeltsin's nemesis, appealed to the regional legislatures in an effort to build an alternative national power base. Since republic leaders had more independence than governors, Yeltsin tended to favor the republics with larger budget subsidies and greater relative autonomy.[3] These concessions were often codified in the form of bilateral agreements between the president and individual leaders. The most generous terms were granted to Tatarstan, Bashkortostan, and Yakutia, the republics with the most potential leverage because of their economic assets.

This battle culminated in the events of September–October 1993, when Yeltsin issued a decree dissolving the parliament. When Khasbulatov and Alexander Rutskoi, Yeltsin's own vice president, resisted and attempted to seize power by force, Yeltsin responded by having tanks shell the building. The new political context led to fundamental changes in regional politics.

First was the drafting of the 1993 constitution that enshrined the concepts of federalism, including the creation of a new legislature with an upper house to represent the regions—the Federation Council—with the right to veto laws passed by the lower house—the State Duma. The Federation Council comprised two representatives from each federal entity, a change from past practice that had given the fifty-seven Russian regions and thirty-two non-Russian republics equal weight in the upper house. (This change led many republics to vote against the constitution in the December 1993 referendum.) Governors often won election to this body and thus achieved additional independence and legitimacy. Yeltsin could not remove members of the Federation Council without its agreement, and council members also received immunity from criminal charges. A second consequence of the 1993 events was the dissolution of regional legislatures (though not in the republics) that had been elected in 1990. As a third consequence, political power in the regions shifted dramatically toward the executive branch of government. Executive power in the regions was further strengthened in the mid-1990s when Yeltsin gave in to the demand by regional executives for popular elections of governors. Yeltsin's last set of appointments to the post of governor took place in late 1995–early 1996, when he appointed thirteen.[4] After that, all governors were elected to office. This gave governors added legitimacy and made their removal by Yeltsin almost impossible.

In 1994–1995, new regional legislatures were elected. The new assemblies were smaller in size than the soviets of 1990, and their powers were substantially reduced. With just a few exceptions, the new deputies tended to be local officials, employees from sectors funded by the government (education and health care), or the regional economic elite—all groups that were dependent on the executive. Only a small proportion of deputies were full-time legislators, and in their legislative role they were both unwilling and unable to challenge the region's governor or president. Very few legislatures had more than token representation by national political parties.[5]

A year after the October 1993 attack on parliament, Yeltsin once again attempted to use force to solve a political problem—this time in Chechnya. Unlike republics such as Tatarstan and Bashkortostan, Chechnya refused to enter into a dialogue with the Kremlin and instead pressed for full independence. Under the leadership of General (and President) Dzhokhar Dudayev, Chechnya created its own military forces and expelled representatives of virtually all central Russian ministries, including the FSB and the Ministry of Finance. It should be said, however, that the Russian leadership did not make a serious attempt to achieve a negotiated solution to Chechnya's complaints, which contributed to the Chechens' resolve to secede. In December 1994, Yeltsin ended several years of neglect of the Chechen problem and ordered Russian Army and Interior Ministry troops into Chechnya in hopes of a quick military victory. The result was a disaster: the army was ill-prepared for a guerrilla war and suffered many casualties while directing much of its military might against the civilian population.

The war in Chechnya and ineffective policies in a number of other areas threatened defeat for Yeltsin in the 1996 presidential elections, and he again turned to regional leaders (as well as the business elite) for help. It was at this time that over twenty new bilateral treaties with *oblasts* and *krais* were signed. Yeltsin further strengthened the status of regional leaders by initiating a change in how the Federation Council was formed. Starting in 1996, governors and the chairs of regional legislatures would automatically have seats in the Federation Council. With the help of regional "administrative resources" such as control over the local press, government workers, and simple vote fraud in some cases, Yeltsin came from behind to win reelection.

These serial political crises took place against a background of persistent economic emergencies that were stabilized in the mid-1990s only by resorting to "virtual" economics and financial trickery. These schemes eventually collapsed in the August 1998 devaluation and default. One common mechanism to formally balance tax receipts and expenses, which was used by both central agencies and regional governments, was sequestering funds—in other words, reducing expenditures by not paying salaries and not meeting obligations to suppliers of goods and services. In this way, the federal government effectively lost control of many of its agencies in the regions. Shortfalls in tax collection and nonpayment meant regional leaders were almost forced to step in to provide funds or in-kind payments (office space, transportation, heat, hot water, electricity, and even food) in order to support the continued operation of federal institutions such as the criminal police, tax police, prosecutors, courts, and even Yeltsin's presidential representatives (created in 1991 to serve as his "eyes and ears" in the regions). Inevitably, federal entities in the regions shifted their loyalty from the center to the regions. Even the Russian military became increasingly dependent on regional leaders for logistical support. The result was "a sustained trend towards increasing compartmentalization and region-alization of military structures, driven primarily by the shortage of resources and underfinancing."[6] It should be emphasized that this was not a power play by regional leaders. In the face of the failure by the Kremlin to carry out its responsibilities, the regions were simply trying to cope.

Another feature of Yeltsin's policies toward the regions was the personal-ized and bilateral nature of many of the center-region relationships. This was in many ways a continuation of the informal operation of regional lob-bying of the central institutions during the Soviet era; both Yeltsin and most regional leaders had practical experience dating back to the Brezhnev era. Some of this bilateralism was formally institutionalized in treaties negotiated between the Yeltsin administration and regional leaders. The first of these agreements was with republics; it provided a set of exceptions and exemp-tions that went far beyond what other regions were allowed under the "1992 Federation Treaty" and the 1993 constitution. These agreements had the effect of making Russian federalism extremely asymmetrical, but in a way that was unsystematic and nontransparent.[7] Much of the enabling documentation at the ministerial level was kept secret. Later, most *oblasts* and *krais* also ne-gotiated bilateral treaties with the center, though under less favorable terms. The personalization of politics meant that Yeltsin often turned a blind eye to violations in a region as long as its leader demonstrated loyalty to him in federal elections.

Overall, the institutional framework and dynamics of "federalism, Russian style" had a number of dysfunctional elements and allowed regions con-trol over other areas of federal responsibility that were atypical of a normal federal system.[8] The nature of federal relations also undermined efforts to democratize the political system as well as efforts to marketize the Russian economy. Governors and republic presidents obstructed the development of a national party system and used their powers to harass political opponents and independent news media. In an effort to protect local industries and markets, regional leaders created barriers to free trade between regions. They also preserved an economic climate that was hostile to outside investment and the rise of small business.[9]

PUTIN'S RECENTRALIZATION POLICIES

Putin's election to the presidency was closely linked to the second Chechen war (1999–2004), which employed massive force to restore Russian federal control over the region. At the same time, he began a series of policy initiatives toward the regions that included the following centralizing measures:

1. Establishing the seven federal districts ("super-regions") headed by presidential envoys, five of whom initially were generals.
2. Increasing central control over federal agencies in the regions, including the courts, police, and television.
3. Bringing the Federation Council under Kremlin control by replacing sitting governors and chairs of regional legislatures with full-time representatives who would be named by governors and legislatures with substantial input from the presidential administration (in the process, regional executives and the heads of regional legislatures lost parliamentary immunity).
4. Adopting laws that allowed the president, under certain conditions, to remove governors and dismiss regional parliaments.
5. Creating a new body for governors (the State Council) to advise the president on policy matters. As a consolation for losing their seats in the Federation Council, all regional leaders are members. Its working organ is a presidium (whose membership changes every six months) made up of one governor/president from each of the seven federal districts. Putin directed that several of these reports serve as the basis for government drafts of new legislation, for example, on policy toward exploiting Russia's timber resources. Other reports, especially ones that reflected the governors' perspectives on administrative reform and federalism, were ignored.
6. Changing the balance in interbudgetary relations through a new tax code, which increased the center's share and gave the federal government greater control over tax receipts and expenditures.
7. Ending direct popular elections of regional leaders after the terrorist attack in Beslan in September 2004, and starting in 2005 presidential appointment of governors and republic presidents with formal approval by regional assemblies.
8. Taking the first steps toward reducing the number of federation subjects by merging administrative entities. A particular target were autonomous *okrugs*, which began to be absorbed by larger entities that surrounded or adjoined them. Putin's purpose was to simplify and improve the effectiveness of management and allow budget optimization.
9. Creating a new national political party, United Russia, that would be given enormous advantages allowing it to dominate the legislatures and city councils of almost every Russian region by 2006. At the same time, regionally based parties were banned. Since April 2008, Vladimir Putin has been leader of United Russia.
10. Changing the electoral system to eliminate single-member districts (direct regional representation) with party list voting, first at the national level and then in elections to many regional assemblies.

THE FEDERAL DISTRICTS AND
PRESIDENTIAL ENVOYS

The first and most important of Putin's innovations, issued in the form of a presidential decree in May 2000, divided Russia into seven administrative districts. The ultimate goal of this new structure was not to replace existing regions, but rather to increase the ability of the center to coordinate the operation of federal agencies in the regions through a framework that was totally controlled by Putin's Kremlin. (Under Yeltsin, horizontal ties between regions had developed in the form of regional economic associations. These largely disappeared under Putin.) The federal districts were not drawn anew based on any particular political or administrative purpose; they corresponded completely to the regional command structure of the Soviet/Russian Interior Ministry troops.[10] The "capital" or administrative center of each district in every case corresponded to the location of the headquarters of the corresponding Interior Ministry district.

The top official in each of these new federal districts was called the "plenipotentiary presidential representative"—*pol'nomochnyi predstavitel' prezidenta*, or *polpred* for short—a term that had been used by Yeltsin to designate his representative in each region. Putin abolished this post in the regions; henceforth, most regions would have a "chief federal inspector" who would be directly subordinate to (and appointed by) the presidential representative for the corresponding administrative district.

The decree creating presidential envoys provided for their direct accountability to the president. Yeltsin had initially given the same degree of access to his representatives, but later they were subordinated to a department within his administration.[11] In practice, though, while Putin appointed each of his representatives, they did not report solely to the president. The *polpreds* were still part of the presidential administration, which meant they were supervised by the head of Putin's staff. This was a source of some consternation among the presidential representatives, since they wanted to be closer to the ultimate source of authority at the top of the administrative ladder. A symbolic indicator of the status of the seven representatives was Putin's decision to give each a seat on his Security Council, a body that has been important in establishing strategic priorities in government policy, both foreign and domestic. The *polpreds* were also given a role in meetings of the Russian government chaired by the prime minister.

Putin's "magnificent seven," as they were initially referred to with some irony in the media,[12] were drawn for the most part from the *siloviki* or "power ministries": FSB, military, police, and prosecutors. The contrast with the early Yeltsin period could not be more vivid. In 1991, Yeltsin created a new institution of "presidential representatives" to be placed in each region. The largest number of this first set of *polpreds* was drawn from the ranks of radical democrats who had worked with Yeltsin in the Soviet and Russian parliaments. In effect, the early Yeltsin appointees to this post were the type of people that several of the Putin appointees had worked to put in prison camps or psychiatric wards! (Later though, Yeltsin replaced his initial appointees with career bureaucrats, including several FSB officials, a trend accelerated by Putin on becoming acting president in January 2000.)

In each of the regions within a district, chief federal inspectors were appointed, taking the place of the officials who had previously been called *polpreds*. Many of these inspectors, while appointed centrally, had roots in the regions to which they were assigned. In especially troublesome regions, however, outsiders—usually from Moscow—were named to the post. Unlike the practice that had emerged in the Yeltsin period, governors and republic leaders were not, as a rule, consulted. However, the ethnic factor was carefully taken into account in appointments to many of the more assertive ethnic republics (Tatarstan, Bashkiria, and Chechnya, for example). The backgrounds of chief federal inspectors are also revealing. There was a heavy predominance of inspectors who came from the "power ministries"; of those for whom biographical data are available, approximately three of every four came from the military, FSB, or Ministry of Internal Affairs (MVD). The majority of federal inspectors were in their mid-forties, all were men, and virtually none of them had a background in any elective office.

Much of the work performed by presidential representatives is secret; as a result, their actual role remains hidden.[13] Putin met regularly with his seven representatives in order to discuss future priorities and initially emphasized three basic tasks. The first was to restore the preeminence of federal law. Much of the early work of the presidential representatives was spent overseeing the process of bringing regional legislation (including republic constitutions and regional charters) into conformity with federal law and the Russian constitution. By the end of the first year's work, it was reported that thousands of regional laws had been "corrected." The effectiveness of this effort is questionable, however, since bringing regional laws into conformity with federal laws was approached as a technical exercise. Given the problems Russia has yet to address in establishing the rule of law, a massive effort to improve the content of laws appears to be premature. Russia, and this is even truer of the regions, is a country where the letter of the law often counts for little in the face of arbitrariness, incompetence, politicization, and corruption in the judicial system and in the bureaucracy.

The second task was to define the division of powers between the center, regions, and local government. Starting in the latter part of 2001, a major effort was undertaken to formalize relationships between center and regions. Part of this initiative has been to clarify the nature of bilateral treaties that were signed between over half of the regions and Yeltsin's government. A commission headed by the then deputy head of Putin's staff, Dmitri Kozak, took the lead in formulating the proper relationship between regions and the center, and it worked with the presidential representatives in this area. The general perspective of the Putin team was that the bilateral agreements signed during the Yeltsin period had limited legal standing; in effect, almost any other form of law or presidential decree took precedence over them.

Part of the division of powers consists of defining the role that would be played by subregional government. Under Yeltsin, the term "local self-management" meant that cities and rural districts enjoyed considerable autonomy. This was an element of both the 1993 constitution and the 1995 law on local government. However, resistance from governors turned these provisions into empty promises. Local budgets are completely inadequate to take on the obligations assigned to them, which puts local officials in the role of supplicants to regional leaders. In October 2003, Putin signed a new "Law on Principles of Organizing Local Self-Management," which replaced the 1995 law. The law increases the control of regional authorities over local officials, bringing mayors also into the "vertical of authority." The law establishes a new system of municipal entities that will encompass the entire country and will vastly expand the number of municipal officials. In 2005, implementation of most of the law's provisions was repeatedly postponed, but the undermining of local government autonomy proceeded without delay. In 2007–2008, numerous mayors were indicted on corruption charges in an apparent campaign similar to that launched against governors a few years earlier.

The third task Putin set for his presidential representatives was to coordinate and optimize federal agencies' activity in regions, including a role in appointing and monitoring personnel in federal agencies in the regions. This actually is an extension of actions taken in 1997–1998, when collegia of federal agencies under the chairmanship of the presidential representative were created in most regions. These never worked well. Given the nature of the coordinating function, it is logical to expect appointments of FSB officers to play the coordinating role. No one else, after all, would have the authority to coordinate such powerful agencies as the FSB, the Federal Agency on Governmental Communication (FAPSI, the agency that controls communications security), the Ministry of Internal Affairs, the tax police, and federal prosecutors. As is shown in table 3.1, during Putin's first term in office there were substantial personnel changes in the two key force ministries in the regions: the MVD and FSB. Over half the top regional officials at this level were replaced from 2000 to the end of 2003. Turnover remained high in 2004–2005, and regional prosecutors and police chiefs continued to be replaced regularly in the years that followed.

Perhaps more important than the stated functions of Putin's presidential representatives were the undeclared ones. It is here the need for FSB functionaries becomes even clearer. These more or less covert assignments

Table 3.1.   Replacement Rate of Key Regional Officials, 2000–2007

Year	Heads of Regions	MVD	FSB	Chief Federal Inspectors	Prosecutors
2000	15/89	10/88	15/87	13/75	28/89
2001	6/89	22/88	17/87	18/75	17/89
2002	6/89	16/88	19/87	9/75	17/89
2003	7/89	24/88	15/87	9/75	17/89
2004	8/89	9/88	19/87	7/75	17/89
2005	13/89	20/88	9/87	13/80	23/89
2006	4/88	20/87	13/86	18/83	24/88
2007	11/86	16/85	8/85	18/82	20/86

Note: The table is based on available data, which are incomplete in some categories. The total number of officials is less than the number of regions because some officials are in charge of several regions, and this pattern changed over time. The number of regions was also changing due to regional mergers.

included bringing military, police, and security organs out from under governors and back under the control of the center. This had been largely accomplished by 2002. Presidential representatives created security collegia in their districts, replacing informal structures of this type that had arisen outside the control of the center. Presidential representatives also helped the center establish control over the MVD. In this they were aided by a change in the law in June 2001, which eliminated the governors' effective veto on appointments of regional MVD chiefs.

A second assignment was to oversee and control the process of gathering compromising material (*kompromat*) on regional leaders. Officials from the Kremlin's Main Oversight Department have a substantial presence on the *polpred*'s staff. Also playing a role in monitoring corruption was the Auditing Chamber, which set up offices in the districts and regions. In effect, the Auditing Chamber branches formed a new "financial vertical of power," in the words of its director, Sergei Stepashin. In 2003–2004, for the first time serious criminal investigations were launched against a number of sitting governors, most typically those the Kremlin labeled as weak and ineffective. While none of these cases were brought to trial, they helped Putin establish his primacy in the period before he began appointing regional leaders.

A third assignment was to influence political developments in the regions. During Putin's first term, *polpreds* were clearly involved in efforts to remove from power those regional leaders who were considered obstacles by the Kremlin. Prior to 2005, when regional leaders were still elected, the Kremlin succeeded in removing from the political stage the heads of a number of regions—Kaluga, Kursk, Krasnodar, Primor'e, Yakutia, Ingushetia, and St. Petersburg. Elections were a time of particular vulnerability (much like a crab that has molted and not yet grown a new shell). The Kremlin tried to influence elections both openly and covertly: for example, Putin used his popularity to endorse favored candidates. In addition, secretive, behind-the-scenes maneuvering was common. Methods included exerting influence over the election commission or the local judiciary to remove a candidate from the ballot. In some cases, *kompromat* gathered on regional leaders was employed to pressure them not to seek another term in office (the use of blackmail, in other words). Overall, as is shown in table 3.1, approximately one-third of Russia's regional leaders were replaced during Putin's first term.

From the beginning, presidential envoys were denied many of the instruments of real power to control developments in the regions—the right to direct financial flows from the center, for example, or the power to appoint federal officials in the regions. They have, however, found other ways to attain leverage. *Polpreds* worked to expand their links with important regional actors, such as the business community. *Polpreds* also influenced personnel decisions by federal agencies and the president in their district through their recommendations for promotions. Over time, they were able to create a web of cadres in the district that facilitated the center's "penetration" of the regions. They also presided over a massive expansion in the number of federal officials in the regions. Between 2001 and 2006, the number of federal executive-branch employees in the regions (not including law enforcement agencies) grew from 348,000 to 616,000, according to the Russian statistical agency.

In the aftermath of Beslan, Putin significantly enhanced the role of the presidential envoy in the Southern Federal District, which includes the republics of the North Caucasus. In a shift away from the *siloviki* (power ministries) pattern of appointment, the new envoy was Putin's longtime aide and troubleshooter Dmitri Kozak. Kozak was given the power to oversee federal ministries through a special commission that he chaired and which required federal ministers to participate under his authority. Kozak remained in his post for three years and then was returned to Moscow as minister for regional development. (In October 2008, he was promoted to the post of deputy prime minister with a mandate to organize the construction and preparations for the 2014 Winter Olympics, to be held in Sochi, as well as oversee all regional development issues.)

PRESIDENTIAL APPOINTMENT
OF REGIONAL LEADERS

With the end of popular elections in 2005, *polpreds* were assigned the additional role of presenting candidates for consideration by the president when there was a vacancy for a regional leadership post. It is unclear how much of the decision making on regional leadership appointments is affected by *polpreds* and how much was exercised in the Kremlin, and it likely varies from case to case. It is apparent, though, that the end of elections has for the first time led to an outcome that would be hard to imagine otherwise: the choice of outsiders to head regions. In a sense, this brings to mind the Stalin-era practice of horizontal rotation, designed to break up entrenched regional elites. In 2005, about a third of Putin's newly appointed governors had few or no ties to the region. These included three former members of Moscow Mayor Yuri Luzhkov's team, Valery Shantsev, Georgy Boos, and Mikhail Men', whom Putin chose as governors of Nizhnii Novgorod, Kaliningrad, and Ivanovo, respectively. Other early outsider appointments included the new governor of Altai *krai*, Aleksandr Karlin—previously head of the presidential administration's civil service department—and the new Irkutsk governor, Aleksandr Tishanin—previously director of the East Siberian railroad. Tishanin came into conflict with local elites and was replaced in 2008 by another outsider, Igor Yesipovsky, who had worked in the arms sales agency (Rosoboroneksport) and served the previous year in the Duma from the Amur *oblast* United Russia list. In other cases, new governors had some local connections but were clearly chosen because of their perceived loyalty to the Kremlin. Generally, when ethnic republic leaders were replaced, the new chief executive was drawn from the same ethnic group. An exception was in Buriatia, where Putin in 2007 appointed Vyacheslav Nagovitsyn, a Russian who had been deputy governor in Tomsk. (This violated Buriatia's constitution, which requires that the republic president speak Buriat.)

It would be misleading, however, to conclude that Putin used his power of appointment to bring about wholesale changes in cadres governing Russian regions. Most governors and republic presidents who had been elected to their posts prior to 2005 remained in power. A procedure was adopted that allowed elected leaders to seek Putin's "vote of confidence," most often through a personal meeting with him, prior to the end of their term in office. In the vast majority of cases, Putin responded favorably without even considering other candidates and submitted the current governor's name to the regional assembly for reappointment. An important consequence of the end of elections is the de facto end of term limits for Russia's regional leaders. There was some speculation that this was the main purpose of the change: it would permit the reappointment of leaders viewed by the Kremlin as hard to replace. In many cases, the Kremlin has decided entrenched loyal elites are preferable to the alternatives. Among those reappointed were the president of Tatarstan, Mintimer Shaimiev, who has been in charge of the republic since 1989, and Yegor Stroev, Orel *oblast* leader since 1985. Both were then Communist Party first secretaries, and both have proven loyal to the Kremlin on numerous occasions.

In determining whom to retain and whom to replace as governor, Putin late in his second term introduced a new system for evaluating performance.

The system comprised forty-three socioeconomic indicators, among which were economic output totals, new housing construction per capita, education expenditures per pupil, crime rates, and the percentage of the population that engages in physical exercise or sports. Polls would also be conducted to determine the level of satisfaction with education, health care, and the performance of regional government, including access to information. The first list ranking the top twenty regions using a collection of these indicators was publicized by the government in November 2008. It was not made clear how the rankings were done, but as a reward each region was promised a share of a grant package worth 2 billion rubles. Meetings between Putin and governors, which continued after Putin moved into the post of prime minister, were often characterized by detailed reports and questions about which indicators showed progress and which were lagging in a particular region. In effect, the purpose is to provide an accountability mechanism that would substitute for popular elections: accountability to the Kremlin rather than to the voters.

An additional mechanism for evaluating regional performance, instituted in January 2006, has been placed directly under government (Putin's) control. These are monthly sessions of the government that review socioeconomic conditions in a different region each month. This practice grew out of the problems exposed when the Russian government attempted to monetize social benefits in 2005 and encountered mass protests in many regions. In these meetings, the governor or republic president is brought before assembled government ministers and provides an overview of his or her region and its problems. On the one hand, governors can use this opportunity to lobby for special projects for their regions with the chief decision makers all in attendance. At the same time, the sessions allow Putin to assess the performance of governors and hold them to account for failings in their work. Starting in April 2008, regions that were developing at a slow pace or underperforming compared to other regions became the chief focus of these sessions.

PARALLEL VERTICAL STRUCTURES

The scheme that Putin established for improving the coordination of federal policy was replicated by many other government agencies at the direction of the president. The strategy was to strengthen the vertical chain of command from the Moscow-based ministries or agencies to the federal district agencies, and from there to ministry officials in the regions.

New territorial structures were established in the seven federal districts by the most important federal agencies and ministries—in all, about twenty federal agencies. To illustrate, within a year of Putin's reform, there were nineteen federal agencies represented in the Volga federal district. These included the prosecutor's office, the Ministry of Justice, the Tax Police, the Federal Tax Service, the Federal Agency on Governmental Communication, the Ministry of the Interior for Internal Troops, the Federal Criminal Police, the Federal Service on Financial Restructuring and Bankruptcy, the State Courier Service, the Committee on State Reserves, the Federal Securities Commission, the Property Ministry, the Federal Property Fund, the Ministry on Publishing and TV and Radio Broadcasting, the Ministry of Natural Resources, the Pension Fund, the Ministry of Transportation, the Health Ministry, the State Committee on Statistics, and the Ministry of Anti-Monopoly Policy (the latter two had other regional branches within which they established federal district departments).[14]

Some of the most important changes in administrative subordination took place in the Ministry of Internal Affairs (MVD). When Putin came to power, there was a symbiosis between police generals at the center and regional leaders that seemed to be unbreakable. Putin employed chesslike maneuvers to reassert dominance over this key lever of control. Instead of immediately appointing his own man as minister, he began by establishing a new intermediate level that separated the regional bottom from the central top. Seven MVD district directorates were created, headed by high-ranking police officials who are directly subordinate to the minister of internal affairs and appointed by decrees issued by Putin.[15] It took a year of personnel changes at the regional level to break up existing networks of relationships, with the *polpreds* providing a mechanism for restoring control by the central ministry over regional police chiefs. This was a source of some dissatisfaction later, when *polpreds* came into conflict with newly centralized police operations. The system of informal governors' control over prosecutors was broken as well, with seven prosecutors' general deputies appointed to head new district offices.

It should be emphasized, however, that none of the heads of the new district agencies is subordinate to the *polpred*. While such a change would make sense from the standpoint of a clear and single vertical chain of command, it would represent a major assault on the prerogatives of the Moscow-based ministries. Ever since Khrushchev's attempt to undermine the ministries and transfer their powers to regional economic councils (the *sovnarkhozy*), the ministries have effectively fought reorganizations that would decentralize power to the district or regional level. The presidential representative could not order the federal agencies in his district to do anything, though he or she could complain to Putin if they resisted.

The FSB was one of the few federal ministries that did not create a new territorial structure based on the federal districts. This suggests the administrative district scheme was conceived by and was, in some respects, an extension of the FSB. Otherwise, the FSB would have sought a voice of its own at the federal district level. Under Putin, the role of the FSB in governing increased dramatically at the national and regional levels. In February 2006, Putin announced the creation of a new federal structure, the National Anti-Terrorism Committee, headed by the FSB chair. Each region's antiterrorism committee (none were created at the federal district level) would be headed by the governor or president of the region. The result was a new "antiterror vertical." On matters concerning terrorism and its prevention, which can be broadly construed, governors were subordinate not just to Putin but to Nikolai Patrushev, then the FSB chair. In each region, the local FSB head (also subordinate to the FSB chief, not the regional leadership) served as the head of the operational staff for antiterror operations and preparations. In 2007, an "antidrug vertical" was added as well, under the State Committee to Combat Narcotics. It paralleled the antiterror vertical, and some analysts concluded that it was designed to act as a counterweight to the FSB or at least allow Putin to monitor its regional activities.

RESTORING ST. PETERSBURG'S CAPITAL ROLE

Putin and Medvedev were the first of the country's Soviet and post-Soviet leaders who were born and raised in St. Petersburg, Russia's imperial capital, rather than coming from a far-flung province. (Interestingly, none has come from Moscow.) Unlike his predecessors, Putin did not spend a lengthy period in Moscow prior to becoming leader. This had two major consequences. First, there has been a significant flow of elites from "Piter" (as St. Petersburg is known colloquially) to Moscow. The old eastern capital (Moscow) is now besieged by young, Westernizing newcomers. It is reported that on Monday mornings, a traffic jam of limousines waits outside the Leningrad railway station in Moscow to pick up officials returning from a weekend with their families in Piter. Second, some capital city functions have shifted from Moscow to Piter. Putin and Medvedev visit the city often, and the Constantine Palace has been restored as an official presidential residence.

There were numerous proposals to move key institutions of the judiciary to St. Petersburg, thus giving substance to its informal designation as Russia's "second capital." In December 2005, Putin announced he had decided to move the Constitutional Court to St. Petersburg, in spite of opposition from the justices. One argument advanced was that by being at some distance from Moscow, the court would be less susceptible to political pressure from government officials in the capital. The Constitutional Court began operating out of the renovated Senate building in 2008. A number of practical problems complicated the move, including the refusal by about two-thirds of the court's research staff to relocate from Moscow to St. Petersburg.

St. Petersburg's growing clout can be considered, at least partly, the consequence of Putin's reliance on his former colleagues from the Leningrad/

St. Petersburg KGB/FSB.[16] However, the picture is more complicated than this, even in terms of personnel policy. There are at least three other sources of Petersburg elite recruitment in addition to the FSB: lawyers—including Medvedev—and former colleagues from Mayor Anatoli Sobchak's administration,[17] liberal economists,[18] and so-called unallied individuals.[19] In addition to top presidential aides and government officials, the speakers of both the State Duma and Federation Council are from St. Petersburg.

One explanation for the dominance of the "Leningrad group" is Putin's and Medvedev's need to fill key posts with people they trust and who have demonstrated their loyalty. Another factor, though, is a desire to systematically dismantle the old Moscow-based bureaucratic machine. Officials from Piter, following long-standing practice, tend to bring with them their own subordinates, so there has been an exponential explosion in the number of mid-level officials from St. Petersburg as well.

CONCLUSION

The state of center-region affairs under Yeltsin was not sustainable—the regions had become too strong at the expense of the center. But it would appear Putin has swung the pendulum too far in the opposite direction. The policies he has undertaken threaten both federalism and democratic development in Russia.[20] There is a Soviet-era joke about a machinist from a defense plant who made Kalashnikovs (machine guns). When he retired from the factory, he decided to make toys for the children in his neighborhood. But whatever he made, whether it was a rocking horse, a doll, or a model ship, it always came out looking like a Kalashnikov! The Putin approach to the regions seemed to suffer from a set of limitations that reflected his life experiences and background. Putin's choice of instruments and personnel made it almost inevitable that his policies for dealing with the regions would end up "looking like a Kalashnikov," a recentralized, unitary system.

The methods used by Putin and his team were in large part derived from the standard operating procedures of the KGB and its successor organization, the FSB. These included gathering compromising materials against "targets," using this information to blackmail the targets in order to gain their cooperation, planning and carrying out extralegal operations with a maximum degree of secrecy, and using diversions and feints to direct attention away from the real purpose of an operation. In the case of the shift of powers to the federal districts, a part of Putin's strategy seemed to be to create new institutions that at first seem merely to duplicate functions of existing institutions, but that could later take their place. The emphasis on discipline, carrying out orders without question, and strict hierarchical relations also reflects the internal ethos of the KGB. Democracy and an effectively operating federal system, on the other hand, call for other modes of operation: politics as the sphere for resolving disputes; an emphasis on transparent, lawful action within existing political institutions; and the use of methods such as negotiation, persuasion, and compromise.

If one sets aside the obvious exception of Chechnya, the Yeltsin presidency relied heavily on compromise and negotiation to achieve settlements with the regions. What prevented Yeltsin from building a more balanced system of federalism was the center's political and economic weakness. This weakness was exploited by republic presidents and governors to carve out substantial autonomy. Putin, with much higher levels of public support, an effective working majority in the Duma, and a much more favorable economic-budgetary situation, had a much stronger basis to exert leverage. The improvement of the Russian economy after the August 1998 crisis and as a result of higher oil prices cannot be overestimated in this regard. This led to enhanced tax collection and greater budgetary resources that could be used to pay off past debts and to finance federal institutions. Putin preferred to use his strength to force the changes he wants largely without bargaining and without employing constitutional mechanisms.

How did Putin's policies work in practice? The evidence is contradictory. On the one hand, the new policies did seem to remove some gubernatorial control over the military, police, and federal agencies that rightfully belonged under federal jurisdiction. On the other hand, there was little recognition among Putin's advisors that this strategy could go too far, or that excessive centralization was one of the weaknesses of the Soviet system. It is clear from Putin's statements on "restoring" vertical power that his main reference point was the USSR. To someone who was a product of the Soviet system, the elimination of checks and balances appears to increase the manageability and effectiveness of the political system. This may have been true in the short run, but there was a serious downside. A highly centralized system runs the risk of collapsing in the face of a crisis or rapidly changing conditions.

A July 2005 meeting of the State Council examined the question of turning over powers again to the regions, now that regional leaders were under the Kremlin's direct control. Putin promised, in effect, to "redecentralize" to the regions over one hundred functions performed by the federal government. The need for a change in the distribution of powers was particularly emphasized by Putin's *polpred* in the Southern Federal District, Dmitri Kozak—who, ironically, as presidential advisor was the author of the proposals that recentralized state power in Putin's first term. Later, from his perspective in Russia's most unstable region, Kozak argued it was wrong to expect governors and republic presidents to act responsibly if they aren't given real responsibility.[21] Nevertheless, decentralization had plenty of enemies among federal ministries who had no desire to surrender functions and reduce their own power.

Russia's leaders have only a hazy notion of what constitutes federalism. To an extent this parallels Soviet-era misunderstandings about the nature of a market economy. The absence of a planned or command system for allocating resources was equated with chaos and anarchy. Similarly, the absence of a clear chain of command in the political-administrative sphere is viewed as disorder or a situation that is "out of control" (*bezobrazie*). The idea that certain important decisions would actually be made in Russian regions without a directive from the center is alien to this mind-set.

The idea that officials at any level should be responsive to voters and citizens is even more alien. The creation of parallel vertical power structures does nothing to facilitate Russia's political maturation. Ultimately, the political center of gravity should be in the regions. In the 1990s, normal political institutions, the organizations that constitute civil society, and independent media were victimized by the disproportionate power wielded by Russia's governors and republic presidents. If the center had used its power to guarantee political freedoms and rights in the regions, it would encourage participation and democratization. Instead, Putin's policies were designed to create new levels of decision making above the regions. This made policy less dependent on governors, but it also puts important policy decisions out of the reach of citizens and their nascent organizations. The end of elections of governors was the logical outcome of this process.

Putin's policy toward political parties and elections to regional legislatures further illustrates this point. Rather than encouraging pluralism and allowing the "bottom-up" development of grassroots parties, Putin pushed for the creation of a national super-party through the merger of three of seven parties represented in the Duma: Unity, Fatherland, and All Russia. This new party, United Russia, was highly centralized under the control of Putin loyalists. As a result of the 2001 law on political parties, regionally based parties were not allowed to register and compete in national elections. The presidential representatives were mobilized to assist in party formation in federal districts, obviously to benefit United Russia. The Kremlin then mobilized the considerable "administrative resources" of governors and republic presidents to help elect an overwhelming pro-Putin majority in the new State Duma elected in December 2003. Later, the Kremlin succeeded in changing the rules on electing regional legislatures to require a mixed single-member and proportional representation system (by party list). This allowed United Russia to establish a dominant role in most regional legislatures. After Putin began appointing governors, most of those remaining outside United Russia rushed to join. By the time of the 2007 Duma elections, almost all governors had become members of the party and they had a direct interest in insuring the best possible performance for United Russia in regional and national elections.

Thus, Putin's vision for Russia was one that created multiple instruments of vertical control: administrative (based on federal districts and presidential representatives), police, FSB (especially the new Anti-Terrorism Committees), antidrug, financial monitoring, a dominant political party, and others. Meanwhile, the development of other political parties and nongovernmental organizations was threatened by increased bureaucratic obstacles, while a Kremlin-loyalist Public Chamber presented itself as the only legitimate forum for civil society. The result is a vertically integrated and horizontally fractured state.

Dmitri Medvedev, who at least initially has played the role of a loyal protégé of Putin, had very little to say about regional policy prior to becoming president. In a November 5, 2008, speech to the Federal Assembly, Medvedev presented his first detailed proposals for reforming Russian democracy, in order to create what he called "a just society of free people" and "a flourishing and democratic country." Among the proposals were several changes in regional policy. Medvedev endorsed, without providing details, "further decentralization" along with a reduction in the number of federal agencies in the regions. The only vaguely democratic measures he advanced were steps to allow greater competition in regional parliamentary elections. The currently prohibitive deposits required for parties to participate in regional elections would be eliminated, while the number of party members required for registering a party and the number of signatures required for a party to get on the ballot would be decreased. (Administrative methods, however, could still be employed to prevent opposition parties from registering using signatures.)

Medvedev also proposed revising the method by which members of the Federation Council would be chosen, for the fourth time since the upper house was created in 1994. Henceforth, the pool of potential senators would be deputies elected either at the regional or municipal level. From these, the governor and regional assembly would each presumably select a senator. While this appears to increase the democratic threshold required to become a senator, in fact it is not difficult to arrange a victory for any desired candidate in a municipal or regional race—most simply by placing that person on the party list of United Russia at one of these levels. A recent limitation on senators, a residence requirement in the regions they represent, would be dropped before it had even been implemented.

Medvedev's other proposals do little to facilitate democracy and in fact strengthen the dominant role of United Russia in the regions. (Putin, of course, became the leader of United Russia in 2008.) Medvedev proposed a change in the system for nominating candidates for governor, which are then submitted to the president for his choice. Previously the nominations were at least formally made by presidential envoys in the federal districts who were expected to consult with major political forces in a region (though appointment of governors with no experience in the region meant that these consultations would lack substance). In the future, the largest party in the assembly would now have an exclusive role in nominating candidates for governor.

In the present context, this means turning the nomination process over to United Russia, since it has a majority in nearly every regional parliament. Depending on the particular case, this could put decisions on governors in the hands of Vladimir Putin, as the leader of the United Russia vertical, or to governors, since party organizations in regions are often controlled by the governors. Thus, the new mechanism guarantees either centralized control from above or the "circularity of power." Governors, chosen by the Kremlin, determine who is in the parliamentary majority, which in turn determines who will be nominated for governor.

In another proposed change, mayors and municipal executives, the only elected executive posts in Russia other than the presidency, would now be subject to removal by city councils or municipal assemblies. Medvedev justified this by saying it would increase the accountability of local executives for the results of their work, a problem "long in need of a solution." The dominance of United Russia in representative bodies at all levels gives governors—or the Kremlin, should it choose to intervene—unprecedented power to overrule the electorate and eliminate potential opponents.

In general, Medvedev's first year in office did not bring any essential changes in the regional dimension of the political and managerial system constructed by Putin. Even trends and informal practices remained the same. Perhaps a deepening financial-economic crisis will stimulate changes: a lack of funds to support the regions could promote the transformation of the current excessively centralized and unitary state into one that is more flexible and effective, with more pronounced federalist features.

SUGGESTED READINGS

Evans, Alfred B., and Vladimir Gel'man, eds. *The Politics of Local Government in Russia*. Lanham, Md.: Rowman & Littlefield, 2004.

Golosov, Grigorii. *Political Parties in the Regions of Russia: Democracy Unclaimed*. Boulder, Colo.: Lynne Rienner, 2004.

Hale, Henry. *Why Not Parties in Russia? Democracy, Federalism, and the State*. New York: Cambridge University Press, 2006.

Reddaway, Peter, and Robert W. Orttung. *The Dynamics of Russian Politics: Putin's Reform of Federal-Regional Relations*. Vols. 1 and 2. Lanham, Md.: Rowman & Littlefield, 2004 and 2005.

Ross, Cameron, and Adrian Campbell, eds. *Federalism and Local Politics in Russia*. London: Routledge, 2009.

NOTES

1. See Graeme Gill, *The Origins of the Stalinist Political System* (Cambridge: Cambridge University Press, 1996); and Gerald Easter, *Reconstructing the State: Personal*

Networks and Elite Identity in Soviet Russia (Cambridge: Cambridge University Press, 1996).

2. Peter Jordan, "Regional Identities and Regionalization in East-Central Europe," *Post-Soviet Geography and Economics* 42, no. 4 (2001): 235–65.

3. Daniel Triesman, "The Politics of Intergovernmental Transfers in Post-Soviet Russia," *British Journal of Political Science* 26, no. 3 (1996): 299–335; and Daniel Triesman, "Fiscal Redistribution in a Fragile Federation: Moscow and the Regions in 1994," *British Journal of Political Science* 28, no. 1 (1998).

4. Michael McFaul and Nikolai Petrov, *Politicheskii Al'manakh Rossii 1997*, vol. 1 (Moscow: Carnegie Center, 1998), 149.

5. Darrell Slider, "Elections to Russia's Regional Assemblies," *Post-Soviet Affairs* 12, no. 3 (1996): 243–64.

6. Pavel K. Baev, "The Russian Armed Forces: Failed Reform Attempts and Creeping Regionalization," *Journal of Communist Studies and Transition Politics* 17, no. 1 (2001): 34.

7. Steven Solnick, "Is the Center Too Weak or Too Strong in the Russian Federation?" in *Building the Russian State*, ed. Valerie Sperling (Boulder, Colo.: Westview, 2000).

8. Alfred Stepan, "Russian Federalism in Comparative Perspective," *Post-Soviet Affairs* 16, no. 2 (2000): 133–76.

9. Darrell Slider, "Russia's Market-Distorting Federalism," *Post-Soviet Geography and Economics* 38, no. 8 (1997): 445–60.

10. Nikolai Petrov, "Seven Faces of Putin's Russia: Failed Districts as the New Level of State Territorial Composition," *Security Dialogue* 33, no. 1 (2002): 219–37.

11. Mathew Hyde, "Putin's Federal Reforms and Their Implications for Presidential Power in Russia," *Europe-Asia Studies* 53, no. 5 (2001): 719–43.

12. The reference is to the movie *The Magnificent Seven*, which was one of the first American films to be widely shown in the Soviet Union during the Cold War. The film, a western, was extremely popular in the 1960s when Vladimir Putin was growing up.

13. The most detailed examination of the early role of the federal districts and *polpreds* is Peter Reddaway and Robert W. Orttung, *Putin's Reform of Federal-Regional Relations*, vol. 1, *The Dynamics of Russian Politics* (Lanham, Md.: Rowman & Littlefield, 2004).

14. An additional eighteen federal agencies had regional offices in another location, while forty-three had no intermediate structures between their central headquarters and regional branches. "Federal Agencies on the Territory of Nizhniy Novgorod *Oblast*," chart prepared by the Volga federal district administration (2001).

15. The number of staff (150) assigned to the federal district MVD offices was greater than that assigned to the staff of the presidential representatives.

16. Nikolai Patrushev (FSB director until 2008, now secretary of the Security Council), Sergei Ivanov (first deputy prime minister, former defense minister, currently deputy prime minister), Aleksandr Bortnikov (current FSB chair, previously head of FSB economic security department), Viktor Ivanov (assistant to the president, in charge of personnel in the Putin administration, currently head of State Commit-

tee to Combat Drug Trafficking), Victor Cherkesov (Putin's chair of the State Committee to Combat Drug Trafficking, currently head of the arms procurement agency), Igor Sechin (Putin's deputy chief of presidential administration, currently deputy prime minister), Georgy Poltavchenko (*polpred* in the Central Federal District that includes Moscow), Viktor Zubkov (chair of the Ministry of Finance's Financial Monitoring Committee, later prime minister at the end of Putin's second term, currently deputy prime minister), Vladimir Yakunin (head of the public corporation that runs the national railroad system), Sergei Verevkin-Rokhal'sky (former MVD deputy minister and former head of tax police), Boris Boyarskov (Rosokhrankultura, the media censorship organ), and Aleksandr Grigor'ev (Rosrezerv, the agency that oversees government supply reserves). The most complete examination of changes in the Russian elite in Putin's early years can be found in Olga Kryshtanovskaia, *Anatomiia Rossiiskoi Elity* (Moscow: Zakharov, 2005).

17. Dmitri Medvedev was in this category (first deputy prime minister, former chief of presidential administration prior to Putin's selection of him as successor), as were Igor Sechin (deputy head of presidential administration under Putin, currently deputy prime minister), Sergei Naryshkin (deputy prime minister; under Medvedev, chief of the presidential administration), Aleksandr Beglov (assistant to the president; under Putin, head of Chief Control Commission; under Medvedev, head of the Kremlin chancellery), Oleg Markov (head of the Financial Monitoring Committee after Zubkov's promotion, currently Medvedev's chief of personnel in the Kremlin), Alexei Miller (chief of Gazprom), Dmitri Kozak (presidential aide to Putin, then *polpred* and later minister for regional development, currently deputy prime minister), Vladimir Kozhin (head of Presidential Administration Property Department), Ilya Yuzhanov (minister of antimonopoly policy and entrepreneurship), Anton Ivanov (chair of Supreme Arbitration Court), Konstantin Chuichenko (head of the Main Oversight Department under Medvedev), Aleksandr Konovalov (*polpred* under Putin; Medvedev named him minister of justice), Vitali Mutko (minister of sport and tourism under Medvedev), and Nikolai Vinnichenko (head of bailiff's office).

18. Anatoli Chubais (head of United Electrical Systems, currently head of the Russian nanotechnology corporation), German Gref (minister for economic development and trade, currently chair of Sberbank), Alexei Kudrin (finance minister and deputy prime minister), Andrei Illarionov (until January 2006, chief economic advisor to the president), Mikhail Dmitriyev (head of the presidential "think tank," the Center for Strategic Research, former first deputy minister for economic development and trade), Dmitri Vasilyev (Federal Securities Commission chair).

19. Boris Gryzlov (speaker of the Duma, former minister of internal affairs), Ilya Klebanov (*polpred* in the Northwest Federal District that includes St. Petersburg), Leonid Reiman (minister of communications under Putin; currently advisor to Medvedev), Sergei Stepashin (head of the audit chamber), Yuri Shevchenko (former health minister), Sergei Mironov (Federation Council speaker and leader of the party A Just Russia), Valery Yashin (director general of Svyazinvest, communications monopoly), Vladimir Kirillov (Rosprirodnadzor, the environmental protection agency).

20. For an overview of the impact of Putin's federal reforms on law enforcement, the courts, Federation Council, local government, political parties, and business

(along with other issues), see Peter Reddaway and Robert W. Orttung, *Putin's Reform of Federal-Regional Relations*, vol. 2, *The Dynamics of Russian Politics* (Lanham, Md.: Rowman & Littlefield, 2005).

21. Darrell Slider, "Putin's 'Southern Strategy': Dmitri Kozak and the Dilemmas of Recentralization," *Post-Soviet Affairs* 24, no. 2 (2008): 177–97.

Chapter Four

The Law in Post-Putin Russia

Kathryn Hendley

Law has had a checkered history in Russia. The rule of law, as evidenced by an independent judiciary that applies the law in an evenhanded manner to all who come before it, has been mostly absent. During the Soviet era, the leaders of the Communist Party used law in a blatantly instrumental fashion. This began to change in the late 1980s, when Gorbachev put forward the goal of a *pravovoe gosudarstvo*, or a "state based on the rule of law."[1] The leaders of post-Soviet Russia reiterated this goal, yet their actions indicated ambivalence. The heavy-handed prosecutions of political opponents of the Kremlin suggest that the willingness to use law as a weapon to achieve short-term goals is a vestige of Soviet life that lives on in post-Soviet Russia. Though these prosecutions have become the most well-known feature of the Russian legal system, both domestically and internationally, they do not tell the whole story. They have occurred within a legal system that has undergone remarkable institutional reforms over the past two decades. Focusing on its many persistent shortcomings is easy but unfair. Moreover, what sorts of changes will be wrought under President Dmitri Medvedev's leadership remain to be seen. During his first year in power, he repeatedly decried the "legal nihilism" of Russians and called for renewed attention to judicial reform.[2]

The contemporary Russian legal system is best conceptualized as a dual system, under which mundane cases are handled in accordance with the prevailing law, but under which the outcomes of cases that attract the attention of those in power can be manipulated to serve their interests.[3] To put it more simply, justice is possible and maybe even probable, but it cannot be guaranteed. This lack of predictability is unfortunate but does not make Russia unique. Law is inherently messy. Many countries aspire to the rule of law, but none has yet achieved it in full measure. Articulating the rules is always easier than applying them to concrete circumstances. Some gap between the

83

law on the books and the law in practice is inevitable. The efforts to bridge this gap in Russia are the subject of this chapter.

HISTORICAL OVERVIEW

The role of law in any society is not dependent solely on written laws and formal legal institutions.[4] It is also influenced by how these laws and institutions are understood and how they are used (or not used) by the powerful and the powerless within that society. These attitudes, often referred to as legal culture, are neither uniform nor consistent. They are influenced by many factors. Primary among them are the common perceptions of the responsiveness of law and legal institutions to the interests of society. For some, these perceptions are shaped by their own experiences. But in Russia, much as in the rest of the world, the vast majority of citizens have had no firsthand encounters with the formal legal system. Their attitudes toward the legal system are influenced by beliefs about how law has worked in the past as well as by mass media accounts about how the legal system is presently functioning or anecdotal accounts of the experiences of friends or family. As a result, making sense of the role of law in Putin's Russia requires some knowledge of what came before.

The Soviet Union is often referred to as a lawless society. Taken literally, this was not true. The Soviet Union possessed all the elements of a typical legal system.[5] It had a complex body of statutory law as well as a series of constitutions. It had a hierarchy of formal courts that mirrored what would be found in any Western democracy, as well as a well-developed system of alternative dispute resolution that allowed for neighborhood mediation in so-called "comrades' courts." But all of these institutions were firmly under the thumb of the Communist Party. Though the constitutions prominently proclaimed their commitment to the principle of judicial independence, the absence of judicial review made the constitutions largely symbolic. The legislature, though composed of representatives who were ostensibly popularly elected, operated as a rubber stamp for decisions made by Communist Party leaders. Likewise, judges tended to toe the party line.[6] All understood that anyone who diverged would not be invited to stand for reelection, and the short five-year terms ensured that judges were kept on a short leash. This should not be taken to mean that party officials dictated the outcomes of all cases. Judges were left alone to resolve many (perhaps most) of the cases they heard in accord with the law and their consciences.[7] But judges knew that at any moment the telephone might ring and they might be told how to decide a specific case. The specter of "telephone law" hung over all cases and gave rise to a culture of dependency within the judiciary. Over time, fewer and fewer calls were needed as judges developed an instinct for what the party wanted. Not surprisingly, ordinary citizens grew skeptical of the power of the law to protect their interests. This legal culture of distrust persists to some extent to the present day and has stymied efforts to reform the legal system.

Mikhail Gorbachev was the first Soviet leader to make a systematic effort to change the role of law.[8] He regularly invoked the goal of creating a *pravovoe gosudarstvo* in his public statements. Moreover, he took concrete actions. His reforms to the electoral system brought an end to the era of the rubber-stamp legislatures. Under his tenure, the judicial selection system was overhauled, eliminating the Communist Party's stranglehold and granting judges life tenure. Though these reforms were certainly necessary to achieving judicial independence, they were far from sufficient. Judges could not shake off the mantle of dependency so easily. Citizens were likewise slow to abandon their skepticism regarding the capacity of judges to rule in an evenhanded manner without clear proof of a shift in judicial behavior. Along similar lines, Gorbachev introduced the principle of judicial review to Russia. He created the Committee on Constitutional Supervision.[9] Although not a full-fledged constitutional court, this committee was empowered to review acts of the executive and legislative branches, making it an early (albeit feeble) attempt at checks and balances. The members demonstrated a commitment to human rights and to requiring the state to live up to its obligations under the law that had previously been absent. The committee issued only twenty-three decisions in its short two-year (1990–1991) life and was ineffective in enforcing them.[10] Once again, its impact was largely symbolic. How far Gorbachev would have pushed the reforms of the legal system had he not lost power is unknowable. What is clear is that he initiated a series of key institutional reforms that pushed Russia away from its Soviet legacy and toward an embrace of a legal system grounded in the rule of law.

Reform to the legal system was less of a marquee issue under Yeltsin but continued throughout the 1990s. In some ways, the challenges were mitigated by the disintegration of the Soviet Union. No longer did reformers have to concern themselves with how reforms would play out in all the republics, which became independent countries in 1992, but the immense size of Russia as well as its federal character left reformers with their hands full. At the same time, Yeltsin's decision to abandon the halfway reforms that characterized *perestroika* and to embrace the goals of creating a democracy and a market economy complicated the task of legal reformers. The institutional infrastructure for both democracies and markets is grounded in law. Much of the Soviet-era legislation and legal institutions were inadequate to the task. Russian reformers turned to Western advisors for assistance in writing the new laws and creating the necessary institutions. Many of these advisors approached Russia as if it were a *tabula rasa*, disregarding what existed on paper as well as the prevailing legal culture. Almost no area of law was left untouched by the legislative whirlwind of the 1990s. The top-down nature of these reforms and the unwillingness to pay attention to the needs of those who would be impacted felt familiar to Russians, who recognized the *modus operandi* from their Soviet past, albeit under a new banner.[11] The result was a continued skepticism toward the usefulness of law, a sentiment that only deepened as the new institutions were rocked by a series of corruption scandals.

Snapshots of the judicial system taken at the beginning and end of the 1990s would reveal dramatically different pictures. Though the basic court system remained intact and continued to handle the bulk of cases, other more specialized courts were introduced. The most well-known is the stand-alone Constitutional Court. The Constitutional Court represented a dramatic break with Russia's autocratic tradition. Through its power of judicial review, the court was entitled to declare acts of the legislative and executive branches unconstitutional, thereby making the judicial branch into an equal partner for the first time in Russian history. In its early days, the court took some highly controversial positions, most notably siding with the legislature against Yeltsin in the lead-up to the October events of 1993.[12] Yeltsin disbanded the court during this crisis. When it was reconstituted in early 1994, the justices, having learned their lesson, shied away from disputes with political overtones.[13] Less well known, but essential to the development of a market economy, was the emergence of a hierarchical system of *arbitrazh* courts in 1992. These courts were not created out of whole cloth but were built on the foundation of the Soviet-era system for resolving disputes between state-owned enterprises. Critical changes were made in terms of the status of the decision makers (raised from arbiters to judges) and jurisdiction (expanded to include disputes involving private firms as well as bankruptcy), but the *arbitrazh* courts represent a creative adaptation of Soviet-era institutions to serve the needs of the new Russia.[14] (See below for a more detailed discussion of each of these court systems.)

In addition to the structural innovations, the depoliticization of the process of selecting judges, begun under Gorbachev, was consolidated under Yeltsin.[15] The constitution approved by popular referendum in December 1993 provided that judges be appointed by the president, with the proviso that nominations to any of the top courts be confirmed by the Federation Council. The seemingly unchecked power of the president to select lower-level judges might seem an example of the expansive (perhaps overly expansive) powers granted to the president by this constitution. In reality, however, it constituted the final step in a system intended to preference competence over political reliability, a noteworthy reversal from the previous system in which judges served at the pleasure of the Communist Party. Under the new system, anyone with a law degree who was at least twenty-five years old and had at least five years of work in the legal profession was eligible to become a judge. Applications were assessed by judicial qualification commissions, who forwarded their recommendations up the bureaucratic chain. Though the president was entitled to reject these recommendations, he rarely did.[16] After an initial three-year probationary period, judges on the courts of general jurisdiction and the *arbitrazh* courts received life tenure, subject to a mandatory retirement age of sixty-five. Allegations of judicial corruption and other malfeasance were handled by the judicial qualifications commissions, which had the power to sanction and even to remove judges.

A review of the legal infrastructure at the close of Yeltsin's tenure reveals many of the necessary building blocks for the rule of law. The introduction of judicial review, combined with the efforts to insulate judges at all levels from political pressure, are critical to creating judicial independence. But below the surface lurked the culture of dependency that had developed over the decades of Soviet power. Many Russian citizens doubted that these judges would be willing to take on the Kremlin to protect citizens' rights. The emergence of the Constitutional Court as a vigorous defender of human rights helped but could not entirely erase their suspicions. Russia is a superb example of the difficulty of changing legal culture. Changing the underlying institutional structure is a necessary but not sufficient condition to achieving this goal.

LEGISLATIVE REFORMS UNDER PUTIN

Putin's consolidation of power within the Duma and his emasculation of the Federation Council allowed for legislative reforms that had eluded Yeltsin. During the 1990s, a number of key pieces of legislation, such as the labor code, the tax code, the criminal procedure code, and the land code, had stalled due to opposition within the Duma. Those affected had to hobble along using either stopgap presidential decrees or Soviet codes, which had been amended so many times that they had come to resemble a patchwork quilt. Not only did this undermine the predictability of law by making it difficult to discern what the rules were, but it left the guiding principles of the Soviet era in place, at least on paper. Under Putin, codes were finally passed that marked a principled shift away from Soviet-era norms, but the manner in which they were passed may signal a return to the Soviet style of rubber-stamp legislatures.

The criminal procedure code in effect when Putin took office was originally passed under Khrushchev. Although it was much amended, human rights activists argued that it still failed to protect the rights of the accused. A new code, which enhanced the rights of judges at the expense of the police, got bogged down in the Duma in the latter years of Yeltsin's tenure. Under Putin, United Russia (the Kremlin-affiliated party) was able to take advantage of both its numbers and the ability of its leaders to enforce party discipline and build coalitions to push Putin's legislative agenda through the Duma.

The new code came into effect in 2002.[17] Under its terms, the police are required to obtain warrants for investigative activities that previously could be carried out without judicial supervision. The code also limits the circumstances under which the accused may be kept in pretrial detention. Whether all of these procedural niceties are observed in practice is a different question. The question of whether judges do a better job of safeguarding individual rights has also come into question. The Khodorkovsky case, in which the Yukos chief was jailed while awaiting trial on fraud charges despite not meeting the prerequisites of the code, shows that the rules regarding pretrial detention can and will be disregarded when inconvenient for the Kremlin.[18] Judging a system solely on high-profile cases can be dicey. The extent to which the state lives up to its obligations in more mundane cases is unclear, but the strong culture of backdoor dealings between judges and prosecutors creates grounds for suspicion. Passing a law is just the beginning. Changing ingrained behavior of state officials is infinitely more difficult and pales in comparison to trying to change the attitudes of ordinary Russians toward the legal system. One key institutional player that has proven resistant to change is the procuracy. The procuracy is a uniquely Russian component of the legal system that is charged not only with prosecuting crime but also with supervising justice more generally. It has stubbornly held out against numerous reform efforts aimed at making its activities more transparent.[19]

The labor code was the subject of much discussion during the 1990s. Everyone understood that the Soviet code, which dated back to the Brezhnev era, was inadequate. It created strong protections for workers, making it almost impossible for management to fire them, whether for cause or not. The code reflected a societal commitment to full employment that was at the heart of state socialism. Yeltsin's decision to transform Russia into a market economy meant that featherbedding could no longer be tolerated. Yet the law lagged behind this political reality. Competing drafts of a new labor code began circulating in the late 1990s. The version supported by the Kremlin broke with tradition by allowing management to fire workers at will. Not surprisingly, trade union activists opposed this version and put forward a draft that would have tilted the balance toward workers. The situation stalemated as representatives of the Communist Party resisted the market-driven principles of the Kremlin's draft.[20] Once Putin took power, he was able to break this logjam and get his preferred version passed in late 2001.[21] He accomplished this not through the power of persuasion but through brute force. The message seemed to be that the fledgling experiment with a lawmaking process in which the views of society are reflected and respected is over. Putin's style harkens back to the Soviet period when the legislature took its cues from the Kremlin and obediently approved anything put before it. This top-down view of law leaves no room for society to feel any sense of ownership in the law and may contribute to a renewal of the disdain and distrust of law exhibited during the Soviet era.

Putin's behavior with regard to the law monetizing pension benefits and the law governing relations between the state and nongovernmental organizations (NGOs) certainly extinguished any lingering doubt as to whether Putin sees law as a reciprocal process in which both state and society participate. In the summer of 2004, the Kremlin proposed replacing in-kind benefits for pensioners and invalids (such as free bus passes and medical care) with monetary grants. These plans were met with howls of disapproval by the groups affected, who feared that the cash grants would be inadequate to meet their needs and that they would not keep up with inflation. Pensioners mounted a series of public protests but were unable to stop the bill from being enacted.[22]

Along similar lines, a bill aimed at making NGOs more accountable to the state was passed in December 2005 over the strong objections of many, both domestically and internationally, who believed the law would fatally compromise the independence of NGOs. The law required all NGOs to reregister, a tactic familiar from the Soviet era, when it was used as a way to purge undesirables from the Communist Party. The fear of NGO activists that reregistration would be used as a pretext to get rid of those NGOs that are distasteful to the authorities was realized when the law went into effect. Echoing a tactic from the Soviet era, the law is riddled with vague language that gives authority considerable discretion in terms of enforcement. Similarly, the law on extremism, which was passed in 2002 to fight terrorism, has been used to outlaw political parties not in sync with the Kremlin.[23] This demonstrates the Kremlin's willingness to use law instrumentally.

JUDICIAL POLITICS UNDER PUTIN

Judicial Selection and Supervision

The method of selecting judges and supervising them once they are on the bench has profound implications for the independence of the judicial system. Ideally, judges should look only to the law in resolving disputes; politics should not factor into their decisions. But when judges feel beholden to a political benefactor (whether an individual or a party) for their appointments or for their continued tenure in office, their impartiality can be compromised. Lifetime tenure is a potential solution but could create a judicial corps detached from society because they answer to no one. Judges, even those with lifetime appointments, must be held accountable if they misbehave. Some sort of oversight is necessary. Yet it requires a delicate touch; otherwise it risks undermining independence. As this suggests, maintaining a judicial system grounded in the rule of law is excruciatingly difficult and highly political. Striking an acceptable balance between independence and accountability can be elusive.

Locating this equilibrium point in post-Soviet Russia has proven particularly vexing. Initially, the primary goal seemed to be ensuring independence. Judges were granted lifetime tenure. Judicial qualifications commissions (JQCs) were created in the late 1980s. Composed entirely of judges, they were charged with vetting applications. Their recommendations were then forwarded to the president, who had final authority over who was to be appointed. The selection process included objective criteria, such as a standardized written exam, as well as more subjective elements, such as an oral interview and a comprehensive background check. Empowering judges to pick their colleagues signals a preference for competence over political reliability.

Under Putin's leadership, concerns about the lack of judicial accountability gave rise to subtle but important changes in the selection system.[24] The composition of the JQCs was altered. Judges no longer enjoy a monopoly but still make up two-thirds of the membership of the JQCs at all levels, leaving them with effective control if they act in concert.[25] In theory, opening JQC membership to nonjudges might seem democratic, in that it creates an avenue for societal concerns to be expressed. Judges saw it differently, fearing an effort by the Kremlin to exert more control over the courts. The change allows other voices into the decision-making process, but most other European countries with organs analogous to the JQCs include a mixture of judges and laypeople.[26] As part of Putin's effort to consolidate power in the wake of the Beslan tragedy, a more radical proposal was put forward that called for equal representation of judges and laypeople on the JQCs, with an additional nonjudge to be appointed by the president. Though this proposal was approved overwhelmingly by the Federation Council, it was withdrawn before being taken up by the Duma. Precisely why is unclear, but perhaps the resistance to the reordering of the JQCs by the heads of the three top courts (see figure 4.1) combined with the strong opposition by certain Duma representatives contributed.[27] While the floating of this sort of proposal seemed to indicate that Putin wanted greater control over the courts, especially the three courts of last resort, he failed to push this agenda. The requirements of prior legal experience and of passing an exam remain intact, ensuring some minimal level of qualifications. Opening JQC membership to nonjudges creates an avenue for societal concerns to be expressed.

In addition to selecting judges, the JQCs have sole responsibility for disciplining judges. This brings some level of accountability into the mix. Possible sanctions range from private reprimands to dismissals. Such deci-

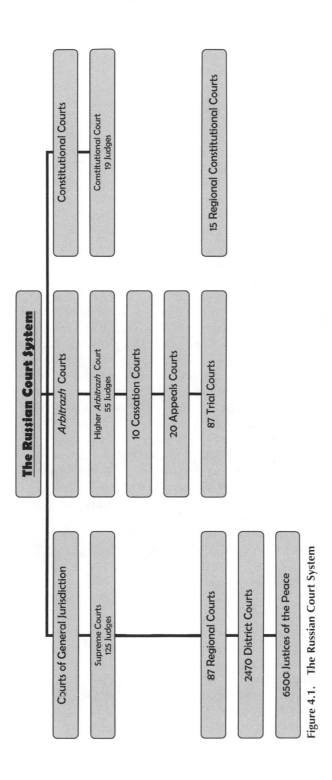

The Russian Court System

Courts of General Jurisdiction

Supreme Courts
125 Judges

87 Regional Courts

2470 District Courts

6500 Justices of the Peace

Arbitrazh Courts

Higher *Arbitrazh* Court
55 Judges

10 Cassation Courts

20 Appeals Courts

87 Trial Courts

Constitutional Courts

Constitutional Court
19 Judges

15 Regional Constitutional Courts

Figure 4.1.   The Russian Court System

sions are made in two contexts. Russian judges receive life tenure only after successfully completing a three-year probationary period, and the decision to retain these newcomers is made by the JQCs.[28] Such decisions are supposed to be based on job performance, but some contend that JQCs are using this opportunity to purge the judicial corps of anyone who threatens to rock the boat politically. The paucity of reliable data makes such allegations difficult to substantiate. Once judges have gotten over this hurdle, any and all complaints about their behavior are referred to the JQCs. The number of complaints has grown by about 10 percent since 2000. Although litigants raised more than 26,000 complaints before JQCs in 2006, this represented less than .02 percent of the cases brought before Russian courts. Motives for filing complaints varied. Over half of the complaints brought from 2001 through 2006 were based on alleged procedural violations (including delays). Another third came from litigants dissatisfied with the judge's decision (even though the more appropriate avenue would be to appeal). Relatively few (about 7 percent) alleged unethical or illegal behavior by judges.[29] Hidden within these statistics are litigants who are acting strategically. Because any complaint must be investigated and, even if later deemed to be frivolous, causes embarrassment to the named judge, litigants may attempt to influence judges by threatening to file a complaint. Had the proposal to equalize the membership of JQCs between judges and laypeople been adopted, it would likely have contributed to more politically driven sanctions, including dismissals. Under the current system, powerful anecdotal evidence of dismissals of judges who refused to toe the line exists,[30] but the actual number of dismissals are relatively few, constituting only 73 in 2006 (67 from the courts of general jurisdiction and 6 from the *arbitrazh* courts). An additional 385 were subjected to lesser forms of discipline (356 from the courts of general jurisdiction and 29 from the *arbitrazh* courts).[31]

In contrast to the U.S. judicial system, in which legal professionals go onto the bench after a fairly lengthy career in some other legal arena, becoming a judge in Russia is a career choice made at a much earlier stage of life. Those interested in becoming a judge typically go to work for the courts as an assistant to a judge immediately after completing their legal education in order to gain the necessary experience to apply for a judicial post. Once they get onto the bench, most stay for their entire work life.[32] The gender makeup of the Russian judiciary has shifted from being primarily female during the Soviet era to being more evenly divided.[33] Though the prestige of the judiciary has risen considerably since the demise of the Soviet Union, it remains lower than in the United States. This general phenomenon is not unique to Russia but is common to countries that share a civil law legal tradition.[34] The situation in Russia has been complicated by the salaries available to judges, which are lower than those available to lawyers in private practice (but higher than those who work in-house for corporations) as well as by the ongoing threats to the physical security of judges who rule against those associated with organized crime groups. Under Putin, both issues were addressed. He pushed for better and more consistent funding for the courts, resulting in increased judges' salaries.[35] That also facilitated the hiring of more judges, which decreased their workload. Those who apply to become judges stand a better than even chance of succeeding. In 2006, about 70 percent of those who applied passed the qualifying exam. Of the candidates remaining, almost all (96 percent) were recommended for judicial posts by the JQCs.[36] Better funding has also ensured better protection for judges on the job. Most courthouses screen entrants, allowing only those with pending cases to enter.

Notwithstanding these improvements, it remains difficult to recruit a sufficient number of judges to staff the courts. Institutional efforts aimed at enhancing the status of the judiciary represent a starting point but are effective only if accompanied by societal trust. This has been slow to develop, as evidenced by public opinion polls indicating that a majority of Russians do not think the courts have earned their trust.[37]

The Constitutional Court

The Constitutional Court is a post-Soviet innovation. Its purpose is to ensure that the constitution remains the preeminent legal authority in Russia. To that end, it is empowered to invalidate legislative and executive acts it deems unconstitutional, making it one of the few institutions capable of standing up to Putin. Before analyzing the extent to which it has taken advantage of its apparent power, a few words of background are in order.

From a technical legal point of view, the Constitutional Court stands on equal footing with the Supreme Court and the Higher *Arbitrazh* Court (see figure 4.1), but it is unlike them in several important respects. First, it does not stand at the apex of an elaborate hierarchy of courts that stretch across Russia. It is a stand-alone court.[38] Second, it is a small court with only nineteen judges, who are organized into two chambers for working purposes. The background of these judges is quite different from that of their counterparts on the other two top courts, most of whom have worked as judges for their entire careers. By contrast, many members of the Constitutional Court are drawn from the top ranks of legal scholars and come to the bench only after several decades of working in universities or research institutes. This means that they are free of the legacy of dependence that hangs over the rest of the Russian judiciary. Because they mostly come from a scholarly background, their opinions are more literate and lengthier, providing a clearer window into their thinking than is possible with opinions from the other courts. This is facilitated by the fact that only this court enjoys the right to write dissenting opinions. Finally, the decisions of the Constitutional Court are unique in that they serve as precedent. As is the norm in other European countries that share Russia's civil law legal heritage, the decisions of the courts of general jurisdiction and the *arbitrazh* courts are binding only on the parties to the specific cases.

The Constitutional Court receives approximately 15,000 petitions per year.[39] Almost all come in the form of individual complaints centering on alleged violations of constitutional rights. The remaining cases stem from claims initiated by the president, a group of legislators (at least 20 percent of the members of either chamber), or regional governments. The president has enjoyed greater success than others in getting his claims heard. Between 1995 and 2006, the court heard 78 percent of presidential petitions while taking only about half of those initiated by legislators, about a quarter of those from the regions, and less than 5 percent of the individual petitions.[40] Its decisions take several forms. Not all involve an up or down vote on the constitutionality of a particular law or regulation. Many of its opinions lay out the justification for legal norms' constitutionality. These "authoritative interpretations" can have the effect of rewriting the law under the guise of ensuring its constitutionality. They have given the court tremendous influence in many areas of law (including taxes, contracts, and social benefits) that would not appear to fall under its jurisdiction.[41] The court has further expanded its jurisdiction by issuing rulings that declared contested legal norms "noncontradictory to the constitution," but their interpretations of these laws are considered binding on all Russian courts.[42]

Since its reconstitution following the October events of 1993, the Constitutional Court has been reluctant to immerse itself in political controversy. Its ability to do so has been institutionally constrained by the decision to limit its jurisdiction to cases brought to it; the court can no longer take up cases on its own initiative.[43] The court has also adopted a more deliberative pace for resolving cases. In contrast to the chaotic practices of the early 1990s, when decisions were sometimes issued on an overnight basis, cases now take eight or nine months to wind their way through the system, allowing time for the sorts of back and forth discussions among the judges that are familiar to students of the U.S. Supreme Court.[44] In terms of the substance of its decisions, the Constitutional Court has consistently been supportive of Putin's agenda to curtail regional power, including the elimination of popular elections for governors.[45] Even when the regions prevail, as in the March 2003 case brought by the legislatures of Bashkortostan and Tatarstan, the court is careful to note that regional governments are entitled to expand their powers only to the extent that they do not infringe on the federal system. The court seemed to feel emboldened by the Kremlin to bring the regions to heel. One member of the court noted, "We struck down the key clauses of 7 constitutions of the republics in June 2000 only after President Putin announced his crackdown on recalcitrant regions; we would not have been brave enough to do this under Yeltsin."[46]

Getting its decisions enforced is a problem that the Constitutional Court shares with the courts of general jurisdiction and the *arbitrazh* courts.[47] Enforcing judgments is not just a problem in Russia; it is a problem that plagues courts everywhere. For the most part, litigants are expected to live up to the obligations imposed by the courts out of a combination of respect for the institution and a fear of being identified as noncompliant and shamed. The lack of societal trust in courts turns these assumptions upside down in Russia. Flouting judicial orders brings no disgrace. The Constitutional Court has attempted to remedy the problem by creating a department charged with monitoring its decisions. But the small size of the department (four people) and intransigence of the underlying political issues have hampered efforts at improving the record on implementation. For example, there have been a series of decisions, dating back to the Committee on Constitutional Supervision, declaring the system of residence permits to be an unconstitutional restriction on freedom of movement. Yet regional leaders, particularly in Moscow, have consistently ignored these decisions with no repercussions. While Putin mimicked Yeltsin in looking the other way on residence permits, he was more aggressive in forcing compliance on issues that interested him. For example, after the court struck down the gerrymandering law in Orenburg, local officials complied only after being strong-armed by Putin's staff.[48]

The Courts of General Jurisdiction

The courts of general jurisdiction are the workhorses of the Russian judicial system. Any case that is not specifically allocated to the Constitutional Court or the *arbitrazh* courts lands in their lap. In 2007, the workload of these courts, constituting almost 16 million cases, was over sixteen times greater than that of the *arbitrazh* courts. They employ over 30,000 judges. They handle all criminal cases as well as any civil or administrative case that affects an individual (rather than a firm).[49] The number of cases heard by these courts rose at a steady pace of over 10 percent per year under Putin, an increase driven by civil cases; the number of criminal cases actually decreased in recent years. The rise in civil claims is particularly intriguing, given that these are cases brought by individuals. Whether this reflects a fundamental shift in attitudes toward the legal system, namely a greater willingness on the part of Russians to use the courts to protect their interests, is unclear. Making such a determination would require an investigation capable of tracking all potential disputes and assessing why they never evolved into full-fledged lawsuits.[50] This sort of research has yet to be undertaken. Yet it is fair to assume that, as elsewhere, most disagreements are settled through negotiations, and therefore that relatively few disputes proceed to court. However, the way in which Russia's judicial system was compromised during the Soviet era may make Russia a special case. Results from public opinion polling seem to indicate that many dismiss the idea of going to court as absurd and even dangerous, but the caseload data suggest that the truth may be more complicated.[51]

The courts of general jurisdiction can be found in every administrative district, making them the most accessible of the Russian courts. This increased under Putin with the introduction of a new layer of courts, the justice of the peace (JP) courts (see figure 4.1). The JP courts were first authorized in late 1998 and were intended to provide a way to siphon off simpler cases, thereby alleviating the burden on the already existing courts.[52] Creating thousands of new courts proved to be easier said than done. When Putin took over, none existed, but by the end of 2007, JP courts existed in every part of Russia except for Chechnya. From an institutional perspective, they have lived up to their promise. In 2007, almost all (95 percent) administrative cases, 75 percent of all civil cases, and over 40 percent of criminal cases originated in these courts.[53] Thanks in large measure to this, delays throughout the entire system have been lessened.[54] The JP courts have also benefitted litigants by making courts more accessible, both geographically as well as in terms of the simplified procedure. Those dissatisfied with the JP courts are entitled to appeal the judgment to a higher court, though relatively few exercise this right, suggesting that most are satisfied with their treatment in JP courts.[55]

As figure 4.1 indicates, these courts have a traditional pyramidal structure. Most cases that have not been diverted to the JP courts originate in the district courts, which are located in each rural or urban district. More serious matters are heard for the first time by the regional courts (which also serve as courts of appeal for the district courts).[56] The court of last resort for this system is the Supreme Court of the Russian Federation. In addition to its pure judicial function of reviewing individual cases, the Supreme Court is also charged with overseeing the general development of judicial practice. To this end, it periodically issues guiding explanations of legislation that has been interpreted in contradictory fashion by lower courts. These explanations are binding on the lower courts. Ironically this gives the Russian Supreme Court greater institutional latitude than that enjoyed by the U.S. Supreme Court, though few would argue that the political clout of the Russian court approaches that of its American counterpart.

Putin's control of the legislature allowed for thorough reforms of the three procedural codes (administrative, civil, and criminal) that govern the day-to-day operations of the courts of general jurisdiction. Some of the innovations of the new criminal procedure code have been discussed above. The code also changed the operation of the courts by institutionalizing jury trials throughout Russia. Jury trials, which had not been available during the Soviet era but which had been part of the tsarist legal heritage, had been employed on an experimental basis since 1993 in nine regions.[57] Defendants charged with serious felonies can opt for a jury trial, and they have been doing so with increasing frequency. Jury trials accounted for 14 percent of such trials in 2007, compared with 8.3 percent in 2003.[58] Defendants tend to fare better with juries than with judges. While in 2007 less than 5 percent of defendants were acquitted in bench (nonjury) trials, over 20 percent of defendants in jury trials were acquitted.[59] Juries are clearly more mercurial than judges. Whether this will continue to be tolerated is unclear. Jury verdicts, including acquittals, have been subject to appeal from the outset. In 2007, for example, the Supreme Court reversed 23 percent of jury acquittals.[60] As politically sensitive cases have begun to reach juries, the FSB has called for cases involving crimes against the state to be declared off-limits for juries.[61] The FSB does not relish being embarrassed by acquittals, as they were in the Danilov case, in which the defendant was acquitted of spying charges by a jury on the grounds that the information he conveyed was not classified.[62] The FSB ultimately got a conviction, thanks to the overturning of the first jury verdict and a retrial which produced the desired guilty verdict by another jury.[63] But the messiness was distasteful. Though the law has not been changed to accommodate the preferences of the FSB, subsequent politically charged trials have been fairly blatantly manipulated to achieve the desired outcomes.[64]

The broader impact of the availability of jury trials on Russians' attitudes toward the legal system is unclear. Elsewhere, juries have been justified on the grounds that they allow defendants to be judged by their peers and that they provide jurors with hands-on experience in how a democratic system operates. The relatively small number of Russians who have served on juries undermines any argument that they are building support for democracy. Russians seem ambivalent about their merits. In an October 2007 public opinion survey, when asked whether juries were (1) fairer and more independent than judges, (2) less knowledgeable and experienced than judges and more likely to be influenced by the parties, or (3) basically the same as regular courts, respondents were less sanguine than they had been when surveyed in 2004.[65] Of course, juries have been in full operation for only a few years. It is perhaps premature to expect any societal impact.

The *Arbitrazh* Courts

The basic mission of *arbitrazh* courts remains unchanged; reforms have been aimed at solving nagging practical problems rather than consolidating the Kremlin's control over the courts. These courts continue to handle economic disputes, though their relevance to economic actors has been questioned. The mass media as well as a number of social scientists have argued that Russian firms avoid the courts, preferring to resolve their disputes with the assistance of organized crime groups.[66] Support for this argument is provided by anecdotal evidence as well as the many public opinion surveys that document Russians' distrust of the courts. Yet targeted empirical research has consistently shown that, notwithstanding their vociferous complaints about the legal system, managers are using these courts in ever increasing numbers.[67] The number of cases brought to the *arbitrazh* courts grew by over 200 percent from 1997 to 2007.[68] The willingness of economic actors to submit their disputes to the *arbitrazh* courts is driven by the comparatively low costs and speed of the process. This is not to say that litigation is the only or even the preferred mechanism of resolving disputes. For Russian managers, much as for their counterparts elsewhere, turning to the courts is a last resort, used only when efforts at negotiation have failed. Rather, the point is that litigation is a viable option for commercial disputes in Russia.

The jurisdiction of the *arbitrazh* courts is threefold: (1) disputes between firms (irrespective of ownership structure), (2) disputes between firms and the state, and (3) bankruptcies. At the outset, almost all cases fell into the first category, but the docket has shifted. Comparing the case distributions for 1997 and 2007 for two of the largest *arbitrazh* courts illustrates the point well. In 1997, disputes between firms dominated the docket, constituting over 80 percent of the cases decided by these courts. By 2007, however, the tables had turned. These disputes made up only about half of the cases decided. The dramatic increase in the percentage of cases involving the state can be partially explained by the general economic recovery under Putin, which led to fewer debt recovery cases. Given that the vast majority of cases involve tax disputes, this shift also indicates that citizens are becoming less tentative about suing the state and that the state is becoming more aggressive in collecting what is owed to it. As plaintiffs, both taxpayers and the state enjoy a robust success rate of over 70 percent, suggesting that *arbitrazh* judges may be guilty of a pro-petitioner bias, but contradicting the common wisdom that they are in the pocket of the state.

Like the courts of general jurisdiction, the *arbitrazh* courts are organized hierarchically. All subjects of the Russian Federation have a trial-level court, typically located in the capital city of the subject. When resolving cases, *arbitrazh* judges generally limit themselves to written evidence; they rarely hear the testimony of witnesses. Anyone dissatisfied with the result is entitled to appeal. The first appeal is heard *de novo*, meaning that the three-judge panel reviews the evidence submitted at trial for factual and legal errors. Until recently, these appellate courts were institutionally embedded in the trial courts. This meant the same set of judges was empowered to hear both trial and appellate cases. Litigants were troubled by this state of affairs, worrying that judges' reluctance to overrule their colleagues would hamper their chances at reversals. In 2003, responding to the concerns of litigants, these two courts were separated institutionally. The number of appellate courts was decreased to twenty, organized on a regional basis. The other parts of the appellate structure remained unchanged (see figure 4.1). The final and ultimate appeal is to the Higher *Arbitrazh* Court. In addition to hearing appeals, this court also routinely issues interpretations of legislation and administrative regulations that are binding on the *arbitrazh* courts.

The reworking of the *arbitrazh* procedural code in 2002 further demonstrates the pragmatic character of the Putin-era reforms. This new code made a multitude of changes aimed at streamlining the work of the courts, such as limiting the number of cases requiring a three-judge panel at the trial level. The prior code had empowered single judges to resolve interfirm disputes on their own, and the new code expands this to include most cases involving the state. Bankruptcy cases still require a three-judge panel. While this change allows cases to be processed more quickly, it may have the unintended consequence of facilitating corruption, in that one judge is easier to sway than three. The new code also clarifies that disputes involving competing claims to stock ownership are within the *arbitrazh* courts' jurisdiction. Because the prior code had denied access to the *arbitrazh* courts to individuals (non-firms), disputes involving both individual and corporate shareholders ended up being brought simultaneously in the *arbitrazh* courts and the courts of general jurisdiction, and sometimes led to inconsistent outcomes, which undermined the public's faith in the courts.[69] The decision to assign all these cases to the *arbitrazh* courts reflects a respect for their greater expertise.

The European Court of Human Rights

With Russia's accession to the Council of Europe in 1996 and its ratification of the European Convention on Human Rights in 1998, it now falls within the jurisdiction of the European Court of Human Rights (ECHR) in Strasbourg. Were Russians as nihilistic about law as is typically assumed, this would have made no difference. But Russians have flocked to the ECHR in record numbers. From 1998 to 2006, more petitions to the ECHR originated from Russia than from any other country.[70] This tells us that Russians still believe justice is possible and that they are searching out ways of holding their courts and government to account. At the same time, the fact that less than 1 percent of these Russian petitions are declared admissible reveals that Russians remain unclear about the precise function of the ECHR. Moreover, a 2008 public opinion survey revealed that only 7 percent of respondents would appeal to Strasbourg if their rights were violated.[71]

The Russian government has a mixed record at the ECHR. When the decisions have gone against it, they have been accepted and paid without question. The impact of these decisions on governmental policy is more difficult to assess. For example, in *Kalashnikov v. Russia*, decided in 2002, the petitioner argued that the conditions of Russian prisons violated his human rights.[72] The Russian government essentially conceded his point, attempting to defend itself on the grounds that all prisoners were treated abysmally and that they were not singling out the petitioner. The ECHR was unswayed and ruled against Russia, but it is doubtful that its opinion prompted an improvement in prison conditions. On the other hand, the availability of recourse to the ECHR has undoubtedly affected judicial behavior. A substantial number of the Russian petitions are grounded in complaints about treatment at trial, such as unreasonable delays and inability to enforce civil judgments. Russian judges, worried that their opinions will become the subject of appeals to the ECHR, are taking more care to live up to their procedural obligations. Though it might be more gratifying if such behavior stemmed from a commitment to the rule of law, fear of public humiliation can be a powerful stimulant, and perhaps the behavior will become ingrained. Regardless of the incentive for the behavioral change, it inures to the benefit of litigants and the legal system.

THE POLITICS OF THE LEGAL
PROFESSION UNDER PUTIN

In many countries, lawyers are potent catalysts for legal reform. Their comprehensive knowledge of the law makes them well qualified to identify where changes are needed. Such changes may be either iterative or fundamental. Their willingness to embrace these changes and to operationalize them through their clients can have a profound impact. Merely passing a law is only a first step. More difficult is integrating new norms into daily life. Lawyers can be integral in this process.

The legal profession in Russia has not traditionally performed this sort of role. The reasons are complicated. As in other countries with civil law traditions, lawyers tend to act more as technicians than as social activists. The divided nature of the profession in such countries also contributes to its political passivity. In Russia, for example, no single organization speaks for lawyers, nor is there any uniform system for licensing lawyers. This inevitably gives rise to a fragmented profession. The Soviet heritage, under which lawyers were heavily regulated and their independence was constrained, has only deepened this natural instinct.

Most of the state regulations governing lawyers were eliminated or ignored in practice during the initial transition. The traditional distinction between litigators (*advokaty*) and business lawyers (*iuriskonsul'ty*) broke down during the 1990s. Private law firms, which had been outlawed during the Soviet era, sprang up and included both varieties of lawyers. Courts treated them similarly. This permissiveness was viewed with dismay by many *advokaty*, who had long viewed themselves as the elite of the legal profession. Admission to the *advokatura* had always been a rigorous and selective process, in contrast to becoming a *iuriskonsul't*, which simply required advanced legal education. *Iuriskonsul'ty* took advantage of the laxness of the regulatory regime to establish themselves as experts in business law, a specialization that had been more or less nonexistent during the Soviet era and an area of law not much exploited by *advokaty* (who tended to focus on criminal defense work). This laxness may also have contributed to a doubling in the *advokatura*, which grew from 23,400 in 1995 to 48,800 in 2002.[73] This number is actually only a fraction of the total lawyers in Russia, which would also include procurators and *iuriskonsul'ty*. It does, however, reflect the growing popularity in legal education, as evidenced by a spike in the number of law schools.[74]

Drafts of a law that would restore the *advokaty* to their preeminent role were floated but never passed during the 1990s. Under Putin, this state of affairs changed. His legislative dominance allowed for the passage of a law dealing with the legal profession in 2002.[75] Though the law did not create a monopoly on courtroom practice, as desired by *advokaty*, it certainly made them the default option. In criminal cases, for example, defendants must use an *advokat* unless being represented by a family member. The law also established a standard process for gaining entry to the *advokatura*. Much like judges, prospective *advokaty* must satisfy the requirements of a qualifications commission, which include an oral exam. Though the questions come from a pre-approved list, some have argued that the subjective nature of evaluation leaves the door open for preferential treatment and for discrimination.[76] The law takes an important step toward institutionalizing the independence of the legal profession by establishing a privilege for attorney-client communications. Precisely what this means in practice remains unclear. The Kremlin's decision to expand the attack on Yukos and Khodorkovsky to include the defense lawyers buttresses skepticism.[77] The procurators' threat to move for disbarment of several of Khodorkovsky's lawyers for abuse of process harkens back to the Soviet era, when such threats were often used to keep *advokaty* from mounting a vigorous defense of their clients in politically motivated trials.[78] On the other hand, there is no evidence of efforts to undermine the attorney-client relationship in nonpolitical cases.

CONCLUSION

This review of the role of law in contemporary Russia illustrates that easy conclusions are not possible. The reasons for criticism of Putin's regime on this score are obvious. Under both Putin and Medvedev, the Kremlin's legislative agenda was pushed through with a heavy hand and often with the result of curtailing human rights. Putin's willingness to use the courts as a weapon for punishing his political opponents quite rightly calls their independence into question. Such policies would be troubling in any context but are particularly disquieting in post-Soviet Russia. They are disturbingly reminiscent of problem-solving tactics employed by Soviet leaders that would seem to have been renounced as part of the transition to a state based on the rule of law, *pravovoe gosudarstvo*. On the other hand, the Putin era witnessed institutional innovations aimed at moving Russia toward a *pravovoe gosudarstvo*. The introduction of the JP courts increased the responsiveness of courts to citizens and eased the strain on the district and regional courts. Along similar lines, the introduction of appellate courts within the *arbitrazh* courts responded to nagging complaints about the perceived influence of trial judges on appeals. The use of courts has continued to grow, suggesting a societal willingness to turn over disputes to the courts.

These seemingly contradictory indicators make sense only when the Russian legal system is analyzed as a dualistic system. The institutional progress cannot be dismissed as mere window dressing. After all, the vast majority of the millions of cases heard each year within the Russian judicial system are resolved on the basis of the law on the books, as interpreted by the judge, and without any interference from political authorities. Justice is not out of reach in Russia; it is the likely outcome in most cases. But the continued willingness of those with political power to use law in an instrumental fashion to achieve their short-term goals means that justice can sometimes be out of reach. It also means that the commitment to the basic principle of the rule of law, namely that law applies equally to all, irrespective of their power or connections, is not yet complete. A gap between the law on the books and the law in practice exists in Russia, as in all countries. Surely it has receded from the chasm it was during the Soviet era. But whether it will increase or decrease under Medvedev remains to be seen.

SUGGESTED READINGS

Burnham, William, and Jeffrey Kahn. "Russia's Criminal Procedure Code Five Years Out." *Review of Central and East European Law* 33, no. 1 (2008): 1–93.

Burnham, William, Peter B. Maggs, and Gennady Danilenko. *Law and Legal System of the Russian Federation*. 3rd ed. Huntington, N.Y.: Juris, 2004.

Solomon, Peter H., Jr., and Todd S. Foglesong. *Courts and Transition in Russia: The Challenge of Judicial Reform*. Boulder, Colo.: Westview, 2000.

Trochev, Alexei. *Judging Russia: Constitutional Court in Russian Politics, 1990–2006*. Cambridge: Cambridge University Press, 2008.

NOTES

1. For background on the meaning of *pravovoe gosudarstvo*, see Harold J. Berman, "The Rule of Law and the Law-Based State (*Rechsstaat*)," *Harriman Institute Forum* 4, no. 5 (1991): 1–12.

2. Medvedev raised the issue of "legal nihilism" during the presidential campaign, emphasizing it during a January 2008 speech to a citizen's forum in Moscow. See www.edinros.ru/news.html?id=126928. Since his election as president, he has raised it in almost every public appearance, including his interviews with Western news outlets. Aleksandr Gamov, "Interv'iu Dmitriia Medvedeva informagenstvu 'Reuter'," www.kp.ru/daily/24120.4/342034/.

3. The conceptualization of the Russian legal system as dualistic was first suggested by Robert Sharlet with regard to the Stalinist system. See Sharlet, "Stalinism and Soviet Legal Culture," in *Stalinism: Essays in Historical Interpretation*, ed. Robert C. Tucker (New York: Norton, 1977), 155–56. He, in turn, was drawing on the ideas of Ernst Fraenkel, *The Dual State: A Contribution to the Theory of Dictatorship* (London: Oxford University Press, 1941).

4. For an overview of the role of law, see Lon L. Fuller, *The Morality of Law* (New Haven: Yale University Press, 1965); and Philippe Nonet and Philip Selznick, *Law and Society in Transition* (New York: Harper and Row, 1978).

5. Harold J. Berman, *Justice in the U.S.S.R: An Interpretation of Soviet Law* (Cambridge, Mass.: Harvard University Press, 1963).

6. George Ginsburgs, "The Soviet Judicial Elite: Is It?" *Review of Socialist Law* 11, no. 4 (1985): 293–311.

7. George Feifer, *Justice in Moscow* (New York: Simon and Schuster, 1964).

8. Kathryn Hendley, *Trying to Make Law Matter* (Ann Arbor: University of Michigan Press, 1996): 34–45.

9. Herbert Hausmaninger, "The Committee of Constitutional Supervision of the USSR," *Cornell International Law Journal* 23, no. 2 (1990): 287–322.

10. Alexander Blankenagel, "Toward Constitutionalism in Russia," *East European Constitutional Review* 1, no. 2 (1992): 25–28.

11. Kathryn Hendley, "Legal Development in Post-Soviet Russia," *Post-Soviet Affairs* 13, no. 3 (1997): 228–51.

12. In addition, the court famously took on the question of the legality of the Communist Party, giving rise to a lengthy and rather bizarre trial. Yuri Feofanov and Donald D. Barry, *Politics and Justice in Russia: Major Trials of the Post-Stalin Era* (Armonk, N.Y.: M. E. Sharpe, 1996), 294–308; David Remnick, *Lenin's Tomb: The Last Days of the Soviet Empire* (New York: Vintage, 1994), 494–530. The text of the court's decision is available in *Vestnik Konstitutsionnogo Suda*, no. 4/5 (1993): 37–64. An English-language summary of the decision is set forth in William Burnham, Peter B. Maggs, and Gennady M. Danilenko, *Law and Legal System of the Russian Federation*, 3rd ed. (Huntington, N.Y.: Juris, 2004), 173–75.

13. Robert Sharlet, "Russia's Second Constitutional Court," in *Russia in the New Century: Stability or Disorder?* ed. Victoria E. Bonnell and George W. Breslauer (Boulder, Colo.: Westview, 2001), 59–77.

14. Kathryn Hendley, "Remaking an Institution: The Transition in Russia from State Arbitrazh to Arbitrazh Courts," *American Journal of Comparative Law* 46, no. 1 (1998): 93–127.

15. Peter H. Solomon Jr. and Todd S. Foglesong, *Courts and Transition in Russia: The Challenge of Judicial Reform* (Boulder, Colo.: Westview, 2000).

16. In 1997, only 2 percent of the recommendations forwarded to the president were rejected. Solomon and Fogelsong, *Courts and Transition in Russia*, 30.

17. Steven Lee Myers, "Russia Glances to the West for Its New Code," *New York Times*, July 1, 2002, A1; Leonid Orland, "A Russian Legal Revolution: The 2002 Criminal Procedure Code," *Connecticut Journal of International Law* 18, no. 133 (2002): 133–56.

18. Mikhail Khodorkovsky was arrested in the fall of 2003 on charges of fraud, tax evasion, and theft of state property in the course of privatization. At every stage of the process, the authorities skirted on the edge of legal proprieties, typically obeying the letter of the law (though not always) but trampling on its spirit. Western commentators have been uniformly critical of the process. See, for example, Timothy L. O'Brien and Erin E. Arvedlund, "Putin vs. the Jailed Tycoon: Defining Russia's New Rules," *New York Times*, January 2, 2004, A1; Bob Dole, "Russia Has Put Itself in the Dock," *Financial Times*, June 16, 2004, 16. Russians' views are more nuanced. Public opinion polls reveal that, while most abhor the tactics used by the Kremlin, they are fairly evenly split on whether Khodorkovsky was actually guilty of the charges. See www.levada.ru/press/2005020304.html. Khodorkovsky was, in fact, convicted of all charges. His company, Yukos, was found to have underpaid its taxes. Key assets were auctioned off by the state to pay these debts, gutting the company. For an assessment of the case, see William Thompson, "Putting Yukos in Perspective," *Post-Soviet Affairs* 21, no. 2 (2005): 159–81.

19. Gordon B. Smith, "Putin, the Procuracy, and the New Criminal Procedure Code," in *Public Policy and Law in Russia: In Search of a Unified Legal and Political Space*, ed. Robert Sharlet and Ferdinand Feldbrugge (Leiden: Martinus Nijhoff, 2005), 169–85.

20. Sarah Karush, "Proposed Code Has Labor up in Arms," *Moscow Times*, December 1, 2000, 1.

21. Robin Munro, "New Labor Code Goes into Force," *Moscow Times*, February 4, 2002, 3.

22. Francesca Mereu, "Benefits Bill Steamrollered Through," *Moscow Times*, August 4, 2004, 1.

23. Osadchuk, "National Bolshevik Party Declared Extremist," *Moscow Times*, April 20, 2007.

24. Alexei Trochev, "Judicial Selection in Russia: Towards Accountability and Centralization," in *Appointing Judges in an Age of Judicial Power: Critical Perspectives from around the World*, ed. Peter H. Russell and Kate Malleson (Toronto: University of Toronto Press, 2006).

25. The Higher Judicial Qualification Commission, which is responsible for recommending judges for the top courts, has twenty-nine members, of which eighteen are judges drawn from various corners of the judicial system. The remainder include ten members of the public appointed by the Federation Council and one presidential representative. The emasculation of the Federation Council means that all of these eleven members are, effectively, the president's representatives. The membership of lower-level JQCs is smaller but similarly structured, with judges representing about two-thirds. Article 11, "Ob organakh sudeiskogo soobshchestva v Rossiiskoi Federatsii," *Sobranie zakonodatel'stva*, no. 11, item 1022, March 18, 2002.

26. Peter H. Solomon Jr., "Threats of Judicial Counterreform in Putin's Russia," *Demokratizatsiya* 13, no. 3 (2005): 325–46.

27. Former Moscow City Court Judge Olga Kudeshkina commented: "The judiciary system is already under the Kremlin's influence, but if this terrible bill is approved, it means that we will lose any hope of seeing an independent judiciary system in Russia, since it will be completely in the hands of the Kremlin." Kudeshkina was allegedly removed as a judge because of her unwillingness to toe the Kremlin's line in the notorious "Three Whales" (Tri Kita) scandal. Francesca Mereu, "Judges Who Lost Their Jobs Speak Out," *Moscow Times*, October 6, 2004. See also Anna Zakatnova, "Spokoino, grazhdane sud'i! Vladimir Putin uteshil tret'iu vlast'," *Rossiiskaia gazeta*, October 21, 2004, www.rg.ru/2004/10/21/sudii.html.

28. The possibility of moving from life tenure to term appointments was raised by a high-level commission appointed by Putin and headed by German Gref, the minister of the economy. The idea was quickly quashed. Peter H. Solomon Jr., "Courts in Russia: Independence, Power, and Accountability," in *Judicial Integrity*, ed. András Sajó (Leiden: Martinus Nijhoff, 2004), 242–44.

29. "Obzor rezul'tatov deiatel'nosti za 2006 god," www.vkks.ru/ss_detale .php?id=856.

30. See, for example, Guy Chazan, "In Russia's Courts, a Judge Speaks Up—And Gets Fired," *Wall Street Journal*, August 4, 2004, 1.

31. "Obzor rezul'tatov deiatel'nosti."

32. Several regions have supported unusually high turnover rates for judges of the justice of the peace courts due to the heavy workload of these courts and salary levels below that for other judges. For example, in Kurgan *oblast*, almost 30 percent of the justices of the peace left during 2007. "Tekuchest' kadrov sredi mirovykh sudei v Zaural'e sostavlyaet pochti 30%," www.nakanune.ru/news/2008/03/12/2112225.

33. According to the data of the UN Economic Commission for Europe, about 60 percent of Russia's judicial corps is composed of women. This has held constant from 2000 to 2006, though the total number of judges has increased by about half (from 18,695 to 28,905), due to the need to staff the justice of the peace courts. http://w3.unece.org/pxweb/Dialog/varval.asp. Court leadership tends to be male. In 2008, only 14 percent of the chairs of *oblast* courts of general jurisdiction were women and 27 percent of the chairs of *arbitrazh* courts were women. In 2004, women were a slight majority (56 percent) of all judges in the courts of general jurisdiction but constituted more than two-thirds of all *arbitrazh* court judges. "Davaite vspomnum te goda," *Sud'ia*, November 2004, 17.

34. For background on the differences between common law and civil law legal traditions, see John Henry Merryman, *The Civil Law Tradition: An Introduction to the Legal Systems of Western Europe and Latin America*, 2nd ed. (Stanford, Calif.: Stanford University Press, 1985).

35. In 2006, judicial salaries were increased by 32 percent. In 2007, they were increased by another 7.5 percent. Government officials explicitly linked these salary increases to a desire to blunt incentives on the part of judges to take bribes. Nina Vazhdaeva, "A Sud'i s chem? Kakuiu zarplatu poluchaiut liudi v mantiiakh, tak do kontsa i ne iasno," *Nove Izvestia*, January 20, 2006, www.newizv.ru/print/38755.

36. "Obzor rezul'tatov deiatel'nosti." In 2006, 7,508 individuals applied for judicial posts. Of these, 2,165 failed to pass the written exam. Of the remaining 5,344, 5,155 were recommended to the president by the JQCs.

37. An ongoing series of polls conducted by the well-respected Levada Center between 2001 and 2007 asked Russians to assess their level of trust in various institutions. Though a solid majority of Russians said they trusted the president, the courts consistently fared worse, with less than 20 percent responding that they fully believed in the courts (with an additional 33 percent saying they were somewhat trustful and about 25 percent saying they had absolutely no faith in the courts). http://wciom.ru/arkhiv/tematicheskii-arkhiv/item/single/9934.html. At the same time, the Levada Center found that Russians do not view the shortcomings of the court as a particularly serious problem. Surveys conducted between 2005 and 2008 reveal that over 70 percent of respondents saw inflation as a serious problem, while only 5 percent saw the inability to get justice in the courts as a serious problem. www.levada.ru/press/2008070103.html.

38. The 15 regional constitutional courts are not institutionally linked to the Russian Constitutional Court. Alexei Trochev, "Less Democracy, More Courts: The Puzzle of Judicial Review in Russia," *Law and Society Review* 38, no. 3 (2004): 513–38.

39. http://ksportal.garant.ru/contact/review_old.html. In 2007, the Constitution Court received 16,612 petitions. http://ksportal.garant.ru/contact/review.htm.

40. Alexei Trochev, *Judging Russia: Constitutional Court in Russian Politics, 1990–2006* (Cambridge: Cambridge University Press, 2008), 126.

41. Sharlet notes that this power was absent prior to the reconstitution of the court in 1994. Sharlet, "Russia's Second Constitutional Court," 62.

42. Trochev, *Judging Russia*, 122–23.

43. Sharlet, "Russia's Second Constitutional Court," 62.

44. Trochev, *Judging Russia*, 120–21.

45. Trochev thoroughly analyzes this line of cases. *Judging Russia*, 139–59.

46. Alexei Trochev, "The Zigzags of Judicial Power: The Constitutional Court in Russian Politics, 1990–2003," doctoral dissertation, Department of Political Science, University of Toronto, 2005, 177.

47. For an analysis of the challenges of enforcing judgments in the other courts, see Peter L. Kahn, "The Russian Bailiffs Service and the Enforcement of Civil Judgments," *Post-Soviet Affairs* 18, no. 2 (2002): 148–81.

48. Kahn, "The Russian Bailiffs Service."

49. In terms of numbers of cases, the courts of general jurisdiction are dominated by noncriminal cases. In 2007, only 8 percent of cases were criminal (down from 12 percent in 2004). Administrative cases constituted 35 percent, while civil cases made up 57 percent. How much time was taken up by the various categories is not clear from the statistical data. Statisticheskaia spravka; "Obzor deiatel'nosti federal'nykh sudov obshchei iurisdiktsii i mirovykh sudei v 2004 godu," *Rossiiskaia iustitsiia*, no. 6 (2005): 26.

50. William L. F. Felstiner, Richard L. Abel, and Austin Sarat, "The Emergence and Transformation of Disputes: Naming, Blaming, Claiming," *Law and Society Review* 15, nos. 3–4 (1980–1881): 631–54.

51. The New Russian Barometer has tracked trust in a variety of institutions over the course of the transition. Its data show a gradual increase in Russians' confidence in courts. In 1994, only 17 percent of respondents trusted the courts, whereas a decade later, the level of trust had risen to 24 percent. The comparison with the change in trust in the president put the court data into perspective. Between 1994 and 2004,

the trust level increased from 18 to 76 percent. Richard Rose, "Russian Responses to Transformation: Trends in Public Opinion since 1992," *Studies in Public Policy*, no. 290 (2004): 19.

52. Peter H. Solomon Jr., "The New Justices of the Peace in the Russian Federation: A Cornerstone of Judicial Reform?" *Demokratizatsiya* 11, no. 3 (2003): 380–96.

53. "Statisticheskaia spravka o rabote sudov obshchei iurisdiktsii za 2007," www .cdep.ru/material.asp?material_id=330.

54. Solomon and Foglesong report that in the mid-1990s, the statutorily imposed deadlines for resolving cases were not met in more than 25 percent and 15 percent of criminal and civil cases, respectively. *Courts and Transition in Russia*, 118–19. By contrast, in 2004, this delay rate was down to about 9 percent for civil cases. "Sudebnaia statistika: Grazhdanskie dela," *Rossiiskaia iustitsiia*, no. 9 (2005): 44. Determining the delay rate for criminal cases is trickier because each component part (e.g., pretrial detention, investigation, trial, appeal) has separate guidelines. Burnham, Maggs, and Danilenko report that these guidelines are routinely violated with impunity. These delays have served as the basis for a significant number of the cases brought to the European Court of Human Rights. *Law and Legal System of the Russian Federation*, 478–79, 506–7. Statistics are available on the length of the actual judicial process, revealing that most cases are resolved within six weeks. "Statisticheskaia spravka."

55. In 2007, about 3 percent of the cases decided by the JP courts were appealed. Litigants were more likely to appeal criminal cases (6.9 percent rate of appeal) and administrative cases (4.3 percent rate of appeal) than civil cases (1.8 percent rate of appeal). "Statisticheskaia spravka."

56. In 2007, only 0.4 percent of criminal cases and less than 0.001 percent of civil cases originated in the regional courts.

57. Stephen C. Thaman, "The Resurrection of Trial by Jury in Russia," *Stanford Journal of International Law* 31, no. 1 (1995): 61–272 (including an appendix reporting on specific cases); Sarah J. Reynolds, "Drawing Upon the Past: Jury Trials in Modern Russia," in *Reforming Justice in Russia, 1864–1996*, ed. Peter H. Solomon Jr. (Armonk, N.Y.: M. E. Sharpe, 1997), 374–96.

58. "Statisticheskaia spravka"; "Obzor deiatel'nosti federal'nykh sudov obshchei iurisdiktsii i mirovykh sudei v 2004 godu," *Rossiiskaia iustitsiia*, no. 6, (2005): 29. Peter Solomon reports that there are enormous regional variations in the preference for jury trials. In Ivanovo, for example, juries were used in 53 percent of eligible cases. "Threats of Judicial Counterreform," 335.

59. "Statisticheskaia spravka."

60. www.cdep.ru/material.asp?material_id=330.

61. Solomon, "Threats of Judicial Counterreform," 336.

62. Anatoly Medetsky, "Danilov Acquitted by a Jury," *Moscow Times*, December 30, 2003, 1.

63. Steven Lee Myers, "2nd Russian Jury Convicts a Physicist Who Was Acquitted of Spy Charges," *New York Times*, November 6, 2004, A10.

64. In the Sutyagin case, the first judge abruptly resigned. His replacement was a judge who had handled a series of politically charged cases. Jury selection was skewed to favor the prosecution; several members of the jury had worked for the FSB at some point. Solomon, "Threats of Judicial Counterreform," 336.

65. In 2007, only 28 percent of respondents assessed juries as fairer and more independent, whereas 34 percent held this view in April 2004. Results reported at www.levada.ru/press/2007102907.html.

66. See, for example, Jonathon R. Hay and Andrei Shleifer, "Private Enforcement of Public Laws: A Theory of Legal Reform," *American Economic Review* 88, no. 2 (1998): 398–403; Vadim Volkov, *Violent Entrepreneurs: The Use of Force in the Making of Russian Capitalism* (Ithaca, N.Y.: Cornell University Press, 2002).

67. For example, a 1997 survey of 328 industrial enterprises found that 70 percent of these enterprises had been to court within the past year. Kathryn Hendley, Peter Murrell, and Randi Ryterman, "Law, Relationships, and Private Enforcement: Transactional Strategies of Russian Enterprises," *Europe-Asia Studies* 52, no. 4 (2000): 627–56.

68. "Osnovanie pokazateli raboty arbitrazhnykh sudov v 1996–1997 godakh," *Vestnik Vysshego Arbitrazhnogo Suda*, no. 4 (1998): 21–23; "Spravka osnovanykh pokazatelei raboty arbitrazhnykh sudov v 2006–2007 godakh," www.arbitr.ru/_upimg.

69. Kathryn Hendley, "Reforming the Procedural Rules for Business Litigation in Russia: To What End?" *Demokratizatsiya* 11, no. 3 (2003): 367–68.

70. Alec Stone Sweet and Helen Keller, "Assessing the Impact of the ECHR on National Legal Orders," in *A Europe of Rights: The Impact of the ECHR on National Legal Systems*, ed. Alec Stone Sweet and Helen Keller (Oxford: Oxford University Press, 2008), 790.

71. Results reported at http://wciom.com/archives/thematic-archive/info-material/single/9815.html.

72. No. 47095/99, 36 Euro. H. R. Rep. 34 (July 15, 2002).

73. *Prestupnost' i pravoporiadok v Rossii: statisticheskii aspekt* (Moscow: Goskomstat Rossii, 2003), 60.

74. Burnham, Maggs, and Danilenko report that 271 law schools were operating in Russia in 2004, only 108 of which were accredited. At the outset of the transition in 1986, there were only 100 law schools, all of which were state run. *Law and Legal System of the Russian Federation*, 133–34.

75. "Ob advokatskoi deiatel'nosti i advokature v Rossiiskoi Federatsii." *Sobranie zakonodatel'stva Rossiiskoi Federatsii*, no. 23, item 2102, June 10, 2002.

76. Eugene Huskey, "The Bar's Triumph or Shame? The Founding of Chambers of Advocates in Putin's Russia," in *Public Policy and Law in Russia: In Search of a Unified Legal and Political Space*, ed. Robert Sharlet and Ferdinand Feldbrugge (Leiden: Martinus Nijhoff, 2005), 149–67.

77. See, for example, Catherine Belton, "Yukos Accused of 'Filthy Theft,'" *Moscow Times*, December 14, 2004, 1 (two Yukos lawyers jailed on embezzlement charges); and Tim Wall, "Canadian Defense Lawyer Expelled," *Moscow Times*, September 26, 2005 (one foreign lawyer expelled and demands from procurators that three Russian defense lawyers be disbarred).

78. Dina Kaminskaya, *Final Judgment: My Life as a Soviet Defense Attorney*, trans. Michael Glenny (New York: Simon and Schuster, 1982).

Chapter Five

The Media and Political Developments

Maria Lipman and Michael McFaul

The Russian media have been the subject of quite different assessments. In the 2008 World Press-Freedom Index compiled by Reporters without Borders, Russia was ranked 141 out of 173 countries in terms of freedom of the press.[1] On the other hand, during his presidency, Vladimir Putin repeatedly denied accusations that media in Russia are constrained by the government. His main argument was that Russia has tens of thousands of operating media outlets, and the government simply did not have the technical capacity to keep all of them under control.[2]

In fact, both assessments of press freedom in Russia are inadequate. Russia has a combination of tightly controlled mass-audience media (this applies first and foremost to national television networks) and smaller-audience outlets that pursue reasonably independent editorial lines (these are found among print dailies and weeklies, radio, the Web, and occasionally also smaller-audience TV channels). To the extent that media freedom is interpreted as the availability of outlets that convey uncensored messages, report news, or voice opinions, Russia has this freedom. It appears to be more appropriate, however, to describe it as *freedom of expression* as opposed to *freedom of the press*, if the latter implies that the press is a public tool that helps keep the government accountable on the people's behalf. Today's Russian media cannot accomplish this mission, because there is no democratic polity in the country. In order to make an appropriate assessment of media freedom in today's Russia, one should view it in the context of the country's political system and the mind-set of the Russian people.

During Putin's presidency, all political power was concentrated at the top of the executive branch, and government decision making was sealed from the public eye. By the time Putin formally stepped down in the spring of 2008, he had ensured secure control over Russia's political life. As soon as Putin's handpicked successor, Dmitri Medvedev, was voted into the presidency,

Medvedev nominated Putin as prime minister, and the emerging ruling tandem shared uncontested and unchecked political authority.

A variety of terms have been used to describe the regime that Vladimir Putin built during his eight-year presidency. During his first term, Russian supporters of Putin referred to it as a "managed democracy" and later as "sovereign democracy." One can just as well call the regime "competitive authoritarianism" with even the traces of "competitiveness" steadily eliminated in the course of Putin's second term.[3]

Upon becoming president in 2000, Putin emasculated the Federation Council (Russia's equivalent of the U.S. Senate), tamed regional barons who once served as a powerful balance to Yeltsin's presidential rule, intimidated Russian oligarchs into submission through arrest or the threat of arrest, weakened the reach of independent political parties, and made the State Duma subservient to Kremlin interests.[4] Expanding the state control over mass-audience media was one of Putin's major goals; his campaign against privately owned national television was launched within days of his inauguration.

Russia's media tycoons who emerged during Yeltsin's presidency may not have been ardent advocates of a free and independent press. Rather, they were profit seekers with questionable business ethics and controversial political agendas,[5] but their media offered alternative views, different from that of the state. This pluralism made nongovernment media a challenge that was unacceptable in Putin's vision of governance as a heavily centralized operation by the Kremlin administration.

PUBLIC/PRIVATE SPHERES IN POSTCOMMUNIST RUSSIA

For most of the twentieth century in Russia, there was virtually no space for political, economic, or social life independent of the state. The Soviet regime aimed to manage the economy: in the USSR private property was outlawed and commercial entrepreneurship was a crime. Communist rulers monopolized political activity, controlled the media (every word printed or broadcast was to be authorized by Communist Party censors), and destroyed almost all autonomous associational life. To the extent that organized social or economic groups existed outside of the family, they were atomized, apolitical, or illegal. At the same time, the Soviet system crowded private life with myriad social, political, and press organizations that mimicked their counterpart organizations in the West in name, but in practice helped to control society.

In the late 1980s, Gorbachev began to liberalize the Soviet political system under the rubric of perestroika. In the name of glasnost, Gorbachev allowed several newspapers, literary journals (the "thick journals"), and weekly magazines greater editorial license to criticize the Soviet system, especially its past, and in particular Stalin and Stalinism. Soon thereafter, the era of preliminary state censorship came to an end. Gorbachev's glasnost, however, was more about political proclamations, emotionally charged opinion, and disclosures of the dark totalitarian past than the development of a media industry. But it gave birth to a new generation of independent-minded journalists and commentators. During the peak years of perestroika, writers in *Moscow News*, *Argumenty i fakty*, *Ogonyok*, and *Izvestiia* were ahead of the political class and civil society in leading the charge for democratic reform.[6] Liberalization of television was much slower. Only in the spring of 1991 did the government of the Russian Soviet Federative Socialist Republic (RSFSR, then a constituent part of the Soviet Union) succeed in compelling the Soviet state to give the Russian republic its own television station, RTR.[7] Yet the general trajectory of more pluralism had even begun to penetrate electronic media by the end of the Soviet era. Significantly, however, the state—be it the Soviet Union or the RSFSR—still owned or subsidized every major media outlet in Russia.[8] In other words, a paper such as *Moscow News* could not have survived without assistance from the federal or local government. But because Gorbachev showed a degree of tolerance toward critical press, *Ogonyok* and *Izvestiia* (from the liberal front), or *Den'* (on the nationalist one) could pursue their editorial lines. Referring to the late 1980s, a prominent Russian journalist said, "As the Soviet power was fast declining, we, journalists, were fighting against the state on its own money and with its own newspapers and magazines."[9] In 1990, a year before the Soviet Union collapsed, the first nongovernment newspapers began to emerge, but prior to the transition to a market economy they, too, relied on some form of government subsidies (for instance, *Nezavisimaia gazeta* relied on subsidized rent for office space).

After the collapse of Soviet communism and the establishment of an independent Russian state, President Boris Yeltsin's reforms created new opportunities for independent political, social, and economic activity. The new Russian media were no longer just about expressing ideas and voicing opinions; they were developing professionally and commercially, guided by editorial standards of independence, objectivity, and accuracy as well as business factors, such as ownership, competition, or advertising revenues.

The 1990s were a time of unconstrained press, though the causes of this freedom were many. During the political turmoil of the last years of the Soviet Union, Yeltsin evolved as a fierce anticommunist, and this turned him, at some fundamental level, into a proponent of an independent press. He didn't intervene to mute criticism of himself or exposure of abuse of authority by government. Rhetorically, he lauded Russia's independent and critical media as an achievement of his democratic reforms. Very early in his tenure, Yeltsin's government succeeded in passing a very progressive law on mass media.[10] At the same time, during most of the early Yeltsin years leading up to the 1996 presidential campaign, Yeltsin and the press were allies against a common threat—a communist comeback.[11] This alliance was forged with little normative commitment to loftier principles of democracy. And the Yeltsin government was also weak. Fighting many political and economic battles simultaneously, the Russian state simply did not have the capacity to control the media. Even the state's own media—such as ORT, Russia's largest and most watched television network—was under the de facto control of a private actor, Boris Berezovsky.

THE RISE OF PRIVATELY OWNED MEDIA

Market reforms initially helped to stimulate still further the growth of media outlets not controlled by the government—including, first and foremost, television.[12] NTV, the first private television network, started by Vladimir Gusinsky in 1993, provided a source of information that was truly independent of the government and that reached beyond Moscow.[13] NTV quickly earned its credentials as a serious news organization when it provided critical coverage of the first Chechen war. This coverage shaped the Russian public opinion of the war in much the same way that the coverage of the Vietnam War shaped the opinion of the U.S. audience. Every day, the mercilessly horrible scenes from Chechnya appeared on the television screens in Russian homes. The government was enraged, but it couldn't do much about this coverage that became overtly antiwar. Evgeni Kiselev, NTV's cofounder and popular political host, had no doubt about what they were doing: "We had a good understanding that information was a powerful tool in our hands," he told a Western reporter.[14] NTV generated antiwar sentiments and broad disapproval of Yeltsin and his government. In the end, Yeltsin was forced to initiate a peace process with Chechnya, otherwise there was no chance for reelection in 1996.

NTV also produced the puppet show *Kukly*, an angry political satire that spared no one. Yeltsin's chief of staff called NTV managers to ask them to stop *Kukly*, but they wouldn't listen. NTV quickly achieved a new level of post-Soviet professionalism, quality, and style that the rival state channels Ostankino and RTR lacked. By producing and hosting *Itogi*, a Sunday-night wrap-up show on politics, Kiselev became a national celebrity.

Before starting NTV, Gusinsky already had begun to publish his own daily newspaper, *Segodnia*. He also bought a stake in a popular radio station, Ekho Moskvy, and in 1995 founded a weekly magazine, *Itogi*, published in partnership with *Newsweek*, making his company Media-Most a media powerhouse. Other financial tycoons followed in Gusinsky's wake, believing that the media, especially television, were an important political tool.[15] Through an inside deal arranged by the Kremlin, Boris Berezovsky acquired part ownership and de facto control of Ostankino, Russia's largest television network, which was renamed ORT (Russian Public Television).[16] Since there was no law on public television, this "public" status hardly meant anything, except the emergence of another powerful media tycoon and another national television asset under private control. Berezovsky also obtained a major stake in a smaller channel, TV-6. Russia's small group of financial houses and oil and gas companies also gobbled up most of the Moscow-based, mainstream daily newspapers.[17]

These outlets were not unbiased, as the new tycoons would occasionally use them to pursue their own political and business goals. But since they were permanently engaged in fierce rivalry, the tycoons' interests were different. So if the Russian media environment of the 1990s did not meet high democratic and ethical principles, at least it ensured pluralism and independence from the state.[18] But the "private" ownership of the media was shaky, and a decade after the collapse of communism, the economic or political independence from the state remained fragile. The state—or more aptly in Russian, *vlast'* (the power)—may have been dramatically weakened after the political turmoil following the collapse of the USSR and the economic meltdown, but it retained some leverage in different strategic sectors, including the media. For example, the Russian federal government was still the majority shareholder in ORT and owned 100 percent of RTR, while regional administrative leaders still controlled the major television networks in their territories and subsidized most local print media. For periods in the 1990s, the state, and especially the Russian federal government under Yeltsin, did not exercise its property rights, creating the false sense of independence for some state-owned media outlets.

When Vladimir Putin emerged as Russia's new leader, first as acting president, then as a popularly elected president, his primary goal was to reassert the power of the state; this implied, first and foremost, reinstating the dominant authority of the nation's top leader. In his book of interviews published in time for his presidency, Putin said, referring to the 1990s: "At some point many people decided that the president was no longer the center of power. I'll make sure that no one ever has such illusions anymore."[19] During his presidency, he effectively and steadily fulfilled his pledge.

RECONSOLIDATION OF THE STATE

Even before Putin came to power, the state began to slowly reclaim the media territory it had lost to the oligarchs in 1998–1999. The first major step was the creation of a government agency in charge of the media and a consolidation of state broadcasters under the federal auspices. In 1998, regional TV stations, which until then had been controlled by local governors, were brought together and subordinated to VGTRK (All-Russian State Radio and Television Company), whose main asset was the national channel RTR, renamed Rossiia channel in 2001.[20]

State-owned television was strengthened organizationally and financially, so the Kremlin could draw on this resource in the election cycle of 1999–2000. The timing for reasserting government control over its media property was not accidental. In 1998, Russia was struck with a financial crisis that led to political turmoil and posed a grave threat to the elite surrounding Yeltsin. In addition, the crisis dealt a dramatic blow to the advertising market. The informal (and mostly unregulated) control over TV assets was no longer a lucrative opportunity that facilitated a gradual reinstatement of state control.

In the aftermath of the 1998 financial crisis, the political elites were sharply divided. The group opposing the Kremlin was associated with the former prime minister Evgeni Primakov and Moscow mayor Yuri Luzhkov. Those who rallied behind them included quite a few of Russia's regional governors. In early 1999, this group emerged as a serious challenge to the Kremlin and was determined to win the parliamentary election and then the presidency.

The oligarchic media played a very significant role in the political campaign of 1999–2000. But unlike the 1996 presidential election, when Gusinsky and Berezovsky combined their efforts, and their television channels were instrumental in Yeltsin's reelection, this time the two media tycoons ended up on different sides. Berezovsky committed his channel, ORT, to support the Kremlin.[21] Gusinsky's channel, NTV, however, would not support the Kremlin's hastily masterminded party Edinstvo (Unity) in the parliamentary race, nor would he back Putin in the March 2000 presidential election.

The Kremlin defeated its rivals. The pro-Kremlin Edinstvo party gained control over the Duma, and Yeltsin's anointed successor, Vladimir Putin, was elected president. This made Berezovsky the winner (and Putin's kingmaker) and Gusinsky the loser. But the consequences for their media properties as well as for themselves were not dissimilar. Soon thereafter, both ended up in exile, stripped of most of their media assets.

THE CAMPAIGN AGAINST OLIGARCHIC MEDIA

Gusinsky's Media-Most was the most financially independent media company in the 1990s. Different from other major media assets, Gusinsky's empire was not a privatized Soviet-era enterprise but was created from scratch, meaning the state did not initially own shares in his companies. But even Gusinsky acquired his initial capital from connections with the Moscow city government (his Most Bank served as the city's banker for several years). He obtained additional control over Channel 4, on which NTV broadcast, as reward for his cooperation with Yeltsin during the 1996 presidential election.[22] Gusinsky then offered an equity stake to Gazprom, a largely state-owned gas company, to finance his expansion plans. Before the Russian financial crash in August 1998, Gusinsky's business plan and debt-to-equity ratios looked ambitious but within reason. The crash, however, made Gusinsky's company vulnerable: the Kremlin took advantage of his indebtedness to the state-controlled gas monopoly.

Gusinsky and his media were occasionally attacked as early as 1999, but it was after Putin's inauguration that attacks were launched in full force.[23] The Kremlin, however, carefully avoided harassing or persecuting journalists or editors. Instead, the campaign was mostly disguised as business litigation, but other strategies aimed at seizing NTV and dismantling Media-Most were also pursued. One of them was to threaten Gusinsky personally—to use the prosecutor's office to bring criminal charges against Gusinsky and to intimidate him into submission. According to the Russian weekly magazine *Kommersant-Vlast'*, for a period of about two years, a court hearing involving Media-Most was held every 4.3 days.[24] Finally, in the spring of 2001, Gusinsky's media company was taken over by Gazprom. Promptly thereafter, the new owner changed the management of NTV. Quite a few of the journalists protested against the takeover and quit, though others stayed and the channel continued its operation. Eventually, though not straight away, its editorial line was also taken under control and kept firmly in line with the Kremlin's political goals. In subsequent years, Gazprom's top management would come to be dominated by Kremlin appointees, and by late 2005 the government would hold controlling interest through the purchase of shares of stock. In effect, Gazprom became an extension of the state and expressed its power through both the purchase of media outlets and the opening of a commercial bank network throughout Russia.

Media-Most, once the biggest privately owned media group in Russia, was destroyed. The daily newspaper *Segodnia* was closed by the new owner, and the entire staff of the news weekly magazine *Itogi* was ousted. The radio station Ekho Moskvy survived; as of this writing, it is among the most prominent media outlets that still pursue reasonably independent editorial lines (see more on this in the section "Beyond Direct Control, but at the Kremlin's Mercy," below).

The destruction of Media-Most took a lot of the government's time, money, and effort. Moreover, it cost Putin many an embarrassing moment during his foreign visits, when he faced criticism for his crackdown on the media's freedom. But the Russian president remained firm in accomplishing his objectives. After the takeover of NTV, it gradually became clear that the government's goal with regard to the media was much more ambitious than eliminating a defiant tycoon (in late 2000, Gusinsky was forced to flee abroad and never came back) and taming his media. The longer-term objective was to bring under state control all national television networks with political broadcasting. This task was greatly facilitated by the fact that the majority of the Russian public did not regard the crackdown on the media as a violation of people's rights.[25] Business and political elites were fragmented, and even liberal politicians would not stand up for Media-Most. They chose either to accept the government interpretation that the whole NTV/Media-Most affair was a conflict of economic interests, or to believe in "authoritarian modernization," which Putin would deliver at a cost of sacrificing some civil liberties. Likewise, the journalistic community failed to show solidarity with their Media-Most colleagues.

ORT, the channel controlled by Berezovsky, was reclaimed by the state at about the same time as NTV. While Gusinsky was regarded as a rival and an enemy, Berezovsky had been perfectly loyal and very useful to the Kremlin. It may be argued, however, that his significant role in Putin's election was one of the reasons Putin wanted to get rid of him. Putin likely wanted no powerful kingmaker by his side. Besides, some of Putin's first steps were not to Berezovsky's liking, and he tried to oppose the new president's moves.

The campaign aimed at regaining control over ORT took much less time than the takeover of NTV and was mostly hidden from the public eye. The way Berezovsky was stripped of his television asset remains murky. The most common theory has it that Roman Abramovich, a tycoon believed to be very close and loyal to Putin, in a secret deal bought this media asset from Berezovsky. The latter was threatened with criminal prosecution, left Russia, and went to live abroad. The purchase of ORT was believed to be a special favor to the Kremlin. Abramovich did not claim control over the channel, so the Kremlin could use this information tool as it saw fit. The ownership of ORT, renamed Channel One in 2002, remains opaque.[26]

In 2001–2002, there were two failed attempts to launch new, privately owned, national television channels. Through various techniques, the Kremlin made sure that both projects would be short-lived.[27] By the middle of 2003, the Kremlin had full control over political coverage of all major national television networks. In 2004, the government control was further tightened: live political talk shows were closed, and political satirical shows were eliminated. Several popular hosts were barred from television. Federal television, whose outreach far surpasses all other Russian media, was turned into a political tool of the government.[28]

MANAGED TELEVISION COVERAGE

A comparison of the coverage of three tragedies that broke out in Putin's tenure—the 2000 sinking of the submarine *Kursk*, the 2002 terrorist siege of a Moscow theater, and the 2004 terrorist attack on a school in Beslan—

provides insight into the Kremlin's expanded control over television broadcasting. Back in 2000, quite a few of the Russian media, including national television, tried their best to cover the sinking of the *Kursk*, which took the lives of all 118 sailors on board. Russian officials, both uniformed and civilian, sought to cover up the inefficiency of the rescue operation and the poor condition of the Russian Navy. Their public statements conflicted with each other. Russian journalists did their best to investigate what caused the disaster and to report what the government sought to hide. Putin was furious and didn't care to conceal his anger. He lashed out at "people in television" who "over the past ten years have destroyed that same army and navy where people are dying today."[29] But aside from expressions of anger, no steps were taken against reporters or TV stations.

In 2002, a group of terrorists seized a Moscow theater with over 800 people inside. In a badly bungled rescue operation, at least 129 hostages were killed, almost all of them by the poisonous gas used by the rescuers. This time, federal television was mostly tame, but the journalists of NTV, taken over by Gazprom the previous year, retained their professional instincts. They tried to produce professional coverage of the tragic developments, even as government officials instructed the channel's top manager to temper the journalistic effort. Once again, Putin was infuriated.[30] Within three months of the event, the NTV top manager was fired.

In September 2004, over 1,100 people, most of them children, were taken hostage in a school in Beslan, in the Caucasus region of North Ossetia-Alania (in southern Russia). During the siege and subsequent attack on the terrorists, at least 334 hostages were killed. The rescue operation left serious doubts about the competence of the government officials in charge as well as state security and other government agencies. By this time, however, all federal television channels had been brought under tight government control. For the federal TV channels, cooperation with the government appeared to be a much higher priority than professional skills or ethics.[31] Their broadcast was thoroughly guided by the government authorities, and as soon as the rescue operation was over, they put a lid on their coverage. No eyewitness accounts, independent experts, survivors, or victims' relatives appeared on the screen. In the aftermath, Putin made no remarks about the coverage or TV reporters' performance. Shortly after this tragedy, significant political changes were introduced.

TIGHTENED CONTROL OVER POLITICAL AND PUBLIC SPHERES

Very soon after the tragedy at Beslan, Putin announced a major political change: regional governors would no longer be elected by popular vote. The

Kremlin may have planned this measure earlier as a way to consolidate political control in view of the forthcoming election cycle of 2007–2008. The horrible terrorist attack in Beslan was used as a formal pretext, though the connection between the attack and the restriction of people's voting rights was never made clear. Putin argued that the terrorist attack was the result of negligent regional officials, and to prevent future attacks, regional governors had to be accountable directly to the Kremlin. This argument was never very persuasive. Nonetheless, new legislation was readily enacted by the rubber-stamp Duma that essentially granted the president the authority to appoint local governors, including the mayors of Moscow and St. Petersburg. A series of other measures amounted to full-blown political reform. For example, the selection method for State Duma deputies was changed, doing away with single-mandate district elections and opting only for party-list seats. The threshold for party representation was raised from 5 percent to 7 percent, starting with the 2007 Duma election. Basically, electoral legislation was thoroughly revised so the Kremlin would have unlimited capacity to bar any unwelcome force or figure from Russian political life.[32] The Kremlin made the rules, oversaw their implementation, and exercised selective enforcement in order to get rid of unwanted political actors.

The end of 2004 was also marked by dramatic political developments on Russia's border. The Orange Revolution in Ukraine evolved as a serious clash between Russia and the West, first and foremost with the United States. The Kremlin, and Putin in particular, were deeply alarmed by the Orange Revolution, which witnessed people's political power from below to resist and eventually overturn a fraudulent election, and to bring to power a pro-Western government and president in the person of Viktor Yushchenko. The Kremlin perceived events in Ukraine as a Western plot to install a pro-Western regime on the Russian borders with the help of foreign-funded NGOs fomenting antigovernment sentiments. In the eyes of the Kremlin, the Rose Revolution in Georgia and then the Orange Revolution in Ukraine represented stark encroachments on Russia's natural sphere of influence. In addition, Putin got personally involved in Ukraine's presidential campaign in an attempt to achieve a desired election result, only to see his effort dramatically fail. The frustration over this failure further aggravated the sense of alarm. Putin and his inner circle feared that the spirit of the Orange Revolution would reach Russia and challenge their power. The Russian government rhetoric following the final victory of the "orange coalition" bordered on hysteria. Kremlin officials and loyalists spoke about Russia as a "besieged fortress," about "the enemy at the gate," and "the frontline running across every house and every yard."

The Orange Revolution pushed the Kremlin to further tighten its grip on power and to expand control beyond the political sphere to the public realm, including various forms of public activism, NGOs, especially those sponsored from abroad, and youth movements.[33] To handle the public sphere, the Kremlin mostly relied on manipulative methods such as cooptation of the compliant and marginalizing or discrediting those who would not pledge allegiance to the state. Another commonly used method was imitation. The Kremlin created and supported groups and organizations (the youth group *Nashi* is the most prominent among them) that serve the political interests of the Kremlin and overshadow genuine public initiatives. Abundant financial resources provided by increasing oil prices and the generally apathetic, fragmented public contributed to the success of this manipulative strategy vis-à-vis the societal activism. Only in rare cases did the government resort to harassment or repression.

By the middle of Putin's second term, the Kremlin ensured absolute control over the political system. Putin stood at the top of a radically deinstitutionalized political system; he did not have to worry about political competition or public accountability; his authority was unchallenged and unchecked. In the public realm, the government sent a clear message that autonomous public activism was not acceptable and those who would not comply will face the consequences. By the 2007–2008 election cycle, any remaining independent political groups and activists were scarce, fragmented or marginalized, and generally reduced to political irrelevance. The dominant mood of the people was passive compliance. The public at large accepted the habitual paternalistic pattern Putin offered. The state-society relationship that took shape during Putin's presidency and especially during his second term may be described as a nonparticipation pact: the government delivers better living standards, and the public doesn't meddle in politics. The compact with the educated, entrepreneurial, advanced elites was not very dissimilar from that with the masses. They accepted the paternalistic political pattern and did not mind being pushed away from decision making, as long as they enjoyed comfortable lifestyles, individual freedoms, and opportunities of drawing high business profits.

Controlled national television constituted a major element in the Russian political system under Putin. The mass-audience channels, especially Channel One and Rossiia, as well as NTV, have been effectively used as a tool to shape public opinion in a way best suited to the Kremlin's goals. To the more sophisticated and critically minded audiences, the political and public affairs coverage of the national TV broadcasters may look like heavy-handed propaganda; for political news and opinion, these groups would rely on other sources of information (on the remaining media independence, see the section "Beyond Direct Control, but at the Kremlin's Mercy"). But the federal channels mostly target those who constitute the electoral base of Putin's political regime: the broad masses, the less advanced, the less wealthy, the less educated, the less urbanized, and the older rather than the younger.

CONTROLLED TELEVISION AS A TOOL
OF POLITICAL CONTROL

National television channels played a major role in President Yeltsin's reelection in 1996 and in Putin's ascension to the presidency in 2000. The 2003 State Duma election, which further consolidated the Kremlin's control, was criticized by the Organization for Security and Cooperation in Europe (OSCE) monitoring mission, which pointed to biased media coverage favoring the incumbent.[34] Putin's reelection in 2004 was a heavily manipulated affair with a preordained result: Putin won handily, with 71 percent of the vote.[35]

The 2007–2008 election cycle was a bigger challenge. Having served for two terms, Putin was not eligible to run for a third consecutive term unless he changed the constitution. He had to think of a political configuration that would enable him to stay in charge. During his time in office, Putin had presided over a major redistribution of power and property, and he alone was recognized as the arbiter by the competing power-and-property clusters. In the deinstitutionalized political system of his creation, Putin stood as the safeguard of stability. By the end of his second term, his control was virtually absolute, and there was no doubt that whatever scheme he would think of would be readily accepted by the Russian public and the political elites. But since the scheme had to have an appearance of a public choice, state-controlled TV was to play an essential role in its implementation.

The television tool was fine-tuned to boost whatever figure Putin chose as his successor. When he promoted two of his high-ranking officials, Dmitri Medvedev and Sergei Ivanov, and pushed them to the fore, national television channels began to give both ample airtime. The public and the elites got the message: these two are the finalists. Television managers saw to it that neither would have the advantage over the other until Putin made his final decision. When Medvedev was picked, he was immediately featured on television almost as prominently as Putin. This way, the nation learned whom it should vote for, and it did not fail the Kremlin. In the March 2008 presidential election, Medvedev received 70 percent of the vote.

The use of television as a tool goes way beyond election campaigns. With the public alienated from politics and policy making, and the channels of feedback between state and society clogged, state-control television serves as a "one-way communication tube" used by the government to communicate to the nation the appropriate picture of Russian life and to shape the public perception of the political reality and, in part, public affairs. It may be argued that the overall strategy of television during Putin's tenure was to foster a mood of passive compliance. Political coverage was shaped so the public would not be inappropriately stirred, and the rest of airtime is intended to distract and entertain. In the words of Russian sociologists Lev Gudkov and

Boris Dubin, the society in Putin's Russia was a "community of viewers," which in their theory is opposed to a "democracy of participants."[36] In this framework, the primary functions of television include positive coverage of the top leadership and of the government decisions and policies.[37] Television coverage does not portray Russia as a country with no problems, yet the focus is not on the problems per se, but on the top leader who stays firmly in charge and effectively handles any problem that comes along. National TV channels can boost, play down, or ignore any force, figure, or development. For example, in recent years Russian television promoted anti-Ukrainian, anti-Georgian, and anti-American sentiments, portrayed Mikhail Khodorkovsky (the head of Yukos who funded opposition parties and expressed interest in running for president) and Mikhail Saakashvili (president of Georgia) as ultimate villains, and presented foreign-funded NGOs as agents of a hostile West. Unlike Soviet times, however, television is not subject to preliminary censorship across the board. Beyond the political coverage, even on federal news channels there remains relative pluralism, and various shows offer different, sometimes conflicting visions.

Controlled television coverage is not the result of coercion. The managers of the federal channels are willing, cooperative, and creative partners of the Kremlin. They jointly shape the agenda of the political and public affairs coverage during their weekly meetings.[38] During Putin's presidency, the oversight of the television coverage was entrusted with Putin's pressman, Alexei Gromov. When Putin stepped down to become the prime minister, he left Gromov in charge of this vital function (Gromov serves as President Medvedev's deputy chief of staff).

In addition to weekly meetings with the top TV managers, Gromov stays in touch with them as the week goes by; he follows the week's developments and talks on the phone with them. Together they fine-tune the news coverage. What makes this operation especially effective is that national television is a successful business model. While national TV channels do not compete in news coverage—the news is fairly bland and hardly differs channel to channel—the competition for viewers as well as the advertisers' ruble is fierce. Channels try to win audiences with all sorts of entertainment shows, some of them high quality, some playing to lowly tastes. The latter is the subject of constant laments by TV critics, scholars of Russian society, and part of the public. But shows savoring dark sides of human nature, violence, ugly human stories, and gory scenes work very well in any culture—Russia is no exception—so people are glued to the screens and stay on the same channels for news.

Advertisers attracted to large audiences eagerly commit their budgets to government-controlled TV. State-controlled television channels in Putin's Russia have thus evolved as lucrative businesses,[39] with the top managers also being the top beneficiaries. Besides, the federal TV channels, as a key element in the structure of state power, are subsidized by the state.[40]

BEYOND DIRECT CONTROL,
BUT AT THE KREMLIN'S MERCY

Outside the federal television channels, political control is much less tight. Publications whose editorial policies are relatively independent of the Kremlin include print dailies and weeklies (published and mostly distributed in Moscow; a small fraction of their circulation is distributed in other large urban centers), the radio station Ekho Moskvy, and a variety of online publications (the Internet in Russia remains free).[41] Some degree of editorial freedom may be found on smaller-audience television channels. These outlets are much less bound by loyalty to the government; some are guided by professional skills and standards and expose abuse of government authority when they discover it. Others assume an openly antigovernment stance and reduce their operation to critical opinion (this is especially true of a number of websites). The picture of Russia as it emerges from reportage, analysis, and opinion of those outlets is entirely different from the image offered by federal TV channels.

The problem with media freedom in Putin's Russia is not the absence of alternative sources of information. In the system of securely controlled politics, the Kremlin can afford not to stifle every voice. In fact, the media that pursue editorial independence may even be useful for the Kremlin, as they help the more advanced and critically minded constituencies to let off steam and are also good for show. So Putin and Medvedev are able to say that they do not, or even cannot, control all the Russian media.

The problem with media freedom in Putin's Russia is therefore not just the state-imposed constraints; it is also in large part a factor of the nonfree political environment and the apathy of the public. In a more open political environment, some of the stories reported by those relatively independent media would become the subject of a parliamentary discussion or probe; others would generate political scandals. Not so in Russia. When there is no political opposition and no competitive politics, when the legislative branch is tightly controlled by the executive, when the judicial decisions are easily bent to the Kremlin will, and when autonomous public activism is thoroughly marginalized, the existing elements of free media cannot make a difference in policy making. They remain politically irrelevant.[42] They may generate political news, but they are incapable of turning it into political events.

Such media outlets have limited audiences and distribution, and the Kremlin makes sure that they stay marginal. First and foremost, the media in question are securely insulated from mass-audience television. Stories reported by smaller-audience media are not picked up by federal TV channels. A format such as *Meet the Press* is inconceivable in today's Russia; independent-minded print, Web, or radio reporters are barred from federal TV news shows.

Restricted access to information and newsmakers is another constraint on media freedom. Decision making in Putin's Russia is reduced to a very limited number of people and is fully closed from the public eye. Top-ranking executives do not hold regular, public briefings where informed reporters ask pointed policy questions. The Kremlin press pool is a handpicked group of loyal reporters who never fail their Kremlin bosses.[43] This policy has paid off: throughout his presidency Putin was never publicly exposed to a single unfriendly question from a domestic reporter. During his presidency, Putin held one press conference per year, attended by about 1,000 reporters from all over Russia, but these events looked more like publicity stunts for the president.

The Kremlin tolerates a degree of free expression, but it has additional control tools that may be used to further crack down on the media, which therefore remain at the mercy of the Kremlin. The change of ownership that worked so well in the takeover of NTV during the years of Putin's presidency was expanded to other media assets. As a result, nearly all the media are in loyal hands, so the ruling elites, if they deem it necessary, can draw on loyal owners to do what it takes to ensure the appropriate editorial policy. The government also has full control over lawmaking and law enforcement. For example, shortly before the 2007–2008 election cycle, new amendments infringing on the operation of the media were made in the anti-extremism and antiterrorism legislation.[44] These amendments would enable the government to suspend media outlets or even shut them down. Vague phrasing facilitates arbitrary, selective enforcement. Provincial journalists and media outlets are more likely to fall victim to such arbitrary treatment at the hands of local government authorities. Moscow media may feel less threatened: the Kremlin generally refrains from heavy-handed methods such as harassment of individual journalists or closure of publications. But nobody feels secure, and those media, even the most prominent among them, that dare to challenge government policies are aware that if they go too far, the Kremlin may move against them.[45] This environment is conducive to self-censorship, which is a common practice among the Russian media, though the degree of self-restriction may vary a great deal.

CONCLUSION

In 2008, Russia was hit by the economic crisis that began in the United States and spread throughout the world. By the end of 2008, forecasts in Russia were extremely pessimistic. The best Russian mainstream daily, *Kommersant*, was writing about an "industrial catastrophe" and predicting a dramatic production slump.[46] Print dailies and weeklies, online media and blogs, and Ekho Moskvy radio were filled with alarming reports of the fast economic decline and growing public discontent. Allegations were made that under the guise of anticrisis measures, the Kremlin would conduct a redistribution of property in favor of its cronies. The tone of the commentary was distinctly gloomy. Opinion writers commonly blamed the government for Russia's dysfunctional banking system, for misunderstanding the nature of the crisis, and for using the wrong remedies, as well as for not listening to the independent, out-of-government experts, and so on.

The federal TV channels, on the other hand, presented a different picture. No doomsayers were allowed to address the nation. The focus of the coverage was not the crisis per se but the leadership of the country taking the right steps for the benefit of the people. The most unpleasant developments were ignored.[47]

The economic crisis presents the Russian government with an extremely tough challenge. During his presidency, Putin effectively consolidated his power. Thanks to high oil prices, Russia was awash in cash, and Putin used this blessing to keep the public reasonably content. As long as the government delivered better living standards, the public didn't question policies. Likewise, the Russian elites were reconciled to this paternalistic political pattern as long as they were assured of benefits such as high business profits. With an abrupt drop of oil prices by the end of 2008 (less than one-third of what it was in the summer of 2008), the government lost the main resource that ensured loyalty across the board and minimized political risks. Moreover, in a system based on political subservience rather than competition, the quality of governance is inevitably low. The empowered, unaccountable bureaucracy is not good at handling crises; it is inefficient and reluctant to assume responsibility. But the problems generated by the economic crisis quickly built up and called for fast, responsible, and well-coordinated effort.

The growing economic difficulties may lead to social discontent. In late 2008, protests in the Far East were probably the most significant public action in Russia, but they were not unique, as smaller-scale protests were reported from other Russian regions. Social unrest is fraught with political risks, especially if the economic crunch deepens the existing cleavages among the Russian elites. Throughout his presidency Putin was universally recognized as the ultimate arbiter by the conflicting elite groups fighting for more clout and property, and he was able to keep these rivalries in check. But if the infighting aggravates as a result of diminishing resources, Prime Minister Putin and President Medvedev may find it much harder to perform this balancing act.

This should be a serious challenge to government tolerance of the elements of free media. The authoritarian logic dictates a crackdown on the remaining rights and freedoms, freedom of expression included, as a response to the growing risks. The first alarming signs were already appearing in late 2008.[48]

Federal TV channels have been an invaluable tool for the Kremlin to maintain political stability, and at least at the onset of the current economic crisis, the Kremlin could still draw on them to keep the nation under control. But if there is a serious split at the top, the three national TV channels could be a major indicator. If the channels stop speaking in one voice on politically sensitive issues, this would imply a breach in the consolidation of the elites and an attempt by rival factions to win over public sympathies—in other words, a reemergence of public politics in Russia.

SUGGESTED READINGS

Baker, Peter, and Susan Glasser. *Kremlin Rising: Vladimir Putin's Russia and the End of Revolution*. New York: Lisa Drew/Scribner, 2005.

Fishman, Mikhail, and Konstantin Gaaze. "Efir dlia dvoikh." *Russian Newsweek*, August 4, 2008.

Fossato, Floriana. "The Russian Media: From Popularity to Distrust." *Current History* 100, no. 648 (2001): 343–47.

Hoffman, David. *The Oligarchs: Wealth and Power in the New Russia*. New York: Public Affairs, 2002.

Kachkaeva, Anna. "Transformatsiia Rossiiskogo TV." In *Sredstva Massovoi Informatsii Rossii*. Moscow: Aspekt, 2006.

———. "Glamurny totalitarizm: Televizionnaia industriia v epokhu stabil'nosti (2004–2007)." In *Teleradioefir: Istoriia i sovremennost'*. Moscow: Elitkomstar, 2008.

Lipman, Maria. "Constrained or Irrelevant: The Media in Putin's Russia." *Current History*, 104, no. 684 (2005): 319–24.

———. "Svoboda pressy v usloviakh upravliaemoi demokratii." Carnegie Moscow Center Briefing Paper 8, issue 2 (March 2006).

McFaul, Michael, Nikolai Petrov, and Andrei Ryabov. *Between Dictatorship and Democracy: Russian Post-Communist Political Reform*. Washington, D.C.: Carnegie Endowment for International Peace, 2004.

NOTES

1. See www.rsf.org/IMG/pdf/cl_en_2008.pdf.

2. Vladimir Putin used this argument on several occasions. See, for instance, his speech at the 59th Congress of the World Association of Newspapers, where Russia was harshly criticized for government encroachment on media freedom. Putin stated that "53,000 periodicals are published in Russia today. We can't control all of them, even if we want to, even if the government had such a desire. . . . And over 3,000 TV and radio channels." See www.kremlin.ru/appears/2006/06/05/1528_type63374type63376type82634_106494.shtml.

3. On these regime definitions, see Steven Levitsky and Lucan Way, "The Rise of Competitive Authoritarianism," *Journal of Democracy* 13, no. 2 (2002): 51–65.

Diamond has reclassified Russia as competitive authoritarianism. See Larry Diamond, "Thinking About Hybrid Regimes," *Journal of Democracy* 13, no. 2 (2002): 21–35.

4. For a complete accounting of these democratic reversals, see Michael McFaul, Nikolai Petrov, and Andrei Ryabov, *Between Dictatorship and Democracy: Russian Post-Communist Political Reform* (Washington, D.C.: Carnegie Endowment for International Peace, 2004).

5. David Hoffman, *The Oligarchs: Wealth and Power in the New Russia* (New York: Public Affairs, 2002).

6. On the emergence of civil society in the USSR, see M. Steven Fish, *Democracy from Scratch* (Princeton, N.J.: Princeton University Press, 1993); and Geoffrey Hosking, *The Awakening of the Soviet Union* (Cambridge, Mass.: Harvard University Press, 1991).

7. Control over television was a major issue for Russia's anticommunist forces before the collapse of the Soviet Union. One of the biggest demonstrations in downtown Moscow in 1991 was devoted to demanding a Russian television station. On Yeltsin's efforts to gain control of RTR, the Russian station, see Ellen Mickiewicz, *Changing Channels: Television and the Struggle for Power in Russia* (Oxford: Oxford University Press, 1997), 92–97.

8. Some political parties had their own newspapers, and a few human rights organizations published newspapers and newsletters with support from Western foundations. But the circulation of these kinds of publications was a tiny fraction of the state-controlled newspapers.

9. Mikhail Berger, oral communication, international economic conference in Belokurikha, February 2007.

10. The Russian law on mass media, adopted in December 1991, was preceded by a Soviet media law framed the previous year by the same group of liberal experts and inspired by a desire to legally enforce that media be independent of the state. See www.medialaw.ru/e_pages/laws/russian/massmedia_eng/massmedia_eng.html.

11. Michael McFaul, *Russia's 1996 Presidential Election: The End of Polarized Politics* (Stanford, Calif.: Hoover Institution Press, 1997).

12. Mickiewicz, *Changing Channels*.

13. On the channel's creation, see the detailed account in chap. 7 of Hoffman, *The Oligarchs*.

14. Hoffman, *The Oligarchs*, 293.

15. Floriana Fossato, "Russia: Changes Sweep Through Two TV Networks," Radio Free Europe/Radio Liberty (RFE/RL), November 5, 1997.

16. Russian Public Television (ORT) gained control of the first national television channel in Russia through a presidential decree (no. 2133) on November 29, 1994, and began broadcasting on April 1, 1995. In the company's charter, fourteen organizations were listed as shareholders, including state institutions such as the State Property Committee of Russia, Ostankino Russian State Television, and Radio Broadcasting Corporation, as well as private companies such as Menatep, National Kredit, and Stolychny banks; Gazprom; and Berezovsky's own company, Logovaz. See *Russian Public Television: Collection of Constituent Documents* (Moscow: ORT, 1995), 18. The private companies purchased 49 percent of the new company and faced no competition for their purchase. Berezovsky's Logovaz owned 8 percent of the shares, while the share of the state owners totaled more than 50 percent. Nonetheless, Berezovsky used

side payments and bribes to gain control of the company's operations and editorial policy. See Paul Klebnikov, *Godfather of the Kremlin: Boris Berezovsky and the Looting of Russia* (New York: Harcourt, 2000), 159–61. Under Putin, the state regained control over ORT and forced Berezovsky out of the country.

17. Mark Whitehouse, "Buying the Media: Who's Behind the Written Word?" *Russia Review*, April 21, 1997, 26–27; and Oleg Medvedev and Sergei Sinchenko, "The Fourth Estate—Chained to Banks," *Business in Russia* 78 (June 1997): 38–43.

18. On the distorting influences of private ownership on editorial lines, see Laura Belin, "Political Bias and Self-Censorship in the Russian Media," in *Contemporary Russian Politics: A Reader*, ed. Archie Brown (Oxford: Oxford University Press, 2001), 323–44.

19. Nataliia Gevorkyan, Natalia Timakova, and Andrei Kolesnikov, *Ot pervogo litsa: Razgovory s Vladimirom Putinym* (Moscow: Vagrius, 2000), 172–3. See also an English version: Vladimir Putin, *First Person* (New York: Public Affairs, 2000).

20. Anna Kachkaeva, "Transformatsiia Rossiiskogo TV," in *Sredstva Massovoi Informatsii Rossii* (Moscow: Aspekt, 2006), 303.

21. The 1999 parliamentary election turned out to be Russia's last truly competitive election, and the competition was fierce and at times ugly. The operation of Berezovsky's television was shocking even by Russian standards. The use of television as a tool for smearing the Kremlin's political rivals was driven to grotesque proportions by TV journalist Sergei Dorenko, hired to fulfill this mission by Boris Berezovsky. The latter thereby emerged as the Kremlin savior and Putin's kingmaker. See Hoffman, *The Oligarchs*, 464–70.

22. Hoffman, *The Oligarchs*.

23. For more detail about the campaign against Gusinsky and his media, see Maria Lipman and Michael McFaul, "Putin and the Media," in *Putin's Russia: Past Imperfect, Future Uncertain*, 2nd ed., ed. Dale R. Herspring (Lanham, Md.: Rowman & Littlefield, 2005), 59–64.

24. "Sud kazhdye 4.3 dnia," *Kommersant-Vlast'*, no. 14 (April 10, 2001).

25. At home, few thought of the campaign against NTV as an encroachment on press freedom. Though the campaign against NTV caused public protest and two large protest rallies were held in Moscow, national polls suggested that "only four percent of the public regarded the NTV takeover as a government attempt to limit media freedom." See Floriana Fossato, "The Russian Media: From Popularity to Distrust," *Current History* 100, no. 648 (2001): 343.

26. Kachkaeva, "Transformatsiia Rossiiskogo TV," 305.

27. The fates of two channels, TV-6 and TVS, are discussed in more detail in Lipman and McFaul, "Putin and the Media," 64–67.

28. According to Russia's leading TV expert, Anna Kachkaeva, "Fast development of cable TV and the Internet notwithstanding . . . Russia still remains a country of traditional . . . television. Almost 90 percent of the Russian population watch TV every day." Anna Kachkaeva, "Glamurny totalitarizm: Televizionnaia industriia v epokhu stabil'nosti (2004–2007)," in *Teleradioefir: Istoriia i sovremennost'* (Moscow: Elitkomstar, 2008), 41.

29. Peter Baker and Susan Glasser, *Kremlin Rising: Vladimir Putin's Russia and the End of Revolution* (New York: Lisa Drew/Scribner, 2005), 89. See his even more emotional statements quoted in *Kommersant-Vlast'* 34 (August 29, 2000).

30. Baker and Glasser, *Kremlin Rising*, 174–75.

31. Baker and Glasser, *Kremlin Rising*, 34–35.

32. For an analysis of electoral reforms carried out during Putin's second term, see Nikolai Petrov, "Kakaia vlast'—takie i vybory, kakie vybory—takaia i vlast' (ob itogakh izbiratel'nogo tsykla 2007–2008 gg.)," Carnegie Moscow Center Briefing Paper 10, issue 2 (March 2008).

33. The campaign against NGOs intensified in late 2005; it included a smear campaign on state-controlled television and in other loyal media. Foreign-funded NGOs were portrayed as political agents of the West or even spies. The Duma passed a bill aimed at restraining their operation. See, for instance, http://news.bbc.co.uk/2/hi/europe/4547872.stm.

34. "We have serious concerns regarding the lack of media independence. State media failed to provide balanced coverage of the campaign," said the head of the Long-Term Observation Mission deployed by the OSCE Office for Democratic Institutions and Human Rights. See www.osce.org/item/7974.html.

35. Maria Lipman, "In Russia It's No Contest," *Washington Post*, December 1, 2004, www.carnegieendowment.org.

36. Lev Gudkov and Boris Dubin, "Obshchestvo telezritelei: Massy, massove kommunikatsii v Rossii kontsa 90–kh godov," *Monitoring obshchestvennogo mneniia*, no. 2 (March–April 2001): 31–45.

37. See www.memo98.sk/en/data/_media/russia_2nd_report_final.pdf. Russian daily *Kommersant* prints on a daily basis the amount of airtime the president and prime minister are given on the three major channels. Since Medvedev was elected president, his time on air, with very rare exceptions, exceeds that of Putin.

38. *Russian Newsweek*, August 4, 2008.

39. On media as business, see Kachkaeva, "Glamurny totalitarizm"; Maria Lipman, "La scène médiatique en Russie: Déclin des institutions et montée en puissance de l'industrie," *Outre-Terre*, no. 19 (2007), 2.

40. For instance, signal transmissions to smaller cities (under 200,000 residents) are subsidized by the state. Mikhail Fishman and Konstantin Gaaze, "Efir dlia dvoikh," *Russian Newsweek*, August 4, 2008.

41. There was speculation that the government had the Internet on its list of outlets to regulate further in the latter Putin period. In his November 2008 state of the union speech, President Medvedev supported free speech and stated that no government officials would be allowed to hinder discussions on the Internet. See *Moscow News Weekly*, December 26, 2008–January 15, 2009, 3.

42. Maria Lipman, "Constrained or Irrelevant: The Media in Putin's Russia," *Current History*, 104, no. 684 (2005): 319–24; and Maria Lipman, "Svoboda pressy v usloviakh upravliaemoi demokratii," Carnegie Moscow Center Briefing Paper 8, issue 2 (March 2006).

43. Peter Baker, "In Russian Media, Free Speech for a Select Few," *Washington Post*, February 25, 2005.

44. See www.rg.ru/2006/07/29/ekstremizm-protivodejstvie-dok.html. For comments, see www.newsru.com/russia/28jul2006/extreem.html. This bill was withdrawn at the end of December 2008 for further work.

45. For example, in late August 2008, popular radio station Ekho Moskvy (its daily audience reached about 900,000 in September–October 2008) brought Putin's

anger upon itself. Ekho Moskvy is a political talk radio which broadcasts political news and other live political shows. According to rumors, the political leadership, Putin in particular, decided that Ekho coverage of the Georgian war was insufficiently patriotic, that some of the commentators and reporters displayed wrong sympathies and the station would be closed down. On August 29, 2008, Putin brought together a group of the country's most prominent editors, mostly TV and wire services, Kremlin loyalists all. The editor of Ekho Moskvy, Aleksei Venediktov, was also invited, even though he hardly belonged in this crowd. Such meetings take place every once in a while, but the top editors never make them public—such are the rules. Putin indeed reprimanded the Ekho editor, yet contrary to the gloating expectations of Venediktov's subservient colleagues, Putin wouldn't announce that he was fired or that his station would be closed. Instead, he told Venediktov that he could go on working but would be held personally responsible for everything broadcast on his airwaves. The Russian media wouldn't mention this story until it was reported by foreign publications. See David Remnick, "Echo in the Dark," *New Yorker*, September 22, 2008; and Philip P. Pan, "In Wake of Georgian War, Russian Media Feel Heat," *Washington Post*, September 15, 2008.

46. Aleksei Shapovalov and Dmitri Butrin, "Obval'noe stalo yavnym," *Kommersant*, December 16, 2008.

47. For example, federal news channels almost completely ignored mass protests staged in Vladivostok in mid-December 2008. Thousands blocked traffic in the city center, protesting against the government decision to raise the tariffs on imported cars, a measure aimed at protecting domestic automakers. Used Japanese cars are the most commonly driven vehicles in this eastern region, and the rise of the tariffs would gravely affect the local automobile business, which includes shipment, sales, car repairs, etc. The protesters demanded that the decision be revoked; they also raised political demands, including the resignation of Putin's cabinet.

48. Two bills submitted in December 2008 introduced new legal restrictions potentially infringing on rights and freedoms, though not in the media sphere. One of them, adopted by the Duma on December 12, 2008, limits the authority of jury courts. See www.newsru.com/russia/12dec2008/pris.html. In Russia, not all court cases are heard in the presence of a jury; in some courts, the judge makes the final ruling. Jury rulings are harder to manipulate; they also tend to be softer. The other bill, which has not yet been enacted as of this writing, dangerously broadens the definitions of state treason and espionage. See Aleksei Nikol'sky, Natalia Kostenko, and Mariia Tsvetkova, "Rezhim sekretnosti usilen," *Vedomosti*, December 15, 2008. If adopted, this bill will enable the state to criminalize undesired contacts with foreign nationals and organizations. In the media realm, there have been consistent attempts to restrict the Internet and extend to Internet publications the legal responsibility of the media for the "dissemination of extremist materials." See Maksim Glikin, Natalia Kostenko, and Anastasia Golitsyna, "Kak zakryvat' saity," *Vedomosti*, December 4, 2008.

Part Two

THE ECONOMY AND SOCIETY

Chapter Six

Russia's Population Perils

Timothy Heleniak

There have been a growing number of media reports on Russia's declining population, with contributions by both demographers and nondemographers inside and outside Russia. These border on the apocalyptical, with recent headlines such as "Russia Is Sliding into a Demographic Abyss,"[1] "The Emptying of Russia,"[2] "The Passing Away of Mother Russia,"[3] and "A Sickness of the Soul."[4] Most of the reports in the mass media are expressed in quite emotive and dramatic terms, and they tend to be quite deterministic, making direct links between population decline and various economic and security disaster scenarios. While admittedly there is not much to be optimistic about when it comes to current Russian demographics, this chapter seeks to provide a more nuanced link between the various elements of Russia's current demographic situation and what it means for the future of the country.

The population of Russia peaked in 1993 at 148.6 million. It has since declined by 6.6 million to 142.0 million at the beginning of 2008.[5] This population decline resulted from deaths exceeding births by 12.2 million and a net immigration of 5.5 million, which only partially compensates for the negative natural increase (see figure 6.1). Deaths began to exceed births in 1992, and it is only coincidental that that was the first year of Russia's independence. A combination of declining fertility, high mortality, and an aging population has contributed to negative natural increase. In recent years, there have been some indications that the magnitude of the population decline is lessening. From 1993 to 2005, deaths exceeded births by an average of 850,000 a year. In 2007, there were 470,000 more deaths than births, as Russian women gave birth to the largest cohort of babies in the post-Soviet era. This was partly due to women having more children, but also there were more women in the higher-fertility ages of 20 to 29. Mortality also decreased slightly, and recorded net immigration was up in 2007.

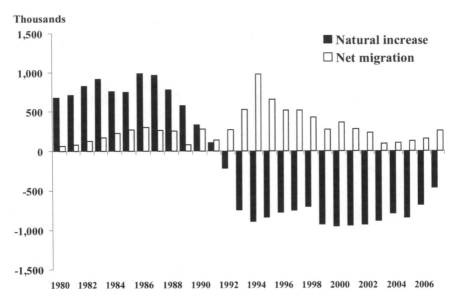

Figure 6.1. Net Migration and Natural Increase in Russia, 1980 to 2007
Source: Rosstat, Demograficheskii ezhegodnik (various years)

Deaths exceed births in a number of other countries in Eastern and Western Europe. In Russia, however, the absolute amount by which deaths exceed births is the largest in the world, and the rate is second to that of Ukraine. The trends of natural decrease and net immigration insufficient to stem population decline are expected to continue into the future, pointing to the demographic dilemma that Russia faces. To avoid the decline, Russia needs to raise fertility, lower mortality, or increase immigration, while some question whether attempting to reverse population decline is even the wisest policy to pursue. The term *population decline* can refer to many different phenomena: a decline in the size of a population; a decline in the rate of growth or the fertility rate; an aging of the population; a decline in the proportion of the majority or dominant ethnic group; or a decline in attributes often attributed to a growing population, such as innovation, mobility, risk-taking, and optimism, for which are substituted conservatism, immobility, risk-aversion, and pessimism.[6] Russia is hardly the first country to fear population decline, nor is this the first time that Russia has worried about declining or negative rates of growth.

This chapter has several aims. The first is to analyze Russian demographic trends from the late Soviet through the Yeltsin, Putin, and Medvedev eras and into the future. The second is to determine what these demographic trends portend for Russia's political and economic future. The third is to assess the effectiveness of population policy in Russia. The chapter examines fertility, mortality, composition of the population, migration, and the spatial distribution of the population in Russia, ending with a discussion of population projections and population policy.

FERTILITY

By the 1960s, Russian women had completed the fertility transition and adopted the two-child family as the norm. The total fertility rate declined to replacement level in the early 1960s and stayed at that level throughout the Soviet period.[7] In 1989, of the cohort of women who had just completed their childbearing, only 3.5 percent had never married and only 7.9 percent were childless.[8] Thus, fertility in Russia at the beginning of the transition period was characterized by nearly universal marriage and childbearing, both of which occurred at young ages. Because of these trends of early marriage and childbearing, there was a much larger contribution of younger cohorts to total fertility than in Western countries, where women delayed childbearing while pursuing education or careers. Russian women typically had children relatively early and then relied on abortion for future fertility regulation, as contraceptive rates were rather low.

The number of births fell from a recent peak of 2.5 million in 1987, during a period of pro-natalist policies, to a low of 1.2 million in 1999, then increased to 1.6 million in 2007 (see figure 6.2). The mortality increase in Russia has been well publicized, but the fertility decline actually has had the largest numerical impact. The annual number of deaths has increased by 549,000 since 1987, while the number of births has declined by 890,000. The fertility rate in Russia also peaked during the pro-natalist period in 1987 at 2.194 children per woman, the last time it was above the replacement level. Thereafter, it declined sharply, reaching a low of 1.157 in 1999 before increasing to 1.406 in 2007, possibly influenced by a package of pro-natalist measures put into place by the government. Even the recent rise is quite minuscule and portends continued overall population decline. The fertility rate in Russia places it among what demographers refer to as "lowest-low" fertility, along with a group of countries in Western and Eastern Europe that includes a number of other former Soviet states with fertility rates below 1.3.[9] Most analysts believe that lowest-low fertility is not likely to be just a short-term phenomenon in Russia and other Central and East European states.

As the trade-off between children and education/careers shifts in favor of the latter, the fertility pattern in Russia is shifting toward that seen in Europe, where the highest fertility rates are among women ages 25 to 29 and overall rates are lower. Between 1989 and the nadir of fertility in Russia in 2000, women at all ages had fewer children, with the largest decline among

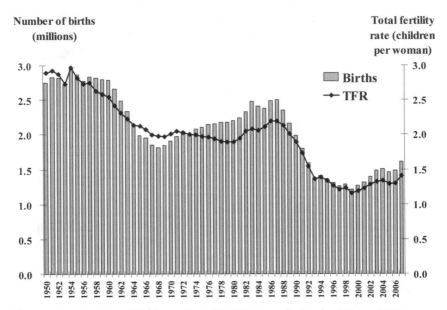

Figure 6.2. Number of Births and Total Fertility Rate in Russia, 1950 to 2007
Source: Rosstat, *Demograficheskii ezhegodnik* (various years)

women ages 20 to 24. Three-quarters of the increase since then is attributable to increased births among women ages 25 to 34, with the fertility of women ages 20 to 24 further declining. The mean age at childbearing increased from 24.6 in 1994 to 26.6 in 2006.[10] Changes in annual total fertility rates can reflect changes in the average number of births, which is known as the quantum effect, or they can reflect shifts in the timing of births, which is known as the tempo effect. The main factor driving the decline in Russia is the reduction in the quantum of fertility, in particular the low propensity to have a second child, as studies show evidence of a shift to a one-child family norm in Russia.[11] During the transition period in Russia, there was a rapid increase in the returns to education, which played a role in the fertility decline.[12] The number of children that Russian women had at each educational level stayed roughly the same between the 1989 and 2002 censuses. What explains much of the decline in fertility is the increase in the number of women pursuing higher education, with the largest increases among younger persons 16 to 29 years of age, when women are in their prime fertility ages.

One issue that Russia will confront is that the smaller cohorts of women born in the late 1980s will soon enter their peak childbearing years. The number of women of childbearing age peaked in 2003 at 40 million and is expected to fall to 32 million by 2020. More crucial is that the number of women aged 20 to 29 will peak by the end of the decade at 12 million and then fall almost in half to 7 million by 2020. In Russia, women in these ages give birth to 65 percent of children. Without a massive increase in fertility levels, the number of births in Russia will decline from its current level of 1.6 million to less than 1 million per year in 2025.

Demographers have identified four proximate determinants that account for the majority of the differences in fertility levels among societies and within societies over time: the share of women who are married or in a union; the prevalence of contraceptive use; abortion rates; and level of postpartum breast-feeding (though the latter is of little importance in a low-fertility country like Russia).[13] Social and economic factors in a country work through these proximate determinants to influence the fertility rate. In Russia, this includes the steep income declines in the 1990s and increases in the direct costs of children during the transition period.

The annual number of marriages fell from 1.4 million in the late 1980s to a low of 850,000 in 1999 before increasing to 1.3 million in 2006. The ratio of divorces to marriages has also recently fallen. Both factors increased the share of women and the length of time in union, where they are engaging in regular intercourse and are exposed to the possibility of becoming pregnant. This is important for fertility levels because of the continued importance of marital fertility to the overall fertility level in Russia. From the peak of fertility in 1987, the annual number of marital births fell by 1.1 million while the contribution of nonmarital births increased by only 114,000. The share of births that occur outside of marriage increased from 13 percent in 1987 to 29 percent in 2006. Though marriage and childbearing are no longer as synonymous as they once were, the decline in the number of marriages in Russia can still explain a significant portion of the overall fertility decline.

With the economic transition and the opening of the Russian economy, the levels of contraceptive use have increased considerably. The contraceptive prevalence rate went from 31.5 percent in 1990 to 73 percent in 1999.[14] The bulk of this increase was greater use of more effective, modern contraceptive methods (e.g., the pill, IUDs, condoms, sterilization). Soon after the Bolsheviks took power, abortion was legalized. Over time, an abortion industry emerged, and abortion became the cheapest and most readily available form of fertility regulation. From 1960 to 1990, the abortion ratio (number of abortions per 100 births) averaged about 220.[15] The abortion ratio fell from 205 in 1989 to 107 in 2006.[16] However, the historical legacy of reliance on abortion remains, as this ratio means that over half of all conceptions are terminated in abortion. Legislation enacted during the 1990s further increased the grounds under which a woman could obtain an abortion upon request. Russia continues to have among the highest abortion rates in the world, and abortion remains a major fertility-inhibiting factor.[17]

Like other low-fertility countries, Russia would prefer to raise fertility rates rather than increase the flow of migrants. Starting in January 2007, a new package of pro-natalist policies was introduced, designed to halt or reverse the steep decline in Russia's birth rate. The package included large child benefits of $113 a month for a second child, longer maternity leaves of eighteen months at 40 percent salary, and a payment of $9,000 to each woman who had a second child.[18] Russian women are increasingly reluctant to leave the labor force to have and care for children, and the policy has clauses to guarantee reentry into the labor market. There are also components that seek to address the poor social status of parents, to make having children more desirable. Given the sensitivity of fertility to income in Russia, the extra payments seem to be working. Births were up by 9 percent in 2007 over 2006. The long-term effectiveness of these policies remains to be seen, but the leadership should be commended for adopting positive measures rather than negative ones, such as reduced access to contraception or restrictions on abortion. However, empirical evidence has shown that pro-natalist programs typically encourage couples to have children sooner but not to increase the overall number of children born.[19]

MORTALITY

The mortality situation in Russia has received considerable attention and for good reason. Mortality levels and patterns of death and disease in Russia are far out of line for a country at its level of development. Russia is a literal "point off the curve" in combining relatively low child mortality levels with very high adult levels.[20] It is the exceptionally high working-age mortality where Russia differs, with mortality three to five times that for males and twice for females among countries with similar income levels.[21] Studies have shown that the key factor driving increases in mortality during the transition period in Russia is acute psychosocial stress, brought about when individuals are called upon to adjust to new situations for which they have few coping mechanisms.[22] This is evidenced in the pattern of causes of death: increases in deaths due to cardiovascular diseases, suicides and accidents, and ulcers and cirrhosis of the liver. The transition period in Russia and the other transition countries was marked by unemployment, rapid labor turnover, job insecurity, family instability, distress migration, and increased social stratification. Less-educated and more socially marginalized groups tended to have much higher mortality levels as there was widening of the life expectancy gap during the 1990s between those with high and low levels of education. Most studies have demonstrated that absolute deprivation, the collapse of the health-care system, and environmental pollution were not major contributing factors.

There was a temporary decline in deaths during the anti-alcohol campaign of the late 1980s, which saved an estimated 930,000 lives over the years 1985 to 1992 (620,000 male lives and 310,000 female lives).[23] There was a sharp upturn between 1990 and 1994, when the number of deaths increased from 1.7 million to 2.3 million, at the time the Soviet Union was breaking up and the economic transition began. There was a decline after this until 1998, the year of the financial crisis, when deaths increased again, peaking in 2003. Since then, there has been a steady decline in the number of people dying in Russia so that in 2007, there were a quarter-million fewer deaths than in 2003.

Life expectancy in Russia rose from quite low levels in the first part of the twentieth century, and levels approached those of the United States and other developed countries in the mid-1960s (see figure 6.3). After that time, life expectancy in Russia remained stagnant (for females) or declined slightly (for males) while in the rest of the world it continued to rise. One noticeable feature that keeps overall life expectancy in Russia low is the large female advantage. Globally, women live three years longer than men, but in Russia they live thirteen years longer.[24] Aside from the anti-alcohol period of 1986 to 1988, the highest life expectancy that Russian males achieved was in 1964. Following the peak in 1988, when life expectancy was 64.9 years for males and 74.4 for females, it plunged for both to lows in 1994 of 57.5 for males and 71.1 years for females, at which time the female-male gap reached its apex of 13.6 years. After 1994, life expectancy rose to 1998 and then fell following the ruble crisis. If there is any hopeful sign, it is that with the recent period of economic growth, life expectancy has increased since 2003 and the female-male gap has narrowed slightly.

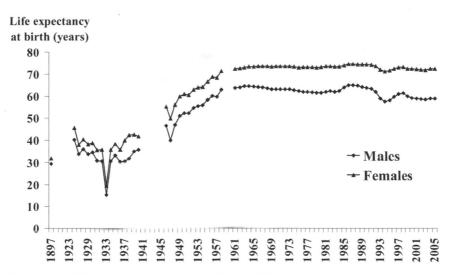

Figure 6.3. Life Expectancy in Russia, 1897 to 2006
Source: Rosstat, *Demograficheskii ezhegodnik* (various years)

More so than in other countries, life expectancy in Russia seems influenced by short-term fluctuations in economic and social currents. Long-term mortality trends in Russia are influenced by cardiovascular diseases, while external causes (suicides, murders, accidents, and poisonings) tend to be responsible for short-term fluctuations.[25] Periods of mortality increase in Russia are marked by increased deaths from heart and circulatory system diseases and external causes among working-age males, while during periods of decrease, deaths from these causes among males decline the most. The fluctuations for working-age females are usually somewhat less than for males, and females typically have larger increases in deaths from circulatory system causes and less from external causes. Death rates among children and the elderly account for very little of the fluctuation in life expectancy in Russia. Infant mortality has steadily declined from 21 infant deaths per 1,000 births in 1985 to 10 per 1,000 in 2007. While Russia does not have anywhere near the lowest infant mortality rate in the world, it is not high enough to have a very significant impact on overall mortality levels, though the poor health of newborns and children affects the population later in life. The improved education and health of Russian children is critical to developing the well-educated and skilled human capital needed for Russia's economic and social development.

Poor diets with an abundance of protein-rich, fatty foods with high cholesterol content have increasingly marked the Russia diet since the 1970s.[26] High blood pressure, high cholesterol, and tobacco account for 75 percent of all deaths in Russia. Low fruit and vegetable consumption, high body-mass indexes, alcohol consumption, physical inactivity, and urban outdoor air pollution are other leading risk factors. Noncommunicable diseases and injuries account for the ten leading causes of death in Russia. There are substantial gains to be made, both demographic and economic, from reducing these causes of death.[27]

In a country where 54 percent of physicians continue to smoke, the antitobacco movement in Russia lags far behind that of the West. Russia is one of a handful of countries that has not signed the Framework Convention on Tobacco Control. The tobacco lobby in Russia has hampered measures that have been effective elsewhere, such as advertising limits, price increases, warning labels on cigarette packages, bans on marketing to children, and restrictions on public smoking. Russian females rank 27 of 131 countries in terms of smoking prevalence, while Russian males have the highest smoking rates in the world.[28] The smoking rates among those aged 13 to 15 also place Russia among the top 20 countries in the world, a sign that the problem of smoking and smoking-related morbidity and mortality show no signs of abating soon.

High and increased levels of consumption of alcohol have played a major role in explaining changes in mortality levels in Russia over time and between Russia and other countries, as Russia ranked fifth in the world in levels of alcohol consumption.[29] A substantial portion of the increase in mortality in the early 1990s can be attributed to alcohol.[30] Alcohol consumption in Russia is characterized by high levels of binge drinking, drinking large amounts of high-alcohol-content *samogon*, and higher levels of consumption of spirits. Three-quarters of alcohol-caused deaths were either binge drinking or alcoholic cardiomyopathy—chronic long-term abuse of alcohol leading to heart failure.

HIV-AIDS came late to Russia but over the past few years has had among the highest incidence rates in the world. According to official data from the Russian Federal AIDS Center, at the end of 1995, there were barely 1,000 reported HIV-AIDS cases in the country and only 364 deaths from the disease.[31] By mid-2008, the number of persons living with HIV-AIDS had skyrocketed to 433,827 and the number of reported deaths was 27,341, while other estimates put the true prevalence level at 940,000 to 1.3 million.[32] There is a different epidemiology of transmission of HIV-AIDS in Russia, with intravenous drug use becoming a major mode of transmission in the late 1990s. This helped fuel a major increase in the incidence rate in Russia in 1996. The epidemic is now growing among the non-drug-using heterosexual population, and over 80 percent of those infected are under age 30.[33]

Many attribute at least part of the health problems in Russia to an inadequate response of the health-care system, stemming from the legacy of the output-oriented Soviet health-care system. The health-care system plays a role in explaining differences between Russia and Western European countries, but it cannot explain a majority of the differences. With infusions from the National Priority Health Program, spending levels have now risen to pre-transition levels. But even with increased health spending, the system is very inefficient, with too many resources aimed at hospitalization and too few devoted to primary and preventative care. Estimates are that in 2005, 150,000 deaths could have been prevented by referrals to primary prevention.[34] There have also been increased funds available for HIV-AIDS prevention, including a 20-fold increase in spending since 2006, targeted in part toward scaling up access to antiretroviral drugs. A World Bank policy note on the Russian health situation suggested four key interventions: controlling excessive alcohol consumption, controlling tobacco consumption, promoting changes in diet and physical activity, and improving road safety. In addition to the quantitative decline of the population acting as a deterrent to economic growth, the qualitative decline in terms of poor health is also a factor.

COMPOSITION OF THE POPULATION

The links between population decline and economic contraction and loss of international power are complex. While the quantitative aspects of Russia's demographic situation are important, so are the qualitative. This section examines four important disaggregations of Russia's population: sex ratios, age structure, educational levels, and ethnic composition.

Sex Ratios

In the 2002 census, there were 77.6 million females enumerated versus 67.6 million males, a difference of 10.0 million and a slight increase over the 1989 census, when females outnumbered males by 9.6 million caused by the increasing female-male gap in life expectancy during the 1990s. This situation of a large excess of females over males has persisted in Russia for quite some time. Males suffered the brunt of the devastating losses during World War II, and at the end of the war the sex ratio was 74.7 males per 100 females, among the lowest ratios ever recorded for a sizable population. The sex ratio gradually increased to a peak of 88.4 males per 100 females in 1995, before declining again to 86.2 males per 100 females in 2007, making it among the lowest in the world.[35] There are more males than females until age 33, so there is limited effect on the marriage market. From that age onward, higher male mortality continues to pull down the sex ratio, so that over age 85, there is only 1 male per every 5 females.

There are several implications of this unequal sex ratio for Russian society and the economy. The primary one is that the population would obviously be a lot higher if not for the large male mortality. The effects of Russia's unbalanced sex ratio are akin to a country involved in war or experiencing large-scale emigration of males. One study examining the effects of Russian women who were in their 20s during WWII found that women in cohorts or regions with lower sex ratios had lower rates of marriage and fertility, and higher rates of out-of-wedlock births and abortions than those less affected by the war.[36] While current male mortality in Russia is not at levels found during wartime, it is extremely high, which might impact on marriage and fertility decisions, as Russian women can expect to spend much longer portions of their lives as widows.

Age Structure

As in many countries, the population of Russia is aging, though Russia does not appear on a list of the world's oldest countries because so many Russians, especially male, do not live long enough to see old age. Because fertility was at or above replacement for most of the twentieth century, the size of the working-age population was growing as a share of the total population, contributing to overall economic growth.[37] As the smaller cohorts of the past two decades replace larger cohorts that are retiring, the size of the working-age population is expected to peak in 2006 and then decline, possibly acting as a brake on economic growth. The size of the labor force will decline from its current peak of 90.4 million to 74.8 million in 2025, a drop of 15.6 million. To maintain economic growth, labor productivity will have to match or exceed this labor force decline. Further exacerbating this problem is that even within the working-age population there is aging. Of the projected decline in the working ages of 11 million persons between now and 2025, 95 percent will be in the 15 to 39 age group. Thus, to avoid further declines, labor participation rates will have to be raised among those in the older working ages or among other groups with traditionally lower participation rates.[38] The challenges will be to sustain economic growth through improved productivity and to manage the fiscal costs associated with aging.

A recent World Bank study labeled the demographic transition of rapidly aging and shrinking populations in Russia as the "third transition" after the political and economic transitions. What makes Russia unique is that the demographic transition is going on at the same time as the other two. This will lead to further economic decline unless productivity and labor-force participation are raised and health care, elder care, and pension expenditures are reduced. Russia's challenges because of aging are more complex and less demographically deterministic than suggested by conventional wisdom. First, the impact of aging on total expenditures in health is low, as many drivers of increased expenditures are technological, independent of aging. Second, aging is one factor that affects level of pension spending, but so do pension-system parameters. One suggestion is to equalize retirement ages between men and women and to perhaps increase them as the duration of working careers are four years less than in countries of the Organization for Economic Cooperation and Development (OECD). With women living much longer than men in Russia, there is little reason other than tradition for maintaining this. The study's conclusion is that changes in population size and composition are not highly influential factors in overall health-care expenditures over the medium and long runs.

In the age-sex structure of the Russian population on January 1, 2008, what is important for future population change is the very narrow base at the bottom, with nearly every cohort from age 20 to age 5 being smaller than the one above it (see figure 6.4). This is the major factor contributing to the declining Russian population in the recent past and in the future. In the last few years, there has been a moderate increase in cohort size from a combination of actual fertility increases and the larger size of cohorts a generation earlier.

One area where the decline in births will be felt most keenly is the military, where current plans seem to be at odds with demographic reality.[39] This decline in male births has cut in half the conscription pool since the mid-1980s, at a time when the plan is to maintain the armed forces at 1.1 million until at least 2011. Simultaneously, the plans call for reducing the term of conscription from two to one year, which implies doubling the number of conscripts

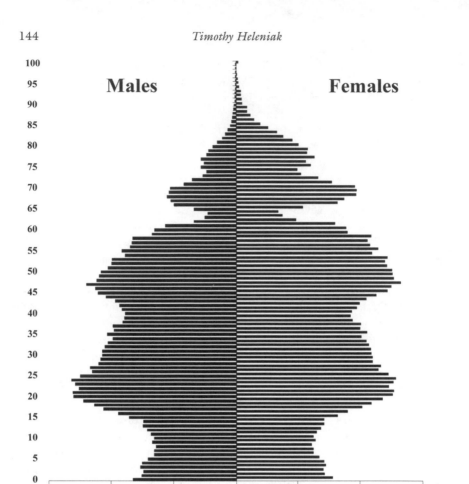

Figure 6.4.   Age-Structure of the Population of Russia on 1 January 2008
Source: Rosstat, *Chislennost' naseleniia Rossiiskoi Federatsii po polu i vozrastu na 1 ianvraia 2008 goda*
(Moscow: Rosstat, 2008), 9

annually. A number of the current deferment categories are to be abolished, but this will not likely matter much, since at present about 70 percent of re-cruits are rejected at the medical-board stage. It appears that the change to a one-year conscription will cause a manpower crisis of an unprecedented scale and a host of security, social, economic, and policy consequences.

Educational Levels

At the beginning of the transition period, Russia could be rightly proud of the achievements of its education system. As part of the education reforms in Russia, there has been a move away from rote learning toward problem-solving and life-long learning. There has been a decreased demand for technical training in vocational schools and engineering at higher levels, and an increased demand for courses in the humanities, economics, finance, languages, and other skills needed for new labor markets. The wage structure under the Soviet economic system was rather narrow but has widened considerably under market conditions, causing a large increase in returns to education.[40] The increasing returns to education brought about by the economic changes of the transition period are evident in the increased shares of the population obtaining higher-level degrees. Those with a higher or graduate degree increased from 11.3 percent in 1989 to 16.0 percent in 2002. Between 1989 and 2002, the share of the population with higher degrees (higher, secondary professional, or primary professional) increased from 34 to 59 percent of the population aged 15 and older. However, there are worrying signs that while overall levels of education are rising, outputs as measured by scores on standardized tests are declining. Russia's scores in mathematics and science in the Program for International Student Assessment (PISA) for grade 8 students declined between 1995 and 2003. And its scores declined in both absolute and relative terms on the Trends in International Mathematics and Science Study (TIMSS) assessment between 2000 and 2003.

This might be due to growing disparities in education access and quality among the regions in Russia. Available funds for education spending are closely linked to per capita gross regional product (GRP), causing growing regional inequalities in education spending and a partial breakdown in Russia's "common educational space."[41] At the bottom end of the education spectrum, there are some tentative signs of the breakdown of universal education and children dropping out of the education system.

Nationality Composition

The complex ethnic mosaic that was the Soviet Union was always difficult to manage and played a part in its demise. There were fears before the last Soviet census that Russians would lose their demographic majority, but they just managed to cling to it as they made up 50.8 percent of the population in 1989.[42] One of the fears of population decline is the decline of the titular ethnic group, but according to official census data, the ethnic Russian population only declined from 81.3 to 79.8 percent of the population between 1989 and 2002, a share that has not changed much since the first Soviet census in 1926 when Russians made up 78.0 percent of the population. Russia has always had an uneasy relationship with the Muslim world of which it is part by virtue of having a larger and growing Muslim population of its own, and having Muslim states along its southern periphery, which figure prominently into Russia's internal and foreign policy agenda. The Muslim population in Russia increased from 7.9 to 10.2 percent of the total population between the 1989 and 2002 censuses. Russia already has troubled ethnic and religious tensions, and if it needs to recruit non-Russians from the other states of the former Soviet Union and beyond to compensate for its demographic shortfall, this will only exacerbate the situation.[43]

INTERNATIONAL MIGRATION

The breakup of the Soviet Union added 28 million persons to the world stock of migrants, and Russia, with 12 million, has the second largest stock of migrants after the United States.[44] There was actually an increase in the percentage of "foreign born" in Russia between the 1989 and 2002 censuses, from 7.8 to 9.3 percent of the population, due to continued immigration of nonnative groups and a natural decrease of ethnic Russians.[45] These are often termed "statistical migrants," as they became migrants not by moving but by virtue of the Soviet Union breaking apart. International migration has become a major internal issue for population and economic growth as well as social cohesion in Russia. It is also an external issue in Russia's relations with other former Soviet states, as the treatment of migrants is often seen as a form of soft power that Russia exerts over its neighbors. The sheer number of migrant workers from Central Asia and the Caucasus seeking work in Russia has forced these other former Soviet states to maintain contacts with what had been the imperial center.[46]

Net migration into Russia rose from 115,000 in 1989 to a peak of 810,000 in 1994 then declined to just 39,000 in 2003 before increasing again to 240,000 in 2007.[47] The first decade after the breakup of the Soviet Union was a period of porous borders with visa-free travel among the Commonwealth of Independent States (CIS). Most of what is recorded in migration statistics are movements for permanent migration, and a considerable portion of the movement into Russia is temporary and quasi-legal. One problem that Russia confronts in formulating migration policy is that it has not fully developed a migration statistics system adequate for the new flows that are taking place.[48] The broad pattern of migration by country for Russia is one of net immigration from the other former Soviet states and net emigration to countries outside the former Soviet Union. The bulk of the net immigration from within the former Soviet states has come from Central Asia and the Caucasus. Most emigration to outside states has been toward Germany, Israel, and the United States.

One issue facing Russian migration policy is that the current migration into the country, both documented and undocumented, is extremely ethnically homogenous. Since 1989, ethnic Russians made up two-thirds of the recorded migration into Russia.[49] If undocumented migration were included, the majority would be of non-Russians. In the immediate post-Soviet period, many of the migration movements across the post-Soviet space were ethnically motivated, people returning to their ethnic homelands or fleeing ethnic violence. More recently, the motivations have been economically motivated, driven by the large income disparities between Russia and the non-Russian former Soviet states. For persons from the low-income former Soviet countries, the returns to migration are large. Moldova, Tajikistan, and Armenia are among the top countries in the world in terms of remittances as a share of GDP, most earned in Russia.[50] The shares of the labor forces of some non-Russian states of the former Soviet Union working permanently or seasonally in Russia is quite significant, with estimates ranging from 10 to 30 percent of the labor forces of Moldova, Armenia, Azerbaijan, Georgia, Tajikistan, Kyrgyzstan, and Uzbekistan.[51] In 1998, there were an estimated 4.0 to 4.5 million illegal immigrants in Russia, of which 3.5 to 3.8 million were working illegally.[52] Current estimates put the number at 5 to 10 million illegal workers in Russia.[53] As in other migration magnet countries, a dual labor market is developing in Russia, with migrants occupying large sectors of the workforce in trade, construction, transport services, and agriculture, and working quite separate from local residents. Being illegal or quasi-legal, these migrants are subject to the same abuses and exploitation as in other migrant-destination countries, perhaps more so in Russia with its history of discrimination against "others." Since the mid-1990s in Russia, there has been a documented rise in acts of violence toward ethnic or religious "others," many of whom are migrants.[54] In Russia, there is a tension between more conservative groups who see only the ills of migration and seek better control over frontiers and more liberal approaches which recognize the inevitability and even desirability of foreign labor migration. Russia's authoritarian political culture allows a stricter enforcement of border crossings and migration movements than is possible in a liberal democracy.

The first formative phase of Russian migration policy during the years 1992 to 1994 was characterized by assistance toward involuntary migrants from the other former Soviet states, the establishment of the Federal Migration Service, passage of key migration and refugee law, abolishment of the *propiska* system, and the signing of key international migration and refugee conventions. While there was concern for the Russian diaspora during this period, there were not strenuous efforts to encourage their return in large numbers. The second half of the 1990s saw further passage of key migration legislation such as laws on labor migration. This period of more liberal attitudes toward migrants ended in 2000 when the Federal Migration Service was abolished and its functions transferred to the Ministry of Internal Affairs and the overall thrust of migration policy became one of combating illegal migration. In 2002, a somewhat restrictive Citizenship Law was passed, Russia quit the Bishkek Agreement allowing visa-free travel among the former Soviet states, and began to negotiate entry and labor migration on a bilateral basis. The years 2006–2008 have seen a shift in migration policy and legislation toward a realization of the inevitability of migration into Russia and its possible benefits both demographically and economically. There was also the realization that efforts were needed to better regulate and protect those migrants who were in the country. Regulations have been passed to increase enforcement of policies toward illegal migrants but also to make the process of registering for work permits easier. As a result, there was a surge in the number of work permits issued in 2007, to four times that of the previous year.[55]

This policy shift is partially the result of the increased necessity for "replacement migration," the use of migration to compensate for declining populations or labor forces. According to a set of UN simulations of replacement migration, for Russia to maintain the same population size over the first half of the twenty-first century, there would have to be a net migration of 25 million people, and to maintain the same labor-force size, there would need to be a net migration of 36 million. This would require immigration levels to exceed those of the 1990s, when there was a net immigration of 4.5 million.[56] Belatedly, Russia is trying to tap into the remaining Russian diaspora for some of this immigration with a program aimed at facilitating their return to Russia.[57] Plans call for the migration to Russia of an additional 3–4 million people during the next decade.[58] However, the prospect for this massive immigration of fellow Russians appears slim, as most of the Russian diaspora view their current state of residence as their homeland, and thus a move to Russia would be a migration away from their homeland.[59] For centuries, and most of the Soviet period, Russia was a major sending state and is making an uneasy transition to being a major migration destination.

SPATIAL DISTRIBUTION OF THE POPULATION

Just as the rise in GDP disparities among the former Soviet states was a major driver of post-Soviet migration among the states, rising income disparities among Russian regions drove internal migration patterns. The Soviet Union attempted to equalize incomes among all regions through centrally administered wages, prices, and subsidies that made disparities lower than what they would have been under market conditions. Between 1990 and 2002, the ratio of regions with the highest gross regional product per capita to the lowest rose from 5 to 36.[60] The restructuring of the regional economic geography of Russia has caused two major internal movements. The first is out of Siberia, the Far East, and the North toward central Russia, and the second is movement up the urban hierarchy.

Between 1989 and 2006, there was an out-migration of 17 percent of the population from the regions that make up the Far North.[61] At the extreme were the two regions in the far northeast, Magadan and Chukotka, which respectively had net out-migration of 57 and 74 percent of their populations. According to Hill and Gaddy, the overpopulation of Siberia and the North was one of the mistakes of Soviet central planners when it came to determining the spatial allocation of population and economic activity.[62] Among others were the lack of medium-size cities, which are often the engines of economic growth, and the lack of connectedness among urban centers. Since the transition, Moscow has grown from 8.9 to 10.5 million, from 6.0 to 7.4 percent of the population in 2008.[63] This trend of population growth in the primate city during the period of economic transition also occurred across many of the former Soviet Union and Eastern European countries. Within Russia, there has been a trend of population concentration into the *oblast* centers and the dying out of many smaller villages as the cost of living in smaller and more distant settlements has became prohibitively expensive with the withdrawal of subsidies on transport.

While the above description of internal migration trends points to considerable movement, migration turnover has declined considerably over the course of the transition period. In 1991, 3 percent of the Russian population changed residences, while in 2005 only 1.5 percent did so. An increasing share of the movements that were taking place were intraregional, as various barriers to migrating remained high, most importantly the cost of doing so.[64] The reforms of the housing and mortgage markets appear to be incomplete, leaving many without the ability to migrate to more prosperous regions. It seems as if spatial poverty traps are developing where people have insufficient liquidity or funds needed to move.[65]

While many think that the depopulation of Siberia is a positive development, some in the Russian government and others fear that with fewer people, the periphery will be unprotected, especially the southern regions of the Far East bordering on China.[66] This notion seems somewhat absurd, as any attack across the Russian border is unlikely to come via its Arctic or Far East coastlines. There are more Chinese in central Russia than in the Far East, and most who are there are carefully monitored. But with recent economic growth, China has had little interest in engaging in grabs of practically vacant land in Russia.

POPULATION PROJECTIONS AND IMPLICATIONS

Population projections for Russia are routinely done by four different agencies: Rosstat, which is the state agency for statistics in Russia,[67] the United Nations Population Division,[68] the World Bank,[69] and the U.S. Census Bureau.[70] The projections done by the latter three agencies extend to the year 2050. All expect that Russia will continue to have a negative natural increase where deaths exceed births, and that Russia will continue to be a net immigration country. Deviations from replacement-level fertility of 2.1 children per woman greatly influence rates of population change. For Russia and other low-fertility countries, there is no expectation that fertility will ever rise again to replacement level. Projections of the fertility rate for Russia in 2050 range from 1.21 to 2.21 children per woman. It is these differing assumptions regarding future fertility levels that explain much of the difference among the projections of Russia's future population size by different organizations and among the different variants. Similar to fertility, assumptions are made regarding the future levels of life expectancy and the age distribution of mortality. The general assumption is that with improvements in wealth, health care, and technology, life expectancy will continue to rise. All agencies project improvements in life expectancy for Russia, albeit to different levels. The range of projections of life expectancy in 2050 is from 68.5 to 72.3 years for males and from 77.9 to 80.2 years for females. However, little in Russia's recent demographic past or current social policy points toward improvements in life expectancy of the magnitudes embedded in the projections.

The impact of HIV-AIDS on Russian population change, economic growth, and society has been the subject of considerable speculation. There have been a variety of "back of the envelope" projections about the future course of HIV-AIDS in Russia. The modeling work done at the U.S. Census Bureau is one careful study of AIDS which uses adjusted data on the disease to produce likely scenarios based on paths of transmission seen elsewhere in the world.[71] The study starts with an infected population of 1.3 million in 2004 and projects that the number of infected persons will peak at about 2.6 million between 2010 and 2015 before gradually declining to 870,000 in 2050. HIV-AIDS-related deaths will increase to 250,000 annually in 2015 before declining to about 100,000 annually in 2050. Overall, HIV-AIDS is expected to account for 8.6 million deaths in Russia in the first half of the century and 8.3 percent of total deaths. The study concludes that HIV-AIDS will have a relatively minor impact on the Russian population and that the disease will not be as catastrophic as in some parts of Africa, though its impact will not be insignificant.

Migration is the most volatile and difficult to project component of population change because it involves so many exogenous economic, political, and social factors. It is also the component that could have the most significant impact on the Russian economy and society and Russia's relations with its neighbors. Since the breakup of the Soviet Union, net migration into Russia has averaged 360,000 annually.[72] The UN projects that net migration into Russia will remain positive at 50,000 persons a year from 2005 to 2050, and the World Bank projects a similar level of immigration. The Rosstat low, medium, and high migration scenarios project an annual average immigration into Russia of 220,000, 415,000, and 840,000 from 2005 to 2025.

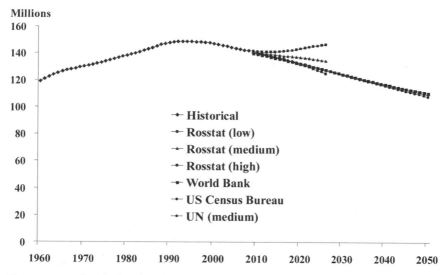

Figure 6.5. Historical and Projected Population of Russia, 1960 to 2050
Sources: Rosstat, *Predpolozhitel'naia chislennost' naseleniia Rossiiskoi Federatsii do 2025 goda: Statisticheskii biulleten'* (Moscow: Rosstat, 2005), 9–11; UN, World Population Prospects; World Bank, World Development Indicators; U.S. Census Bureau, International Data Base.

Barring unforeseen political events, economic differentials between Russia and its neighbors will determine future levels of migration into the country, as well as rates of population growth.

The population history of Russia and various projections are shown in figure 6.5. In 1946, after the devastation of World War II, Russia's population was 97.5 million, rising steadily to a peak of 148.6 million in 1993 before declining. The three different Rosstat projections range from 125.0 million to 146.7 million in 2026, the latter being the only one of the eight scenarios to project a population increase.[73] The three different UN projections range lower than the three Rosstat projections, from a low of 119.4 million to a high of 135.2 million in 2026. The low UN projection scenario shows the largest decline of any, indicating a population decline of 23 million or 16 percent in just two decades. Projecting further out to midcentury, the three UN projections bracket those of the World Bank and U.S. Census Bureau and range from a low of 89 million to a high of 130 million, with a medium scenario of 108 million.

GLOBAL IMPLICATIONS OF
RUSSIA'S POPULATION DECLINE

For the last several centuries, the Russian Empire or the Soviet Union was the third largest country in the world in terms of population size, behind

China and India, and just ahead of the United States. When the Soviet Union broke apart, Russia became the sixth most populous country in the world; by 2008, it had fallen to ninth.[74] Russia is expected to fall to twelfth in 2025 and to fifteenth by midcentury. Population size is just one determinant of a state's capabilities. Others include size of economy, territory, technological level, size and equipment of armed forces, and qualitative attributes such as organizational effectiveness and morale, as well as location, climate, and topography.[75] The relative weights of these factors change over time, and having a large territory is less important than factors such as size of economy and technological capability. Classifying countries as a function of the size of territory, population, and GDP, the Soviet Union/Russia has fallen out of the category of super-giants where it had been during the Soviet era (others were Britain, China, and the United States), below the category of giants, and is now classed as a subgiant, with the United States and China being the only remaining super-giants.[76] This is not just because Russia has declined in population rank but more because its economic size has fallen from second to tenth in the world. One source, speculating broadly on global trends in the first half of the twenty-first century, notes that Russia has an unmatched treasure trove of energy resources, but its current weaknesses, including overall population decline and decline in ethnic Russian majority, might keep it on the sidelines of the great-power game.[77]

One study identified six security implications of global population change, many of which apply to Russia.[78] These include disproportionate growth in large and Muslim countries, shrinkage in population in EU and former Soviet states, differential age structures between developed and developing countries and increased migration between those groups, and the impact of AIDS. As the report points out, given these trends, leaders of affected countries, including Russia, must concentrate on mitigation measures, none of which will be easy.

Russia seems destined to fall to about fifteenth place among the world's populations by midcentury, when it will have a population just one-quarter the size of the United States. How Russia deals with this new demographic reality and how well it deals with the other elements of state power and national wealth will determine its future place among great powers. Counting Russia out as a great power just because of its current dire demographics might be a bit premature.[79]

CONCLUSION

During the 1990s, demographic issues were largely ignored by the Russian government, but in his 2006 state of the nation address, Putin identified the demographic decline as the country's largest problem. His speech addressing population policy is without parallel by a European head of state.[80] He laid out programs to lower the death rate, increase the birth rate, and more effectively manage migration. Following that speech, Putin issued a decree to adopt the "Concept on Demographic Policy of Russia until 2025."[81] The program is expected to be implemented during 2008–2010. Some of the specifics of the program remain to be spelled out, but its introduction comes at a time when Russia has the financial resources to commit. It is too early to fully measure the effectiveness of these policies but it is a positive sign that the government is taking the dire demographic situation seriously and taking concrete steps to address them.

Not surprisingly, President Dmitri Medvedev is likely to continue the demographic policy agenda laid out by Putin. In his first state of the nation address in November 2008, Medvedev reemphasized the importance of increased education, healthy lifestyles, ethnic tolerance, internal mobility, and regulation of immigration, including recruitment of those highly skilled.[82] However, there is only so much a government can do to affect fertility, mortality, and migration trends. The federal government, regional governments, business, the media, and most importantly, the population itself all must contribute, and success depends on social and economic factors outside government control. Empirical evidence has shown that there is a two-way relationship between economic growth and improved health.[83] If Russia can use its recent economic prosperity to improve its dire demographics, the rumors of its demise may indeed have been premature.

SUGGESTED READINGS

Becker, Charles M., and David Bloom, eds. *World Development*, Special Issue: The Demographic Crisis in the Former Soviet Union, 26, no. 11 (1998): 1913–2103.

Bobadilla, Jose Luis, Christine A. Costello, and Faith Mitchell, eds. *Premature Death in the New Independent States.* Washington, D.C.: National Academy Press, 1997.

Chawla, Mukesh, Gordon Bethcherman, and Arup Banerji. *From Red to Gray: The "Third Transition" of Aging Populations in Eastern Europe and the Former Soviet Union.* Washington, D.C.: World Bank, 2007.

Cornia, Giovanni Andrea, and Renato Paniccia, eds. *The Mortality Crisis in Transitional Economies.* New York: Oxford University Press, 2000.

David, Henry P., ed. *From Abortion to Contraception: A Resource to Public Policies and Reproductive Behavior in Central and Eastern Europe from 1917 to the Present.* Westport, Conn.: Greenwood, 1999.

World Bank. *Dying Too Young: Addressing Premature Mortality and Ill Health Due to Non-Communicable Diseases and Injuries in the Russian Federation.* Washington, D.C.: World Bank, 2005.

NOTES

1. "Doomsday Demographics: Russia's Population Declines Sharply as Births Drop, Nation's Health Falters," *Washington Times*, December 1, 2004, www.washington times.com.

2. Nicholas Eberstadt, "The Emptying of Russia," *Washington Post*, February 13, 2004, www.washingtonpost.com.

3. Patrick Buchanan, "The Passing Away of Mother Russia," *American Cause*, February 26, 2003, www.theamericancause.org.

4. "A Sickness of the Soul: Russian Health and Demography," *Economist*, September 9, 2006, 51–52.

5. Rosstat, www.gks.ru.

6. Michael S. Teitelbaum and Jay M. Winter, *The Fear of Population Decline* (San Diego: Academic, 1985), 10–11.

7. The total fertility rate is the number of children per woman, with 2.1 children per woman considered replacement level.

8. CIS Statistical Committee, *1989 USSR Population Census CD-ROM* (Minneapolis, Minn.: Eastview, 1996).

9. United Nations Population Division, *World Fertility Patterns 2007* (New York: United Nations, 2008).

10. Rosstat, *Demograficheskii ezhegodnik Rossii* (Moscow: Rosstat, 2007), 158.

11. A. Avdeev, "The Extent of the Fertility Decline in Russia: Is the One-Child Family Here to Stay?" paper presented at the IUSSP Seminar on International Perspectives on Low Fertility: Trends, Theories and Policies, Tokyo, March 21–23, 2001.

12. Louise Grogan, "What Caused the Post-Transition Fertility Decline in Central and Eastern Europe and the former Soviet Union?" Discussion Paper no. 2002-5, University of Guelph, September 18, 2002.

13. John Bongaarts, "A Framework for Analyzing the Proximate Determinants of Fertility," *Population and Development Review* 4, no. 1 (1978): 105–32; John Bongaarts, "The Fertility Inhibiting Effects of the Intermediate Variables," *Studies in Family Planning* 13, nos. 6/7 (1982): 179–89.

14. U.S. Bureau of the Census, "International Data Base," www.census.gov/ ipc/www/idb/; U.S. Department of Health and Human Services, *Reproductive, Maternal, and Child Health in Eastern Europe and Eurasia: A Comparative Report*, April 2003, 62.

15. Henry P. David, ed., *From Abortion to Contraception: A Resource to Public Policies and Reproductive Behavior in Central and Eastern Europe from 1917 to the Present* (Westport, Conn.: Greenwood, 1999), 232–33.

16. UNICEF Innocenti Research Centre, *TransMONEE 2008 Database*, released May 2008, www.unicef-irc.org.

17. United Nations Population Division, *World Abortion Policies 2007* (New York: United Nations, 2007).

18. Elizabeth Brainerd, *The Baby Decision amid Turmoil: Understanding the Fertility Decline in Russia of the 1990s*, National Council for Eurasian and East European Research Working Paper, February 2007.

19. Central Intelligence Agency, *Long-term Global Demographic Trends: Reshaping the Geopolitical Landscape* (Washington, D.C.: CIA, July 2001).

20. Christopher J. L. Murray and Jose Luis Bobadilla, "Epidemiological Transitions in the Formerly Socialist Economies: Divergent Patterns of Mortality and Causes of Death," in *Premature Death in the New Independent States*, ed. Jose Luis Bobadilla, Christine A. Costello, and Faith Mitchell (Washington, D.C.: National Academy Press, 1997), 184–219.

21. United Nations in Russia, *Demographic Policy in Russia: From Reflection to Action* (Moscow: United Nations, 2008), 28.

22. Giovanni Andrea Cornia and Renato Paniccia, eds., *The Mortality Crisis in Transitional Economies* (New York: Oxford University Press, 2000), 27–34.

23. Vladimir M. Shkolnikov and Alexander Nemtsov, "The Anti-Alcohol Campaign and Variations in Russian Mortality," in *Premature Death in the New Independent States*, 239–61.

24. Population Reference Bureau, *2008 World Population Data Sheet* (Washington, D.C.: PRB, 2008).

25. Vladimir M. Shkolnikov, France Mesle, and Jacques Vallin, "Recent Trends in Life Expectancy and Causes of Death in Russia, 1970–1993," in *Premature Death in the New Independent States*, 34–63.

26. Renato Paniccia, "Transition, Impoverishment, and Mortality: How Large an Impact?" in *The Mortality Crisis in Transitional Economies*, 105–26.

27. Patricio Marquez, Marc Suhrcke, Martin McKee, and Lorenzo Rocco, "Adult Health in the Russian Federation: More than Just a Health Problem," *Health Affairs* 26, no. 4 (2007): 1040–51.

28. World Health Organization, *World Health Statistics 2007*, www.who.int/tobacco/global_data/en/index.html.

29. World Health Organization, *WHO Global Status Report on Alcohol 2004*, www.who.int/globalatlas/default.asp.

30. Charles M. Becker and David Bloom, eds., *World Development*, Special Issue: The Demographic Crisis in the Former Soviet Union, 26, no. 11 (1998): 1913–2103.

31. Russian Federal Scientific-Methodological Center for the Prevention and Treatment of AIDS, http://hivrussia.org.

32. United Nations in Russia, *Demographic Policy in Russia*, 35.

33. U.S.-Russia Working Group against HIV/AIDS, *On the Frontline of an Epidemic: The Need for Urgency in Russia's Fight against AIDS* (New York: Transatlantic Partners, 2003).

34. United Nations in Russia, *Demographic Policy in Russia*, 38.

35. United Nations Population Division, *World Population Prospects: The 2004 Revision and World Urbanization Prospects: The 2003 Revision*, http://esa.un.org/unpp.

36. Elizabeth Brainerd, *Uncounted Costs of World War II: The Effects of Changing Sex Ratios on Marriage and Fertility of Russian Women*, National Council for Eurasian and East European Research Working Paper, October 2007.

37. Working ages are 16 to 59 for males and 16 to 54 for females.

38. Mukesh Chawla, Gordon Betcherman, and Arup Banerji, *From Red to Gray: The "Third Transition" of Aging Populations in Eastern Europe and the Former Soviet Union* (Washington, D.C.: World Bank, 2007), 110.

39. Kier Giles, *Where Have All the Soldiers Gone? Russia's Military Plans versus Demographic Reality*, Russia Series 06/47 Defence Academy of the United Kingdom, October 2006.

40. Yuriy Gorodnichenko and Klara Sabirianova Peter, *Returns to Schooling in Russia and Ukraine: A Semiparametric Approach to Cross-Country Comparative Analysis*, IZA Discussion Paper Series no. 1325, September 2004.

41. Mary Canning, Peter Moock, and Timothy Heleniak, *Reforming Education in the Regions of Russia*, Technical Paper Series no. 457 (Washington, D.C.: World Bank, December 1999).

42. Goskomstat SSSR, *Natsional'nyi sostav naseleniia SSSR* (Moscow: Finansy i statistika, 1991).

43. "The CIA Director on Demographics and Security," *Population and Development Review* 34, no. 3 (2008): 593–94.

44. United Nations Population Division, *Trends in Total Migrant Stock: The 2005 Revision*, http://esa.un.org/migration.

45. *1989 USSR Population Census* and Rosstat, www.gks.ru.

46. Sebastein Peyrouse, *The Russian Minority in Central Asia: Migration, Politics, and Language*, Kennan Institute Occasional Paper no. 297, 2007, 1.

47. Rosstat, *Demograficheskii ezhegodnik Rossii* (annual editions) and Rosstat, www.gks.ru.

48. Yuri Andreinko and Sergei Guriev, *Understanding Migration in Russia*, CEFIR Policy Paper no. 23, Center for Economic and Financial Research at the New Economic School, November 2005.

49. Timothy Heleniak, "Migration of the Russian Diaspora after the Breakup of the Soviet Union," *Journal of International Affairs* 57, no. 2 (2004): 99–117.

50. Ali Mansoor and Quillin Bryce., eds., *Migration and Remittances: Eastern Europe and the Former Soviet Union* (Washington, D.C.: World Bank, 2007).

51. Leonid Rybakovsky and Sergey Ryazanstev, *International Migration in the Russian Federation* (New York: UN Population Division, 2005).

52. Goskomstat, *Registration of International Migration in the Russian Federation*, Working Paper no. 2, Conference of European Statisticians, Geneva, May 21–23, 2001.

53. Natalia Voronina, "Outlook on Migration Policy Reform in Russia: Contemporary Challenges and Political Paradoxes," *Migration Perspectives Eastern Europe and Central Asia*, ed. Roger Rodriguez Rios (Vienna: International Organization for Migration, 2006), 71–90.

54. Mikhail A. Alexseev, *Fortress Russia: An Overview of the 2005 Russian Federation Survey on Immigration Attitudes and Ethnic Relation*, Working Paper no. 139, Center for Comparative Immigration Studies, University of California, San Diego, May 2006.

55. "FMS to Discuss Priorities of Migration Policy for 2008," *ITAR-TASS (Russia)*, January 31, 2008, www.itar-tass.com/eng/.

56. United Nations Population Division, *Replacement Migration: Is It a Solution to Declining and Ageing Populations?* (New York: United Nations, 2001).

57. Timothy Heleniak, "An Overview of Migration in the Post-Soviet Space," in *Migration, Homeland, and Belonging in Eurasia*, ed. Cynthia Buckley and Blair Ruble (Washington, D.C.: Woodrow Wilson Center Press; and Baltimore, Md.: Johns Hopkins University Press, 2008), 29–67.

58. Rybakovsky and Ryazanstev, *International Migration in the Russian Federation.*

59. Lowell W. Barrington, Erik S. Herron, and Brian D. Silver, "The Motherland Is Calling: Views of Homeland among Russians in the Near Abroad," *World Politics* 55, no. 2 (2003): 290–313.

60. Goskomstat Rossii, *Regiony Rossii* (Moscow: Rosstat, various years).

61. Timothy Heleniak, "Migration and Population Change in the Russian Far North during the 1990s," in *Migration in the Circumpolar North: New Concepts and Patterns*, ed. Chris Southcott and Lee Huskey (Edmonton, Alberta, Canada: Canadian Circumpolar Institute Press, University of Alberta, 2009).

62. Fiona Hill and Clifford Gaddy, *The Siberian Curse: How Communist Planners Left Russia out in the Cold* (Washington, D.C.: Brookings Institution Press, 2003).

63. Rosstat, www.gks.ru.

64. Timothy Heleniak, "The Role of Attachment to Place in Migration Decisions of the Population of the Russian North," *Polar Geography*, Special Issue: Circumpolar Migration, ed. Wayne Edwards (2009).

65. Y. Andrienko and S. Guriev, "Determinants of Interregional Labor Mobility in Russia," *Economics of Transition* 12, no. 1 (2004): 1–27.

66. Yasmann, Victor, "Russia; Health Ministry Considers Solutions to Population Decline," Radio Free Europe/Radio Liberty (RFE/RL), February 28, 2006.

67. Rosstat, *Predpolozhitel'naia chislennost' naseleniia Rossiskoi Federatsii do 2025 goda: Statisticheskii biulleten* (Moscow: Rosstat, 2005).

68. United Nations Population Division, *World Population Prospects: The 2006 Revision*, http://esa.un.org/unpp.

69. World Bank, *World Development Indicators CD-ROM 2007* (Washington, D.C.: World Bank, 2007).

70. U.S. Census Bureau, *International Data Base*, www.census.gov/ipc/www.

71. Dennis Donahue, "HIV Prevalence in the Russian Federation: Methods and Estimates," paper presented at the 2004 annual meeting of the Southern Demographic Association, Hilton Head Island, South Carolina, October 14–16, 2004.

72. Rosstat, *Demograficheskii ezhegodnik* (Moscow: Rosstat, 2005), 41; and Rosstat, www.gks.ru.

73. There are three projection scenarios done by Rosstat and the UN and one each by the World Bank and U.S. Census Bureau.

74. U.S. Census Bureau, "International Database," updated June 18, 2008, www.census.gov/ipc/www/idb.

75. Geoffrey McNicoll, "Population Weights in the International Order," *Population and Development Review* 25, no. 3 (1999): 411–42.

76. Andrei Treyvish, "A New Russian Heartland: The Demographic and Economic Dimension," *Eurasian Geography and Economics* 46, no. 2 (2005): 123–55.

77. Vaclav Smil, "The Next 50 Years: Unfolding Trends," *Population and Development Review* 31, no. 4 (2005): 605–43.

78. Jack A. Goldstone, "Flash Points and Tipping Points: Security Implications of Global Population Changes, 2005–2025," paper prepared for the Mackinder Forum, Minster Lovell, UK, March 14–15, 2006.

79. Smil, "The Next 50 Years."

80. "Vladimir Putin on Raising Russia's Birth Rate," *Population and Development Review* 32, no. 2 (2006): 385–89.

81. United Nations in Russia, *Demographic Policy in Russia: From Reflection to Action* (Moscow: United Nations, 2008).

82. Dmitri Medvedev, "Address to the Federal Assembly of the Russian Federation," November 5, 2008, www.kremlin.ru/eng/.

83. Patricio V. Marquez, *Better Outcomes through Health Reforms in the Russian Federation: The Challenges in 2008 and Beyond* (Washington, D.C.: World Bank, December 2007).

Chapter Seven

The Oligarchs and Economic Development

Peter Rutland

The age of the oligarchs as a political class came and went. Ten years ago, they seemed to have seized control of the commanding heights of Russia's economy and its political institutions. But just as quickly as they appeared, they retreated, in the face of Vladimir Putin's assault at the head of a rejuvenated Russian state. Is oligarchic rule a feasible option for Russia, or was it only a transitional phase? What is the role that the oligarchs play in Putin's Russia? Are they a boon or an obstacle to democracy?

According to Aristotle, oligarchy, which he defined as rule by the wealthy few, was the least stable and hence least desirable form of government. Oligarchs were sufficiently few in number to easily collude to promote their private interests against the public interest. This danger has animated a distinguished line of political thinkers from James Madison on. At the same time, oligarchs are too numerous, and their interests too mutually antagonistic, to be able to come to a stable consensus on public policy. Hence Aristotle argued they would soon be displaced by an autocrat, or an aristocracy—a small group that differs from an oligarchy in being based on heredity and virtue, as opposed to the haphazard accumulation of wealth that is characteristic of an oligarchy.

Aristotle's warning that oligarchy is inherently unstable seems to have been borne out by the Russian experience since 1991. The Russian oligarchs came out of existing (and rapidly expiring) Soviet era institutions—such as academic institutes, or the Komsomol (Communist Youth League). They essentially started as individuals but quickly created a network of institutions (e.g., saunas, tennis clubs, private restaurants) for the purpose of factional collusion. The oligarchs did not have the opportunity or capacity to form a core set of shared values; they did not have the experience of being raised and educated as a cohesive elite. This is a point of difference from the established oligarchies that have effectively ruled countries in Latin America, the Philippines, and Japan for decades. Thus, Russian oligarchy seems to be a political-economic model as yet unable to reproduce itself over time, a one-shot phenomenon that arose in the chaos of the Soviet collapse and that retreated as the Russian state reasserted its authority.

THE ECONOMIC BACKGROUND

The Russian economy has gone through a wrenching decade, with unpredictable developments that brought risk and opportunity in equal measure. Economic recovery was disrupted by a series of political crises: the struggle for power between President Boris Yeltsin and the parliament in 1992–1993, Yeltsin's bid for reelection in 1996, and the search for a successor in 1999. These were interspersed with economic crises: privatization scandals, bank crises, and above all the August 1998 financial crash. After 1998, the crises receded, and GDP grew about 7 percent a year during 1999–2007. But fear of a return of the earlier chaos still shapes the mind-set of many political and economic actors, to which has been added a new fear—of growing state authoritarianism. The global financial crisis that hit Russia in the summer of 2008 revived doubts about the sustainability of Russia's energy-driven economic development model.

Two positive trends nevertheless emerged during the 1990s. First, Russia became a market economy as officially recognized by the European Union (EU) in 2002, albeit one with "Russian characteristics." The centralized, command economy was dismantled. Seventy percent of economic activity now takes place in legally independent private corporations, and price controls on most goods have been abolished.[1] (The most important exception is the price that Russian consumers pay for natural gas, electricity, and housing utilities.[2]) Second, Russia has become much more integrated into the global economy than was the Soviet Union. Foreign trade went from 17 percent of GDP in 1990 to 48 percent in 2004.[3] And most of Russia's trade is with Europe, not with the former Soviet states. By 2007, the Commonwealth of Independent States (CIS) only accounted for 15 percent of Russia's exports and 23 percent of its imports.

The main question mark hanging over Russia's economic future is that of governance. In the 1990s, Russia gave birth to several dozen successful and internationally prominent business corporations. In fifteen years, Russia went from a society where entrepreneurship was a crime to one that had produced thirty-six billionaires by 2004, the third highest number in the world.[4] In a World Bank–sponsored study of industrial concentration, the country's twenty-three largest firms were estimated to account for 30 percent of Russia's gross domestic product in 2001, and those firms were effectively controlled by a mere thirty-seven individuals.[5] A 2005–2006 study of a sample 1,000 firms similarly found that 35 percent had a single majority shareholder.⁶ By international standards, this is an astonishing concentration of wealth and industrial power—all the more so given that Russia is a large country, with the world's eighth largest economy, and private ownership had been outlawed during the decades of Soviet rule. Not a single capitalist had existed legally in the country just fifteen years earlier.

Western observers were initially uncomfortable with the rise of the oligarchs, whose ascendance coincided with a wave of lawlessness, contract killings, and grotesque displays of wealth. But the oligarchs at least seemed to refute the argument that Russians were innately incapable of behaving like entrepreneurs—of taking risks and reaping the rewards. Soon, Western economists were arguing that the oligarchs were playing a necessary role in creating the Russian market economy, akin to the U.S. robber barons of the late nineteenth century.⁷ Some economists have argued that the concentration of ownership in individual hands is a rough and ready solution to the problem of enforcing property rights in absence of strong rule of law.⁸ The oligarchs pushed out communist-era bureaucrats and managers, and in the pursuit of personal gain they turned the sow's ear of Soviet enterprises into the silk purse of profit-seeking firms. Liberal reformers such as Prime Minister Yegor Gaidar were convinced that the oligarchic capitalism that they helped to construct in Russia beat the alternative—which they portrayed as a return to central planning.⁹

But to function in the textbook manner, free markets require multiple producers and free entry of new firms, plus a set of institutions conspicuously absent in Russia (rule of law, free press, banking system, regulatory agencies, etc.). No matter. The reformers assumed that oligarchic capitalism was a transitional phase that would give way to liberal capitalism after the economic system matured. Once the oligarchs had accumulated some wealth, they would have a strong personal interest in seeing the rule of law take hold, in order to protect their wealth from the next wave of oligarchs. They would not want to go through life looking over their shoulder at the next asset-stripper, driving around in columns of heavily armored vehicles, and hiding their families from kidnappers, sequestered behind high dacha walls and on foreign estates. The counterargument was that the oligarchs had a vested interest in trying to preserve the status quo of partial reform, since further liberalization would compete away their oligopolistic profits.¹⁰

However, the structure of ownership in the new Russian economy was very opaque. The security of the property rights of the new captains of Russian industry was unclear, and under President Vladimir Putin the state seemed bent on reasserting its control over Russian industry. The key turning point was the arrest on October 25, 2003, of the richest man in Russia, Mikhail Khodorkovsky, the head of Russia's largest oil company, Yukos. Khodorkovsky was subsequently sentenced to eight years in jail for tax evasion.¹¹

One could not ask for a more vivid illustration of the limits of business independence in Russia. The fact that business evolved into a narrow oligarchy made it relatively easy for the state to recapture the commanding heights of the economy under Vladimir Putin. Even as late as 2003, most observers assumed that the system of oligarchic capitalism had stabilized: few foresaw Putin's crackdown. But since then a new model of state capitalism has emerged in Russia.

THE RISE OF THE OLIGARCHS

With the collapse of the USSR in December 1991, a huge void of political and economic power opened up in the post-Soviet states. Key institutional structures such as the Communist Party and the central planning system were dismantled in Russia, and the new entities that emerged in their wake (the presidential administration, the State Committee for the Administration of State Property, regional governors) were hard-pressed to expand their effective zone of control.

In the chaos of transition, power shifted from formal political institutions to informal networks of influence among individuals who had political connections or economic resources at their disposal. While market forces penetrated large sections of economic activity, the Russian economy was only partially marketized by the liberalization reforms. A whole parallel barter economy sprang up, accounting for perhaps half of all business-to-business transactions. The interface between polity and economy was mediated by corruption and mutual favors, instead of political orders as under the old regime.

The first period of chaotic liberalization in 1992 saw the rapid emergence of a multitude of independent economic actors—from street traders, who were now allowed to buy and sell in public markets, up to factory directors, now free to manage their still-state-owned factories without supervision by central planners. They often seized the opportunity to route sales through intermediary firms that they (or their relatives) owned, enabling them to skim off the profits from the firm's operations. This process saw a leakage of power from state to nonstate actors, and from the federal center to the regions. Individual regional leaders signed bilateral "treaties" with President Boris Yeltsin on the division of responsibilities with the federal center, beginning with Tatarstan in 1994. (By 1996, forty-six of Russia's eighty-nine regions had signed such treaties.)

This early period also saw the breakdown of respect for the law and a surge of crime and corruption. Alarmingly, businesses started using criminal groups and not the courts to enforce contracts and secure their property rights.[12] This criminalization of Russian business was a highly volatile process that opened the door to a later counteroffensive by state security organs. The lack of a firm legal basis for their rapidly acquired wealth made the new business elite vulnerable to attack by the state, the guardian of legality. The rapidity and rapaciousness of their enrichment meant that they lacked a strong social basis of support, so when the state came knocking on their door, it would be with strong public approval.

The first phase of "wild privatization" was followed by a period of gradual consolidation. More powerful competitors pushed out their weaker rivals, and economic power was concentrated in the hands of a small number of individuals. These figures headed business corporations, but they had close connections to the political leadership at the national or regional level. Russia had dismantled an autocracy, but instead of rule by the many (democracy), it had arrived at rule by the few (oligarchy).

Most of these oligarchs headed private corporations formed on the basis of former state enterprises, such as regional oil companies, banks, or metallurgical plants. They typically made their first million through commodity trading, importing scarce goods or financial brokering, and then grew by acquiring state assets as they were privatized.[13] Most of the first wave of oligarchs was concentrated in the banking sector (see table 7.1). Banking was a lucrative business since the banks served as intermediaries reaping profits from Russia's booming natural resource exports, exploiting the gap between the ruble-denominated domestic economy and the dollar-denominated foreign trade. Also, banks were the main vehicle for many of the most lucrative privatizations of state-owned assets.

Pivotal in the transition to oligarchy were the loans for shares auctions in 1995–1996, when key firms such as Norilsk Nickel and the Sibneft oil company were sold off at bargain prices to politically favored businesspeople. The auctions were rigged to exclude competitive bidding and were structured in

Table 7.1.   The 1997 Oligarchs

Name	Initial Core Assets
Boris Berezovsky	ORT (TV station), Logovaz (auto dealer), Aeroflot (airline)
Vladimir Potanin	Interros (metals)
Mikhail Khodorkovsky	Rosprom (industrial holding company), Menatep (bank)
Vladimir Gusinsky	Most Bank, NTV (TV station)
Oleg Deripaska	Rusal (aluminum)
Vladimir Vinogradov	Inkombank (bank)
Mikhail Fridman	Alfa Group (bank)
Pyotr Aven	Alfa Bank (bank)
Aleksandr Smolensky	SBS-Agro (bank)
Rem Viakhirev	Gazprom (natural gas)

Note: Berezovsky's estimated net worth in 1997 was around $3 billion, Potanin's $1.5 billion, and the others around $1 billion.

the form of a loan to the state treasury against which the company's shares were pledged as collateral—to avoid giving the impression of a direct sell-off of state assets. After one year, if the loan was not repaid, the new owner could take possession of the shares. The scheme was introduced by presidential decree: there was no way that the opposition-dominated State Duma would have approved it. In return, these oligarchs helped President Boris Yeltsin win reelection in June 1996 by putting their financial and organizational resources at his disposal. Above all, it was the mobilization of their press and TV empires that pulled Yeltsin through to victory.

The oligarchic consolidation in 1994–1996 coincided with a degree of macroeconomic stabilization. Inflation came down from 1,500 percent in 1992 to 25 percent in 1996 and 12 percent in 1997. GDP even recorded a slight growth of 0.7 percent in 1997, after seven years of decline. It was at this point that the term *oligarch* entered the Russian political lexicon.[14] In spring 1997, the word was taken up by Boris Nemtsov, a deputy prime minister who was pushing for a new round of liberal reforms, along with fellow deputy premier Anatoli Chubais. Nemtsov and Chubais wanted to cut corruption and introduce more competition into the "crony capitalism" that had been forged between the newly emerged oligarchs and the weakened state.

The 1997 reform drive failed in the face of energetic opposition from regional governors and business oligarchs, who mobilized their supporters in the State Duma. Moreover, the macroeconomic stabilization proved illusory. The government was borrowing heavily to cover its budget deficit, and the Asian financial crisis in 1997 caused a slump in world oil prices that eroded Russia's account surplus. That led to a run on the ruble and the dramatic devaluation and debt default in August 1998, during which most private banks collapsed and the ruble lost 75 percent of its value.

The demise of oligarchic capitalism was due to deep contradictions in the model, and not merely contingent factors such as Yeltsin's incompetence or the August 1998 financial crash. Two contradictions stand out. First, the oligarchs were parasitic on the Russian state. They were draining it of assets and revenues to the point where the soaring budget deficit and profiteering from high-interest treasury bonds helped trigger the 1998 crash. Second, the oligarchs lacked a political strategy for legitimating their rule in the eyes of the Russian public. The cynical manipulation of public opinion through campaign shenanigans and pre-election budget spending may have secured Yeltsin's reelection in 1996, but there was no guarantee that such tactics could work in each future election. Third, the oligarchs were deeply divided among themselves. They did not trust each other, fighting bitterly, for example, over the privatization of the telecom holding company Svyazinvest in summer 1997.

They were also split over the Yeltsin succession. The oligarchs did not have an institutional procedure for resolving disputes among themselves. The only "mechanism" they had was appeal to Boris Yeltsin. Given that Yeltsin was physically incapacitated most of the time during his second term, this meant the oligarchs competed for the favor of the Kremlin courtiers (the "Family") who controlled access to the president. Yeltsin's second and final term as president was due to end in March 2000, and the oligarchic system did not have any procedure in place for picking a successor.

Thus at the end of the Yeltsin era, Russia's evolution toward what is regarded in the West as a "normal" market economy was stalled in midstream. Powerful leaders had a vested interest in preserving the status quo, and there was no significant coalition of groups with a stake in further reform. The economy had been sufficiently liberalized to enable the oligarchs to enrich themselves, but not so much as to expose them to effective competition (from foreign companies, for example). This situation was inefficient and morally indefensible, but it was unclear whether it was politically and economically stable. Could it continue indefinitely, or would it require a fresh round of market reform? In the end, Russia moved in an unexpected third direction, neither the status quo nor a resumption of reform—the return of state control.

PUTIN TAKES CONTROL

Yeltsin went through a series of prime ministers in 1998–1999, searching for a reliable successor who could maintain the political system that he had created. In August 1999, he appointed Vladimir Putin. After a wave of apartment-house bombings the next month, attributed to Chechen terrorists, Prime Minister Putin sent federal forces back into Chechnya.

The December 1999 State Duma election was seen as a sort of presidential primary: it was assumed that the leader of the winning party would be well placed for a run at the presidency. The oligarchs funded rival parties that fought a bitter and dirty media campaign. The Kremlin slapped together a pro-Putin Unity party that managed to win second place after the communists. Yeltsin then preempted the race for the presidential succession by resigning ahead of schedule on December 31, 1999, nominating Putin as acting president. Putin proceeded to sweep the March 2000 presidential election, winning in the first round with 52 percent of the vote.

Putin said that his intention was to continue market reform and not to revisit Yeltsin's privatization program. It looked as if Putin wanted to strengthen the power of the state but not break the pluralistic character of the system as a whole.[15] Adding to the sense of continuity was the fact that many key figures from Yeltsin's inner circle were kept on, such as chief of staff Aleksandr Voloshin and Prime Minister Mikhail Kasianov. It was also noteworthy that Putin retained the services of Anatoli Chubais, the former privatization chief and for many on the political left the most hated face of the Yeltsin reforms. Putin kept Chubais on as head of the electricity monopoly Unified Energy System (RAO EES) and tasked him with privatizing the firm—Russia's biggest company: a project that was to stretch over eight years.

Putin proved more independent than many observers had supposed, and he moved swiftly to distance the oligarchs from the center of political power. In the summer of 2000, Putin seized control of the two national TV stations owned by Boris Berezovsky and Vladimir Gusinsky, driving them into exile.[16] This was accomplished by sending in the tax police and threatening them with long jail terms. Most of the other oligarchs assumed that so long as they kept away from mass media (television in particular), it would be business as usual.

Still, some of the oligarchs envied the power of the president. In spring 2003, Mikhail Khodorkovsky, the founder of the Yukos oil company and the richest man in Russia, started signaling his interest in a political career. Rumors began circulating that Khodorkovsky intended to run for the presidency in 2008—if not in 2004. Yukos was active in buying the loyalty of Duma deputies, and the company did not hesitate to use its leverage to block legislation it disliked, such as higher oil excise taxes and revisions to the 1995 law on production sharing (an arrangement that allowed approved foreign companies to recoup their investments in oil and gas fields before they started paying taxes). In the December 2003 State Duma election, Khodorkovsky poured money into parties across the political spectrum. Yukos-linked analysts were floating the idea of introducing a parliamentary system of government, in which the government would be answerable to the State Duma (presumably oligarch controlled) rather than to the president.[17]

On the economic front, Khodorkovsky tried to strengthen his position by adopting international accounting standards and adding Westerners to the Yukos board, with a view to offering a large stake in the company to a Western oil major.[18] This would enable him to cash out some of his share holdings, valued at their peak at $15 billion. To increase Yukos's attractiveness, he tried to develop new export possibilities, outside the state-owned Transneft pipeline system. He pursued an agreement with China to finance a $3 billion pipeline to carry oil from Angarsk in Siberia to Daqing in China. He also mounted an aggressive international public relations campaign, funding international charities, and getting himself appointed to worthy foundation boards, such as that of the International Crisis Group. He thought that these steps would make it too risky for Putin to take him down. But his strategy backfired. The more successful he was, the greater the threat he represented to the Kremlin. In the summer of 2003, Putin gave the green light for the arrest of Khodorkovsky and half a dozen other Yukos executives and the dismemberment of Yukos.

This set the scene for a sweeping victory for the pro-Putin United Russia in the December 2003 State Duma election. United Russia won 37.6 percent of the popular vote in the party-list race that fills half the 450-seat chamber, giving them 120 seats, plus another 126 seats in single-mandate races. After the election, 60 independents who won in single-seat races joined United Russia, raising their numbers to 304—above the two-thirds majority required to change the constitution. The Yukos affair also led to the departure of the remaining key members of Yeltsin's "Family" from the Kremlin. Chief of Staff Voloshin resigned in November 2003 shortly after Khodorkovsky's arrest, and Putin fired Prime Minister Kasianov one month before the March 2004 presidential election.

The oligarchs underestimated Putin's power and his political acumen. Putin had the vast resources of the Russian state at hand, a cornucopia of sticks and carrots that soon won the loyalty of virtually all the regional bosses and business leaders. The security apparatus of the Soviet state, the renamed Federal Security Service (FSB), had shrunk in size but was still intact and eager to expand its sphere of action once its former leader became president. Putin also enjoyed huge popular legitimacy, having been directly elected in March 2000 and again in March 2004 (with over 71 percent of the vote), and maintaining approval ratings above 70 percent in the intervening period.

The new business corporations were very powerful political actors, with considerable economic resources and direct access to the political power elite. But the headlong speed of their rise meant their popular legitimacy was fragile and their base of support in society very narrow.[19] In Russia, both the state and society are suspicious of business, a value orientation that has deep roots in Russian culture. This was true in the tsarist period, in Soviet times, and in the post-Soviet era. In each period, the rationale behind the hostility shifted in a new direction, but in all three periods big business was associated with injustice and exploitation. According to a 2003 ROMIR poll, 45 percent considered the influence of big business on the economy negative and only 25 percent saw it as positive. Their influence on politics was seen as negative by 49 percent and positive by 17 percent.[20] In a FOM poll of June 2003, 71 percent agreed with the statement that you cannot earn a lot of money without breaking the law.

Oligarchs aside, public attitudes toward the market economy and business in general are quite positive. In one late 2004 survey, 65 percent of respondents below pension age expressed approval of the market economy, and only 15 percent disapproval. Among pensioners, the corresponding figures were 34 percent and 42 percent.[21] On the other hand, if asked to choose between a stronger state and developing private enterprise, the state prevailed by 82 percent to 12 percent.

The main obstacle to the spread of market competition is the delayed privatization of the electricity industry. Before privatization can succeed, the prices paid by consumers need to be raised, in order to make regional electricity companies attractive to private investors. Ever since 1991, some of the rents from energy exports have been channeled to subsidize Russian households and domestic manufacturers. The main vehicle for cross-subsidization is the maintenance of artificially low prices for domestic consumers of gas and electricity. The biggest beneficiaries have been the energy-intensive metals producers, who have enjoyed an export boom thanks to electricity prices that are one-quarter those in Europe. As of March 2008, Gazprom was only permitted to charge $60 per 1,000 cubic meters of gas to domestic industrial customers and $50 for households, while export prices had reached $370.[22] The national electricity holding company RAO EES was officially dissolved in July 2008, but the new private regional energy companies are struggling because prices are still regulated and are too low to finance investment to replace the aging capital stock.

BUSINESS STRATEGIES

In retrospect, we can see that oligarchic capitalism was highly unstable, since the economic fate of the individual oligarchs was too closely tied to the course of state policy. Who would be given the right to acquire the remaining assets of state industry as they were put up for privatization? For how long would the government retain control over the "natural monopolies" such as the railways, Gazprom, Unified Energy System, the oil pipeline operator Transneft, Gazprom, the telecom holding Rostelecom? How could the public be persuaded to bite the bullet and accept postponed but necessary reforms of the tax system, cuts in social benefits, and increases in utility prices?

Yeltsin's political economy was built around horizontal bargaining between a plurality of actors, and it did not provide a clear and decisive answer to any of these questions. Putin replaced Yeltsin's system with a centralized, authoritarian hierarchy, what came to be called the "power vertical." By 2004, it was increasingly clear that the Yeltsin regime had given way to a system of what we may as well call "state capitalism." Alexei Zudin argues that Putin set out from the very beginning with such a goal in mind: to fundamentally weaken the oligarchs and turn them into a subordinate group, an instrument of state rule.[23] Sergei Peregudov in contrast sees more of a balance, an "iron triangle" of a bureaucratic elite, the presidential apparatus and business corporations.[24] There is no doubt that the oligarchs had the ability to veto certain policy initiatives during Putin's first term, thanks to their influence in the State Duma.[25] But the Yukos affair destroyed this balance.

What, then, is the role of business in the state capitalist system which Putin has fashioned? Albert Hirschman famously analyzed the basic political options as exit, voice, and loyalty.[26] The oligarchs certainly had an exit strategy: they could always cash out and vacation on the French Riviera, or buy a British soccer team. Roman Abramovich is the poster child for the internationalization of the Russian oligarchy. He acquired a "navy" of luxury yachts, including one that cost an estimated $300 million. He spent a similar amount acquiring the Chelsea soccer club and buying up top players. But pride, greed, and patriotism prevented some of the oligarchs from exercising the exit option. "Voice," meaning organized political activity in defense of their interests, was gradually squeezed out of the range of options by Putin's systematic restoration of the "power vertical"—beginning with the TV stations, continuing with the State Duma election, and ending with the abolition of elected governors.

That leaves "loyalty" as the only available strategy. It is not only that oligarchs must now be personally loyal to the Kremlin and stay out of politics. They must conduct their business in more transparent ways, following Russian laws and paying Russian taxes. They are also expected to play an active role in helping the Kremlin to realize its political, economic, and social agenda, dipping into their coffers to subsidize Kremlin-approved social programs.[27]

The Yukos affair dramatically revealed that the tax inspectors, the courts, and the security services are all willing tools of the Kremlin. The introduction in 2000 of seven federal districts headed by presidential representatives restored the president's ability to exert direct control of the power organs in all regions of Russia. In the absence of clear property rights that can be defended in an independent court system, Russian business remains very vulnerable to state pressure.

Businesses had various strategies to insulate themselves from such uncertainties. They have actively pursued vertical integration, seeking to protect themselves by controlling the entire production cycle (e.g., metal companies buy ports to ensure the security of their exports). They tried rooting themselves into regional bastions, buying off regional administrations, if not running for governor themselves.[28] That door was slammed shut with Putin's surprise decision to abolish elections for regional leaders in September 2004, a step ostensibly taken in response to the Beslan school crisis. After 2004, future governors and republic presidents are to be nominated by the president, subject to approval by regional legislatures.

Then there is the global dimension. The Russian political economy was not a closed system. It was very open to international influences and opportunities. Both Putin and his oligarch rivals sought international support as part of their strategy to acquire and consolidate power. This made the balance of forces between Putin and the oligarchs inherently unstable and unpredictable. Not all the relevant variables and actors were within the Russian Federation. At first the internationalization of business took the form of entrepreneurial activity to take advantage of the vast gulf between Russia's domestic prices and global prices by importing manufactured goods and exporting resources. That was accompanied by exploitation of the international financial system to hide revenue from Russian tax authorities through the use of shell companies, offshore bank accounts, and transfer pricing. Some of the most detailed information about the extent of these practices came out in the Yukos trial.[29] Even state-controlled institutions such as the Central Bank and Gazprom were heavily engaged in these activities in the 1990s.

Some of them also considered an exit-and-return strategy, thinking that the West could offer both political legitimation and practical financial support. This strategy was exemplified by Berezovsky and subsequently Khodorkovsky. However, the internationalization strategy failed. International condemnation was not strong enough to deter Putin from arresting Khodorkovsky and dismantling Yukos. An appeal to a Houston court against the bankruptcy of Yukos by its holding company, Menatep, did cause some Western banks to pull back from financing the purchase of its subsidiary, Yuganskneftegaz, in December 2004. But the Kremlin brazenly pushed ahead with the auction, using a phony subsidiary to transfer the assets to state-owned Rosneft, which was in the process of merging with Gazprom.

Some commentators thought the transition from Putin to Dmitri Medvedev as president in 2008 would lead to the restoration of a more open and pluralist system. Medvedev never served in the ranks of the Federal Security Service, and he had espoused a strong commitment to engagement with the West. But the impact of the global financial crisis that erupted in the summer of 2008 made that look increasingly unlikely.

RUSSIA'S NEW CAPITALIST ELITE

Even though Putin beat back the political challenge of the rising capitalists, the oligarchs as a class have not disappeared. On the contrary, under Putin they increased in number and saw their wealth multiply. Cases like Khodorkovsky and Berezovsky were exceptions and did not presage the destruction of the capitalist class. They signaled the new rules of the political game, and capitalists who followed those rules were allowed to hold onto their businesses. Moreover, the political stability and economic growth that Russia experienced during Putin's presidency enabled them to increase their wealth many times over. The oligarchs benefited from the sustained boom in global oil and metals prices, and from Russia's surging economy and soaring stock market. An important element was global integration—roughly half of the money in the Russian stock market came from foreign investors, and Russian firms in turn were listing their shares on Western stock markets and launching IPOs (initial public offerings) of their shares abroad. For example, in July 2006, Rosneft sold off 15 percent of its stock in an IPO on the London stock exchange, raising $11 billion. In 2007, foreigners bought $26.6 billion of assets inside Russia, while Russian firms spent almost as much—$23.3 billion—in foreign acquisitions.[30] Stock market capitalization rose to 44 percent of GDP by 2005, while the RTS index went from 300 in 2000 to 2,360 in December 2007.[31] By 2007, the market capitalization of the 200 biggest Russian firms was in excess if $1 trillion (one-third of which was Gazprom).

Forbes magazine reported there were thirty-three individuals in Russia in 2006 with personal assets above $1 billion, the third highest number of billionaires in the world. Their ranks had risen to eighty-seven by 2008, putting Russia in second place after the United States[32] (see table 7.2). *Forbes* estimates their combined assets doubled from $90 billion in 2005 to $172 billion in 2006, and more than doubled again to $455 billion by spring of 2008 (though the subsequent global crash wiped out at least half their wealth). Only a dozen or so of the oligarchs on the *Forbes* 2007 list are based primarily in the oil and gas industry. Banking is the largest single source of wealth (much of that coming from the recycling of petrodollars). But there are also several dozen metals-based billionaires, and a half-dozen coal tycoons. There are even oligarchs with fortunes based in humble commodities such as cement or vodka. A new cluster of magnates whose wealth was generated in retailing and real estate has appeared in the last few years.

This all testifies to some degree of "spreading around" of wealth from the oil and gas sector (if not exactly "trickling down" to the mass of society). The sectoral and regional dispersion of the new capitalist elite suggests that it might not be so easy for Russia's hypercentralized state and personalized decision-making process to monitor and control the activities of these billionaires.

Of the original ten on the 1997 list, by 2007 one was in jail (Khodorkovsky), two were in exile (Berezovsky and Gusinsky), three had dropped out of the billionaire league (Smolensky, Vinogradov, and Viakhirev), and only four were still on the *Forbes* list—Potanin, Deripaska, Fridman, and Aven. (The exiled Berezovsky was still on the list, at no. 897, with an estimated net worth of $1.3 billion.)

LOBBYING PRACTICES

Russia has evolved into a vibrant, capitalist economy with dozens of independent private owners commanding internationally influential businesses. This is about as far removed from the Soviet centrally planned economy as one can imagine. And yet this pluralistic and dynamic economy exists alongside—and within—a political framework that became increasingly

Table 7.2. Russian Oligarchs in Top 300 World Ranking, 2007 (listed according to 2007 world ranking)

Name	World Ranking in 2007	World Ranking in 2005	Estimated Net Worth in 2005 ($ billion)	Estimated Net Worth in 2007 ($ billion)
Oleg Deripaska	9	84	5.5	28.0
Roman Abramovich	15	21	13.3	23.5
Alexei Mordashov	18	107	4.8	21.2
Mikhail Fridman	20	60	7.0	20.8
Vladimir Lisin	21	60	7.0	20.3
Mikhail Prokhorov	24	117	4.4	19.5
Vladimir Potanin	25	117	4.4	19.3
Suleiman Kerimov	36	—	—	17.5
German Khan	54	306	2.1	13.9
Vagit Alekperov	56	122	4.3	13.0
Dmitri Rybolovlev	59	—	—	12.8
Iskander Makhmudov	63	413	1.6	11.9
Aleksandr Abramov	65	272	2.3	11.5
Viktor Vekselberg	67	94	5.0	11.2
Alexei Kuzmichev	72	413	1.6	10.8
Viktor Rashnikov	73	151	3.6	10.4
Vladimir Yevtushenkov	77	258	2.4	10.0
Igor Zyuzin	77	437	1.5	10.0
Alisher Usmanov	94	366	1.8	9.3
Nikolai Tsvetkov	113	306	2.1	8.0
Leonid Fedun	149	321	2.0	6.4
Boris Ivanishvili	149	228	2.6	6.4
Sergei Popov	149	548	1.2	6.4
Andrei Melnichenko	158	548	1.2	6.2
Kirill Pisarev	160	—	—	6.1
Yuri Zhukov	160	—	—	6.1
Dmitri Pumpyansky	164	—	—	6.0
Pyotr Aven	178	—	—	5.5
Aleksandr Frolov	178	—	—	5.5
Leonid Mikhelson	214	—	—	4.7
Elena Baturina	253	507	1.3	4.2
Vasili Anisimov	260	—	—	4.0
Mikhail Balakin	260	—	—	4.0
Andrei Molchanov	260	—	—	4.0
Gleb Fetisov	277	—	—	3.9

Source: "The World's Billionaires," *Forbes*, May 3, 2008, www.forbes.com.
Note: All those listed above are Russian citizens.

closed and authoritarian in the 2000s. On one hand, post-Soviet Russia has a large number of social, economic, and political actors (companies, labor unions, social organizations, etc.) that exist outside the state apparatus—both in law and in reality. On the other hand, the rule of law is exceptionally weak, and the state is able to exert strong influence over the conduct of most social actors.

Putin made some efforts to institutionalize business-state relations, but the context became one of control rather than dialog. He instituted regular face-to-face meetings between the president and leading business executives, about twice a year. On July 28, 2000, Putin met with twenty-one leading businesspeople in the Kremlin, mostly from energy companies.[33] In contrast to previous meetings between Yeltsin and business leaders, this time it seemed to be the president laying down terms to the oligarchs, rather than the other way around. Putin cautioned the oligarchs to stay out of politics and pledged to maintain "equidistance" from them as president, not favoring one over the other.[34] Subsequent meetings were usually low-key affairs discussing issues like trade policy and customs reform, and even these modest gatherings ground to a halt in the wake of the Yukos affair. Business leaders were fearful that Putin would give in to pressure from the nationalists in the Duma and the security bloc (*siloviki*) in his own administration and would embark on wholesale renationalization of the industries privatized in the 1990s.

In November 2000, Putin selected the Russian Union of Industrialists and Entrepreneurs (RSPP) as the designated interlocutor with the business community. Putin issued a "royal command" for all Russian business leaders to unite in the RSPP and to submit all complaints via this body, collectively, after working out a common opinion.[35] The RSPP was a rather staid, decade-old organization representing traditional state-owned factories, but in 2001 it found itself taken over by the brash new oligarchs. However, the reformed RSPP was still deeply split between neoliberals and neostatists, which inhibited its ability to give clear advice to government development plans.

The Kremlin, deciding to spread its bets, lest the RSPP become too independent minded, encouraged the formation of alternative groups such as Delovaia Rossiia and the United Entrepreneurs' Organizations of Russia (OPORA), which was supposed to reach out to small and medium enterprises. In December 2001, former prime minister and Putin supporter Evgeni Primakov was appointed head of the Chamber of Commerce and Industry (TPP).[36]

Most business lobbying under Putin, as under Yeltsin, took the form of direct approaches to government officials by business groups, either individually or by industrial sector. They lobby for tax breaks, protective tariffs, and government contracts. Their efforts ebb and flow depending on national and international trading conditions. For example, the steel industry, dominated by the Big Four companies (Novolipetsk, Severstal, Magnitka, and Evrazholding), was lobbying for state protection in 2001, but by 2004 they were born-again free traders.[37]

The legislative branch attracted a lot of attention from businesspeople in the late 1990s. In the elections of 1995 and especially in 1999, many businesspeople spent hefty sums to try to win a seat in the Duma. Their motives were often more individual than political. A Duma deputy is immune from prosecution unless the body votes to strip him or her of this privilege. Also a Duma seat would bring contacts useful for spreading their business beyond their home region. Business-connected deputies were so influential in the Duma, and even more so in the Federation Council (where they held more than half the seats), they were effectively substituting themselves for the role conventionally played by political parties. Leading corporations like Yukos and Gazprom were the most politically active, with Gazprom supporting an estimated 130 candidates in the 1999 elections.[38] In the 2003 election, roughly 20 percent of the candidates were directly linked to business corporations, even including the communist nominees (24 percent of whose candidates were thus identified).[39] These business-friendly representatives served their paymasters well, blocking new legislation on everything from the closure of tax loopholes to new production-sharing legislation that would allow in more foreign investors.

THE RISE OF STATE CORPORATISM

It is important to remember that not all Russian industry is privately owned. Alongside the private oligarchs there are also what could be called "state oligarchs," individuals who are government officials delegated to manage or supervise state-owned companies. After taking office, Putin moved to ensure that the leading state corporations were headed by people loyal to him. In May 2001, he ousted the long-standing Gazprom chief, Rem Viakhirev, and replaced him with Alexei Miller, a young and trusted economist from Putin's hometown of St. Petersburg. Gazprom's exports ($15 billion in 2001, rising to double that by the end of the decade) make it Russia's largest single cash earner. Later in 2001, Putin removed the head of Russian Railways, Nikolai Aksënenko, who was dogged with accusations of corruption. He also removed Viktor Gerashchenko, head of the Central Bank, in March 2002 and replaced him with Sergei Ignatiev, who was serving as deputy finance minister.

Even before the Yukos affair of 2003, the state still held a 100 percent stake in some 100 companies, including the oil company Rosneft, the oil pipeline monopoly Transneft, the aircraft maker Sukhoi, and the Russian Railways Corporation. It was holding shares in some 4,000 other companies, including a majority stake in the savings bank Sberbank (62 percent), Aeroflot (51 percent), the electricity giant Unified Energy Systems (51 percent), and the natural gas monopoly Gazprom (38 percent).[40] In 2004, Putin launched a campaign to bring more companies back under state control—beginning with the assets of the bankrupted Yukos corporation.

In the wake of the breakup of Yukos, the share of oil output produced by majority state-owned companies rose, from 10 percent in 2000 to 42 percent in 2008.[41] The overall state share in the economy rose from 30 percent to 35 percent.[42] The main Yukos production unit, Yuganskneftegaz, was sold to state-owned Rosneft for $9.35 billion in December 2004. Its other two main subsidiaries, Samaraneftegaz and Tomskneft, were sold to Rosneft by auction in May 2007 for $13.2 billion. A plan for Gazprom to absorb Rosneft was derailed after months of backroom maneuvering, but the government went ahead with a complex plan to buy 10.7 percent of Gazprom shares in order to raise the state holding to 51 percent, using a loan to be paid off with a public offering of $7.5 billion of Rosneft stock. Gazprom was compensated for its failure to take over Rosneft by being allowed to buy independent gas producer Nortgaz and Roman Abramovich's Sibneft, the fifth largest oil company, in November 2005. Gazprom paid $13 billion for 73 percent of Sibneft shares, close to a market price.[43]

This growing state-controlled sector was acquired and managed through somewhat unorthodox methods. The state was just as complicit as the oligarchs in using shell companies, offshore banking, and other nefarious maneuverings to conceal its economic activity from outside observers. This tradition extends back to the 1990s and includes a broad spectrum of government and para-statal agencies, from the Orthodox Church to the Central Bank. But it became even more entrenched under Putin. The initial sale of Yukos assets, for example, was laundered through a false intermediary company, Baikal trading. One-third of Russian oil is sold through a Swiss-based intermediary, Gunvor (whose principal owner, Gennadi Timchenko, is no. 462 on the *Forbes* list).[44] Russia's gas sales to Ukraine have been channeled through a succession of intermediary companies (first Itera and then RosUkrEnergo), registered through a shadowy network of internationally registered companies whose beneficiary owners are unclear.[45] There was also consolidation in the engineering sector—the three state-owned firms RAO EES, Gazprom, and Rosoboroneksport (the arms exporter) bought the engineering firms Silovye mashiny and OMZ and auto producer Avtovaz, respectively. The state's total shareholding portfolio is estimated to have had a market value of $469 billion in 2007, equal to 40 percent of the capitalization of Russia's stock market.[46]

Government oversight of the companies is achieved through the placement of members of the executive branch on corporate boards, in some cases as the chair. Many of these board members are drawn from Putin's own retinue. For example, in July 2004, Putin's deputy chief of staff, Igor Sechin, replaced Economic Development and Trade Minister German Gref as chair of Rosneft. Presidential aide Viktor Ivanov chairs Aeroflot and the Almaz-Antei arms firm; presidential aide Igor Shuvalov chairs Sovkomflot; First Deputy Prime Minister Sergei Ivanov heads the United Aircraft Building Corporation. Apart from Viktor Ivanov, former KGB men placed on boards included Nikolai Tokarev (Zarubezneft), Sergei Chemezov (Rosoboroneks-port), and Andrei Belyaninov (Federal Arms Procurement Service). Sergei Guriev's 2007 survey found that 29 percent of the firms in their sample had a government representative on their board.[47] One anonymous banker told a journalist, "All big companies have to put people from the security services on the board of directors."[48] Even Arkadi Dvorkovich, the head of the presidential analytical directorate, complained that the new state corporations are exempt from basic audit requirements.[49] Putin assured leaders of the Chamber of Trade and Industry, "We don't want to create state capitalism," but his actions don't correspond to this sentiment.[50]

This all means that many Russian business corporations occupy a gray area—they are not fully independent of the state but are not fully part of it either. Decision making is opaque and hidden from public view, brokered in face-to-face meetings between the leaders of state corporations and top government officials. These companies are run on a commercial basis, reporting profits and losses and paying dividends to shareholders. Many of them have adopted international accounting standards in order to attract foreign investors, and to float their own shares abroad. But they also are expected to obey state mandates (conveyed through backroom communications), which means that they are not profit-maximizers like most other international corporations.

SMALL BUSINESSES

The oligarchs controlled a large chunk of the Russian economy, but not all of it. At the other end of the scale, small businesses have been mostly shut out from the political battle of the giants—and from economic policy making. In 2004, there were 4.7 million sole proprietors and 952,000 small companies in Russia (defined as those with turnover less than 15 million rubles or $550,000 a year and fewer than 100 workers). The number of enterprises had not increased over the previous decade—testimony to the crushing pressure on entrepreneurs from state bureaucrats on one side and mafia protection rackets on the other. Small businesses accounted for 17 percent of GDP: less than half the proportion in comparable economies (and well below the 60 percent level in the United States).[51]

President Vladimir Putin oversaw the introduction of new laws on inspection, licensing, and registration in 2001–2002, which eased the bureaucratic burden on small firms, according to surveys by the Center for Economic and Financial Research. The reforms cut the wait time and reduced the list of business activities that required licenses from 250 to 103.[52] Still, the Transparency International index of corruption perceptions gave Russia the same dismal score (2.3 on a 10-point scale) in 2007 that it earned in 1997.[53]

The most radical measure pushed through by Economy Minister German Gref was a reform of the tax system, under which a progressive income tax of 12 to 30 percent was replaced with a flat tax of 13 percent in 2001. The payroll tax was cut from 40 percent to 26 percent, and corporate profit tax was raised to 35 percent but later cut to 24 percent. The income tax cut was followed the next year by a 25 percent increase in tax revenue, probably due to the reporting of previously concealed income rather than to any incentive effect.[54]

One example of the ineptness of government policy in this area is the fate of the Federal Fund for Support of Small Business (FFPMP), whose closure was announced on March 4, 2005. The FFPMP was created in 1995 with a R25 billion ($1 billion) budget to invest in small business promotion. It set up a network of regional offices and got additional funding, such as a $150 million loan from Dresdner Bank in 1997. However, it was an ineffective bureaucracy that was unable to reach small businesses. An additional complication was that it was competing with a $300 million fund of small business lending set up by the European Bank for Reconstruction and Development. A 2003 survey by the Ministry of Economic Development and Trade found that only 5 percent of entrepreneurs had come across the fund. The Federal Anti-Monopoly Service fought to protect the agency, which was under its jurisdiction, but after a two-year struggle, the FFPMP was shut down.[55]

CONCLUSION

Western perceptions of Russia are now entering their third paradigm shift. The first shift, which took place in 1992, was the conviction that Russia had shed its communist legacy and was building a normal, market economy.[56] That paradigm collapsed with the August 1998 crash, although it still has some adherents. The second shift was the appearance of Vladimir Putin, who brought stability and order to Russian politics while also pursuing a policy of alliance with the West and adherence to a market economy. According to this paradigm, while Putin pursued tough, Machiavellian policies toward Chechen separatists, regional leaders, and his political opponents, he would press ahead with market reforms in order to turn Russia into a modern, efficient economy—the only viable basis for a leading state power in the twenty-first century.

Even this "market autocrat" paradigm recognized that Putin's split personality was reflected in a division within his administration between the Petersburg liberals and the sinister *siloviki*. But it was also widely assumed that Putin was interested in keeping a balance between the two factions, and that he had the political resources and acumen to do so. With regard to the oligarchs, Putin wanted to lay down new rules for the game, quite different from those which prevailed during the Yeltsin era. The oligarchs would have to keep out of politics, in return for which Putin would allow them to keep their business empires and would even adhere to a policy of "equidistance," not favoring one oligarch over another.

However, the Yukos affair—the arrest of Mikhail Khodorkovsky in October 2003 and the forced sale of the company's main asset, Yuganskneftegaz, in December 2004—represented the third shift and raised profound doubts about the viability of the "market autocrat" paradigm. Some suggest that Putin never intended to coexist with the oligarchs, that he was always bent on establishing a vertical hierarchy of power, centered in the Kremlin. First, Putin drove the oligarchs out of the media in the summer of 2000. Then he used the presidential representatives to curb the powers of regional bosses. Finally in 2003, he pushed the oligarchs out of the State Duma by crushing the liberal parties that they financed and which were the main conduit for their lobbying.

Others argue that Yukos is an exceptional case, that Putin was merely creating a stable political environment within which market capitalism can flourish. Putin has no inclination to reverse the privatizations of the 1990s, no desire to "kill the goose that lays the golden eggs." He seems quite happy to work with oligarchs such as Vladimir Potanin, Roman Abramovich, Mikhail Fridman, and Anatoli Chubais. So once the Khodorkovsky case was over, for most of the oligarchs it was business as usual. Generally speaking, where you stand on this issue depends on where you sit. Human rights activists belong to the first camp. Most Western bankers, frustrated at being shut out from the Russian market, and experts of the international financial institutions, belong to the second.

Dmitri Medvedev thus enters the political scene at an interesting juncture in Russia's economic development. In his early months, he spoke of the need to respect the rule of law, to crack down on rampant corruption, and to end what he called "legal nihilism." At the same time, Medvedev entered office as "Putin's man" and did not have his own independent base of power; he was dependent on Putin's circle. The open question is to what extent he will distance himself from trends established during the preceding eight years. Going forward, only time will tell whether the Yukos case was an exception or part of a larger trend in state-business relations, and whether the "market autocrat" paradigm remains intact or retreats to the dustbin of history, replaced by a different paradigm.

SUGGESTED READINGS

Aslund, Anders. *Russia's Capitalist Revolution*. Washington, D.C.: Petersen Institute, 2007.

————. *How Capitalism Was Built: The Transformation of Central and Eastern Europe, Russia, and Central Asia*. Cambridge: Cambridge University Press, 2007.

Freeland, Chrystia. *Sale of the Century: Russia's Wild Ride from Communism to Capitalism*. New York: Crown Business, 2000.

Goldman, Marshall I. *The Piratization of Russia: Russian Reform Goes Awry*. London: Routledge, 2003.

Gustafson, Thane. *Capitalism Russian-Style*. Cambridge: Cambridge University Press, 1999.

Hoffman, David. *The Oligarchs: Wealth and Power in the New Russia*. New York: Public Affairs, 2003.

Klebnikov, Paul. *Godfather of the Kremlin: Boris Berezovsky and the Looting of Russia*. New York: Harcourt, 2000.

Nemtsov, Boris, and Vladimir Milov. *Putin: The Results*, http://russophobe .blogspot.com/2008/03/boris-nemtsovs-white-paper-in-full.html.

Sim, Li-Chen. *The Rise and Fall of Privatization in the Russian Oil Industry*. New York: Palgrave Macmillan, 2008.

NOTES

1. Anders Aslund, *Russia's Capitalist Revolution* (Washington, D.C.: Petersen Institute, 2007).

2. Prices were not entirely deregulated outside the energy sector. In the fall of 2007, the Ministry of Agriculture imposed "voluntary" restrictions on wholesale food prices for some basic products (e.g., bread and some dairy products). These restrictions ended in winter 2008. Also, individual regional and city governments imposed retail price controls in 2007 and into 2008 in response to the extreme increase in commodity prices worldwide, which affected Russian commodity prices and consumer prices.

3. World Bank, *From Transition to Development* (April 2004), www.worldbank .org.ru. The 48 percent share in part reflects the undervalued exchange rate. The World Bank's purchasing power estimate for 2002 boosted Russian GNI from $306 billion to $1,165 billion. This would accordingly reduce the share of trade in GDP.

4. "Rising Tide," *Forbes*, March 15, 2004. The magazine counted zero Russian billionaires in 2000, and 17 in 2003, based on an estimate of their assets.

5. The study was conducted in 2003 and was looking at company structure as of 2001. Sergei Guriev and Andrei Rachinsky, "Oligarchs: The Past or the Future of Russian Capitalism?" Center for Economic and Financial Research (CEFIR), June 15, 2001. www.cefir.org/papers.

6. Sergei Guriev et al., "Corporate Governance Practices and Prospects in Transition Countries," CEFIR, June 28, 2007. www.cefir.ru/papers.

7. Andrei Shleifer and Daniel Treisman, *Without a Map: Political Tactics and Economic Reform in Russia* (Cambridge, Mass.: MIT Press, 2001).

8. Olga Lazareva et al., "A Survey of Corporate Governance in Russia," CEFIR, Working Paper no. 103, June 2007, 13.

9. Yegor Gaidar, *Collapse of an Empire: Lessons for Modern Russia* (Washington, D.C.: Brookings Institution, 2007).

10. Joel Hellman, "Winners Take All: The Politics of Partial Reform in Postcommunist Transitions," *World Politics* 50 (January 1998): 203–34.

11. Natalya Byanova and Andrei Litvinov, "Russian Pogrom against the Oligarchs," *Gazeta*, December 24, 2003.

12. Federico Varese, *The Russian Mafia* (New York: Oxford University Press, 2002).

13. See Rose Brady, *Kapitalizm: Russia's Struggle to Free Its Economy* (New Haven, Conn.: Yale University Press, 1999); Chrystia Freeland, *Sale of the Century: Russia's Wild Ride from Communism to Capitalism* (New York: Crown Business, 2000); Paul Klebnikov, *Godfather of the Kremlin: Boris Berezovsky and the Looting of Russia* (New York: Harcourt, 2000); Li-Chen Sim, *The Rise and Fall of Privatization in the Russian Oil Industry* (London: Palgrave Macmillan, 2008).

14. The word *oligarch* was first used by Aleksandr Privalov of *Ekspert* magazine, which started a regular poll of elites, publishing rankings of those seen as the most influential political and business figures. Olga Romanova, "Novosti," *Vedomosti*, January 29, 2002.

15. Natalya Astrakhanova, "Natural Clan Selection," *Ekspert*, December 2001.

16. Christian Caryl, "Twilight of the Oligarchs," *Newsweek International*, February 5, 2001.

17. "Oligarkhi-zagovorshchiki," *Stolichnaia vechenyaia gazeta*, May 29, 2003; Sovet po natsional'noi strategii, "V Rossii gotovitsia oligarkhicheskii perevorot," www.utro.ru, May 26, 2003.

18. Lyudmila Romanova, "O strategii Khodorkovskogo," *Mirovaia energeticheskaia politika*, May 31, 2003, 18–21. Exxon was assumed to be a likely candidate.

19. Sergei Peregudov, "Korporativnyi capital i instituty vlasti," *Polis*, no. 5, 2002; Sergei Peregudov, *Korporatsiia, obshchestvo, gosudarstvo* (Moscow: Nauka, 2003).

20. N. I. Gorin et al., "Obshchestvo, biznes, vlast,'" *Obshchestvo i ekonomika*, December 2003, 36–63. The only "positive" element in these polls is that respondents are just as suspicious of state officials as they are of businesspeople.

21. Aleksandr Kolesnichenko, "No Aversion to Private Enterprise," *Novye Izvestiia*, March 4, 2005. Survey of 15,000, November–December 2004, by Romir and the Social Projects Institute.

22. Putin meeting with Gazprom board chair, Aleksei Miller, March 14, 2008, www.kremlin.ru; http://eng.gazpromquestions.ru/index.php?id=5.

23. Aleksei Zudin, "Neokorporatizm v Rossii?" *Pro et Contra* 6, no. 4 (2001).

24. Peregudov, "Korporativnyi capital i instituty vlasti."

25. Roland Nash, "Who Needs Politics Anyway?" *Prime Tass*, December 17, 2003.

26. Albert Hirschman, *Exit, Voice and Loyalty: Responses to Decline in Firms, Organizations, and States* (Cambridge, Mass.: Harvard University Press, 1970).

27. Interview with Economic Development and Trade Minister German Gref by Vera Sitnina, *Vremia novostei*, December 22, 2003.

28. Natalya Zubarevich, "Prishel, uvidel, pobedil? Krupnyi biznes i regional'naia vlast," *Pro et Contra* 7, no. 1 (2002).

29. A Paris-based former Yukos associate, Elena Collongues-Popova, revealed details of some of the myriad offshore companies through which Yukos had allegedly evaded taxes. Jeanne Whalen, "A Jilted Banker's View of Khodorkovsky's Empire," *Wall Street Journal*, January 2, 2004.

30. *Vedomosti*, March 13, 2008.

31. Lazareva, "A Survey of Corporate Governance in Russia."

32. There are 1,125 billionaires on the list, including 439 Americans, 87 Russians, and 59 Germans.

33. Inessa Slavutinskaya, "Liberalissimo," *Profil*, August 7, 2000.

34. Boris Vishnevsky et al., "Equidistance in Different Directions," *Obshchaia gazeta*, June 7–13, 2001.

35. Aleksei Bogaturov, "The Kasyanov Cabinet Is Finishing Its Game," *Rodnaia gazeta*, June 27, 2003; Aleksei Yefimov, "The Oligarchs Come Crawling on Their Knees," *Nezavisimaia gazeta*, October 23, 2003.

36. *Izvestiia*, December 11, 2001.

37. Dmitrii Butrin, "Gosplan ekonomicheskogo rosta," Gazeta.ru, April 26, 2004.

38. Sergei Kolmakov, "The Role of Financial-Industrial Groups in Russian Political Parties," *Russia Watch*, no. 9 (January 2003).

39. Francesca Mereu, "Business Will Have Big Voice in Duma," *Moscow Times*, November 13, 2003.

40. Natalya Alyakrinskaya and Dmitry Dokuchev, "State = Board of Directors," *Moscow Times*, June 9, 2004.

41. Miriam Elder, "How the State Got a Grip on Energy," *Moscow Times*, March 14, 2008.

42. Neil Buckley and Arkady Ostrovsky, "Back in Business: How Putin's Allies Are Turning Russia into a Corporate State," *Financial Times*, June 19, 2006.

43. By 2004, the largest companies by share of reserves were: Lukoil 23 percent, Rosneft (including Yuganskneftegaz) 14 percent, TNK-BP 12 percent, Yukos 11 percent, Surgut 9 percent, Gazprom 9 percent, Tatneft 8 percent and Bashneft 3 percent. Energy Information Administration, *Country Analysis Brief-Russia* (Washington, D.C., U.S. Department of Energy, 2006), www.eia.doe.gov/emeu/cabs/Russia/Oil_exports.html.

44. Boris Nemtsov and Vladimir Milov, *Putin: Itogi* (February 7, 2008), 14. Available at http://grani.ru/Politics/m.133236.html#9, and in English at http://russophobe.blogspot.com/2008/03/boris-nemtsovs-white-paper-in-full.html.

45. Global Witness, *It's a Gas: Funny Business in the Turkmen-Ukraine Gas Trade* (London: Global Witness, July 25, 2006).

46. *Vedomosti*, February 6, 2008.

47. Guriev, "Corporate Governance Practices and Prospects in Transition Countries."

48. Francisca Mereu, "Putin Made Good on Promise to FSB," *Moscow Times*, February 8, 2008.

49. E. Belyakov, "Exhausted by State Corporations," *Gazeta*, October 4, 2007.

50. Cited in American Free Press (AFP), December 11, 2007.

51. A. Reut, "We're Stuck between Socialism and Capitalism," *Izvestiia*, July 12, 2007.

52. Yevgenny Yakovlev and Yekaterina Zhuravskaya, "Deregulation of Business," CEFIR Working Paper no. 97, December 2007. "Monitoring of Administrative Barriers to Small Business Development in Russia," December 21, 2004, www.cefir .org.

53. That placed Russia 121 out of 163 countries in 2007, an improvement over 49 out of 52 in 1997. www.transparency.org/policy_research/surveys_indices/cpi/ 2007.

54. M. Keen, Y. Kim, and R. Varsano, "The 'Flat Taxes': Principles and Evidence," IMF Working Paper no. 218, September 2006.

55. Dmitrii Buttrin, "Dirizhiskskaia Panama," Gazeta.ru, March 5 2005.

56. For an elaboration on the "normal country" argument, see Andrei Shleifer, *A Normal Country: Russia after Communism* (Cambridge, Mass.: Harvard University Press, 2005).

Chapter Eight

Crime, Organized Crime, and Corruption

Louise Shelley

Almost two decades after the collapse of the Soviet Union, organized crime and corruption remain intractable problems for the Russian state. Violent crimes rates are high, especially for homicide. Organized crime is no longer as visibly violent, and gang wars are no longer fought for the control of the aluminum industry, as was the case in the 1990s. However, the extent of the crime problem has not diminished and its form has merely transformed over time. President Dmitri Medvedev in mid-2008 launched a new anticorruption campaign, as all previous campaigns proved ineffective and the high levels of corruption have been undermining the state. Yet no one has much optimism that this campaign will prove any more effective than the previous ones.[1] Moreover, the specialized police units to combat organized crime were abolished in September 2008 without any alternative enforcement strategy proffered to address this persistent problem.[2]

Russia's crime problems are not just national; they are international. Russian criminals were among the first to take full advantage of globalization. Russian criminals used their criminalized banks to move their money offshore to safe havens and to finance criminal activity outside Russia. Whereas their activities were once focused primarily on the acquisition of key sectors of the Russian economy, more recently they have become greater participants in the international drug trade. This complements their international role in the trade of women, arms, and endangered species. Moreover, the technical capacity of the criminals has pushed them to the forefront of computer crime, with major involvement in the production of child pornography marketed through the Internet, "phishing," and even wholesale coordinated attacks on the Internet and websites of countries such as Estonia and Georgia.

In Russia, there is a unique integration of the licit and illicit economies. Key sectors of the Russian economy are controlled by oligarchs with criminal pasts or close ties to organized crime. But the parallels once drawn between the oligarchs and robber barons have proven invalid. Robber barons used corruption and coercion to eliminate competition and to intimidate laborers. In Russia, the order has been reversed. Criminality was crucial to the acquisition of key sectors of the energy sector, aluminum, and natural resources. Then violence was used to eliminate competitors.

Russia's licit and illicit economies both operate on a natural resource model. This is not surprising, as illicit business is shaped by the same cultural and historical factors that shape the legitimate economy. The illicit economy merely mirrors the patterns of the legitimate one. Russia was never a society of traders. Before the revolution, Russian trade was dominated by non-Russians, including Armenians, Greeks, Germans, and others who lived in distinct districts of Moscow. Russians did not trade. Instead they sold off the natural resources of fur, timber, and the mineral wealth of their vast empire. With the reintroduction of capitalism, old patterns of business quickly reemerged. Oil sales represent one-third of the national economy, with little thought of diversification. Moreover, little attention is paid to the economic future of Russia when this precious resource is dissipated or when prices drop. The trafficking of women operates on the natural resource model. Russian criminals sell off women like a raw commodity. Women are sold to other crime groups who exploit them in the destination countries, maximizing profits. The Russian state has shown little will to protect its citizens even though Russia faces a severe demographic crisis, and the export and sale of its women of childbearing age threatens the very survival of the nation. The natural resource model of both licit and illicit trade is extremely harmful to the long-term health of the Russian economy and the Russian state.

This chapter is based on a wide variety of sources, including the analyses that have been carried out in Russia by researchers affiliated with TraCCC (Terrorism, Transnational Crime, and Corruption Center) centers in Russia. Over the past decade, these centers have existed in all major regions of Russia. At first, the centers concentrated on the largest cities—Moscow, St. Petersburg, and Ekaterinburg. But more recently, research has been carried out in smaller cities such as Saratov on the Volga, Chelyabinsk near the Kazakh border, and Vladivostok, a crime center of North Asia.[3] Research has also been carried out in Siberia and many other regions that face serious and distinctive crime problems. This has permitted much serious analysis of regional differences in crime. Much insight has been obtained from the sponsored research of these centers that has resulted in the publication of dozens of books and hundreds of articles since the mid-1990s. The multidisciplinary research has focused on particular aspects of crime, such as human trafficking, money laundering, the role of crime groups in the process of privatization, overall crime trends, and many other topics.

Interviews have been conducted with large numbers of law enforcement in Russia and in other parts of the world concerned with post-Soviet organized crime. Legal documents of criminal cases in Russia and abroad have been studied to understand the mechanisms of organized crime activity. Civil litigations in the West among key industrial figures with criminal pasts have also been examined to shed light on the acquisition of businesses through criminal tactics.[4] The author has also read extensively in the Russian press and used Russian national and regional data to understand the evolution and geography of crime in Russia. Analysis of crime data reveals striking differences among regions, with the highest crime rates in many large cities and with crime rates rising from west to east, in part a legacy of the Soviet era, when labor camps were concentrated in Siberia and new industrialized cities without established communities gave rise to particularly high rates of criminality.[5]

OVERALL TRENDS IN CRIME

The growth of crime and the absence of an effective law enforcement response have affected both the quality of daily life, the longevity of the population, and the economy. Beccaria, the Enlightenment thinker, wrote that the certainty of punishment is more important than its severity. In Russia, at the present time, there is no certainty of punishment although there is severity for those who are caught and either cannot pay the bribes to get out of the criminal justice system or are subjects of particular political concern to the government, such as the former oil magnate Mikhail Khodorkovsky.[6]

The following important trends characterize Russian crime and organized crime:

- High rates of homicide.
- High rates of youth crime and child exploitation.
- Very high rates of drug abuse and a rapidly escalating problem of international drug trade.
- Large-scale human smuggling and trafficking both from, into, and through Russia.
- Organized crime involvement in all sectors of the economy.

Each trend is discussed in more detail below.

Homicide

Russia in the immediate post-Soviet period had very high rates of homicide. Homicide in this transitional period was the result of both high rates of interpersonal violence and the contract killings associated with organized crime. Part of this violence was also explained by the availability of weapons, which had been tightly controlled during the Soviet period.[7] The availability of arms, facilitated by the small-weapons trade of Russian organized crime and former military personnel, made many ordinary acts of crime more violent than in the past.[8] The decline in Russian medical care meant that many individuals who in the past had merely been assault victims were now homicide victims. Even though contract killings have declined, intrapersonal violence remains very high. Part of this is a consequence of the enduring problems of alcohol abuse. Consequently, Russia now has 22 homicides per 100,000—a rate that is four times that of the United States and approximately twenty times that of Western Europe.[9]

Youth Crime and Child Exploitation

High rates of youth crime and child exploitation are enduring problems in Russia. This is explained by the high rates of abandoned children, street children, and institutionalized children whose parents have left them or who have been declared incompetent to raise their children.[10] Parents have been determined unfit parents because of alcoholism, drug use, domestic violence, and child sexual exploitation. The number of children now determined to be homeless or abandoned is estimated to be at the same level as after World War II. There are 700,000 orphans and 2 million illiterate youths.[11] Children exposed to high levels of violence in their youth often replicate these patterns in adolescence and adulthood. Moreover, the absence of programs to help deinstitutionalized youth after age 18 return to their communities has made many of the females susceptible to sex traffickers.

Commercial sexual exploitation of children is recognized as an increasing problem although the Duma has not yet passed adequate legislation to combat all aspects of this phenomenon. Much of the production of child pornography marketed on the Internet is produced in Russia and sold internationally. Russia now assumes second place in the production of marketed pornography, contributing 23 percent of international production.[12]

There are now fifty transit homes throughout Russia, but these are intended to provide temporary shelter for children who are found abandoned or begging on the streets. Many children do not enter these homes because they are forced to beg or prostitute themselves by organized crime. Sometimes collusion between the criminals and the police prevents children being brought to the transit homes. The huge influx of migrants from other former Soviet states has contributed to a large number of abandoned and homeless children who are not Russian and may have a poor knowledge of the Russian language, making them even more vulnerable to exploitation.[13]

Drug Abuse

Drug addiction has skyrocketed in Russia, which is estimated to have 5–6 million regular consumers of heroin and other serious drugs.[14] This increase has occurred in the number of users, the geographical reach of the problem, and the variety of drugs used. As the market has grown, large and powerful organized crime groups have been involved, although no monopolization of markets has yet emerged. According to the head of the Federal Service for the Control of Narcotics, the last decade has seen a fifteenfold rise in the number of drug-related crimes and a tenfold increase in the number of drug users.[15]

According to the Ministry of Internal Affairs, there are now 4 million youth who use drugs, starting as young as age 11. The rate of drug abuse is 2.5 times higher among youth than among adults. Mortality connected to drug abuse is now 42 times higher for youth than in the 1980s, while the comparable figure for adults is 12 times higher.[16]

Russian official statistics reveal an alarming trend in the quantity and the distribution of the drug trade. For example, in 1985, the Ministry of Internal Affairs had identified only four regions in Russia with over 10,000 serious abusers of drugs. By the beginning of the twenty-first century, that figure had climbed to over thirty regions. At the present time there is hardly a city in Russia in which there are not drug addicts.[17] Drug abuse is not evenly distributed.[18] If 310 addicts were registered per 100,000 people in Russia as a whole in January 2004, the figure in the Russian Far East was 542 per 100,000.[19] With approximately 500,000 registered users but millions of unregistered users representing 2–4 percent of the Russian population, narcotics now assumes a notable share of the $15 billion of the Russian shadow economy.[20] Mark Galeotti several years ago estimated an even more severe problem than these estimates suggest: over 6 million drug users, of which 2 million are addicts.[21] Russia in a very short period has developed one of the world's most serious problems of drug abuse.

The drug business appears to be employing an ever larger number of Russian citizens annually. Not only are crime groups more actively engaged in the drug trade, but many impoverished Russian citizens serve as drug couriers. Russian governmental sources estimate that the number of organized criminal groups involved in the drug trade has increased by 85 percent since 1993.[22] By 2004, 950 criminal groups were estimated to be involved in the drug trade.[23] Other explanations for the growth lie in the political-criminal nexus and the links Russian organized crime has formed with crime groups in many other parts of the world. In the early 1990s, 30 percent of the drugs in Russia came from abroad, including the near abroad; the comparable figure at the beginning of the twenty-first century is double. In several regions of Russia, for example Moscow, St. Petersburg, and Khabarovsk, 80 percent of the confiscated drugs are of foreign production. The range of countries supplying drugs to Russia includes such a diverse group as Peru and Colombia, the Netherlands, several countries in Eastern Europe, and Central Asian states including Afghanistan.[24]

Russia is also increasingly a transit country for drugs from Afghanistan, Pakistan, and Iran into European markets.[25] In the past decade, the "Northern" route of heroin smuggling has linked Afghanistan via Central Asia to Russia and Europe. This route has become an ever more important part of the drug route out of Afghanistan and has assumed an ever larger share of Afghan's drug exports.[26] Perhaps Russia was first intended to be a transshipment country, but its main importance in the global heroin industry is now as a consumer. Many of the consumers are young, and some are or were military personnel formerly deployed on the borders in Central Asia and in the Chechen conflict.

The actors in this illicit economy range from Russian military personnel, law enforcement, and ordinary criminals to Soviet ethnic crime groups and illegal immigrants from Asian countries. The corrupt relationships which exist between the drug traffickers and local and regional officials allow these crime groups to operate throughout Russia, even in its capital. Furthermore, crime groups from many other countries are active in Russia. These include crime groups not only from the neighboring states of the former USSR but also Eastern Europe, Japan, China, South Korea and possibly North Korea, Vietnam, Nigeria, and Latin America.[27]

The Russian situation also recalls the Colombian situation, as drug trafficking in many cases is used to finance nonstate violent actors, including separatist and terrorist movements.[28] Although the link between insurgencies and the drug trade is not as strong in Russia as in Colombia, there is an important link between drugs and violent conflict. Organized crime including drug trafficking has been a factor prolonging the war in Chechnya, providing income and the motivation to continue warfare on both sides of the conflict.

Human Smuggling and Trafficking

Human trafficking persists on a large scale. This trafficking is not just of Russian women exported for sexual exploitation abroad. Rather, there is a large importation of trafficked women from poorer Soviet successor states. Moreover, there is a significant illegal migrant population, and many of the workers find themselves in situations of severe labor exploitation.

Even as the Russian economy has grown and the middle class has expanded, the problem of sex trafficking of Russian women persists on a large scale because of the poverty, vulnerability, and hopelessness of many adolescents and women in contemporary Russia. Many youth live in poorly supported children's homes. Others are living in the streets, having been abandoned by their parents or having run away from drunken and violent parents. Even teenagers from intact families can be victims of trafficking. In 2007, outside Nizhyni Tagil in the Urals, a pit was found that held the bodies of forty missing women, including the daughter of one of the traffickers who had lured young women with promises of ice cream and then tried to compel them into prostitution. Many young women who resisted were murdered. Many had previously been reported to the police as missing by their families, but there had been no follow-up. When the facts became known, a public outcry followed.[29]

This is just a small element of trafficking victimization in contemporary Russia. With its increasing affluence and a shortage of workers to do hard physical labor, Russia has had a rapid influx of illegal immigrants, primarily from impoverished countries of Central Asia such as Tajikistan and Kyrgyzstan. Russia estimates that there are now 5–10 million illegal migrants in Russia. This figure is in addition to the legal migrants, a new category of workers introduced in Russia that now gives temporary work permits for stays up to three months. Despite this new category of legal migrants, 80 percent of all migrants are employed in the informal or "shadow" economy, receiving a fraction of the wages paid to Russian workers. Recent research revealed that one-quarter of those surveyed knew migrants who had been enslaved: their passports had been taken away and their wages withheld, and they had been kept in confinement by those who controlled them. The number of those subject to labor trafficking is now estimated to exceed the number of victims of sex trafficking.[30]

Despite this massive exploitation, aiding these people is not a priority for Russian citizens or the state. There is very little conception of individual rights, a legacy of the Soviet period and even prerevolutionary traditions. Sixty percent of the population is not ready to help migrants. Yet the number ready to help migrants is greater than the percentage ready to help their fellow citizens who have engaged in deviant behavior. Only 13 percent of the population believes that a prostitute should receive assistance or protection. The majority of the Russian population is not concerned with the rights of prostitutes, alcoholics, or drug addicts. This lack of concern is exploited by criminals.[31]

Organized Crime

Post-Soviet organized crime is distinct from organized crime in many regions of the world because it initially focused its efforts on the legitimate economy and only more recently assumed a larger role in the drug trade and other forms of the illicit economy.[32] Organized crime was able to grow so rapidly in the first decade of the post-Soviet period because of the pervasive corruption of government officials, the incapacity of the demoralized law enforcement, and the perception by the criminals that they could act with almost total impunity. During the Soviet period, party sanctions placed some curbs on government misconduct; but with the collapse of the Communist Party, and in the absence of the rule of law, there were no limits on the conduct of government officials. The crime groups could function effectively because they corrupted or coopted government officials and were rarely arrested and incarcerated.[33] Corruption, bribery, and abuse of power escalated rapidly, but there was a sharp diminution of prosecutions for these offenses.[34]

The law enforcement system, decimated by poor morale and dangerous work conditions as well as the dismissal and departure of many long-term personnel, was ill-equipped to deal with the increasing number of serious crimes. Moreover, law enforcements' inexperience with investigating and prosecuting crimes of a market economy gave organized crime groups the opportunity to greatly expand their financial reach. A whole business of private protection evolved that was often staffed and run by organized crime, and crime groups extracted payments from those in need of protection rather than actually providing a service. They have been named "violent entrepreneurs" by the Russian researcher Vadim Volkov, who studied the phenomenon.[35]

The diversity of post-Soviet organized crime is one of its hallmarks. Crime groups are multiethnic and often involve cooperation among groups that are antagonistic outside the criminal world.[36] Foreign groups not only operate on Russian territory but provide partnerships with Russian crime groups to carry out their activities. For example, Japanese Yakuza work with Russian organized crime in the Far East to illegally secure needed timber and in exchange provide used Japanese cars for the Russian market.

Organized crime groups are not involved exclusively in one area of criminal activity. Certain crime groups may specialize in drug trafficking, arms trafficking, or auto theft, but most crime groups are multifaceted, spanning many aspects of the legitimate and illegitimate sectors of the economy. In any one region of the country, most forms of illicit activity will be present. However, organized crime involvement with environmental crime will be greater in Siberia and the Far East than in the more densely populated regions of Western Russia.

Russian organized crime's involvement in the banking sector since the Soviet collapse undermined the integrity of the banking system and facilitated massive money laundering out of Russia. Russian money laundering, as distinct from capital flight, was so significant in the 1990s that it drained Russia of much of its investment capital.[37] Only after the Russian financial collapse in 1998 and after Russia was cited early in the following decade by the Financial Action Task Force for noncompliance with international money laundering standards were substantial improvements made in the banking sector.[38] But there are still problems of organized crime influence over some banks and large-scale problems of capital flight associated with it.[39]

THE GEOGRAPHY OF CRIME

The vastness of Russia's enormous territory reaching from the borders of Western Europe to Asia results in significant variations by region. Compounding these geographical differences is the fact that many regions of Russia, such as the North Caucasus, Tatarstan, and parts of the Volga region, have strong ethnic influences that also shape the characteristics of crime. Furthermore, certain regions are characterized by particularly high rates of crime, such as the major cities of Moscow, St. Petersburg, and Ekaterinburg as well as the regions of Siberia and the Russian Far East. Crime rates escalate as one moves from the western part of the country east. This phenomenon is a legacy of Soviet-era policies of strict population controls, a massive institutionalized penal population located in Siberia that after release settled close to their former labor colonies, and the development of new cities east of the Urals without necessary infrastructure and social support systems.

Siberia and the Urals

During the Soviet era, new cities were established, particularly in Siberia, that were populated primarily by young men, and there was no planning to attract women to these communities. With the existing internal passport and registration system that restricted mobility, women could not move to these communities without employment. Therefore, these new cities quickly became areas with high rates of alcohol consumption, violent crime, and other forms of criminality.

At the end of the Soviet period, these communities that were the basis of Soviet industrial production went into significant decline. The rich natural resources of the Urals and Siberia, however, provided large revenues for the corrupt bureaucrats and crime groups that appropriated this state property as their own. Furthermore, the Urals region was a major center of the Soviet Union's military-industrial complex. With the decline of Soviet military production, many factories ceased to function, leaving many citizens without incomes. The economic crisis that hit this region helps explain the large number of children at risk. Although economic prosperity has come to many cities in the area in the 2000s, serious problems endure. The Nizhni Tagil case of young women who resisted prostitution found dead in a pit is illustrative of the problems of vulnerability in poverty-stricken parts of the formerly industrialized Urals. Especially high levels of drug addiction characterize Siberia, especially the area around Irkutsk.[40]

The Russian Far East

The Russian Far East has seen a significant decline in population since the collapse of the Soviet Union. The absence of economic development in the region and its isolation from more populous eastern regions of Russia provided an enormous incentive for citizens to leave. The region had extremely high crime rates in the 1970s and continues to be characterized by very high rates of crime and violent crime. Exacerbating the criminality of the region has been the criminalization of the region. Epitomizing this problem was the arrest of the mayor of Vladivostok, Vladimir Nikolayev, in early 2007. An organized criminal with the "klichka" or criminal name of Winnie the Pooh, he was elected in 2004.[41] His ouster was made all the more difficult because he held the second position in Putin's ruling party for the Russian Far East.

Organized crime groups from the Russian Far East work with South Korean, Japanese, Chinese, and Vietnamese crime groups. Much of the criminality is connected with the ports and the massive shipping that flows through this region. Many of the shipping and fishing companies are dominated by organized crime. The impoverished military in the region has contributed to massive unauthorized arms sales to foreign governments and organized crime groups. A sale of Russian helicopters to North Koreans was averted in the late 1990s only when police who were not part of the scheme stumbled on the helicopters just prior to delivery.[42]

Much of the crime is connected with the exploitation of natural resources. Fish and timber represent 93 percent of the exports from the Russian Far East. Fish from overfished waters wind up in Japanese and Korean markets.[43] Since the fall of the Soviet Union, there has been a fourfold decline of forested land.[44] Half the hardwood in the Russian Far East is illegally harvested either by corrupt officials or by gangs in the communities. Japanese and Chinese crime groups are actively involved in the illegal purchase of timber. One investigation revealed that illegally harvested timber was worked in Chinese factories to make furniture for Wal-Mart.[45]

The Russian Far East has been the beneficiary of many valuable financial transfers from the central government to the region. The theft of state budgetary resources was so severe in the 1990s that electricity was rationed. The ouster of the mayor of Vladivostok most likely occurred because of Moscow's concern that state appropriations for the Far East would be stolen by the criminalized government. Since his arrest, many other crime figures in the Far East have been arrested, indicating a strong commitment by the central state to decriminalize the area. The initiative has received strong support from the citizenry, as evidenced by communications to Internet-based media.[46]

Crime in Major Urban Centers

Moscow as Russia's largest city and economic powerhouse is the home of the largest and most important crime groups, such as Soltnsevo and Izmailovo, which have penetrated into the most lucrative sectors of the economy, including banks, real estate, and raw materials. These groups are part of a very diverse picture of criminality in the city. Ethnic crime groups have been deeply involved in the consumer markets for food and goods. Restaurants, clubs, and casinos have been centers of criminal activity and investment. But in this rich investment environment, it is often hard to differentiate where the criminality ends and the corruption of government officials begins.

Moscow has become one of the most expensive cities in the world. The absence of competition, the large sums extracted by organized crime as their share of profits, and the domination of real estate by organized crime groups in cooperation with corrupt officials help explain the extremely high cost of business and of daily life. The same problems in the real estate sector exist in St. Petersburg.[47] The criminalization of real estate continues, even though its form has evolved over time. In the past, many citizens simply lost their apartments and disappeared without trace. No protection was available from the government to protect tenants who were threatened by high-level organized crime. High-level officials in Moscow and St. Petersburg demanded significant bribes even for information about the availability of property for rent and purchase. Companies that built much of the new construction often have organized crime figures as major shareholders or financiers.

Moscow is still a major center of money laundering, despite enhanced controls. The large number of casinos, the cash-reliant economy, and the lack of regulation of financial markets make it relatively easy to move illicit funds and those from the very large shadow economy.

CONCLUSION

Crime rates were suppressed in the Soviet years, a consequence of the high levels of social control, high rates of incarceration, and controls over places of residence. With the liberalization of the Gorbachev era, fundamental changes occurred in crime patterns. Crime rates rose rapidly, and organized crime became a formidable actor in the new economy. The 1990s were traumatic. Many Russians lost their savings in bank failures. Unemployment rose dramatically, particularly among women, and the social safety net collapsed. In the absence of effective state enforcement, organized crime filled the vacuum and became a visible force in society, not only through its displays of violence and its role in private protection but also through the key role it played in privatization and politics in the transitional period.

The Putin years saw greater stability, but Russia has not been able to eliminate the high rates of violent crime, endemic corruption, and pervasive organized crime. High levels of money laundering and export of capital continued to deprive Russia of the capital it needs for investment, although the record profits obtained during the boom years of oil revenues masked the impact.

The crime problems evolved in the years since the collapse of the Soviet Union, but they have remained an important element of the structure of the Russian economy, society, and political system. The homicides associated with organized crime have declined, but overall homicide rates remain high. Conflicts over property are no longer decided by shootings but often instead by expensive litigation in the West, where many of Russia's richest citizens have placed their assets.

Property rights are still not secure. The property acquired by force, deception, and coercion in the early days of the post-Soviet period is now often being redistributed by corporate raiding. Over 70,000 cases in 2007 testify to the force often used to wrest property from its owners. The property can be as small as one residential building or as large as the stakes of British Petroleum.

Russia is an exporter of trafficked women, an importer of large numbers of migrants, and a transit and destination country for trafficking victims. Although Russia has provided temporary work permits for many foreign workers, there are still large numbers of illegal migrants from poor Soviet successor states who come to Russia to earn money. Significant numbers become victims of labor and sexual trafficking.

There has been no concerted state action commensurate with the size of the crime and corruption problems. President Medvedev made a crackdown on corruption a priority during his early months in office, but it is not clear whether he can be any more effective than Putin was, and many analysts suspect that success will be elusive. Without an effective law enforcement apparatus, an empowered civil society, or free media, it is very difficult to curb the rise of organized crime or the pervasive corruption. The criminal trajectories set in motion in the early post-Soviet period have continued without impediment. Organized criminals have so much power because they assumed critical investment positions in key sectors of the economy in the transitional period. Massive collusion with and corruption of politicians have ensured this continued ownership. In fact, many criminals have sought government positions to acquire immunity from prosecution.

Crime in Russia is a major political and economic influence on society. The heavy involvement of criminals and corrupt politicians in the legitimate economy are key explanations for the absence of transparency in Russian financial markets. This contributed to the especially precipitous decline of the Russian markets relative to other international exchanges in fall 2008. Furthermore, the existence of widespread monopolies as a result of organized crime and oligarch dominance of the economy has led to high prices. The pervasive criminal activity is an enormous impediment to entrepreneurship and the emergence of small and medium-sized businesses that are crucial to long-term economic development and a middle class that could be the backbone of a more democratic society.

Suggested Readings

Karklins, Rasma. *The System Made Me Do It: Corruption in Post-communist Societies.* Armonk, N.Y.: M. E. Sharpe, 2005.

Orttung, Robert, and Anthony Latta, eds. *Russia's Battle with Crime, Corruption, and Terrorism.* London: Routledge, 2008.

Stoecker, Sally, and Louise Shelley, eds. *Human Traffic and Transnational Crime: Eurasian and American Perspectives.* Lanham, Md.: Rowman & Littlefield, 2005.

Varese, Federico. *The Russian Mafia: Private Protection in a New Market Economy.* Oxford: Oxford University Press, 2005.

Volkov, Vadim. *Violent Entrepreneurs: The Use of Force in the Making of Russian Capitalism.* Ithaca, N.Y.: Cornell University Press, 2002.

Wedel, Janine R. *Collision and Collusion: The Strange Case of Western Aid to Eastern Europe.* New York: St. Martin's, 1998.

NOTES

1. "Transparency International Calls on Medvedev to Monitor Top Officials," July 7, 2008, www.iht.com/articles/ap/2008/07/07/europe/EU-Russia -Corruption.php.

2. "Medvedev's First Police Reform: MVD Loses Specialized Organised Crime Department," http://inmoscowsshadows.wordpress.com.

3. Numerous publications of these centers can be accessed through http:// policy-traccc.gmu.edu. Look at the section of the website on study centers in Eurasia. The website of the center in Vladivostok, www.crime.vl.ru, has about 800,000 readers annually, making it one of the most read academic websites in Russia.

4. Steven Swinford and Jon Ungoed-Thomas, "Peter Mandelson Oligarch Oleg Deripaska Linked to Mafia Boss," *Sunday Times*, October 26, 2008, www.timeson-line.co.uk.

5. "Crime, Violence, and Political Conflict in Russia," in *Understanding Civil War: Evidence and Analysis,* ed. Nicholas Sambanis (Washington, D.C.: World Bank, 2005), 87–117.

6. Serge Schmemann, "The Case against and for Khodorkovsky," *International Herald Tribune*, October 19, 2008, http://www.iht.com.

7. Louise I. Shelley, "Interpersonal Violence in the Soviet Union," *Violence, Aggression, and Terrorism* 1, no. 2 (1987): 41–67.

8. N. F. Kuznetsova and G. M. Minkovskii, *Kriminologiia: Uchebnik* (Moscow: Vek, 1998), 553.

9. "What's Behind Russia's Crime Wave," www.thepittsburghchannel.com/money/10110784/detail.html.

10. Clementine K. Fujimura, Sally W. Stoecker, and Tatyana Sudakova, *Russia's Abandoned Children: An Intimate Understanding* (Westport, Conn.: Praeger, 2005).

11. "V Rossii, 'tretiia volna' bezprizonosti, beznadzornosti, negramotnosti, i prestupnost' podrostov (statistika)," June 1, 2005, www.newsru.com/russia/01jun2005/generation.html.

12. U.S. Attorney's Office of Eastern District of Wisconsin, www.usdoj.gov/usao/wie/LECC/Newsletter/July_2008.pdf.

13. Discussion by Marina Ryabko, director of the Priyut-Tranzit government-funded shelter for children and teens in St. Petersburg. The event was entitled "Child Trafficking and Exploitation in Russia: Scale and Scope," September 24, 2008, George Mason University, Arlington, Va.

14. U.S. Department of State, Bureau for International Narcotics and Law Enforcement Affairs, *International Narcotics Control Strategy Report*, vol. 1, *Drug and Chemical Control*, March 2007, www.state.gov/documents/organization/81446.pdf.

15. V. Cherkesov, "Otvechaet na voprosi glavnovo redaktora almankha organizovannaia prestupnost, terrorism, i korruptsiia," *Organizovannaia Prestupnost', Terrorizma, i Korruptsiia*, no. 4 (2003): 8.

16. "V Rossii, 'tretiia volna' bezprizonosti, beznadzornosti, negramotnosti, i prestupnost' podrostov (statistika)," June 1, 2005, www.newsru.com/russia/01jun2005/generation.html.

17. B. Tselinsky, "Sovremennaia Narkosituatsiia v Rossii: Tendentsii i perspektivii," *Organizovannaia Prestupnost', Terrorizma, i Korruptsiia*, no. 4 (2003): 21.

18. A. G. Museibov, "Regional'nye praktiki po preduprezhdeniiu nezakonnogo oborota narkotikov," *Sotsiologicheskie issledovaniia*, no. 7 (2003): 125–30.

19. Based on the analysis of Vladivostok branch of the Transnational Crime and Corruption Center, www.crime.vl.ru.

20. U.S. Department of State, *International Narcotics Control Strategy Report*.

21. Mark Galeotti, "Russia's Drug Crisis," *Jane's Intelligence Review*, October 2003.

22. "Narkobiznes—ugroza natsional'noi bezopasnosti," Press Release, Federal Narcotics Control Service, July 15, 2003.

23. Vladimir Vorsobin, "Putin prizval bortsov s narkotikami rabotat' 'na polnuiu katushku,'" *Komsomolskaia Pravda*, March 31, 2004.

24. Tselinsky, "Sovremennaia Narkosituatsiia v Rossii," 6.

25. Tselinsky, "Sovremennaia Narkosituatsiia v Rossii," 23; Kairat Osmonaliev, *Developing Counter-Narcotics Policy in Central Asia* (Washington, D.C.: Central Asia-Caucasus Institute and Silk Road Studies Program, 2005).

26. U.S. Department of State, *International Narcotics Control Strategy Report*.

27. A. N. Sukharenko, "Transnatsionalnaia narkobiznesa v Rossii," www.crime.vl.ru.

28. Tamara Makarenko, "Terrorism and Transnational Organised Crime: The Emerging Nexus," in *Transnational Violence and the Seams of Lawlessness in the*

Asia-Pacific: Linkages to Global Terrorism, ed. Paul Smith (Honolulu, Hawaii: Asia Pacific Center for Strategic Studies, 2004); Kimberley Thachuk, "Transnational Threats: Falling through the Cracks?" *Low Intensity Conflict and Law Enforcement* 10, no. 1 (2001); Sabrina Adamoli et al., *Organized Crime around the World* (Helsinki: HEUNI, 1998); Barbara Harris-White, *Globalization and Insecurity: Political, Economic, and Physical Challenges* (New York: Palgrave, 2002); Ian Griffith, "From Cold War Geopolitics to Post-Cold War Geonarcotics," *International Journal* 30, no. 2 (1993–1994); R. Matthew and G. Shambaugh, "Sex, Drugs, and Heavy Metal: Transnational Threats and National Vulnerabilities," *Security Dialogue* 29 (1998): 163–75.

29. "Na Urale nashli tainoe zahoronenie seks-rabyn," *Komsomolskaia Pravda*, February 2, 2007, http://kp.ru; Valentina Blinova, "Proshchanie," *Ogonek*, no. 7 (February 12–18, 2007): 18–20.

30. Elena Tyuryukanova, "THB, Irregular Migration, and Criminal Gains (Case of Russia)," presented at the OSCE-UNODC-CYPRUS Regional Meeting on Human Trafficking and Money Laundering, September 18–19, 2008, Larnaca, Cyprus.

31. Tyuryukanova, "THB, Irregular Migration, and Criminal Gains."

32. Svetlana Glinkina, "Privatizatsiia and Kriminalizatsiia: How Organized Crime Is Hijacking Privatization," *Demokkratizatsiia* 2, no. 3 (1994): 385–91.

33. G. F. Khohkriakov, "Organizovannia prestupnost' v Rossii," *Obshchestvennye nauki i sovremmenost*, no. 6 (2000): 62–74.

34. See Louise Shelley, "Crime and Corruption," in *Developments in Russian Politics*, ed. Stephen White, Alex Pravda, and Zvi Gitelman (Palgrave: Houndsmills, 2001), 239–53.

35. Vadim Volkov, *Violent Entrepreneurs: The Use of Force in the Making of Russian Capitalism* (Ithaca, N.Y.: Cornell University Press, 2002); Vadim Volkov, "Silovoe predprinimalatel'stvo v sovremennoi Rossii," *Sotsiologiecheskie issledovaniia*, no. 1 (1999): 55–65.

36. Frederico Varese, *The Russian Mafia: Private Protection in a New Market Economy* (Oxford: Oxford University Press, 2005).

37. Center for Strategic and International Studies, *Russian Organized Crime and Corruption: Putin's Challenge* (Washington, D.C.: CSIS, 2000), 32–39.

38. Christopher Kenneth, "FATF Not Satisfied with Russia's Anti-Money Laundering Efforts," April 11, 2002, *Russia Journal*, www.russiajournal.com.

39. N. A. Lopashenko, *Begstvo kapitalov, peredel sobstevennosti i ekonomicheskaia amnistiia* (Moscow: Iuridicheskie programmy, 2005).

40. The problem first identified by Anna Repetskaya a decade ago still endures. See Anna Repetskaya, "Irkutsk Organized Crime Press Review," *OC Watch* 5 (1999): 16.

41. "Vladivostok Mayor Stripped of Power among Corruption Investigation," Associated Press, March 1, 2007, www.iht.com.

42. V. A. Nomokonov, ed., *Organizovannia prestupnost': Tendentsii, perspektivy bor'by* (Vladivostok: Dalnevostochnogo universiteta, 1998).

43. P. V. Korovnikov, "Problemy dekriminalizatsii sfery prirodopol'zovaniia Primorskogo kraiia i nekotorye puti ikh resheniia," in *Rossiia i ATR Problemy bezopasnosti, migratsii i prestupnosti* (Vladivostok: Dal'nevostochnogo universiteta, 2007), 88–89.

44. *Dal'nii Vostok: Khronika organizovannoi prestupnosti (obzor pressy 1997–August 2003)*, www.crime.vl.ru.

45. Raffi Khatchadourian, "The Stolen Forests inside the Covert War on Illegal Logging," *New Yorker*, October 6, 2008, www.newyorker.com.

46. See the thousands of messages sent to the online forum of the Vladivostok Center for the Study of Organized Crime, www.vlcrime.net.

47. See Konstatin Dobrynyn, "Moshenichestvo v sfere nedvizimosti v Sankt-Peterburge: Primaia vzaimosviaz s organivovannoi prestupnost'iu i korruptsiei," research grant done for St. Petersburg Crime and Corruption Center, 2002.

Chapter Nine

Agriculture in the Late Putin Period and Beyond

Stephen K. Wegren

In recent years Russian agriculture has experienced a significant recovery, which is not to deny that significant problems continue to exist in agriculture and more broadly in rural society.[1] While not all problems have been solved, at least the production declines of the 1990s have abated and real growth in the sector has ensued. In the third edition of this book, I characterized Putin's agrarian policies as a "quiet revolution." Putin's quiet revolution replaced Yeltsin's "loud revolution," which essentially was characterized by politicizing agrarian reform, an approach that pursued privatization as a mobilization campaign. I wrote: "Although Putin's revolution may be quiet, the policies being pursued today will shape domestic and international agrarian relations for decades to come. Putin's quiet revolution in agriculture has signaled the politics of confrontation have ended. . . . Putin's quiet revolution is important because it has provided Russia with a more stable foundation for future development in the agricultural sector."[2]

Since 2000, two main stages of governmental agrarian policy may be discerned. The first stage was the creation of an institutional and policy base that would stabilize the agricultural sector and pave the way for economic growth. The second stage has witnessed the introduction of significant financial assistance that is intended to increase domestic production, make Russian agriculture internationally competitive, and reduce dependence on foreign imports. The purpose of this chapter is to trace the government's strategy and policies toward agriculture through these two stages.[3] The chapter also examines not only where Russian agriculture has been under President Vladimir Putin but where it is going, and in this respect the chapter discusses the continuing obstacles that confront President Dmitri Medvedev in the first years of his presidency.

BACKGROUND

Even before Vladimir Putin assumed the presidency in early 2000, he was aware of the deep crisis in Russian agriculture and the need to rectify those problems. In March 1999, Putin stated, "the revival of Russia is unthinkable without the revival of the Russian countryside. An agrarian policy is needed that will organically unite measures of state support and state regulation with market reforms in the countryside."[4] Indeed, the litany of problems inherited by Putin was long and multifaceted. During most of the 1990s, food production had fallen precipitously. Large farms (state and collective farms and their legal successors) suffered the biggest decrease in food production for a variety of reasons. Food production on large farms declined due to input prices that rose faster than wholesale food prices, the shifting of responsibility for rural social services and rural infrastructure to farm budgets, a general shortage of credit to cover seasonal operating and production costs, and a decline in domestic demand for food as a result of rapidly escalating retail food prices. In other words, large farms felt a financial squeeze in both revenue and expenditures. Using an index of physical volume of output (1990=100), in Yeltsin's last year in office domestic agricultural production by large agricultural enterprises declined to 36 percent of their 1990 levels. Moreover, during the 1990s the structure of output changed so that by the end of the decade, households and not large farms were the predominant producer as measured in ruble value.[5]

Despite the privatization of farmland and equipment held by former state and collective farms, farm productivity declined, and debt and unprofitability soared as the terms of trade moved drastically against agricultural producers. Food imports increased significantly during the 1990s, particularly for meat and poultry products to large cities, which in turn led to concerns about the nation's food security. The situation was compounded by alarm over the decline in animal stocks during the Yeltsin years, a decline that even exceeded the first years of Stalin's collectivization.[6] Furthermore, the amount of arable land under cultivation by large farms declined by about 30 million hectares from the end of 1991 to the end of 1999.[7] Agricultural land abandonment was rampant and land reclamation virtually ceased.

Basic food production became a problem, even though domestic demand and consumption were falling due to rising retail prices. During 1995–1997, grain harvests averaged only 73.7 million tons, whereas in 1992–1993 the average was about 103 million tons. The average fell to 56 million tons during 1998–2000. The nadir was reached in 1998 when the harvest totaled only 47.9 million tons, the worst harvest since the early 1950s.[8] By the latter Yeltsin era, the combination of extraordinarily bad harvests, financial default on loans by the government, and devaluation of the ruble in 1998 led to regionally imposed price controls on food products in the fall of 1998 and winter 1998–1999. To prevent starvation, some regions received Western food aid well into 2000. Nor did it appear that Russia's agriculture could rebound quickly, because rural infrastructure crumbled at an accelerated rate during the 1990s as government capital investments dried up. Annually, large numbers of capital stock became unusable as farm equipment fell into disrepair or was removed from use. Thus, in many ways, when Putin assumed the presidency, the agricultural situation was bordering on catastrophic.

PUTIN'S INSTITUTIONAL AND POLICY INITIATIVES IN AGRICULTURE

The first stage in Putin's "quiet revolution" in agriculture was designed to lay an institutional and policy foundation for future development. When Putin became president, it was immediately clear that a primary role of government was to pursue and protect "state interests." In agriculture, this orientation led in turn to: (1) priority attention to the recovery of agriculture and in particular large farming enterprises, in terms of both their financial strength and their food production; (2) starting in 2001, import protection policies for several types of food products that benefited agricultural producers; and (3) government intervention in the domestic grain market for the purpose of "stabilizing" wholesale prices for grain producers, regional supplies, and retail prices for consumers. Since large farms produce the overwhelming majority of grain products, they benefited the most from government intervention.

The government's goals were initially laid out in a document called "Basic Directions of Agrofood Policy to 2010," which former Minister of Agriculture Aleksei Gordeev presented in July 2000.[9] Gordeev indicated that the highest priority of agricultural policy would be increasing domestic food production and lowering reliance on food imports, with the goals of improving the nation's food security in particular and economic security in general. The "Basic Directions" reflected a broad-based strategy of governmental support for agriculture during the next few years. This first stage of the government's agrarian strategy was to create an institutional and policy foundation that would facilitate economic growth, in contrast to Yeltsin's agrarian policies that had largely been destructive. Some of the policies are discussed in more detail below.

Policies for Large Farms

A main priority of the Putin administration was to improve the productive capacity of large farms, and early attention was paid to creating more favorable financial conditions that would allow large farms to expand productive capacity. Towards this end, in 2001 a state-owned and -operated agricultural bank (Rossel'khozbank) was created to channel state credits and loans to agricultural producers. This bank originally opened in Moscow, but regional branches opened in almost every region during the next several years. Other policies were adopted to help large farms: a state-backed crop insurance program was implemented, a consolidated agricultural tax was introduced that simplified the tax system and lowered the amount of tax paid by large farms, and a policy of state price supports for grain crops was enacted that helped to stabilize wholesale prices in years of grain surplus.

The policy of financial relief was further embodied in the law "On the Financial Renewal of Agricultural Producers," which was signed into force by President Putin in July 2002.[10] Prior to the law, during 1999–2002 a series of government resolutions provided partial restructuring of debt for more than 18,000 large farms, totaling 42 billion rubles.[11] In 2004, more than 11,000 large farms participated in the program of debt relief, and by the end of that year more than 60 billion rubles of farm debt had been restructured and about 30 billion rubles of penalties and fines written off nationwide.[12] By April 2008, 12,820 large farms had participated in the program, with more than R84 billion of farm debt restructured and R44 billion of penalties and fines written off. Another 8,751 large farms were not eligible to participate in the program for a variety of reasons, the most common of which was bankruptcy.[13] As a result of financial relief and an increase in domestic food production, the number of unprofitable large farms declined. In 1998, about 89 percent of large farms were unprofitable. In 2005, this number decreased to 42 percent, to 32 percent during 2006, and to 25 percent in 2008. In the first part of 2008, the law on financial renewal was amended so that large farms were given a second opportunity to restructure debt, and the law also allowed them to extend the term for repayment of debt.[14]

Large farms also received other forms of financial assistance. State-owned Rosagrosnab and Rosagrolizing were funded to purchase agricultural machinery and equipment and lease it to large farms and private farms at a subsidized rate, with the government subsidizing the difference. This became one of the main sources of government support for agriculture, and although Rosagrosnab and Rosagrolizing had existed since 1994, funding increased substantially during the Putin administration.

Another important factor contributing to the financial recovery by large farms has been the willingness of the Russian government to intervene in the grain market for the purpose of stabilizing wholesale prices and domestic supplies. This willingness to intervene is important because it sends a signal to producers *not* to reduce grain crops or take land out of cultivation in the wake of a bountiful harvest. Specifically, the methods of state intervention are twofold. The first method is purchase-price support, similar to the practice in the West. This method means that if average domestic market purchase prices fall below a defined minimal level (calculated by the Ministry of Agriculture as sufficient to provide a profit), the government defines a price floor for wholesale purchase prices, thereby creating a minimum price which producers can be assured to receive irrespective of domestic market trends. The government purchases grain at its defined purchase-price levels, with the intent to use "the market" to ease some of the oversupply of grain and stabilize wholesale prices.

The second method of government intervention concerns commodities and occurs when the government sells some of the government-purchased grain, releasing it to the wholesale market in times of bad harvests with the intent to influence wholesale market prices downward. Thus, commodity intervention—the sale of grain purchased by the government—is a method used to stabilize retail bread prices. Export quotas or tariffs are also used in tandem with the two methods just described. In years of bad harvests or when world market wholesale prices are quite high (as in 2008), the government may enact either export quotas or tariffs, or may even prohibit grain exports by Russian producers. Recently, because domestic prices were much lower compared to prices on the international grain market, high export tariffs were applied in November 2007 and exports were prohibited from January 2008 onward in order to prevent producers from exporting too much and creating pressures for higher domestic retail prices. The restrictions on exports were removed in July 2008.

Large farms produce the vast majority of grains for the country, more than 85 percent in recent years, so large farms have been the primary beneficiary from government intervention. The legal basis for federal government intervention in wholesale food markets can be dated to a 1997 law. However, the government intervened in the domestic grain market for the first time following a very good grain harvest in 2001, when the harvest was 85 million tons, up from 65 million tons in 2000. In 2002, with a harvest of 86 million tons, purchase intervention was again used. Since then, with good harvests, grain intervention was used each year during 2004–2007. In 2008, it was first speculated that grain intervention would not be necessary, but thanks to a confluence of good weather and a financial credit policy that seems to be working, Russia achieved a postcommunist high in grain production, over 112 metric tons, including 60 metric tons of wheat, the highest since 1978. The record harvest led the government to announce purchase intervention for the 2008–2009 agricultural year (1 July 2008–30 June 2009). In November 2008, Gordeev indicated that the government planned to spend R36 billion to purchase 6–8 tons of grain. Despite the financial crisis in Russia, the government plans to continue its support of grain producers. At the end of December 2008, Prime Minister Putin stated that it is necessary to retain planned credit and funding levels for agriculture.[15] Going forward, government intervention in the grain market is likely to remain a key policy instrument.

Commodity intervention was used in 2003 when the grain harvest was almost 20 million tons less than in 2002, totaling only 67 million tons. This intervention became necessary when criticism and concerns were voiced over rising bread prices due to reduced grain supplies and increased demand by the population. In order to relieve upward pressures on retail prices, the government sold some grain it had purchased in previous years. Grain sales began in the winter and continued through May 2004. The grain sales were channeled through commodity exchanges that were registered with the government, with prices established by the government. Commodity intervention benefits primarily consumers.

Polices for the Private Sector

Government programs were also introduced that were designed to assist the private sector (private farms and households operating a private plot). In order to assist private farmers, in 2004 a program was introduced that allowed private farmers to lease agricultural machinery at state-subsidized rates (large farms could participate also). This law was important because private farms were chronically undermechanized and often could not afford to purchase agricultural machinery on their own due to the shortage of available private credit. In 2004, a new law on land mortgaging was adopted that allowed private farmers to mortgage privately owned land in order to raise capital for investment in production. In 2007, 35 of Russia's 86 regions had implemented pilot projects that provided financial credit based on land mortgaging.[16] Both private farmers and large farms were eligible to mortgage their land. Private farmers would mortgage privately owned agricultural land, and different sources indicated that private famers were quite active in this sphere, with the average credit line in 2007 totaling R1 million. Large farms could also mortgage agricultural land, and did so by using as collateral land shares that they controlled.[17] Data from Rossel'khozbank show that during 2006–2007, the bank loaned out R6.3 billion, based on over 250,000 hectares of agricultural land as collateral.[18] In early 2007, government resolutions were announced to subsidize private farmers who raised different types of pedigree livestock.

State assistance was also directed toward households and specifically private plot operators. The 2003 federal law on subsidiary agriculture freed private plot operators from taxation on the income earned from the sale of their food production. In addition, one of the main components of the program called "Development of the Agroindustrial Complex" (2006–2007) was the provision of credits to food producers (including private plot operators) for the purchase of farm animals, in particular cattle. The program offered both collateralized and noncollateralized loans for private plot operators. Households also were eligible to receive state subsidized loans. Households could take out loans with repayment terms from two to eight years. For households that operate a private plot, a line of credit of up to R150,000 is available for one individual (with collateral), or R300,000 for a jointly owned plot, repayable within two or five years depending on how the money is to be used.[19] Unsecured loans (no collateral) have a maximum credit line of R30,000. Minister of Agriculture Gordeev noted that financial support was given "only to those who work successfully, who have adapted to market conditions."[20] In early 2007, Rossel'khozbank announced a policy that allowed private plot owners to mortgage land they owned in order to raise capital.

The Effects of Policies

The introduction of state programs and financial assistance to agriculture since 2000 contributed to a rebound in agricultural production compared to the deep depression of the 1990s. Comparing the 1998–1999 averages to 2007, food production increased for all of the major food products except milk, as shown in table 9.1.

Moreover, each of the three major producers experienced an increase in food production, although not at equal rates. Private farms' output since 2001 grew the most rapidly until 2007. As a result, by 2007 the value of private farms' output accounted for more than 6 percent of national production, or more than three times as much as during the 1990s. Output on large farms increased steadily, though not as spectacularly as the value on production from private farms. By 2007, the value of output from large farms accounted for about 41 percent of national production. But because large farms had a larger base from which to begin, even lower growth rates translated into large production increases. Household production, which grew rapidly in the first half of the 1990s and stagnated thereafter, continued to display uneven growth and increased the least among the three main producers, as shown in table 9.2. In 2007, households continued to produce the highest total value of food production, a position they had held since 1997. In 2007, the value of production from households' production accounted for almost 53 percent of national production.

Increased production on large farms contributed to higher export volumes for some products, particularly grain. By 2006–2007, Russia had not only established domestic grain reserves but exported in excess of 10 million tons of grain annually during 2005–2007. More broadly, the value of food exports more than doubled from $1.6 billion in 2000 to $9.1 billion in 2007, most of which was grain. Even with this increase, it should be noted that the export of agricultural products accounted for less than 3 percent of the total value of Russia's exports, as oil and gas exports continued to dominate in terms of value and volume.

Russia's economic growth since 2000 led to increases in real disposable incomes. In 2000, GDP per capita was about $7,600, increasing to over

Table 9.1. Annual Agricultural Production, 1998–2007 (all categories of farms)

	1998–1999	2000–2001	2002–2003	2004	2005	2006	2007	2007 as % of 1998–1999 Average
Grains (million tons)	51.2	75.3	76.9	78.0	78.2	78.6	81.8	160
Sugar beets (million tons)	13.0	14.3	17.5	21.8	21.4	30.9	29.0	223
Sunflower seeds (million tons)	3.6	3.3	4.3	4.8	6.4	6.8	5.7	158
Potatoes (million tons)	31.2	34.5	34.7	35.9	37.3	38.6	36.8	118
Vegetables (million tons)	11.4	12.7	14.0	14.5	15.2	15.6	15.5	136
Meat and poultry (million tons, carcass weight)	4.5	4.4	4.8	4.9	4.9	5.2	5.6	124
Milk (million tons)	32.4	32.4	33.4	31.9	32.2	31.0	32.2	99
Eggs (billion)	32.8	34.4	36.3	35.7	35.8	37.9	37.8	115

Sources: Rossiiskii statisticheskii ezhegodnik (Moscow: Goskomstat, 1999), 363–71; Agropromyshlennyi kompleks Rossii (Moscow: Goskomstat, 2001), 61–81; Rossiia v tsifrakh (Moscow: Goskomstat, 2004), 209–11; www.gks.ru/free; www.mcx.ru; A. I. Manellia, "Sel'skoe khoziaistvo Rossii v 2006 godu," Ekonomika sel'skokhoziaistvennykh i pererabatyvaiushchikh predpriiatii, no. 4 (April 2007): 59–62; and author's calculations.
Note: Data for 1998–1999, 2000–01, and 2002–2003 are averages for the two years. Grain totals after cleaning.

Table 9.2. Growth Rate in Value of Agricultural Production by Sector, 2000–2007 (percentage)

	2000	*2001*	*2002*	*2003*	*2004*	*2005*	*2006*	*2007*
Growth rate for all producers within agricultural sector	7.7	7.5	1.5	1.3	3.0	2.3	3.6	3.3
Growth rate for large agricultural enterprises	6.5	11.1	1.9	−3.9	4.8	3.1	4.3	4.9
Growth rate for private farms	21.5	36.1	16.6	11.4	30.7	10.6	18.0	4.1
Growth rate for households	8.0	3.0	.1	4.2	−.4	.7	1.6	2.0

Sources: *Rossiia v tsifrakh* (Moscow: Rosstat, 2005), 211; *Rossiia v tsifrakh* (Moscow: Rosstat, 2006), 223; *Agropromyshlennyi kompleks Rossii v 2005 godu* (Moscow: Rosstat, 2006), 46; A. I. Manellia, "Sel'skoe khoziaistvo Rossii v 2006 godu," *Ekonomika sel'skokhoziaistvennykh i pererabatyvaiushchikh predpriiatii*, no. 4 (April 2007): 59–62; *Rossiia v tsifrakh* (Moscow: Rosstat, 2007), 232; and www.gks.ru.
Note: Growth expressed as change in value of output from previous year, measured in rubles.
Private farms include individual enterprises.

$16,000 by 2008. The rebound in the domestic economy and the increase in real incomes among consumers facilitated an increase in food consumption. Although variations in consumption levels are evident among different socioeconomic groups and regions, the general consumption trend is upward, particularly for meat, which is a high-preference commodity. Just as consumers adjusted their diets during the 1990s by consuming less meat and high-value animal products when their real incomes were contracting, so too did they adjust their diets as real incomes increased after 2000. In particular, consumption of meat products grew substantially in comparison to the 1996–2000 period.

While domestic producers responded to increased demand by producing more meat, the animal husbandry sector was slower to recover, and herd sizes remained significantly below 1990 levels. The reason for a slower recovery is that the raising of beef cattle in particular remained unprofitable, due in large part to price disparities between feed costs and the wholesale price of beef. While the production and sale of grain was profitable in every year during 2000–2007, the raising and sale of beef cattle was unprofitable in every year during the same period. Because Russia's meat production continued to lag 1990 levels of production, imported meat accounted for more than one-third of total supply after 2000. In mid-February 2008, President Putin stated that Russia's largest cities import 80–85 percent of their meat supply.[21] Overall, during 2003–2007, food imports grew faster than domestic production, thereby reflecting both increased demand and the inability of domestic producers to meet consumer demand. In 2007, as shown in table 9.3, the value of food imports into Russia exceeded $27 billion, three times the value of Russia's food exports.

Table 9.3.   Russia's Food Imports, 2000–2007

	Amount Spent on Food Imports ($ billion)	Meat Imports of All Types (million Tons)	Meat Imports as % of Total Supply
2000	7.4	1.2	21
2001	9.2	2.3	34
2002	10.4	2.5	35
2003	12.0	2.3	32
2004	13.8	2.1	30
2005	17.4	2.7	36
2006	21.6	2.7	34
2007	27.5	2.7	33

Source: I. G. Ushachev, "Nauchnoe obespechenie gosudarstvennoi programmy razvitiia sel'skogo kho-ziaistva i regulirovaniia rynkov sel'skokhoziaistvennoi produktsii, syr'ia i prodovol'stviia na 2008–2012 gody," *Ekonommika sel'skokhoziaistvennykh i pererabatyvaiushchikh predpriiatii*, no. 7 (July 2008): 2; and author's calculations.

STAGE TWO: THE NATIONAL PROJECT

The second stage of agrarian policy under Putin witnessed the infusion of massive financial assistance to agriculture in volumes that previously were unimaginable. This stage was marked by the inclusion of the agricultural sector as one of the national projects, a program called "Development of the Agroindustrial Complex" that ran during 2006–2007.[22] The original plan was to expend more than R30 billion during this two-year period, with about R14.2 billion coming from the federal budget, primarily in the form of loans with subsidized interest rates (the term of the loans could range from two to eight years).[23] In reality, just under R48 billion were directed to agriculture during 2006–2007.[24] The federal subsidies, loans, and credits were channeled through various Russian banks, including Sberbank and Rossel'khozbank. In the first year of the program (2006), Rossel'khozbank expanded its loan profile enormously and made more than 130,000 loans, including loans to 121,000 private plot operators and 5,500 private farms, totaling more than R25 billion.[25] As a result, by the end of 2006, Rossel'khozbank had become one of Russia's ten largest banks. Altogether, during the first year of the project, about R70 billion were loaned out, al-most three times as much as the original plan envisioned. Included in the total sum were about R53 billion loaned out for eight-year terms for the development of the animal husbandry sector, including the construction of animal sheds and the acquisition of pedigree cattle.[26]

The program "Development of the Agroindustrial Complex" consisted of state financial support in three broad policy areas.[27] The first was to develop the animal husbandry sector, leading to an increase in the production of ani-mal husbandry products. In order to facilitate growth in domestic animal husbandry, the state purchased pedigree livestock and modern agricultural equipment abroad and leased the animals and equipment at subsidized rates to farms through the state-owned company Rosagrolizing. During 2006–2007, an agricultural enterprise or private farmer could sign a five-year agreement at 0.8 percent annual interest for pedigree cattle, and a 10-year agreement at 1.9 percent annual interest for machinery.[28] The lessee could elect to begin payment one year after the delivery of the equipment or cattle.[29]

The second broad policy area was to stimulate small farming enterprises (personal and family plots, and private farms), along with various types of rural cooperatives. For the development of small farming enterprises, the program envisioned R13.3 million of subsidized credit available for private plot operators, private farmers, and rural consumer credit cooperatives. The chair of Rossel'khozbank, Yuri Trushin, noted that in 2007 the government increased the amount that could be borrowed to R1 million—up to R300,000 for two years, and up to R700,000 for five years. With 18 million private plots and only 200,000 loans processed, Trushin saw "enormous" potential in expanding the number of loans to be dispersed.[30] The program also envisioned the development of a network of rural cooperatives, including credit and consumer coops. The credit coops were expected to help fill the shortage of private credit in the countryside. The third policy area was the construction of adequate housing for young specialists in the countryside as part of the general personnel policy in agriculture, with the intent to retain young specialists in agricultural employment.[31] The federal government originally planned to allocate R2 billion to subsidize the construction of rural housing for agricultural specialists.

The state program in agriculture was important for several reasons. First, the program represented a shift in strategy, as the production potential of the private farming and individual sector took on new importance, and the necessity of state financial support for private producers once again was on the political agenda. A previous special state-funded program to aid private farmers had ended in 1994, and during 2000–2005 the federal budget did not even contain a budget line for support to private farmers. Under the new program, the creation of credit cooperatives was designed to help small-scale producers, who previously often found it difficult to obtain credit from Rossel'khozbank or other large banks, one of the main complaints of private farmers and agrarian politicians. The former president of the private farmers association (AKKOR), Vladimir Bashmachnikov, indicated that prior to the national project, only about 500–600 private farmers in the whole country obtained credit annually, but under the program some 8,000 farmers received credit in 2006, showing that the program "did not turn into a political slogan, but became a real economic foundation."[32] During 2006–2007, more than 11,600 private farmers received loans totaling more than R15 billion from Rossel'khozbank.[33]

Second, the program was important because it demonstrated a strategy to prepare Russian agriculture for international competition. With Russia to join the World Trade Organization (WTO), Putin wanted agriculture to be ready to compete by strengthening domestic producers in the short term and over the longer term.[34] There was also a strategic element as both Putin and Gordeev repeated many times the desire to lessen dependence on foreign food and to reduce imports. Stronger domestic producers were good for the country.

Third, a consequence of strengthening domestic producers was to make investment into agriculture more desirable. Both foreign and domestic investment into agriculture increased substantially. In 2005, the equivalent of R114.5 billion was invested in the Russian countryside from all sources. In 2007, that total had more than doubled, to R310.8 billion.[35] At the same time, a profitable agricultural sector made land a valuable commodity, and both foreign and domestic investors became interested in purchasing agricultural land.[36] As "raiders" bought up farm members' land shares and even whole farms, "land wars" broke out between ordinary rural dwellers. Minister of Agriculture Gordeev described how urbanite "raiders" with money bought up land shares and agricultural land, thereby dispossessing common rural dwellers of their rights to land: "A new type of raiding has appeared. People with money arrive, with lawyers, and together with all the shareowners they sit in a bus, conducting registration. The shares are entered into some kind of auction and are bought. The new 'owners' summon the director of the farm and say—goodbye, this land is no longer yours, and we have other plans for it."[37] Gordeev responded that steps needed to be taken to protect property rights of land shareholders, and he implied that greater regulation of the land market by the state is required. In July 2008, Gordeev announced the creation of a new department in the Ministry of Agriculture that would work out a new conception of land relations and introduce "corrections" to existing land legislation that would increase state regulation over agricultural land.[38]

Finally, the program was important because the degree of state involvement in the dispersion of state-backed credit and subsidized loans creates dependencies that imply a long-term presence of the state in agriculture, a fact that comports with the increased influence of the state in other segments of the economy, such as energy. From a political angle, the increased role of the state in agriculture comports with the attempt to increase "vertical control" over regions from Moscow. When he was deputy prime minister, Dmitri Medvedev was explicit about the national project and vertical control, stating that "the system of control for the implementation of the national project may become a prototype of general state vertical control."[39] Further, the more that different actors and producers within the agricultural sector depend on state financial support, the more the situation suggests that political loyalty to the Kremlin may become a requirement to continue to receive federal monies.

The introduction of the national project in agriculture and achievements during its first year did not preclude criticism from some circles. For example, the chair of the Agrarian Party and president of AKKOR, Vladimir Plotnikov, argued that the project did not do enough or spend enough to solve the long-standing problems in the agricultural sector. He noted that the amount spent on the project in 2006 was "seven times less than the country spent on imported food."[40] Other problems and complaints of agrarians included continued price disparity and unequal terms of trade between agricultural and industrial products, low salaries for agricultural workers, high fuel prices, and a decline in the percentage of the federal budget expenditures allocated to agriculture.[41]

Despite some criticism of the program, press coverage of progress in the program was waged as a Soviet-style press campaign. During 2006–2007, literally every issue of the agricultural newspaper *Sel'skaya zhizn'* (Rural Life) included an article on fulfillment of the program in a specific region. The paper *Krest'yanskiye vedomosti* (Peasants Gazette) often devoted a whole section of each issue to the program's fulfillment, or would carry an interview with Gordeev or some other agricultural official on progress. About once a month, a leading official (often the president) from Rossel'khozbank was interviewed who provided data on the amount of credit that had been dispersed. With this widespread coverage, to even attempt a summary of the accomplishments in the separate regions would be unwieldy. Thus, a short summary of accomplishments will suffice.

Goals and Results

The program's original goals were: (1) to increase milk production by 4.5 percent and meat by 7 percent in comparison to 2005; (2) to increase the volume of food production from private plots and private farms by 5–7 percent; (3) to purchase and lease out 100,000 head of pedigree cattle; (4) to purchase modern efficient equipment for the creation of 130,000 cattle stations; and (5) to create 2,550 rural cooperatives (550 processing cooperatives, 1,000 service cooperatives, and 1,000 credit cooperatives). As noted by one Russian analyst, "practically all" of the indicators were fulfilled. Milk production increased in 57 regions, and overall production was up by 4 percent in comparison to 2005. Production of meat and poultry increased in 64 regions, and overall rose by more than 13 percent compared to 2005.[42] By the end of 2007, the value of production had risen in the private sector (private farms and households) by almost 16 percent in comparison to 2005, or more than double the original goal.[43] In 2007, private farms produced more than 20 percent of the nation's grain, 12 percent of its sugar beets, and about 30 percent of its sunflowers.[44] More than 105,000 head of pedigree cattle had been added to livestock herds, and 266,000 cattle stations were modernized. Finally, 3,840 rural cooperatives were opened, or 150 percent of the original goal.[45]

The success of the original program led Putin to suggest that the program be extended at the expiration of its original term. In March 2007, Deputy Prime Minister Dimitri Medvedev indicated that the program would continue as part of the five-year state program called "The Development of Agriculture during 2008–2012."[46] During that five-year period, state expenditures for agriculture would increase from R76.3 billion in 2008 to R130 billion in 2012.[47] Overall, during the program's five years, R551.3 billion will be financed from the federal budget and R1.5 trillion from the consolidated budget (regional and federal budgets). The goals of the program are: (1) improve regional rural development; (2) increase rural employment and standards of living; (3) increase competitiveness of Russian food products; (4) achieve financial stability in the sector and modernization of agriculture; (5) accelerate the development of priority subbranches within agriculture; and (6) protect and reclaim land and other natural resources that are used in agricultural production.

Going forward, the continuation of the development of the agricultural sector as a governmental priority was clearly evident as the presidency passed from Putin to Medvedev. In the run-up to the March 2008 presidential election, Putin, who would subsequently assume the post of prime minister, promised to continue financial support and state attention to agriculture, and stated that he intended to remain an advocate for the interests of Russian food producers both domestically and in international markets.[48] During the first six months in his new position, Putin continued to speak out in support of agriculture, first in May 2008 when he discussed the tasks to improve the effectiveness of the government's agrarian policies, including increasing food production, reequipping agriculture with modern machinery and technology, and attaining price stability for both inputs used by farms and for consumers.[49] In July 2008, Putin urged faster development of agriculture,[50] and later in summer 2008 he promised to continue to defend the interests of domestic producers in the WTO.[51]

Similar messages came from Medvedev, first as deputy prime minister under Putin and then during the early months of his presidency. As deputy prime minister and presidential nominee, Medvedev promised to continue the policies of state financial support for agriculture, noting that the national project benefited not only agriculture but the economy and society as a whole and therefore should remain a governmental priority.[52] As president, in one of his earliest speeches, Medvedev indicated that "our long-term priority should be regional rural development" and the resolution of rural social problems.[53] He also spoke about the need to address land ownership questions, as well as the regulation of food markets to ensure supply and price stability.

CONCLUSION

In recent years, significant financial improvement in the agricultural sector and increases in food production have been due to governmental policy initiatives and programs of financial support. The recovery in Russian agriculture since 2000 is not meant to suggest that the rural recovery is complete or that continuing problems do not exist. The recovery in Russian agriculture since 2000 is a good start, but more needs to be done. What are some of the problems that need to be addressed in Russian agriculture during Medvedev's first term?

A key problem is that Russia has difficulty feeding itself, despite an increase in food production from Russia's domestic producers since 2000. Indeed, in 2007 the value of Russia's food imports was about three times the value of its food exports. Among G8 nations, only Japan and Russia are net food importers, and Russia imports almost one-half of the food and agricultural products it consumes each year. Moreover, even with the government program to develop agriculture, in 2008 Russia spent about ten times as much on food imports as was allocated for financial support to domestic producers. There is no single cause to the food problem but rather a confluence of factors that has created the inability of domestic producers to meet demand.

While domestic food production has rebounded from its decline in the 1990s, the chair of the Committee on Agro-food Policy in the Federation Council noted that in recent years the value of gross production in the agricultural sector has lagged growth rates in the economy as a whole and increases in real income.[54] Moreover, many farms are not in a financial position to expand production. Thus, domestic production cannot satisfy increased demand that has resulted from higher real incomes. In particular, the value of total agricultural production in 2007 was just over 78 percent the level of 1990. But there are important sectoral differences. The value of production of plant products in 2007 was 107 percent that of 1990, but the value of animal husbandry production was less than 58 percent the 1990 level. In 2006, meat consumption had almost reached 1990 levels, but the sizes of beef and milk cattle herds were only 38 percent of their 1990 levels, and domestic meat output was about one-half the 1990 level. The inability of Russia to feed itself became especially important in 2008, when commodity prices worldwide drove up food prices for consumers and input prices for food producers. The Russian government responded by imposing limits on grain exports and established regulated retail prices for selected commodities in markets where food retailers controlled more than 15 percent of the retail market.[55]

The rise in food imports has several consequences. Advocates of "food security" assert that Russia is dangerously dependent on imported foodstuffs, and food security as a slogan representing Russian nationalism became more prevalent in 2008 than any other time since 1995.[56] Not only have concerns about national food security arisen, but the exposure to global price increases in commodities fuels inflation within Russia. When talking about the increase in the value of food imports, Gordeev stated that "in such conditions a stable food market is not possible."[57] Moreover, concerns over national food security and food production led the government to reexamine laws regulating agricultural land use with a view toward increasing state regulation. Similarly, concerns over food security created pressures to increase government regulation of trade networks and food trade, up to and including regulating prices of basic foodstuffs.[58]

Why doesn't Russia just produce more if demand is growing, particularly for meat products? One reason is that increases in costs from fuels, feed, and fertilizers have created price disparities between inputs and farm gate prices whereby input prices have risen faster than wholesale prices received by producers, especially those of livestock products. Russian farms today respond quickly to price relationships and adjust product mix, but it takes longer and is more expensive to rebuild herds than to change crops. In Russia, farms have been exposed to worldwide commodity price increases, and rapidly rising feed and transportation costs offset to a certain degree the infusion of state financial assistance to the animal husbandry sector. For example, Rossel'khozbank distributed more than R84 billion in subsidized credit (about $3.2 billion at 2008 exchange rates) to the development of animal husbandry—obtaining heads of livestock and the construction or repair of animal sheds during 2006–2007.[59] But the amount of credit given pales in comparison to the amount spent on meat imports. In the 2008–2012 program, an additional R47 billion will be allocated to the development of the animal husbandry sector from the federal budget.[60]

Another factor restricting production expansion is the shortage of skilled workers and antiquated agricultural machinery and technology. In mid-2008, Gordeev indicated that there was a deficit of 70,000 specialists in the agricultural sector.[61] Because incomes for agricultural workers are at or near the bottom of the national income scale, large farms often lose skilled labor to other professions or other branches of the economy. According to data from the Ministry of Agriculture, in 2006 large farms employed less than 42 percent the number of agricultural specialists as in 1990, 19 percent the number of workers in animal husbandry, and 25 percent the number of tractorists and machinists as in 1990.[62] Lower levels of rural amenities, including educational and cultural opportunities, and substandard rural housing make it difficult to retain skilled rural labor. As a result, less-skilled labor is used, which decreases efficiency and adds to production costs. The need to improve the quality of human capital is especially great if Russia hopes to compete with advanced farming sectors among many EU nations and in the United States, where governments actively support agricultural education and science.

Another problem is to improve the capital stock of large farms and private farms, both quantitatively and qualitatively. It is estimated that much of Russia's technological base in agriculture is two to three generations behind the developed world, a reflection of years of neglect and lack of investment. These shortcomings affect production levels and yields. A related problem is rural infrastructure in general, including roads, food storage, and the export capacity of ports, which after years of neglect are substandard. In the past, state financial support for exports was oriented toward industrial goods, but credits from the federal budget are now included under the rubric of the program to develop agriculture for the export of processed food.[63] In 2008, a program for the development of the transport system was adopted that will expend R14 trillion during 2010–2015. This program is planned to expand railroad lines by 4,700 kilometers and build or repair 7,300 kilometers of roads on federal property.[64]

At present, rural labor is cheaper than machinery, and thus a key to the production problem is an agricultural system that supports sustainable rural communities. In 2002, a program of social development was adopted that was to run through 2010, and in his speech to the Federal Assembly in May 2003, Putin indicated that a substantial reduction in poverty was a national priority. President Medvedev's government has promised to work for an increase in rural standards of living, an increase in rural incomes, and a reduction of rural poverty. Sustainable rural communities are a major budget item in the 2008–2012 program, with more than R107 billion allocated to the improvement of "social infrastructure" and rural development.[65]

The development of sustainable rural communities in Russia has been complicated by widespread rural poverty. Two well-known Russian experts estimate that 77 percent of rural children age 16 or less live in households in which the average monetary income is below the subsistence minimum, 67 percent of workers in agriculture and forestry have monetary incomes below the poverty line, and 54 percent of rural management personnel have monetary incomes below the poverty line.[66] If nonmonetary income is included, the percentages are somewhat lower but still are very high. Only a small percentage of the rural population could be considered well off. [67] Rural poverty is compounded by enduring high unemployment and limited alternative employment opportunities, particularly in remote small villages. Poorer households are disadvantaged in a number of ways that make the alleviation of poverty more difficult. Households in poverty have disadvantages in their demographic structure; they tend to consume more of the food they produce and sell less; they have lower income from entrepreneurial activities; they have smaller land holdings and are more risk averse; and the remoteness of village location influences income.[68]

Building sustainable rural communities is more complex than throwing money at the problem. An integrated program must be funded that addresses many rural problems simultaneously, including but not limited to infrastructure, educational, recreational, and cultural opportunities, rural housing, low incomes and high poverty, and the quality and quantity of human capital and social capital. As Russian leaders have indicated, the long-term health of agriculture depends on rural areas not being an unpleasant place to live and work. But that is easier said than done, especially when considering the extent and size of "rural" Russia. Several of the Western nations in the European Union demonstrate that a large rural workforce is not required for a productive agricultural sector. At the same time, the EU has taken deliberate steps to build sustainable rural communities and has a separate budget line for rural development that is used to alleviate rural poverty and reduce motivations for out-migration. These goals are enormously expensive and have been pursued for several decades. Russia is attempting to undo a historical legacy of unmet goals—we should remember that the Soviet leadership under Brezhnev in the 1960s also posited the goals of raising rural standards of living and bringing living conditions closer to those found in urban areas.

Complicating the problem is the contradiction between building sustainable rural communities and the larger goal of modernizing the agricultural sector. Building sustainable communities implies that rural out-migration will be low, which in turn avoids the ripple effects of housing shortages and dislocation of labor. This goal also implies that the size of the rural population as a percentage of the total population will remain relatively high. This goal further implies relatively higher expenditures on transfer payments as the rural population continues to age. On the other hand, the modernization of agriculture implies a reduced need for labor and a weakening, if not ending, of the symbiotic relationship between large farms and rural households that has existed for decades. Modernization of agriculture implies higher rural out-migration and transfer of labor from rural to urban locales. Thus, it is important to note that some of the macroeconomic goals are contradictory, and it is not clear how those contradictions will be rectified. Going forward, therefore, despite notable improvements in Russian agriculture during Putin's administration, the challenges that lie ahead are formidable, and success is sure to be difficult.

Suggested Readings

Ioffe, Grigory, Tatyana Nefedova, and Ilya Zaslavsky. *The End of Peasantry? The Disintegration of Rural Russia*. Pittsburgh, Pa.: University of Pittsburgh Press, 2006.

Lerman, Zvi, ed. *Russia's Agriculture in Transition: Factor Markets and Constraints on Growth*. Lanham, Md.: Lexington Books, 2008.

O'Brien, David J., and Valery V. Patsiorkovsky. *Measuring Social and Economic Change in Rural Russia: Surveys from 1991 to 2003*. Lanham, Md.: Lexington Books, 2006.

O'Brien, David J., and Stephen K. Wegren, eds. *Rural Reform in Post-Soviet Russia*. Washington, D.C.: Woodrow Wilson Press/Johns Hopkins University Press, 2002.

Pallot, Judith, and Tat'yana Nefedova. *Russia's Unknown Agriculture: Household Production in Post-Socialist Rural Russia*. Oxford: Oxford University Press, 2007.

Wegren, Stephen K. *Russia's Food Policies and Globalization*. Lanham, Md.: Lexington Books, 2005.

———. *The Moral Economy Reconsidered: Russia's Search for Agrarian Capitalism*. New York: Palgrave Macmillan, 2005.

———. "Typologies of Household Risk-Taking: Contemporary Rural Russia as a Case Study," *Journal of Peasant Studies* 35, no. 3 (2008): 390–423.

———. *Land Reform in Russia: Institutional Design and Behavioral Responses*. New Haven, Conn.: Yale University Press, 2009.

NOTES

1. Some of these problems included price disparities between agriculture and other branches of the economy; the lack of a market infrastructure for agricultural machinery, leading to increased dependence on imported machinery; low rural incomes and persistent rural poverty; high expenditures on food imports; and a variety of social problems related to the quantity and quality of rural labor. See *Rossiiskaia zemlia*, no. 2 (January 2005): 5–6, and no. 18 (May 2005): 3; Grigory Ioffe, Tatyana Nefedova, and Ilya Zaslavsky, *The End of Peasantry? The Disintegration of Rural Russia* (Pittsburgh: University of Pittsburgh Press, 2006); A. V. Gordeev, "O gosudarstvennoi programme razvitiia sel'skogo khoziaistva na 2008–2012 gody," *Ekonomika sel'skokhoziaistvennykh i pererabatyvaiushchikh predpriiatii*, no. 9 (September 2007): 6–10; and I. Ushachev, "Nauchnoe obespechenie programmy razvitiia sel'skogo khoziaistva na 2008–2012 gg," *Ekonomist*, no. 4 (April 2008): 19–30.

2. See Stephen K. Wegren, "Putin and Agriculture," in *Putin's Russia: Past Imperfect, Future Uncertain*, 3rd ed., ed. Dale R. Herspring (Lanham, Md.: Rowman & Littlefield, 2007), 147.

3. For a survey of government policies, both those discussed in this chapter and others, see L. Kosholkina, "Gosudarstvennoe regulirovanie APK," *Ekonomist*, no. 7 (July 2005): 81–85; Stephen K. Wegren, *The Moral Economy Reconsidered: Russia's Search for Agrarian Capitalism* (New York: Palgrave Macmillan, 2005); and Zvi Lerman, ed., *Russia's Agriculture in Transition: Factor Markets and Constraints on Growth* (Lanham, Md.: Lexington Books, 2008).

4. Cited in *Rossiiskaia zemlia*, nos. 34–35 (September 2007): 4.

5. Judith Pallot and Tatyana Nefedova, *Russia's Unknown Agriculture: Household Production in Post-Socialist Rural Russia* (Oxford: Oxford University Press, 2007), chaps. 3, 5.

6. Livestock herds were especially hard hit. During the first eight years of contemporary agrarian reform (1992–1999), the number of beef cattle declined by 46 percent and

the number of pigs by 48 percent. To put those declines in perspective, during the first seven years of Stalin's collectivization (1928–1934), the number of cattle decreased by 40 percent and the number of pigs by 33 percent. As a result of declines in contemporary livestock holdings, livestock herds at the end of 1999 were smaller than herds in the late 1950s. *Sel'skoe khoziaistvo v Rossii* (Moscow: Goskomstat, 2000), 66–67.

7. *Rossiiskii statisticheskii ezhegodnik* (Moscow: Goskomstat, 2000), 361.

8. *Sel'skoe khoziaistvo v Rossii* (Moscow: Goskomstat, 2002), 57.

9. See Stephen K. Wegren, "Russian Agrarian Policy under Putin," *Post-Soviet Geography and Economics* 43, no. 1 (2002): 27–28. Gordeev was minister of agriculture from August 1999 into February 2009. On March 12, 2009, President Medvedev signed a decree replacing him with Elena Skrynnik. Because this chapter concerns policies in force under Gordeev's leadership, the remainder of the chapter refers to him as Minister Gordeev instead of former minister.

10. See "O finansovom ozdorovlenii sel'skokhoziaistvennykh tovaroproizvoditelei," *Sobranie zakonodatel'stva Rossiiskoi Federatsii*, no. 28 (July 15, 2002): 7121–30. And see the methodological appendix for calculating the financial status of an agricultural enterprise, embodied in Government Resolution no. 52 on January 30, 2003, published in *Ekonomika sel'skokhoziaistvennykh i pererabatyvaiushchikh predpriiatii*, no. 3 (March 2003): 33. Farms have to meet certain financial criteria to be eligible to participate in the program.

11. L. A. Kosholkina, "Finansovoe ozdorovlenie sel'skokhoziaistvennykh organizatsii," *Ekonomika sel'skokhoziaistvennykh i pererabatyvaiushchikh predpriiatii*, no. 9 (September 2003): 12.

12. *Rossiiskaia zemlia*, no. 7 (February 2005): 2.

13. Data from the Russian Ministry of Agriculture website under the link "financial renewal." See www.mcx.ru.

14. *Krest'ianskie vedomosti*, nos. 20–21 (May 2008): 3.

15. *Sel'skaia zhizn'*, December 18–24, 2008, 1–3.

16. Cited in V. N. Khlystun, "Zemel'no-ipotechnoe kreditovanie: Sostoianie i perspektivy," *Ekonomika sel'skokhoziaistvennykh i pererabatyvaiushchikh predpriiatii*, no. 4 (April 2008): 12.

17. *Sel'skaia zhizn'*, June 26–July 2, 2008, 6.

18. A. Ia. Kibirov, E. V. Sergatskova, and L. V. Gubernatorova, "Vozrozhdenia zemel'noi ipoteki v sel'skom khoziaistve Rossii," *Ekonomika sel'skokhoziaistvennykh i pererabatyvaiushchikh predpriiatii*, no. 5 (May 2008): 17.

19. *Krest'ianskie vedomosti*, no. 37 (September 2006): 4, 7.

20. *Krest'ianskie vedomosti*, nos. 1–2 (January 2007): 2.

21. *Krest'ianskie vedomosti*, no. 8 (February 2008): 2.

22. The original national project included agriculture as one of the national priorities; the other priorities were housing reform, health, and education.

23. Expenditures included R7.45 billion in 2006 and R7.18 billion in 2007 for the development of animal husbandry; and R6.6 billion in 2006 and R9.37 billion in 2007 for the stimulation of small farming enterprises and various types of cooperatives. During 2006–2007, there was a link at the Russian Ministry of Agriculture's website called "The National Project," from which these data were taken. In 2008, this link was replaced with a link called "The State Program," which includes information for the development of agriculture. See www.mcx.ru.

24. A. Slepnev, "Razvitie sel'skogo khoziaistva na blizhayshuiu perspektivu," *APK: ekonomika, upravlenie,* no. 6 (June 2008): 2.

25. *Sel'skaia zhizn'*, May 3–9, 2007, 5.

26. *Krest'ianskie vedomosti,* no. 6 (February 2007): 3.

27. The program was worked out and discussed during 2005. An early description of the program in agriculture was published in October 2005. See *Sel'skaia zhizn'*, October 25, 2005, 1, 3, 4.

28. *Krest'ianskie vedomosti,* nos. 14–15 (April 2007): 6–7.

29. *Krest'ianskie vedomosti,* no. 10 (March 2007): 2.

30. See the interview with Trushin in *Sel'skaia zhizn'*, June 14–20, 2007, 3.

31. "Vystupleniia Ministra," April 7, 2006, www.mcx.ru.

32. *Sel'skaia zhizn'*, March 27, 2007, 3.

33. *Fermerskoe samoupravlenie,* nos. 3–5 (March–May 2008): 5.

34. On Russian agriculture and the WTO, see S. V. Kiselev, ed., *VTO i sel'skoe khoziaistvo Rossii* (Moscow: Teis, 2003); A. V. Petikov, ed., *Agroprodovol'stvennaia politika i vstuplenie Rossii v VTO* (Moscow: Russian Academy of Agricultural Sciences, 2003); and Stephen K. Wegren, "Russian Agriculture and the WTO," *Problems of Post-Communism* 54, no. 4 (2007): 46–59.

35. L. Kosholkina, "Rezul'taty natsional'nogo proekta "Razvitie APK,'" *Ekonomist,* no. 6 (June 2008): 18.

36. Although ownership of agricultural land by foreigners is not permitted by law, this prohibition is easily skirted by setting up Russian-owned subsidiaries that could buy farm land.

37. *Krest'ianskiie vedomosti,* no. 12 (April 2007): 3.

38. *Sel'skaia zhizn'*, July 17–23, 2008, 1.

39. *Krest'ianskie vedomosti,* no. 41 (October 2006): 2.

40. See interview with Plotnikov on the national project in *Rossiiskaia zemlia,* no. 39 (October 2006): 3, and quote from Plotnikov in no. 15 (April 2007): 3.

41. See *Rossiiskaia zemlia,* no. 42 (November 2006): 7, and no. 15 (April 2007): 4; and *Sel'skaia zhizn'*, June 17, 2008, 1–2.

42. Data from Slepnev, "Razvitie sel'skogo khoziaistva na blizhayshuiu perspektivu," 2.

43. Kosholkina, "Rezul'taty natsional'nogo proekta 'Razvitie APK,'" 17.

44. *Fermerskoe samoupravlenie,* nos. 3–5 (March–May 2008): 6.

45. Slepnev, "Razvitie sel'skogo khoziaistva na blizhayshuiu perspektivu," 2.

46. *Sel'skaia zhizn'*, March 20, 2007, 1; the goals of the five-year plan are discussed by Medvedev in *Krest'ianskie vedomosti,* no. 9 (March 2007): 10.

47. The planned expenditures are enumerated at the website of the Ministry of Agriculture, www.mcx.ru.

48. *Krest'ianskie vedomosti,* no. 8 (February 2008): 2.

49. See Putin's speech of May 19, 2008, at www.government.ru.

50. *Sel'skaia zhizn'*, July 15, 2008, 1.

51. *Krest'ianskie vedomosti,* no. 34 (August 2008): 2. In 2008, a website was opened on the national projects with links to health, education, housing, and agriculture. The website also has links to news, including speeches and presentations by Putin and Medvedev, as well as documents, events, and data on fulfillment by federal region. See www.rost.ru.

52. *Krest'ianskie vedomosti*, nos. 1–2 (January 2008): 4; and *Rossiiskaia zemlia*, no. 6 (February 2008): 1.

53. *Krest'ianskiie vedomosti*, no. 10 (March 2008): 2.

54. *Sel'skaia zhizn'*, July 31–August 6, 2008, 3.

55. *Rossiiskaia zemlia*, no. 13 (April 2008): 2.

56. For example, at the end of October 2008, the minister of agriculture spoke before the Federation Council on the status of Russia's food security and measures to ensure it. See www.mcx.ru under the link "Vystupleniia Ministra."

57. *Rossiiskaia zemlia*, no. 21 (June 2008): 5.

58. Toward that end, in November 2008 Gordeev chaired a meeting in the Ministry of Agriculture to discuss state regulation of trade. See www.mcx.ru under the link "Novosti Ministerstva."

59. *Rossiiskaia zemlia*, no. 20 (May 2008): 2.

60. "Gosudarstvennaia programma razvitiia sel'skogo khoziaistva i regulirovaniia rynkov sel'skokhoziaistvenoi produktsii, syr'ia i prodovol'stviia na 2008–2012 gody (prilozheniia)," *Ekonomist*, no. 10 (October 2007): 18. In contrast, the program envisions about R22 billion for the development of the plant-growing sector of agriculture—less than half the total for animal husbandry.

61. *Sel'skaia zhizn'*, June 5–11, 2008, 3.

62. Ushchachev, "Nauchnoe obespechenie programmy razvitia sel'skogo khoziaistva na 2008–2012," 21.

63. *Sel'skaia zhizn'*, June 5–11, 2008, 3.

64. *Rossiiskaia zemlia*, no. 19 (May 2008): 2.

65. "Gosudarstvennaia programma razvitiia sel'skogo khoziaistva i regulirovaniia rynkov sel'skokhoziaistvenoy produktsii, syr'ia i prodovol'stviia na 2008–2012 gody (prilozheniia)," 17.

66. I. Ushchachev and L. Bondarenko, "Kontseptsiia snizheniia sel'skoi bednosti," *APK: ekonomika, upravlenie*, no. 1 (January 2007): 5; and see David J. O'Brien and Valery V. Patsiorkovsky, *Measuring Social and Economic Change in Rural Russia: Surveys from 1991 to 2003* (Lanham, Md.: Lexington Books, 2006), chap. 7.

67. O'Brien and Patsiorkovsky, *Measuring Social and Economic Change in Rural Russia*, chap. 6; and see David J. O'Brien, Stephen K. Wegren, and Valery V. Patsiorkovsky, "Income Stratification in Russian Villages: From Profession to Property," *Problems of Post-Communism* 54, no. 1 (2007): 37–46.

68. See Stephen K. Wegren, David J. O'Brien, and Valery V. Patsiorkovsky, "The Economics of Rural Households in Russia: The Impact of Location," *Eurasian Geography and Economics* 49, no. 2 (2008): 200–14; and Stephen K. Wegren, "Typologies of Household Risk-Taking: Contemporary Rural Russia as a Case Study," *Journal of Peasant Studies* 35, no. 3 (2008): 390–423.

Part Three

FOREIGN POLICY AND THE MILITARY

Chapter Ten

Russia's Foreign Policy

Andrei P. Tsygankov

Early in Putin's second term as president, Russia's foreign policy became much more assertive, but Russia's international course has not become confrontational.[1] Instead, Russia has signaled that it seeks greater stakes in the international system and will no longer accept the status of the West's junior partner as during the 1990s. In addition to its desire to capitalize on its energy competitiveness and break into Western economic markets, Russia no longer viewed the old methods of preserving stability and security as sufficient. Putin's speech at the Munich Conference on Security Policy in February 2007 became a high point in Russia's new assertiveness, at which he was extremely critical of U.S. "unilateralism." Putin accused the United States of "disdain for the basic principles of international law" and having "overstepped its national borders in . . . the economic, political, cultural and educational policies it imposes on other nations."[2] Russia's assertiveness was again evident in August 2008 in response to Georgia's use of force against South Ossetia. Despite worldwide disapproval, Russia cemented its military presence in the Caucasus by defeating Georgia and recognizing the independence of South Ossetia and Abkhazia. Through its actions in the Caucasus, Russia has demonstrated that, while maintaining an essentially defensive security posture, it believes in a more assertive strategy to defend its national interests and is ready to use force in the areas that it views as critically important.

This chapter documents the shift to a more assertive foreign policy in various geopolitical directions—West, East, and the former Soviet region—as a result of Russia's increased material ability and perceived political vulnerability. Contrary to some common views that attribute Russia's assertive behavior to its traditionally imperialist and anti-Western political culture, the primary drivers in the Kremlin's foreign policy are contemporary and domestic. They include new opportunities for economic growth and stability, as well as a need to address increasing security threats. Initially the country's leadership was hoping to develop a grand strategy by engaging Western nations, in particular the United States, in projects of common significance, such as counterterrorism and energy security. However, as the West turned its attention elsewhere and as Russia grew stronger, the Kremlin made important adjustments to its policy. While taking precautions against encroachment on its sovereignty, Russia is far from isolating itself or launching imperial revenge against those vulnerable to its pressures. The concluding section of the chapter offers an assessment of Russia's assertive foreign policy and analyzes challenges ahead.

RUSSIA'S CONDITIONS AND WORLDVIEW

New Conditions

After years of post-Soviet depression, Russia's domestic conditions changed dramatically. By 2007, the economy reached the level of 1990 in terms of GDP, and since 1999 grew about 7 percent annually. The overall size of the economy increased about six times in current dollars—from $200 billion to $1.3 trillion. Russia's per capita GDP quadrupled to nearly $7,000, and about 20 million people have been lifted out of poverty.[3] Russia's middle class now constitutes about 25 percent of the population.[4] During 2000–2005, the average Russian saw a 26 percent annual growth in income, while the average Chinese saw only 10 percent growth.[5] Direct foreign investments to the Russian economy skyrocketed, making it the first in the world among developing economies.[6] Although much of the economic recovery was due to high oil prices, the government continued to work to reduce a reliance on energy exports. In early 2008, for example, industrial production rose an annual 9.2 percent.[7] As a result, there was an increase in the number of Russians who thought that the course of development in Russia was correct.[8] The economic recovery provided conditions for Russia's active business promotion in Europe, where Russia conducts 50 percent of its foreign trade. The Kremlin insisted on long-term contracts with Europeans and greater integration with European markets in order to avoid repetition of the 1985–1986 scenario when a sharp decline in energy prices considerably contributed to the breakup of the Soviet economy.

Because of the economic recovery, the domestic political situation also improved, yet Moscow was fearful of destabilization resulting from the U.S. strategy of global regime change. For three reasons, Russia viewed liberalizing and democratizing instincts coming from the United States as directed against the Kremlin's power and security. First, the Kremlin feared a "color" revolution inside Russia similar to the Orange Revolution in Ukraine. Although the public support for a revolution was weak,[9] the Kremlin's political technologists took the threat seriously, based on the fact that influential elites in the United States maintained contacts with some radical organizations in Russia.[10]

Second, the Kremlin felt increasingly encircled by radical pro-American regimes in the former Soviet region. The color revolutions in Ukraine, Georgia, and Kyrgyzstan during 2003–2005 failed to bring greater stability and prosperity but did politicize the international environment in the region. Georgia and Ukraine expressed their desire to join NATO, which added to Russia's sense of strategic insecurity. In the aftermath of the NATO summit in April 2008, President Putin stated, "We view the appearance of a powerful military bloc on our borders . . . as a direct threat to the security of our country. The claim that this process is not directed against Russia will not suffice. National security is not based on promises."[11] The public also reacted overwhelmingly negatively to the alliance's expansion: 74 percent of Russians polled in March 2008 said that Ukraine's possible accession to NATO posed a threat to the national security of the Russian Federation, and 77 percent expressed a similar attitude toward Georgia's possible membership in the organization.[12]

Third, Russia felt vulnerable to radicalization of Islam. Although some of Russia's problems toward Islamic terrorism could be attributed to its own errors, such as attempts by some of its authorities to close local mosques, another part had to do with U.S. policies that tended to isolate moderate Muslims. In a global world, this translated into a greater support for Islamic radicals inside Russia.

The Kremlin therefore had come to realize that a purely defensive strategy could no longer provide the necessary sense of stability and security, and it was important to take active measures to defend Russia's interests. This explains why the Kremlin trained its own youth organizations, restricted activities of Western NGOs and radical opposition inside the country, and warned the United States against interference with Russia's domestic developments. Russia's elections also demonstrated fear of outside interference and the willingness of Russian politicians to resort to anti-Western rhetoric.[13]

The Vision of a More Assertive Foreign Policy

The broad objectives of Russia's foreign policy have essentially stayed the same, as outlined in Vladimir Putin's 1999 speech "Russia at the Turn of the Millennium."[14] These goals encompass economic modernization, political stability, and enhancement of security. Yet, in response to new economic opportunities and security vulnerabilities, Russia modified the *methods* of pursuing these foreign policy objectives.

In his response to a new foreign policy context, Putin sought to reaffirm Russia's commitment to European values. In his speech delivered to the Federation Council in April 2005, Putin declared that he saw Russia moving toward the same values shared by others in the European continent: "the ideals of freedom, human rights, justice and democracy."[15] In the former Soviet region, this translated into the doctrine of "continuing the civilizational role of the Russian nation in Eurasia." Responding to charges of "imperialism" toward post-Soviet nations in the wake of the color revolutions, Putin insisted that Russia seeks not the post-Soviet states' territory or natural resources, but human dignity and the quality of life for its citizens, whom it regards as its own cultural compatriots. He stated: "Russia, traditionally linked with the former Soviet republics, and now newly independent states, by history, the Russian language and great culture, cannot stay away from the common striving for freedom."[16] Putin was clear, however, that while moving in the same direction of freedom and democracy as Europeans, Russia does so at its own pace and given its own conditions. In the same speech referring to the Western role in the color revolutions in Georgia and Ukraine, Putin insisted on Russia's right to "decide for itself the pace, terms and conditions of moving towards democracy," and he warned against attempts to destabilize the political system by "any unlawful methods of struggle."[17] The motive of noninterference in Russia's domestic developments from outside only became stronger over time, and in his addresses to the Federation Council in May 2006 and April 2007, Putin put an even greater emphasis on the values of sovereignty and strong national defense.[18]

Putin's supporters interpreted his vision using concepts of "sovereign democracy" and "sovereign economy,"[19] insisting on the need for Russia to protect its path of development and natural resources. The Kremlin's leading ideologist, Vladislav Surkov, justified the concept of sovereign democracy by the need to defend an internally determined path to political development and to protect economic prosperity, individual freedom, and social justice from potential threats, which he defined as "international terrorism, military conflict, lack of economic competitiveness, and soft takeovers by 'orange technologies' in a time of decreased national immunity to foreign influence."[20] "Sovereign economy" indicates the state's determination to have an upper hand in deciding conditions on which Western companies participate in Russia's economic development. In the world of growing energy prices, the emphasis shifted from providing macroeconomic discipline and tough fiscal policies toward a desire to capitalize on Russia's reserves of natural gas and oil. In addition, Russia insisted that a more assertive foreign policy would better protect its national security. Putin's speech in Munich,[21] with its strong criticism of U.S. "unilateralism" in world politics, was especially noteworthy as another reminder that Russia was not about to tolerate policies that it viewed as interfering with its sovereignty and security. Importantly, the speech was delivered to a European audience; Putin's supporters have long argued that insistence on sovereignty and security was not inconsistent with European values. From their perspective, by upholding values of sovereignty, Russia was in fact preserving European values that Europe itself could not always sustain when confronted with political pressures from the United States.[22]

Overall, a new foreign policy consensus emerged that an assertive style of achieving the objectives of development, stability, and security suited Russia well at the moment. The new Foreign Ministry report entitled "A Review of the Russian Federation's Foreign Policy," commissioned by the Kremlin and released on March 27, 2007, further elaborated on the new face of Russia's great power pragmatism. It indicated an important change in Russia's thinking since the 2000 Foreign Policy Concept. The 2007 report embraced the notion of multipolarity based on "a more equitable distribution of resources for influence and economic growth,"[23] which it said laid the ground for a more self-confident and assertive Russia. The document presented Russia as ready to actively shape international relations by challenging the actions of others, particularly the United States, if they were "unilateral" and disrespectful of international law. At the same time, the report was not anti-American and did not call for any concerted effort to undermine the United States' global position. Instead, it defended the notion of collective leadership and multilateral diplomacy as an alternative to unilateralism and hegemony in international relations.

Russia's new president, Dmitri Medvedev, has amplified Putin's assertive vision, seeking to position Russia as a global player and a maker of new global rules. Speaking in Berlin in June 2008, Medvedev proposed a broad perspective on Europe "from Vancouver to Vladivostok" and proposed an all-European treaty to establish a new security arrangement by moving beyond NATO expansion and the conflict over Kosovo.[24] In addition to expressing his dissatisfaction with the U.S. role in European security, Medvedev blamed the United States for generating the global financial crisis by trying to substitute for the global commodities and financial markets, and he proposed an overhaul of the international economic order.[25] By this criticism, Russia did not mean to pursue an anti-Western policy. Rather, Russia sought to reengage the West on terms the Kremlin found comfortable—by strengthening membership within a U.S.-EU-Russia alliance, developing ties with growing powers, such as China and India, and sharing the world's economic benefits with poor non-Western nations.

The Domestic Support for Assertiveness

This new vision found support within Russia's political elite. Security threats associated with terrorism and the expansion of Western military infrastructure toward Russian borders strengthened the position of the security class. The security class did not become dominant, as some have suggested,[26] but it was able to influence state decisions more than previously, and it gained a greater presence in commercial companies, especially those that were energy related. The state was not consolidated enough to isolate powerful security influences, yet it did not become a hostage to those influences. Liberals, such as Alexei Kudrin, stayed in the government and continued to make a case for more aggressive liberal economic policies. Members of the security class were unable to assert greater isolationism in economic matters by protecting large companies from international competition,[27] or in politics by forcing Putin to stay for a third presidential term. Increasingly, the state was taking charge in deciding between ideologies of security-driven isolationism and liberal-minded openness.

The state's position has been to stake a middle ground between the two approaches by acquiring a greater prominence in economic affairs, and making Russia more open, not closed, to international competition. Ever since the most powerful oligarchs, such as Boris Berezovsky, Vladimir Gusinsky, and Mikhail Khodorkovsky, were stripped of their economic empires, the state has consistently asserted itself in other key areas. It increased its share in leading energy companies, such as Gazprom and Rosneft. It renegotiated production-sharing agreements with Western companies in some of the most lucrative oil fields in Siberia and the Far East. Foreign energy giants, such as Royal Dutch Shell and British Petroleum, now had to play by different rules as introduced by the more assertive Russian state. In addition to the energy industry and military-industrial complex, the state announced plans to create "national champions," or state-supported companies in the banking, aerospace, automobile, and heavy machinery sectors. Yet the state also argued that the creation of such companies was necessary to position them for successful international competition.[28] Russian officials also insisted on expediting the country's entrance to the WTO. Furthermore, Putin's strategy of a state-dominant capitalism recognized the vital need of foreign investment, particularly from Western nations, for continuing high economic growth.

EUROPE AND THE UNITED STATES

Energy Strategy and Relations with Europe

In relations with European countries, Russia's main focus was greater integration with the EU's economy, and it has concluded a number of important agreements to this effect. Russia's largest natural gas company, Gazprom, agreed to build a direct pipeline to Germany underneath the Baltic Sea. It also negotiated an agreement with Hungary to extend Russia's Blue Stream pipeline from Turkey to Hungary via Bulgaria and Romania. Another important development is a new oil pipeline to Bulgaria and Greece projected to be built by 2010, with Russia owning 50.5 percent. The oil supplies from Russia would be shipped through the Black Sea, bypassing the crowded Bosporus.[29] Russia also managed to achieve greater integration with European economies by exchanging some companies' shares, and it made progress in political relations with the EU by developing a common understanding on solving the Middle Eastern conflict and the issue of Iran's nuclear program. Many Europeans shared the Kremlin's commitment to multilateralism and negotiations, rather than sanctions and force.

Still, the strategy of integration with European countries faced important obstacles. Russia and the EU disagreed on what defines economic security. And the EU perceived Russia's energy disputes with former Soviet republics as a threat to its own interests and insisted that Russia ratify the Energy Charter. The charter had been signed by Boris Yeltsin during the 1990s and stipulated access for third parties to Russia's energy pipelines. The EU also saw the issue in terms of market diversification principles and wanted to have room for changing energy partners should such opportunity present itself. However, Russia was an energy producer, not a consumer, and it wanted to sign long-term contracts. Given the significance of high energy prices for its economic development, Russia wanted to avoid repetition of the 1985–1986 situation, when a sharp decline in oil prices undermined the Soviet economy. In addition, Russia was wary of European efforts to negotiate separate energy agreements with Azerbaijan, Turkey, and other countries of Central Asia. Russia also had limited success in gaining greater access to EU retail markets and distribution networks, as well as shares in prominent European companies.[30]

Other difficult issues included the role of the Organization for Security and Cooperation in Europe (OSCE) in the former Soviet region and bilateral disputes with some Eastern European nations concerning, among other things, their decision to work with the United States in deploying an antimissile system on their territory. Russia saw the OSCE as deviating from its main mission to solve security conflicts, instead concentrating on pushing a particular version of democracy in the region. The Kremlin indicated to the OSCE that it would withdraw its financial contribution should that practice continue. Russia also took a hard line on the missile defense system, claiming that in response it was considering withdrawal from the Intermediate Nuclear Missile Treaty. In November 2008, President Medvedev indicated that Russia may aim some of its missiles at Poland and the Czech Republic, the nations that agreed to host the system on their territory. In addition, Russia refused to yield to pressure from Eastern European states to acknowledge responsibility for the Soviet occupation of their territory following World War II, or to transport energy to Western European countries through Eastern

Europe. Russia-EU summits in Samara (May 2007) and Khanty-Mansiysk (June 2008) failed to secure a "strategic partnership" pact or to produce any substantive agreements.[31]

Cooperation and Rivalry with the United States

In a number of areas, Russia's cooperation with the United States remained strong since the post-9/11 partnership. Both sides were committed to solving issues of nuclear proliferation and joined forces in encouraging North Korea and Iran to halt their movement toward producing nuclear weapons. The United States supported Russia's proposal to reprocess Iran's spent nuclear fuel as a way for Iran to continue with its nuclear program for peaceful purposes. Russia and America also coordinated numerous antiterrorist activities. For instance, in December 2006, U.S. intelligence alerted Russia to a potential terrorist threat to a Moscow metro station, which helped the Kremlin to defuse the threat.

Despite these positive developments, tensions between the two countries grew dramatically and encompassed issues such as Iran, arms sales abroad, energy resources, and the expansion of U.S. military infrastructure toward Russia's borders. The Kremlin became very critical of the U.S. approach to Iran and North Korea, arguing against tough sanctions, let alone use of force, and insisting on comprehensive negotiations instead. Russia also sharply increased its arms sales—against loud protests from American officials—to areas of potential concern to the United States in the Middle East, China, and Latin America.[32] By selling arms, the Kremlin argued that it did not violate any international agreements and only did what the United States was doing by selling its own weapons worldwide, including to areas of Russia's concern such as Georgia and Azerbaijan. An additional issue was Russia's promotion of its energy interests abroad, which generated anxiety in America.[33] As the United States built the alternative Baku-Tbilisi-Ceyhan pipeline and worked hard to persuade potential investors and Central Asian nations to build the Trans-Caspian route under the Caspian Sea, Russia secured a commitment from Kazakhstan, Turkmenistan, and Uzbekistan to increase exports of Central Asian energy via Russia's pipelines.

Finally, there was the issue of expanding the American military presence closer to Russia's borders, which was taking place within and outside NATO. The United States continued its support for former Soviet states, such as Azerbaijan, Georgia, and Ukraine as potential NATO members. In 2007, the United States announced plans to deploy a missile defense system in Eastern Europe. Russia expressed its strong criticism of both developments, viewing them as a threat to its own security. At the April summit in Bucharest, Russia managed to block issuing Georgia and Ukraine Membership Action Plans (MAPs), and it further expressed a strong criticism of a OSCE/NATO-based security system in Europe, arguing against new "lines of division" between nations with a common history.[34] In addition, President Medvedev said Russia was "extremely disappointed" that the United States signed a deal to deploy part of a missile defense system in the Czech Republic and would respond appropriately.[35] By then, the Kremlin had already tested new missiles capable of penetrating the missile defense system[36] and announced plans to reequip its new single-warhead intercontinental ballistic missile with multiple warheads.[37]

ASIA AND THE MIDDLE EAST

Imperatives of Modernization and Security in Asia

Although Russia saw itself as a country of European identity, it sought to take advantage of its strategic proximity to Asia for the purpose of modernizing the economy. It was highly symbolic that after being elected, President Medvedev chose China and Central Asia as the first regions to visit. China and the Asia-Pacific region were important because of the potential to become a gateway for Russia's entrance to the global economy. With one-half of the world's population and one-fifth of global trade, the region was viewed by many as a success story of modernization and globalization. Rich in natural resources, Russia was poised to contribute to satisfying the region's growing demand for energy and modernizing its own domestic economy along the way. Russia moved from a primitive accumulation of capital to the stage of generating a stable flow of investments in the economy. In addition, the region faced several long-standing security challenges, such as the nuclear ambitions of North Korea and China's relations with Taiwan.

Russia's first interest was in increasing its role in solving vital security issues in East Asia. For years, Russia's officials argued for the development of a multilateral security framework in the region and outside. The Kremlin insisted that security problems could only be solved through systematic coordination of state efforts and not through use of force by ad hoc coalitions. For instance, it developed the Shanghai Cooperation Organization (SCO), with China and four Central Asian states, in order to address threats from terrorism and the security vacuum in the area. In East Asia, Moscow advocated multilateral solutions to the nuclear crisis with North Korea and contributed considerably to creating the six-party format for dealing with the crisis. In February 2007, an agreement was reached according to which North Korea would stop production of plutonium and begin closing down its nuclear program in exchange for $300 million in energy supplies. Russia believed the deal became possible due to the prominent role played by China, and because the United States reversed its previously hard-line position.[38]

Russia's most important priority remained economic modernization, and that required determination to win markets in arms and energy. China and India remained Russia's largest buyers, purchasing more than 90 percent of Russia's annual arms exports. While promoting weapons sales in Asia, Putin did so mainly for commercial reasons, not out of desire to create some new strategic "axis" against the United States. Russia viewed itself as connected with Asia whereby Russia, due to richness of natural resources, occupies an appropriately important role and reaps considerable economic as well as political benefits. Although its energy markets remained primarily in Europe and accounted for about 50 percent of foreign trade, Russia continued to aggressively promote itself as an energy pipeline hub connecting Asia, Europe, and North America. Russia's Energy Strategy estimated that by 2020, 30 percent of the country's oil exports would go to Asia (the figure was 3 percent in 2005). During the last two years, Russia's sales of weapons and energy to China decreased,[39] yet the two nations' economic and political interests are compatible, and there is hardly an alternative to their growing cooperation in the future.

Russia's other priorities in the region include nuclear security and political stability. Seeking a nonnuclear status for North Korea, Moscow has worked to develop its ties with that country, and it stayed engaged with Pyongyang during nuclear crises. Close relationships with North Korea helped Russia to increase its participation in security negotiations, and it was ultimately Pyongyang that demanded Moscow join the six-party format. In Russia's view, changes in the region, such as reunification of the two Koreas, should be orderly and not destabilizing.[40] On several occasions, Putin extended his support for unification of the two Koreas if it takes place in orderly fashion and on the basis of inter-Korean dialogue. Russian analysts consider a unified Korea a potential strategic partner, provided that the shape of unification is not overly determined by the United States. For these reasons, Russia has insisted on preserving special and even-handed relations with both Koreas.

Of course, none of this means Russia has been without constraints in advancing its influence in the region. One such constraint had to do with progressive power differentials. As Russia continued to supply China with energy and weapons, and China continued to grow at a considerably higher rate than its northern neighbor, the risk of Moscow becoming a junior partner in a Beijing-led coalition increased. However, a way out of this "relative gains" dilemma was not to reduce bilateral interactions, but rather to continue strengthening multilateral security institutions in the region. In addition, it was important to be versatile in developing economic relations by strengthening relations with the United States and promoting trilateral cooperation with South Korea and North Korea in anticipation of their future unification. Russia could only reap economic and security benefits through development of multiple ties in the region with all the sides involved—China, South Korea, North Korea, the United States, and Japan.[41]

Engaging the Islamic World

Russia also demonstrated a renewed activism in the Middle East and the larger Muslim world. Aside from ambitious economic projects and weapons sales to India, Iran, Syria, and Palestine, the Kremlin encouraged an international conference on Iraq to discuss an American phased withdrawal from the country. In order to address growing suspicions of Iran's intent to obtain a nuclear bomb, it also encouraged Tehran to send its spent nuclear fuel to Russia. Acting independently from the UN-US-EU-Russia quartet, the Kremlin also opened political dialogue with leaders of Hamas, who won the Palestinian elections in the Gaza strip but continued to refuse to renounce violence against Israel or recognize Israel's right to exist as an independent state. In addition, Russia strongly condemned the publication in Denmark and some other European nations of cartoons satirizing the Prophet Muhammad as an "inadmissible" provocation against Muslims.

Russia's assertiveness in the Middle East had roots in global and domestic developments. Globally, the Kremlin was reevaluating its relations with the United States. Many of Russia's post-9/11 expectations did not materialize. Military cooperation in Central Asia and Afghanistan was replaced by rivalry over controlling security space and energy resources. Instead of rebuilding Afghanistan, the United States launched a war in Iraq. The Kremlin no longer viewed Russia-U.S. cooperation in Central Asia and the Middle East as beneficial, and it thought the U.S. presence there invited terrorism, rather than eradicated it. Russia's perception of the U.S. role in the region as destructive corresponded with perceptions by many Muslims across the world, who viewed the U.S. "war on terror" as a war on them. What began as a counterterrorist operation in Afghanistan with relatively broad international support was increasingly turning into a "war of civilizations," or America's crusade against Muslims and their style of living. Instead of engaging moderate Muslims, U.S. policies tended to isolate them.

Implications of the "war of civilizations" were fundamental to Russia's well-being. For a country with 20–25 million Muslims, an involvement in such a war would mean setting fire to its own home. Russia's domestic intercultural ties were far from balanced. A growing influence of radical Islamist ideologies, rising immigration from Muslim ex-Soviet republics, and poorly conceived actions of some of Russia's local authorities in failing to build ties with Muslims created an explosive political environment. Although the situation in Chechnya was much more stable, Islamic radicals were spreading violence and extremist ideology across the larger North Caucasus.

Although Russia's Middle Eastern initiatives were not anti-Western, they signaled that the "war of civilizations" between Western nations and Islam was intensifying. By engaging with Iran and Hamas, Russia sought to compensate for Western policy blunders in the region (e.g., calls to boycott elections in Iran, and clumsy attempts to pressure Palestinian voters), and to find a way out of a developing intercivilizational confrontation. Implicitly, the new Kremlin initiatives recognize that the threat of Islamic radicalism in Russia cannot be successfully confronted without reaching out to the Muslim world. The notion of a dialogue with the Muslim world was strongly endorsed by Russia's political class. Russia called for an "intercivilizational alliance" and "compromise" involving countries in the Middle East. For example, in March 2008, President Putin sent a message to the Organization of the Islamic Conference meeting in Senegal in which he said that "deeper relations of friendship and cooperation with the Islamic world are Russia's strategic course" and that "we share concerns about the danger of the world splitting along religious and civilizational lines."[42] Other officials presented Russia as a country "which is on the junction of Europe and Asia and is a natural inter-civilization bridge" and expressed a desire to have closer ties with the Islamic world.[43]

THE FORMER SOVIET WORLD

New Energy Policy

Consistent with the new vision, Russia moved to strengthen its energy position in world markets. In addition to increasing Russian shares in foreign companies abroad and coordinating its activities with other energy producers, Russia's energy strategy included building pipelines in all geographic directions, raising energy prices for its oil- and gas-dependent neighbors, and moving to control transportation networks in the former Soviet lands. Although many interpreted Gazprom's energy dispute with Ukraine in December 2005 as an attempt by the Kremlin to punish the new leadership of Ukraine for the Orange Revolution,[44] the dispute also aimed to economically normalize relations with Kiev by moving in the direction of establishing market-based prices for energy supplies. Moscow worked to reduce the amount of subsidies to the Ukrainian economy, and Kiev understandably resisted the effort. Russia's decision reflected the Kremlin's long-articulated pragmatic modernization approach in the former Soviet region. Already in February 2001, a former secretary of the Security Council, Sergei Ivanov, announced that previous attempts to integrate the Commonwealth of Independent States (CIS) had came at a very high price and that Russia had to abandon the integration project in favor of a "pragmatic" course of bilateral relations. By the time this announcement was made, the CIS states' debt to Russia had reached $5.5 billion.[45]

Russia's decision also reflected a policy adjustment in the post-Soviet world following the color revolutions. As Ukraine, Georgia, and Moldova moved to challenge Moscow by questioning the Russia-controlled CIS, the Kremlin was determined to secure economic gains in the region. As explained by Putin, "over the last 15 years Russia subsidized the Ukrainian economy by a sum that amounted to $3–5 billion each year," and "each year we raised the issue of whether we should change to the European regime for determining prices."[46] The fact that Russia's close allies in the region, such as Armenia and Belarus, also faced a tripling of gas prices further indicated that the Kremlin's energy strategy reflected imperatives of economic modernization. In an energy dispute with Belarus during late 2006–early 2007, Russia's Gazprom cancelled a preferential price, instead doubling it to $100 per 1,000 cubic meters and acquiring a 50 percent stake in Belarus's state gas pipeline company, Beltransgaz. For oil, Russia imposed a new export duty, thereby increasing domestic revenue and reducing Belarus's chances of reexporting Russian oil. The net gain from both deals for Russia, according to some calculations, amounted to around $4 billion, or over 2 percent of the overall budget.[47]

Importantly, the Kremlin also renegotiated price arrangements with oil- and gas-rich Turkmenistan and Kazakhstan, leaving them with less incentive to sell to Europe and China.[48] With attractive prices and an energy transportation system in place, the Caspian states would be less likely to construct new pipelines favored by non-Russian nations. In addition, the autocratic regimes in Central Asia appreciate that Russia does not aim to "democratize" them.

In Search of Stability and Security

As Russia's economic recovery required preservation of the international status quo, the Kremlin sought to insulate the region from what it saw as politically destabilizing activities. It took different approaches to different parts of the region. In Central Asia, the Kremlin chose to work independently from the West and in partnership with China to address a challenge of a destabilization from local and foreign Islamic radicals. This was a departure from the original policy of working with the West and allowing U.S. and NATO troops to be based in the Central Asian states in order to launch a counterterrorist operation in Afghanistan. In Ukraine, it signaled a desire to move beyond the Orange Revolution and work with all political forces in the country. In Georgia, the Kremlin took a hard-line approach, imposing sanctions, strengthening ties with separatist territories, and practicing containment toward Tbilisi. After Georgia arrested four Russian intelligence officers in September 2006, Moscow reacted with a heavy package of economic and political sanctions that stayed in place even after the officers had returned to Russia.

Even this hard-line approach did not work, and on August 8, 2008, Georgia's President Mikhail Saakashvili ordered troops to attack the South Ossetian capital, Tskhinvali, in attempting to restore control over the rebellious province. Georgian troops killed ten Russian peacekeepers, and by attacking the city with heavy artillery, Georgia inflicted heavy civilian casualties on South Ossetia. Russia responded with overwhelming force that included several armored battalions, air power, and marines, defeating and destroying much of the Georgian military. Russia also recognized the independence of South Ossetia and Abkhazia and imposed areas of security control throughout Georgia. Despite Saakashvili's efforts to present his offensive as a response to Russia's aggression, sources as diverse as intelligence agencies, human rights organizations, the Georgian exiled leader Irakli Okruashvili, and various government analysts agreed that the aggression came from Tbilisi, not Moscow.[49]

Much of Russia's reaction can be explained by a perception of a threat stemming from the expansion of NATO. The West's geopolitical advances into what Russia has traditionally viewed as its sphere of interests, and the desire expressed by the postrevolutionary Georgia and Ukraine to join NATO, exacerbated Russia's sense of vulnerability and isolation. Following the NATO summit in Bucharest, Russia reiterated that it would do everything in its power to prevent expansion of the alliance and extension of NATO membership to Georgia and Ukraine.[50] The "frozen conflicts" were merely leverage in the Kremlin's hands, and until the war in the Caucasus in August 2008, the Kremlin planned to keep them frozen until NATO ceased plans to continue its march to the east. In the aftermath of the summit, to signal its dissatisfaction to Georgia, the Kremlin extended an additional assistance to the secessionist South Ossetia and Abkhazia.[51] Some Russian analysts argue that if membership in NATO is so important to Georgia, then Tbilisi is likely to obtain it at the cost of its territorial integrity.[52] South Ossetia and Abkhazia oppose Georgia's membership in the Western alliance and continue to press for integrating with Russia. Such integration became a few steps closer due to the United States' recognition of the independence of Kosovo and the Kremlin's recognition of South Ossetia's and Abkhazia's independence in the wake of the Caucasus crisis. At the same time, Moscow expedited negotiations with Moldova over incorporation of Transdniestria into Moldova, provided that Kishinev remains neutral and does not join NATO.[53] Moscow may be signaling that the "no NATO membership" in exchange for territorial integrity deal may still be possible to conclude with other republics outside Georgia, such as Ukraine and Azerbaijan.

CONCLUSION

On balance, the shift toward foreign policy assertiveness has been success-ful in defending Russia's objectives. Apart from the conflict with Georgia, Russia did not experience any major threats to its security from terrorist attacks or elsewhere. While pressing for preserving and strengthening secu-rity ties with Western countries, Russia managed to sustain good relations with Iran and other Middle Eastern nations. Middle Eastern nations in par-ticular often had complicated relationships with the United States and the European Union and, no less importantly, had the potential to undermine Russia's security through the funding of religious extremist activities. The Kremlin's effort to reach out to the Muslim world by initiating contacts with its multilateral organizations and developing bilateral ties served Rus-sia well. The overall situation improved in Chechnya, although terrorism in the Caucasus remains an important issue. In the former Soviet regions, Russia strengthened its security standing by maintaining even-handed rela-tions with other states in Central Asia and the Caucasus. The exception was Georgia, against which the Kremlin applied sanctions and ultimately military force.

Russia's foreign policy has been relatively successful in meeting the objec-tive of economic development. The Kremlin's strategy of capitalizing on the country's energy reserves added revenue without alienating potential foreign investors. Russia's drastic decisions to cut energy supplies for some of its neighbors, as well as some other components of its energy strategy, raised concerns among Western countries and former Soviet republics, but on balance it did not do any irreparable damage. More importantly, Russians themselves have been strongly behind the course of foreign policy assertive-ness. For example, in March 2007, 61 percent of respondents evaluated the Kremlin's international actions as well considered and well balanced. Indeed, 16 percent thought that Russia's foreign policy course was too pro-Western, and only 8 percent believed it was hard-line and uncompromising toward the West.[54] This assessment, of course, is subject to how well Russia is going to meet future foreign policy challenges. One can identify at least two groups of such challenges: external and internal.

Russia's main external challenge is to preserve the international status quo in order to continue with the vital program of domestic economic and social modernization. Major economic disturbances, such as a world economic re-cession or a sharp decline in oil prices, are bound to complicate the process. The international financial crisis made itself felt in Russia and may continue to negatively affect its economic development.[55] If those experts who project growing demand for energy among both developed and developing nations, such as China and India, are correct, then in the medium-term Russia should still be able to take advantage of the situation if it is successful in developing its own reserves.[56] Another danger might be related to further destabilization of the Middle East and continued expansion of the Western military presence to Russia's borders. A U.S. troop withdrawal from Iraq that leaves an adequate security framework, or a military confrontation with Iran, would create a large flow of refugees and further destabilize the region. The effects of such destabilization would be felt in the Caucasus and Central Asia and therefore, at least indirectly, in Russia. No less dangerous could be NATO's decision to extend membership to Georgia and Ukraine, or American attempts to place elements of a missile defense system in close proximity to Russia. These kinds of international disturbances may provide ammunition to those inside Russia's political class who resent Russia's great-power pragmatism and want to push an assertive style toward radically anti-Western policies.

A primary internal challenge is the split within the political leadership over how to deal with Western pressure. For many analysts, Russia has become so emboldened by its recent economic recovery that it has forgotten the country's lingering problems. Yet Russia, as the old saying goes, while never as weak as it seems, is never as strong as it says. The country is strong in its growing international presence and energy power, yet it remains weak in such critical respects as population health, demographic dynamics, and the size of middle class. Indicators of poverty, HIV infection, and demographic crisis are plentiful and make a convincing case for the nation's continuing weakness. Despite all the trumpets of great-power revival, Russia remains a vulnerable country in an increasingly volatile environment. For at least for the next decade, Russia will do well to think hard about the linkage between external war and internal instability. Its own experience speaks volumes about the linkage.

SUGGESTED READINGS

Legvold, Robert, ed. *Russian Foreign Policy in the 21st Century and the Shadow of the Past.* New York: Columbia University Press, 2007.

Mankoff, Jeffrey. *Russian Foreign Policy.* Lanham, Md.: Rowman & Littlefield, 2009.

Melville, Andrei, and Tatyana Shakleina, eds. *Russian Foreign Policy in Transition: Concepts and Realities.* Budapest: Central European University Press, 2005.

O'Loughlin, J., G. O Tuathail, and V. Kolossov. "A 'Risky Westward Turn'? Putin's 9-11 Script and Ordinary Russians." *Europe-Asia Studies* 56, no. 1 (2004): 3–34.

Renz, Bettina. "Putin's Militocracy? An Alternative Interpretation of *Siloviki* in Russian Politics." *Europe-Asia Studies* 58, no. 6 (2006): 903–24.

Stent, Angela. "Revolution and Restoration in Putin's Foreign Policy." *Europe-Asia Studies* 60, no. 6 (2008): 1089–1106.

Treisman, Daniel. "Putin's Silovarchs." *Orbis* (Winter 2007): 141–53.

Tsygankov, Andrei P. "Russia's International Assertiveness: What Does It Mean for the West?" *Problems of Post-Communism* 55, no. 2 (2008): 38–55.

————. *Russia's Foreign Policy: Change and Continuity in National Identity.* Rowman & Littlefield, 2006.

NOTES

1. This chapter partly draws on Andrei P. Tsygankov, "Russia's International Assertiveness: What Does It Mean for the West?" *Problems of Post-Communism* 55, no. 2 (2008): 38–55; and Andrei P. Tsygankov, "Two Faces of Putin's Great Power Pragmatism," *Soviet and Post-Soviet Review* 33, no. 1 (2008): 103–19.

2. "Speech at the Munich Conference on Security Policy," Munich, February 10, 2007, www.kremlin.ru.

3. "Russia's Economy under Vladimir Putin: Achievements and Failures," *RIA Novosti*, March 1, 2008; "Russia Turns from Debtor into Creditor Country—Medvedev," *Itar-Tass*, January 27, 2007; Guy Chazan, "Lighting a Spark: Fueled by Oil Money, Russian Economy Soars," *Wall Street Journal*, March 13, 2007.

4. "Russians Rich and Poor," *Russia Profile*, October 11, 2005, www.russiaprofile.org; "Middle Class Grows Atop," *Kommersant*, February 27, 2008.

5. Andrea Crandall, "Invest in China? Invest in Russia," *Johnson's Russia List*, no. 22 (April 19, 2006), www.cdi.org/russia/Johnson.

6. "Russia Is Most Attractive Emerging Economy for Investors," *Kommersant*, February 14, 2008.

7. Paul Abelsky, "Russia Industrial Output Rises 9.2 percent, Nine-Month High," *Bloomberg*, May 20, 2008.

8. "Russians Think Chosen Development Course Correct—Poll," *Interfax*, June 18, 2008.

9. One poll revealed, for example, that Russians valued political order and stability as a result of a successful foreign policy by expressing strong condemnation of revolutionary prospects in the country. They are most positive about such word-symbols as "order" (58 percent), "justice" (49 percent), and "stability" (38 percent). In the same poll, the word "revolution" was among the least popular, with 22 percent viewing it in a negative light. See "Russians Like Order and Justice," *RosBusinessConsulting*, March 28, 2007.

10. Members of the American political class maintained ties with organizations, such as the National Bolshevik Party, while increasing pressures on the Kremlin to "democratize" and respect political freedoms only served to strengthen the perception. See Vladimir Frolov, "Democracy Pretension: Is the United States Promoting Democracy or Leveraging Political Influence in Russia?" *Russia Profile*, April 17, 2007, www.russiaprofile.org.

11. Vladimir Putin, "Press Statement and Answers to Journalists' Questions Following a Meeting of the Russia-NATO Council," Bucharest, April 4, 2008, www.kremlin.ru.

12. "Poll Shows Russians See NATO Membership for Ukraine, Georgia as Threat," *Interfax*, April 1, 2008.

13. Neil Buckley, "Clan with a Plan: All the Contradictions of Vladimir Putin's Russia," *Financial Times*, November 29, 2007; Robert Coalson, "For Russia's Most Powerful Man, Fear Still a Factor," *RFE/RL Newsline*, November 30, 2007.

14. Vladimir Putin, "Rossiia na rubezhe tysiacheletii," *Nezavisimaia gazeta*, December 31, 1999.

15. Vladimir Putin, "Poslanie Federal'nomu Sobraniiu Rossiiskoi Federatsii," April 25, 2005, at www.kremlin.ru.

16. Putin, "Poslanie Federal'nomu Sobraniiu Rossiiskoi Federatsii." In this same speech, Putin also called for granting Russian citizenship to legal aliens from other former Soviet states.

17. Putin, "Poslanie Federal'nomu Sobraniiu Rossiiskoi Federatsii."

18. Vladimir Putin, "Poslanie Federal'nomu Sobraniiu Rossiiskoi Federatsii," May 10, 2006, www.kremlin.ru.

19. Nikita Garadzha, ed., *Suverenitet* (Moscow: Yevropa, 2006).

20. Vladislav Surkov, "Suverenitet—eto politicheski sinonim konkurentnosposobnosti," *Moskovskie novosti*, March 3, 2006, www.mn.ru/issue.php?2006-7-9.

21. Vladimir Putin, "Speech at the Munich Conference on Security Policy," February 10, 2007, www.kremlin.ru.

22. For details, see Andrei P. Tsygankov, "Finding a Civilizational Idea: 'West,' 'Eurasia,' and 'Euro-East' in Russia's Foreign Policy," *Geopolitics* 12, no. 3 (2007): 375–99.

23. "Obzor vneshnei politiki Rossiiskoi federatsii," March 27, 2007, www.mid .ru.

24. "Medvedev Doubts Effectiveness of OSCE/NATO-based Security System," *ITAR-TASS*, June 11, 2008. See also Dmitri Medvedev, "Speech at the Meeting with Russian Ambassadors and Permanent Representatives to International Organizations," Russian Foreign Ministry, Moscow, July 15, 2008, and "Speech at World Policy Conference, Evian, France," October 8, 2008, www.kremlin.ru. Also see the article by Foreign Minister Sergei Lavrov, "A Strategic Relationship: From Rivalry to Partnership," *Russia beyond the Headlines*, May 28, 2008, www.rbth.rg.ru.

25. Dmitri Medvedev, "Speech at the 12th Petersburg International Economic Forum," St. Petersburg, June 7, 2008, www.kremlin.ru.

26. Russian and Western analysts have speculated that the security class has become omnipresent in policy making. See, for example, O. Kryshtanovskaya and S. White, "Putin's Militocracy," *Post-Soviet Affairs* 19, no. 4 (2003); Daniel Treisman, "Putin's Silovarchs," *Orbis* (Winter 2007). For alternative perspectives on the objectives and the role of the security class, see Sharon Werning Rivera and David W. Rivera, "The Russian Elite under Putin: Militocratic or Bourgeois?" *Post-Soviet Affairs* 22, no. 2 (2006); and Bettina Renz, "Putin's Militocracy? An Alternative Interpretation of Siloviki in Russian Politics," *Europe-Asia Studies* 58, no. 6 (2006): 903–24.

27. For instance, in 2006 the energy unit of German chemical giant BASF and Gazprom agreed to exchange equivalent stakes, and similar contracts are planned with French and Italian companies. See Padma Desai, "Putin and Progress," *Wall Street Journal*, February 16, 2007.

28. Dmitri Medvedev, "Dlia protsvetaniia vsekh nado uchityvat' interesy kazhdogo," *Ekspert*, no. 28 (July 24, 2006), http://expert.ru.

29. Andrew E. Kramer, "New Pipeline Will Bypass the Bosporus but Involve Russia," *New York Times*, March 16, 2007.

30. That Russia's leading companies Severstal and Gazprom failed to gain shares in European companies indicated that Europeans were not eager to let Russians in

their markets. However, Europeans remained interested in Russian stakes, despite the Kremlin's pressures on Royal Dutch Shell, BP, and others to give their majority stakes in Russia's lucrative energy shelves.

31. Chloe Arnold, "EU/Russia: Summit to Thrash Out Partnership Pact," *RFE/RL Newsline*, June 26, 2008.

32. "Russian Arms Business Breaks New Records," *RFE/RL Newsline*, March 22, 2007; "Ameriku trevozhit 'boevaia' ekspansiia Rossii," *Izvestiia*, March 23, 2007.

33. Conservative American politicians such as Senator John McCain and Dick Cheney, the vice president under President George W. Bush, issued multiple statements that indicated their concerns with Russia's new "imperialism" and energy "blackmail." In November 2006, Senator Richard Lugar delivered a keynote speech during the NATO summit in Riga in which he called for updating the alliance's basic role to include protection of member countries' energy security from Russia's actions. See Vladimir Socor, "Lugar Urges Active Role for NATO in Energy Security," *Eurasia Daily Monitor*, December. 1, 2006, www.jamestown.com.

34. "Medvedev Doubts Effectiveness of OSCE/NATO-based Security System"; Dmitri Rogozin, "Global Security and Propaganda," *International Herald Tribune*, July 1, 2008.

35. Henry Meyer and Sebastian Alison, "Medvedev Says Russia to Respond to U.S. Missile Deal," *Bloomberg*, July 9, 2008.

36. Robert S. Norris and Hans M. Kristensen, "Russian Nuclear Forces, 2006," *Bulletin of the Atomic Scientists* 62, no. 2 (2006), www.thebulletin.org.

37. "Russia to Re-Equip Its New Mobile ICBMs with Multiple Warheads," *RIA Novosti*, December 15, 2007.

38. "Russian Expert: US Awareness of Mistakes Made Led to Success in N Korea Talks," *Interfax*, February 13, 2007.

39. M. K. Bhadrakumar, "Medvedev Reaches Out to China," *Asia Times*, May 29, 2008.

40. In August 2003, Russia conducted massive military exercises in the Far East to rehearse actions for accepting up to 100,000 North Korean refugees in case of a U.S.-North Korean military confrontation.

41. For development of these points, see Gil Rozman, Kazuhiko Togo, and Joseph Ferguson, eds., *Russian Strategic Thought toward Asia* (New York: Palgrave, 2006), especially the chapter by Aleksandr Lukin.

42. "Putin Wants 'Deeper Friendship' with Islamic World," *RFE/RL Newline*, March 14, 2008.

43. "Russia Ready to Contribute to Alliance of Civilizations Potential," *Itar-Tass*, January 16, 2008; "Minister Hails Ties to Muslim World," *RFE/RL Newline*, January 11, 2008.

44. See, for example, "Black-Belt Ambitions, Orange-Belt Throw," *Transitions Online*, January 10, 2006.

45. *Nezavisimaia gazeta*, February 7, 2001.

46. Vladimir Putin, "Transcript of Meeting with the Leaders of the News Agencies of G8 Member Countries," June 2, 2006, www.kremlin.ru.

47. Andrei P. Tsygankov, "The Test of Belarus," *Johnson's Russia List*, no. 14 (January 19, 2007).

48. Max Delany, "Energy Ties Take Medvedev Eastward," *Moscow Times*, July 2, 2008.

49. See, for example, Special Press-release by Memorial Human Rights Center, "A Month after the War: Violations of Human Rights and Norms of Humanitarian Law in the Conflict Zone in South Ossetia," September 16, 2008; Patrick Armstrong, "The War He Actually Got," *Johnson's Russia List*, no. 170 (September 17, 2008); Brian Rohan, "Saakashvili 'Planned S. Ossetia Invasion': Ex-minister," *Reuters*, September 15, 2008; "Did Saakashvili Lie?" *Der Spiegel*, September 15, 2008.

50. "Russia Again Vows to Block NATO Enlargement," *RFE/RL Newsline*, April 9, 2008.

51. C. J. Chivers, "Russia Expands Support for Breakaway Regions in Georgia," *New York Times*, April 17, 2008.

52. Anatoli Tsyganok, "On the Consequences of Georgia's NATO Entry," *Fondsk.ru*, January 2, 2008, www.fondsk.ru.

53. "Moldovan President, Transdniester Leader Hold Landmark Talks," *RFE/RL Newsline*, April 14, 2008.

54. Leonti Byzov, "Narodnye imperialisty," *Vremia Novostei*, March 13, 2007.

55. "The Financial Crisis in Russia," *Stratfor.com*, October 28, 2008; Robert Skidelsky, "Crisis-hit Russia Must Scale Down Its Ambition," *Financial Times*, October 31, 2008.

56. Jeronim Perovic and Robert Orttung, "Russia' Energy Policy," *Russian Analytical Digest*, April 3, 2007.

Chapter Eleven

Russia and Central Asia's Multivector Foreign Policies

Gregory Gleason

Russian foreign policy is expected to remain the major factor in foreign policy calculations in Central Asian states.[1] To be sure, several other important factors play a role in the foreign policies of the region, including the rising influence of China, the continuing instability in Afghanistan and Pakistan, the threat of insurgency and insurrection, the pressures created by volatility in energy markets, and the marked differences among the Central Asian states themselves over such issues as the water and energy nexus, migration, and transnational commercial interactions. A number of other factors, such as the role of ethnic, clan-based, and familial loyalties, are hard to define and hard to evaluate yet continue to play an important regional political role. Nevertheless, in calculations of Central Asian foreign policy, factors typically play a role not independently but in the context of Russia's policy toward the post-Soviet "South."

Many things contribute to the prominence of Russian foreign policy in the Central Asian region. The historical legacy of Russian influence during the Soviet and tsarist periods, the physical proximity of Russia, the "middleman" position of Russia with respect to European and Western commercial markets, the importance of Russia's role in the production, transshipment, and delivery of energy resources, the entrepreneurial skill of Russia's oligarch "captains of industry," Russia's political influence in the Caucasus and Iran, the rise of Russia's influence in international organizations, and a host of other factors contribute to Russia's importance vis-à-vis Central Asia. Russia's position is so important that it marks a pivot around which Central Asian countries are forced by circumstances to move. The political geometry of these relationships has given rise to phenomena that Central Asian and Russians alike refer to generically as "multivector policies."

Russia's predominant position does not imply that Russian foreign policy determines Central Asian foreign policies; even less so does Russia determine the internal politics of the Central Asian countries. Central Asian leaders determine their own objectives using their own resources and at their own direction, but they typically do so in relation to their expectations, fears, and hopes regarding Moscow's designs. What the Central Asian leaders achieve in foreign policy is not always what Moscow intends or desires. The subtle but profoundly significant recalculations that took place in Central Asian chancelleries following the outbreak of the Russo-Georgian war in August 2008 illustrate the elasticity of Central Asian multivector policies. After occupying and then declaring the independence of Abkhazia and South Ossetia—two territories located within Georgia—Russian leaders sought recognition of their independence from other countries around the world and put exceptional pressure on the Central Asian countries to endorse Russia's policies. In the distinctive style of the multivector approach, the Central Asian countries appeared to side with Russia in the dispute but not to the extent that any Central Asian country recognized the independence of Georgia's breakaway regions.

A multivector policy is a complex stratagem. In practice, multivector foreign policies are essentially risk-avoidant lines of action, emphasizing multiple partners, multiple dimensions, and multiple issues, and relying largely on diplomatic hedging against unreliability, threat, and hard-to-calculate advantage. Multivector foreign policies assign low importance to ideological considerations and high importance to instrumental alliances and calculated advantage.

What a multivector policy means in the context of the Central Asian relationships is that any of the states will have a policy of one vector toward Russia, one vector toward China, one vector toward Europe, and so on. There is logic to the "balancing symmetry" inherent in the calculation of interests in Central Asia. Russia is a factor in every balance. Russia is too big and too close to ignore, too aggressive to contest. At the same time, Russia is not easy to interact with simply as an equal partner. Central Asian policy officials use the concept of "multivector foreign policy" to explain and justify their diplomatic and security relationships with other countries within the Central Asian region and with other countries outside the region and with international organizations.

The idea of a "multivector" foreign policy merits more than mere academic consideration because it has very real policy implications. In algebraic calculations, of course, equal and opposing vectors cancel one another. In geometry, equal and opposing forces will add to zero. But in the world of diplomacy, opposing vectors may continue to retain their values. The idea of multivector relations, technocratic and clinical in its euphemistic expression of diplomatic relationships, is in actuality moved by a profound respect for historically based realism. As a crossroads region, Central Asia forms a bridge, interconnecting the Asian and Eurasian landmasses and providing a territory where outside powers have extraordinary influence in business, government, and international security. In this arena, Central Asian foreign policy makers often choose pragmatism and purpose over doctrine and principle. This is neither weakness nor wisdom. It is simple and stark realism. Central Asian states today occupy territory that has been invaded and overrun by foreigners for millennia. The Central Asian states, while inheritors of ancient traditions, occupy borders existing for the first time in history. Decades of tsarist and then Soviet-era imperialism and Russian great-power national chauvinism are diminished in Central Asia— diminished but not forgotten. Counterbalanced by the new conflicts of today's rapidly changing international environment, the legacies of the past are taking on a new character.

What that character means requires some reflection on the recent past and some extrapolation into the future. That is the goal of this chapter on Russian foreign policy in Central Asia. The chapter considers first the role of Russia's foreign policy toward the post-Soviet Central Asian states of Kazakhstan, Kyrgyzstan, Tajikistan, Turkmenistan, and Uzbekistan. Twenty years ago the analysis of this question would have taken place primarily in the context of doctrine. Today the analysis primarily concerns economic and commercial relationships, particularly regarding energy. Next the chapter turns to a survey of the domestic politics of each of these countries as they influence the foreign policies of the states. The Central Asian states may be described as "top heavy" in the sense that leadership predominates in the politics of the countries; the style and even psychological orientation of the leaders and their close entourages overshadow other factors.

Russia has acted independently in the past and can be expected to do so in the future, but Russia's contemporary foreign policy differs from traditional Russian approaches in the respect that Moscow had developed a distinct preference for acting in the context of multilateral regional international organizations. For this reason, state-to-state political association, alignment, competition, and conflict are most visible in terms of the formal interaction of the Commonwealth of Independent States (CIS), the Eurasian Economic Community (EAEC), the Collective Security Treaty Organization (CSTO), the Shanghai Cooperation Organization (SCO), and the Conference on Interaction and Confidence Building Measures in Asia (CICA), as well as many other organizations such as the Organization for Security and Cooperation in Europe (OSCE) and the Economic Cooperation Organization (ECO). Finally, the chapter considers the implications of these considerations for the Central Asian states as we look ahead.

THE SOVIET LEGACY AND RUSSIA'S
SPECIAL SPHERE OF INFLUENCE

Russian influence expanded to the south in the latter part of the nineteenth century in the preemptive expansion for territorial control. In a struggle with the expanding Victorian-era empires of Europe, Russia eventually played a role in defining the contours of modern-day Asia and the Middle East, through defining the outlines of West China, Afghanistan, and Iran. These borders remain today. The idea of territorial expansion was romanticized in the geopolitical doctrines of nineteenth-century political geographer Halford Mackinder, who is credited with proclaiming that the "hand that controls the heartland of Asia controls the world." Russian influence in Central Asia receded in the period of the First World War, but the Bolshevik leaders in St. Petersburg and Moscow were loath to relinquish any measure of control over the territories of the Russian Empire that they so hated. Mackinder's idea of the heartland of Asia swells Russian spirits today, particularly those of the Eurasianist faction of national expansionists in Russia. The Eurasianists argue for a modern version of Uvarov's concepts of *samoderzhavie, pravoslavie,* and *narodnost*—the nationalist troika of autocracy, Russian Orthodoxy, and populism. These ideas give sustenance to those who argue for the primacy of the state as against the antistatist ideas of liberal commercialism that emerge in association with the maritime empire of Great Britain in the nineteenth century.

The evolution of Russian foreign policy in recent years must be understood in terms of the "lessons" of the disintegration of the USSR. As the first decade of postcommunist experience proceeded, Russia's capacity to exert decisive influence over the regions of Central Eurasia receded. Independent-minded states such as Georgia and Uzbekistan challenged Russia's claim to a dominant voice in the security and economic arrangements in the region. Russia's own internal political disputes, shrinking government revenues, the Russian financial markets crisis in 1998, weak world market commodity prices, and the rising European and U.S. influence throughout the Eurasian region hampered Russia's ability to maintain Moscow's former sphere of influence in the Caucasus and Central Asia. Russia lost the capacity to influence infrastructure development as international organizations and large multilateral lending institutions moved into the region, establishing new mechanisms and new priorities for economic development.

Russian foreign policy makers found their hands tied and their choices constrained. On occasion, Russia attempted to retain control over south Eurasian regional politics and oil development through intimidation, coercion, and surreptitious support for coups and armed conflicts in Azerbaijan and Georgia, by the invasion of Chechnya in 1994, by securing basing rights in Armenia, Georgia, and Turkmenistan, by seeking to block the transport of Kazakhstan oil and gas exports, and by retaliating against independent-minded Uzbekistan through establishing a Russian military outpost in neighboring Tajikistan. Yet these heavy-handed Russian attempts to regain control were usually unproductive and often counterproductive, inclining their south Eurasian partners to seek stratagems of self-help and greater independence.

For these reasons, Russian grand policy toward Central Asian and the Caucasus gradually devolved into a situation in which Russia was conducting numerous parallel but not always complementary bilateral foreign policies. Sometimes this put Russia in a position of being able to divide the countries to its benefit, but more often it simply meant that none of the countries succeeded in even the most basic forms of infrastructure and commercial cooperation. Eventually, dwindling intraregional trade, the failure of international policy harmonization, and a growing concern with threats of insurgency and lawlessness gradually persuaded Moscow to acknowledge that its approach to Central Asia was fragmented, ad hoc, and unsuccessful.

In the early 1990s, Russian leaders were primarily concerned with national consolidation and paid less attention to foreign policy with respect to the "near abroad." The December 1995 election brought changes in the Duma, the lower house of the Russian parliament, such that the non-reformist communist, nationalist, and agrarian parties controlled more than half the votes. President Yeltsin, whose popularity was low and who was facing a difficult race in the June 1996 presidential election, reacted to the strong showing of antireform factions by removing visible reformers from his administration. Yeltsin removed Andrei Kozyrev as minister of foreign affairs in January 1996, replacing him with longtime intelligence chief and Middle East specialist Evgeni Primakov. Primakov set out to develop a new definition of the Russian national interest in the postcollapse situation, with a scaled-back role but more efficient mechanisms. Primakov's analysts began to characterize Russia as a great power that, along with Japan, China, and the European Union, formed the basis of the emerging multipolar global order that was capable of restraining hegemonic tendencies of the United States. In September 1998, Primakov was appointed as a compromise premier following the default crisis. Yeltsin removed him in May 1999, replacing him with Sergei Stepashin.

By the latter part of the 1990s, Russian policy makers looking at trends in the Caucasus and Central Asia realized they would have to regard Russia's Eurasia policy as woefully unsuccessful. International financial institutions had become the driving force in all the countries' national development strategies. Uzbekistan was intransigently defining a foreign policy of self-reliance deliberately antagonistic to Russia. Kazakhstan was wooing Western oil investment with ideas of strategic partnership and the Baku-Tbilisi-Ceyhan pipeline that would in part circumvent Russian pipelines. Afghanistan was still in turmoil, producing violent anti-Russian extremist doctrines and generating frightful amounts of opium-based narcotics flowing through Russia. Turkmenistan was opportunistically looking for gas consumers and investors. NATO was enlarging and indirectly extending influence through Central Asia in the form of NATO's Partners for Peace program.

By the late 1990s, a consensus had emerged within the Russian foreign policy community that the time had come for a new strategy toward the southern Eurasian states. By the time Yeltsin left office, a consensus had already formed in the Ministry of Foreign Affairs that some new approach toward Central Asia was necessary. Putin's public statement in late 1999 that Russia was, after all, a "Eurasian power" set the stage for a reexamination of Russia's strategy toward Central Asia. The Russian National Security Strategy of January 2000 and the Russian Foreign Policy Strategy of June 2000 formalized Russia's reassessment. Important changes were included in the approach to the Central Asian states.[2] Just following the election of Dmitri Medvedev as president in March 2008, a new Foreign Policy Concept was ratified by the president.

Russia and the other member states have put great emphasis on the idea of reestablishing economic linkages severed during the period following the collapse of the USSR. The idea of creating an economic union grew out of the simple goal, common among all the members of the CIS, to establish and sustain a "single economic space" throughout the former Soviet region. The establishment of a single economic space meant different things to different people. In the eyes of some, it represented the restoration of Soviet-era economic if not political relationships. In the eyes of others, it meant only the establishment of a new common region in which trade and commerce could flourish on the basis of market-driven supply and demand. These people saw the establishment of the Eurasian Economic Community (EAEC) as a preliminary step for integration into the world market and international trade organizations.

The EAEC may have been a grand economic design, but it was also the result of a great deal of very practical and down-to-earth political negotiating. After the Soviet collapse, the newly independent states emerged with very different institutional and resource endowments. The states adopted very different policies and assumed separate and often conflicting economic strategies. One of the most ambitious plans for bringing the post-Soviet states together to promote commerce was devised by Kazakhstan's Nursultan Nazarbayev under the aegis of "Eurasian economic integration." Nazarbayev had been a prominent Soviet political official and Communist Party Politburo member. As president of independent Kazakhstan, he began as early as 1994 to urge the other post-Soviet countries to adopt a unified idea of economic integration.

Nazarbayev's Eurasian integration ideas were initially greeted in Kremlin circles with little enthusiasm. But the Kremlin gradually shifted when the Putin administration came to power in Russia. Qualms about Eurasian integration were put aside. Russia first adopted and then grew to be the leading sponsor of the idea of Eurasian economic integration. The Eurasian Economic Community was legally established in October 2000 in Astana, Kazakhstan's capital, to institutionalize a framework of close economic cooperation. Russia became an enthusiastic supporter of further expanding multilateral ties by seeking to parallel economic cooperation with security linkages. Russia was instrumental in promoting the EAEC through investment and assuming the lion's share of the EAEC's administrative costs. At the same time, Russia began enthusiastically promoting the region's most important security alliance, the Collective Security Treaty Organization. The CSTO was established in October 2002 as a formalized and institutionalized version of the original Collective Security Treaty signed in 1992 in the wake of the Soviet collapse.

The EAEC members—Belarus, Kazakhstan, Kyrgyzstan, Russia, Tajikistan, and as of January 2006 Uzbekistan—committed themselves to adopting common policies on customs, trade, labor, migration, education, currency exchange, interbank financial settlement, and infrastructure development. EAEC members adopted specific agreements designed to adopt harmonized labor, monetary, customs, employment, tax, and investment laws and coordinate policies on a region-wide basis. The EAEC members embraced the idea of establishing a free trade area, while eliminating or at least regularizing internal tariffs. The EAEC announced it intended to create common external tariffs. EAEC members also began to expand the overall goal of economic cooperation to the idea of forming a single energy area, a single transport area, a gas marketing alliance, a single securities stock market, and a new ruble zone. Energy supplies, particularly the transport of energy through Russia to European markets, played a key role in integration.

CENTRAL ASIAN STATES

Prior to the breakup of the USSR, leaders of the Communist Party governed the Central Asian region as a whole. Each of the Central Asian republics was administratively managed by a local Communist Party organization in conjunction with the USSR's economic ministries. These institutions were subordinated to Moscow-based, all-union organizations. The independent countries that emerged in Central Asia from the breakup of the USSR— Kazakhstan, Kyrgyzstan, Tajikistan, Turkmenistan, and Uzbekistan—were conceived during the Soviet period. None of these "republics" ever existed as an independent state prior to the Soviet period. They were artificial creations, products of the Soviet Marxist theory of economic and political development for underdeveloped regions. During the Soviet period, these "socialist republics" were not countries at all, but regions managed by Moscow political authorities. Little republic-to-republic interaction took place. Interaction among the Central Asian republics was routinely managed by and through Moscow. Furthermore, despite the religious, cultural, and linguistic traditions that these republics shared with the countries of the Middle East, China, and West Asia, the Central Asian region was physically separated from the rest of the world by nearly impassible southern and eastern Soviet frontiers and by decades of northward-oriented infrastructure development.

When independence came to the Central Asian countries, the Soviet-era leadership embraced it with enthusiasm. The opportunities for democratic progress were substantial. Initially the reform trends were clearly oriented in the right direction. Each of the republics' Communist Party leaders—quickly donning robes of nationalist protectors of the interests of the newly independent states—spoke out in favor of the establishment of secular, democratic, independent governments, market economic relations, and foreign relations recognizing international standards.[3] Kazakhstan's Nursultan Nazarbayev was the most forthright of the leaders in this regard, explaining to his colleagues and fellow citizens that the rejection of communism and the adoption of international standards was "merely common sense."[4]

In 1992, the countries individually began joining major international organizations such as the United Nations, World Bank, International Monetary Fund, European Bank for Reconstruction and Development, and Asian Development Bank.[5] Each of the countries began making progress in establishing national sovereignty and transforming the political institutions of the communist period. Kazakhstan and Kyrgyzstan made notable progress in specific areas toward adopting international standards of good governance, eventually adopting tax laws and civil codes that were considered among the best of the postcommunist world. Uzbekistan, despite a continuing inability to liberalize prices and adjust its currency to international practice, strove energetically to develop a commercially oriented welfare state. Tajikistan, torn by war and internal divisions, clearly moved in the direction of national reconciliation following a series of cease fire agreements with the opposition and then, in June 1997, the signing of a peace accord and a pact for national reconciliation. Even Turkmenistan, the least successful in making the psychological transition to an open, modern society, made some headway in attempting to harmonize its laws with international practice.

Kazakhstan's objectives and capabilities defined its pro-globalization strategy. Kazakhstan emerged from the USSR with a deliberate goal of establishing a democratic system and a market-oriented economy. Kazakhstan's nuclear status, its oil and mineral wealth, its enthusiasm for structural reform, and its mixed Kazakh and Russian populations have been defining influences on the domestic political context of foreign policy making during the first years of independence.

Kazakhstan's integration into the fabric of institutions of the international community proceeded more swiftly and more fully than did that of its neighbors. Almaty quickly became the most significant diplomatic center in the region, home to embassies from all the major countries of the world and representatives of international organizations. During the first years of Nazarbayev's presidential tenure in Kazakhstan, his diplomatic efforts were consistently associated with the concept of "Eurasian-ness," the idea of the close linkages among the peoples of the Central Eurasian landmass. Based on the idea of "Eurasian integration," Kazakhstan's foreign policy followed a careful line, balancing interests based on many factors. Balancing interests implied not turning away from Russia while at the same time not permitting Russia to dominate decision making for Kazakhstan. For Kazakhstan, this meant maintaining a balanced distance from Russia, remaining neither too close nor too distant. Maintaining good relations with the West and international organizations was an ideal instrument for achieving what Kazakh policy makers eventually began to refer to as Kazakhstan's "multivector" foreign policy. A primary motive, perhaps the primary motive, for Kazakhstan's globalization policy was the goal of preventing the reemergence of Russian domination in the region.

Kyrgyzstan's foreign policy was limited by the country's modest resource base and internally divided political situation. After independence, Kyrgyzstan quickly developed a reputation for being the most pro-reform country in the Central Asian region. It was the first ex-Soviet country to follow the advice of the international donor community and withdraw from the ruble zone. It was the first post-Soviet country to adopt a Western-style civil code and a modern legal and regulatory framework, to liberalize prices, to privatize industry, to open the door to foreign civic organizations, and to undertake electoral reform. It was the first country of the CIS to join the World Trade Organization. However, Kyrgyzstan's limited resources constrained the country's progress. By the late 1990s, the International Monetary Fund began to impose limits on Kyrgyzstan's borrowing. Kyrgyzstan's reputation as the "island of democracy" in Central Asia grew tarnished.[6]

Corruption and favoritism by the leaders of the government led to intense criticism of the Akaev government and eventually to the ouster of Akaev in the "Tulip Revolution" in March 2005.[7] A former prime minister, Kurmanbek Bakiev, set a course for political renewal, but Kyrgyzstan's fissiparous internal politics led to scandals and internal divisions. Bakiev found that Kyrgyzstan depended on foreign assistance for economic help and security protection, but that foreign influences often pushed in opposing directions. Rather than choose an Eastern orientation over a Western orientation, or vice versa, Kyrgyzstan authorities sought to support both. Russian military forces were allowed to locate at the Kant airbase not far from Bishkek, and U.S. forces were allowed to be stationed at the Manas Ganci airbase on the other side of Bishkek. Kyrgyzstan's East-West formula was balanced only in the sense that it represented a dynamic tension between two continually contending influences on the Kyrgyz government. This tension continues to be the most salient feature of Kyrgyzstan's foreign policy.

Tajikistan, the smallest, poorest, and most geographically constrained country of the Eurasian region, would likely have moved swiftly in the direction of post-Soviet reform if the country had not fallen victim to an internal contest for power in the first year of independence. The contest plunged the country into civil war. Tajikistan is a landlocked, mountainous country lacking good transportation routes. The war resulted in a blockade by its neighbors, further compressing the already collapsing Tajikistan economy. CIS peacekeeping forces succeeded in stabilizing the country under a leadership well disposed toward Moscow. The Moscow-Dushanbe compact continued to be an irritant with neighboring Uzbekistan for several years, blocking improvement in relations between Moscow and Tashkent. Tajikistan's struggling economy was based almost exclusively on a few mammoth Soviet-era enterprises such as the Turzonzade aluminum smelter and the Vaksh cascade hydroelectric stations.

Its close geographical and cultural ties with northern Afghanistan are major factors in Tajikistan's foreign policy. The scale of the drug trade originating in Afghanistan and transiting through Tajikistan has been so large that it has continued to exert a damaging influence in Tajikistan. A report of the UN Office for Drug Control's (UNODC) *Afghanistan Opium Survey for 2006* showed the area under opium cultivation in Afghanistan reached a record 165,000 hectares in 2006 compared with 104,000 in 2005, resulting in nearly a 60 percent increase in opium production. In contrast, UNODC's *Afghanistan Opium Survey for 2008* showed a sharp decline in opium cultivation to 157,000 hectares, down from the record harvest of 193,000 hectares in 2007. But owing to higher yields, opium production dropped less dramatically, down 6 percent, from 8,200 to 7,700 tons. Afghanistan opium production nevertheless created the single most corrupting influence throughout South Asia. The revenue produced by the production of opium, in the words of Antonio Maria Costa, "is making a handful of criminals and corrupt officials extremely rich . . . [and] is also dragging the rest of Afghanistan into a bottomless pit of destruction and despair."[8] Under present conditions, it is impossible for Tajikistan to insulate itself from the effects of the drug trade, and Tajik foreign policy includes pursuing diplomatic alliances that can counter the situation. Tajikistan is also moving energetically to develop the country's hydroelectric potential, and plans proceed to create larger, region-wide electric transmission grids in the South Asian region.

Turkmenistan's foreign policy goals have been since independence inextricably tied with the personal goals of the country's illustrious leader, who has come to be referred to as "Saparmurad Niyazov Turkmenbashi the Great."

Soon after independence, Niyazov adopted an assertive posture of national self-reliance based on Turkmenistan's gas and oil wealth. Niyazov eventually came to refer to this as Turkmenistan's policy of "positive neutrality."[9] In practice, the policy meant three things. First, Turkmenistan sought to maintain as much distance as possible from Russia without giving up the big Russian gas market and, most of all, without giving up access to Western gas markets that, by virtue of the possession of the fixed pipeline system, Russia in large measure continued to control. Second, it meant wary policies of self-interest with Turkmenistan's southern neighbors. Third, it meant drawing in foreign investment to the extent possible to revitalize the gas-related industry and build a Kuwait-style emirate in Turkmenistan.

At the beginning, Turkmenistan developed the idea of "positive neutrality" to insulate itself from being linked to Russia. The policy was used as the rationale for building new relationships with Azerbaijan, Iran, and Ukraine, outside of Russia's influence. But the Turkmen government's goal of shipping gas through Azerbaijan fell apart, the idea of the trans-Afghan pipeline was stalled, and the Iranian gas sales remained on a minimal level. The Turkmen government reversed its position 180 degrees and applauded positive neutrality as the rationale for reestablishing its warm relations with Russia, as embodied, for instance, in a twenty-five-year marketing contract with Russia's towering natural gas monopoly, Gazprom. Those Turkmen officials who saw the contradiction in this policy were conveniently removed from positions of influence, usually by accusations of corruption followed by prison sentences. International financial institutions discreetly withdrew from conducting many of their operations in Turkmenistan, waiting for an improvement in the governance environment.

Uzbekistan holds a pivotal role in Central Asia, given its physical location in the heart of the region as the only Central Asian country that borders all other Central Asian countries, and it is positioned at the converging point for energy, water, and transportation infrastructure. Moreover, the country's leaders have aimed at re-creating a largely fictional historical role for Uzbekistan as the leading country in the region. After independence, Uzbekistan quickly established itself as defiantly nationalist. In a few short years, the country jettisoned virtually the entire legacy of seventy years of Soviet—and thus essentially Russian—political control and cultural influence. Uzbekistan's heavy-handed president, Islam Karimov, who had been a dutiful communist in his Soviet-era incarnation, soon became an enthusiastic champion of an independent political path and an Uzbek cultural renewal.[10] In ways reminiscent of Turkey's Kemal Ataturk, Karimov engineered a determined national consolidation, a new "Uzbek path." Government, economics, culture, and essentially the entire spectrum of policy arenas were harnessed to the drive to "recover" Uzbekistan. After the collapse of the USSR, Uzbekistan moved toward isolation from Russian influence for several years.

Uzbekistan attenuated Russian cultural influence, ended widespread instruction in schools of the Russian language, suspended military cooperation, and blocked many forms of commercial interactions with Russia. The initial Uzbek neomercantilist strategy aggressively sought diplomatic and commercial ties with a host of countries, partially in order to increase its foreign policy options, but mainly in order to diminish the leverage of Russian diplomats and traders.

After the events of September 11, 2001, Uzbekistan formed a strategic partnership with the United States to aid in ousting the Taliban from Afghanistan.[11] But the U.S. partnership came with a host of conditions relating to standards of practice, governance, and civil rights. After chafing at insistent reminders from U.S. officials over civil rights and the right of free association, Uzbekistan reversed its position, abandoning the partnership and shifting back in favor of closer relations with Russia.[12] The opprobrium that had been heaped on Russia for years turned virtually overnight into dithyrambs. After signing the agreement to join the EAEC, Karimov proudly announced that the reestablishment of close relations with Russia went beyond mere cooperation. Karimov said the new relationship was akin to restoring "union relations" (*soiuznie otnoshenie*), a code phrase harkening back to the Soviet period.

CASPIAN BASIN ENERGY RESOURCES

Hydrocarbon deposits in the Central Asian region are located far from established markets, and the countries' lack of direct access to the hydrocarbon transit sea lanes collectively involves them in competition and cooperation to get the oil and gas to market. When the USSR disintegrated, geographical and political impediments to development tended to separate rather than align the post-Soviet countries. Countries had differing responses to the situation. Kazakhstan's greatest development opportunities were bound up in the oil, gas, and coal resources that were in the ground and far from markets. Newly independent Kazakhstan was highly reliant upon what had become Russian transportation and refining capacity. When the USSR came to an end, Kazakhstan took claim to the natural resources on its territory, including the oil and gas reserves. Much of Kazakhstan's oil wealth was located in the northwestern section of the country, close to the southern Russian border. In 1991, the Kazakhstan government began negotiating what the Kazakhstan press referred to at the time as "the deal of the century" to develop Kazakhstan's Tengiz oil fields.

The Caspian Pipeline Consortium (CPC) was created as a partnership of states and companies to bring the area's gas and oil to market. Geological exploration and a series of finds led to considerable scrambling for access to the resources and raised expectations regarding the prospects for the region competing with the Middle East. The CPC, however, traversed Russian territory and depended on the delivery to international market for transit through the Bosporus. Alternative energy corridors were opened, to deliver oil through a pipeline through the Caucasus and on to Turkey and a pipeline from Kazakhstan to market in China.[13] The U.S. government and oil companies in the mid-1990s began supporting new physical infrastructure development, emphasizing the importance of multiple access routes to markets in order to diminish tendencies toward monopolistic domination. The Baku-Tbilisi-Ceyhan pipeline project (BTC) was one of the first examples of the U.S. policy of promoting multiple forms of access to markets. After a decade of planning, consultation, and multilateral support, the BTC oil pipeline connected Kazakhstan's landlocked oil producers with world markets when it was officially opened in late 2005. The BTC is one element of a larger goal of creating a policy framework and the associated physical infrastructure conducive to conditions for sustainable and equitable growth throughout the region. As Frederick Starr pointed out, "By re-opening ancient east-west and north-south trade routes, the United States and its partners are creating a great new Eurasian economic zone."[14]

Just as energy holds great importance for Central Asia, it also holds great importance for markets. Consequently, energy security holds great importance for the Central Asian states, Caucasus states, and European states. Rising energy costs, the emergence of rapidly growing energy demand in Eastern states, environmental trends, and the increased reliance of high-volume markets on energy imports have sensitized concerns in highly developed countries over the reliability of commercial energy supplies. European countries have become particularly concerned about the pivotal influence of Russian energy suppliers and transporters over energy prices and supply reliability.

European Union (EU) negotiators have long been concerned to enhance energy security through a negotiated foundation for assurances of energy supplies. By "energy security" the negotiators principally had in mind assured energy deliveries at agreed upon prices without the threat of disruption connected to political advantage. The idea that multilateral rules could provide a more equitable and stable framework for international energy commerce led in 1991 to the proposal of a European Energy Charter. The charter was officially signed in December 1994 and came into effect in 1998. Although Russia signed the Energy Charter in 1994, it opted not to ratify the agreement and, particularly after adopting the Russian Energy Strategy in 2000, moved away from initial indications that it would conform to the charter provisions.[15]

Russia's influence over energy resources as an instrument of foreign policy stimulated fears among Europeans regarding dependence on Russian energy resources. The increasingly close coordination between Russian diplomatic goals and Russian energy producers' commercial interests converged to the extent that the two agendas are virtually indistinguishable. In response, at EU initiative, in October 2000 agreements were reached to establish a program of regular consultations and discussions under the auspices of the European Union–Russia Energy Dialogue. The goal of the dialogue was to maintain regular communication regarding energy conservation, improvement of production and transport infrastructures, investment cooperation, and bilateral relations between producer and consumer countries concerning disputes over prices, quality, delivery, conflict adjudication, and related issues.[16] However, the number of disagreements and charges of politically motivated exploitation of vulnerabilities continued to grow over this period.

Critics of Russian policy aver that oil pipelines have been used repeatedly to punctuate the importance of Russian diplomatic goals. Early in 2003, Latvian oil importers were cut off from Russian oil supplies and complained to EU authorities that the cutoff was politically motivated.[17] In early 2006, natural gas supplies to Ukraine were interrupted, causing shortfalls in planned deliveries to European states. Early in 2007, Lithuania sought EU assistance in a commercial disagreement with the Russian oil transportation trust, Transneft, alleging that oil supply interruption, while being represented by the Russian side as a technical-industrial problem, was actually masking a political goal of manipulation.[18] U.S. Vice President Dick Cheney, speaking at a conference in Vilnius, accused the Kremlin of using gas and oil supplies as "tools of intimidation and blackmail."[19] Increasingly anxious efforts to mitigate the danger of cutoffs of gas and oil to European countries mobilized a new concern in Europe in 2006 over political vulnerability.

Oil supplies are generally viewed as less vulnerable than natural gas supplies, as the natural gas market is so heavily tied to the fixed distribution pipeline system. European vulnerability to natural gas supply disruption was underscored by the cutoff of Russian natural gas deliveries to Ukraine in early 2006. The Ukrainian gas crisis was resolved with substantial price increases at the risk of severe economic implications for the Ukrainian economy. While the natural gas delivery price that was eventually settled on ($100 per 1,000 cubic meters) was still far below a world market value, the conditions in which the deal was driven through were widely considered commercial stratagems for the purpose of political influence.

Yet European diplomats continued to stress the importance of finding a negotiated path toward reciprocal relations. As the EU commissioner of external affairs argued in November 2006, "The substantial and reliable flow of revenues that Russia obtains from selling energy to the EU has undoubtedly been one of the key factors in Russia's economic revival. For the EU, the stable flow of reasonably priced energy has been an important factor underlying the EU's economic growth and well-being," and both sides therefore should seek to reinforce this "win-win" situation.[20] But Russia's greatest future comparative advantage in translating energy supplies into political influence may be its access not to the energy markets of Western Europe—which are expected to have only modest future growth—but to the sharply growing energy markets of South Asia and China.

Kazakhstan is the dynamic leader of Central Asian countries, carrying out highly successful postcommunist reforms and anticipating rapid increases in gas and oil exports during the decade ahead. Kazakhstan policy makers have stressed the importance of Kazakhstan's role in international energy commerce. As Kazakhstan's foreign minister, Marat Tazhin, said at the Eurasian Energy Forum in September 2007, "Kazakhstan is fully aware of its new role in providing international energy stability and security. . . . We are pondering large infrastructural projects that will diversify Kazakh deliveries to the world market and ensure stability."[21] Kazakhstan's oil production in 2007 reached nearly 1.5 million barrels a day (see table 11.1). Disagreements over technical issues and new oil discoveries were resolved in January 2008, and the major new Kashagan field is expected to come into production beginning in 2011. Kazakhstan's oil production growth is expected to accelerate in the next decade. Current production from the large Tengiz field is expected to double, while the Kashagan is expected to begin producing an additional 1 million barrels a day after 2011. Oil production has become the basic driving force in Kazakhstan's rapid economic recovery.

The other Caucasus and Central Asian countries are also highly interdependent with respect to energy resources, transportation infrastructure, and markets. Rich oil and gas reserves are located in Azerbaijan, Kazakhstan, Turkmenistan, and Uzbekistan. Much of the oil wealth is located on the Caspian Sea littoral or in remote western Kazakhstan. The potential for increasing oil and gas production in the region is great. Oil industry analysts expect that the region could be exporting as much as 3 million barrels a day by 2010. But because the region's oil-producing countries are mostly land-locked, routes to the market invariably involve shipment through third-party countries.

The Central Asian states form an important part of the larger Caspian Basin hydrocarbon producers. The Caspian Basin as a whole produced in mid-2008 about 2.8 million barrels a day. The major crude oil producers are Azerbaijan, Kazakhstan, and Uzbekistan. Oil and gas are located onshore and offshore in the countries, and the offshore ownership rights are defined by international agreements. More than half of the production of the entire Caspian Basin region is made up by Kazakhstan. Kazakhstan's oil revenues have promoted rapid growth that, according to World Bank analyses, has averaged 9 percent per year between 2001 and 2007. Kazakhstan's combined onshore and offshore hydrocarbon reserves may reach as high as 40 billion barrels. In 2007, Kazakhstan produced an average of nearly 1.5

Table 11.1. Russian and Central Asian Oil Production (thousand barrels daily)

	1997	1998	1999	2000	2001	2002	2003	2004	2005	2006	2007
Russia	6227	6169	6178	6536	7056	7698	8544	9287	9552	9769	9978
Kazakhstan	536	537	631	744	836	1018	1111	1297	1356	1426	1490
Azerbaijan	182	231	279	282	301	311	313	315	452	654	868
Turkmenistan	108	129	143	144	162	182	202	193	192	186	198
Uzbekistan	182	191	191	177	171	171	166	152	126	125	114

Source: See Statistical Review of World Energy 2008, www.bp.com.

million barrels per day, nearly 70 percent of which was exported. The great bulk of crude oil production comes from four very large fields: Tengiz, Karachaganak, Kurmangazy, and Kashagan. Production is expected to increase rapidly in the years ahead as newly exploited fields come into production.

All the Central Asian oil and gas supply contracts hinge on transportation. Russia inherited a number of distribution oil pipelines from the Soviet government. These pipelines are now owned and managed by the state-run oil transportation firm, Transneft.[22] At the time of the Soviet breakup, the Kazakhstan government was intent on finding a new transit route. This resulted in formation of the Caspian Pipeline Consortium in 1992 as a joint venture between governments and private firms.[23] The CPC was designed as a framework for a 1,510-kilometer oil pipeline from the Tengiz field in northern Kazakhstan to the Novorossiysk Marine Terminal on Russia's Black Sea coast. Regular operation of the pipeline started in April 2003. In late 2008, the CPC was shipping on average over 700,000 barrels a day. The crude was processed, then shipped from the Tengiz loading station through a pipeline powered by a number of pump stations to the terminal, where it was loaded on ships destined to travel across the Black Sea, through the Dardanelles, and on to markets. The CPC pipeline is scheduled to become the major export route for the oil from the Kashagan and Karachaganak fields. The CPC is presently the only oil export pipeline in Russian territory not wholly owned by Transneft.

In September 1997, a Framework Agreement was adopted for the development and construction of the West Kazakhstan-China oil pipeline between the China National Petroleum Corporation (CNPC) and the Ministry of Energy and Natural Resources of Kazakhstan, with the idea of constructing a pipeline from Atyrau to Alashankou on the border. This would give CNPC a minimum guarantee in exchange for the construction of the pipeline. In September 1999, this was extended into an agreement on cooperation in the oil and gas sector between the governments of Kazakhstan and China. Kazakhstan agreed to make arrangements for right of way for pipeline construction, safety and security guarantees, stability of the legal regulation for oil export duties, and equipment import duties. Construction of the Kumkol pipeline (Atasu-Alashankou) began in September 2004 and was completed in December 2005. This draws on the Kumkol and crude from the Kenkiyak (Aktobe) that is shipped by railcar before transfer to the pipeline.

The fact that the BTC corridor is not expected to be large enough and secure enough for the shipment of all oil has led to the exploration of other shipment mechanisms. Oil continues to be shipped by train through Russia but at a much higher cost than pipeline shipment. Another option being explored is shipment by barge across the Caspian. Kazakhstan intends to develop a Kazakhstan Caspian Transportation System (KCTS) that will transport by barge oil from western Kazakhstan to Azerbaijan ports for transshipment through Georgia and Turkey.

CONCLUSION

The relations of the Central Asian states with Russia are complex. The political managers of Central Asian foreign policies recognize that Russia, diminished in the period following the collapse of the USSR, has reemerged as an important and influential actor on the world stage. The post-9/11 period witnessed the gathering momentum of an assertive and self-confident Russian foreign policy directed by activist presidents, managed by a cadre of professionally schooled "intellicrats," and supported by a pantheon of well-ensconced and politically resourceful oligarchs. Russia's resurgence was fueled by soaring oil prices and driven by Russia's foreign policy clout resulting from European dependence on natural gas from Eastern suppliers. The Central Asian states witnessed Russia becoming more assertive in former Soviet regions in the context of the diminishing U.S. capacity to unilaterally determine foreign policy outcomes, Russia's fear of encirclement from NATO countries, China's rising economic influence, and Russia's disagreement with OSCE policies and practices. The Central Asian states witnessed Russia embarking on a grand strategy of dividing U.S. and European interests along the lines proposed in Dmitri Medvedev's "Berlin Initiative" announced in April 2008. They viewed Russia's military operation in South Ossetia and Abkhazia in August 2008 as a first skirmish in the plan to restore Russia to a position as one of the world's major powers, along with the United States, the European Union, and Japan. They realized Russia's "north-south dimension"—the relations with the Caucasus and Central Asia, South Asia, and the Middle East—had become one of the three major dimensions of Russian foreign policy.

The rise of Russian influence was supported by many policy makers and analysts in Central Asian capitals. In Ashgabat, Astana, Bishkek, Dushanbe, and Tashkent, many foreign policy strategists at least in part welcomed the restoration of the influence of Moscow. Yet even among Moscow's strongest supporters, few viewed Russia's increased role in Central Asia as an unalloyed benefit. Other strategists were expressly apprehensive. Some analysts feared that the return of an expansive and aggressive Russia to the Central Asian region portended dark aspirations of a return of Russian imperial ambitions. Some feared that the new "liberal imperialism" so enthusiastically endorsed by Russia's erstwhile electric power autocrat, Anatoli Chubais, was merely a strategy for imperial restoration in another guise. Some saw in the outline of Russia's return to Central Asia a stealth strategy to displace America's role as a guarantor of international security. Some saw Russia's rising influence as only the first stage of a vast strategy to unfold a new form of political influence over infrastructure in rail, shipping, air routes, electricity grids, oil and gas pipelines, and finance. With India and China increasing their demand for electricity and gas, some saw Russian shipping, gas, oil, electric supplies, and investment as a means by which Russia's oligarchs might capture the new markets for economic reasons that have both commercial objectives as well as political underpinnings. Some saw Russia's moves to harness the hydroelectric potential of Kyrgyzstan and Tajikistan as the first steps in a strategy for gaining control of power resources throughout the region. And some feared that Russia's historical indifference to civil rights and freedoms was likely to further motivate the willingness of Russian leaders to overlook human rights violations for narrow political interests.

The global economic slowdown that began in 2008 has brought about a reassessment of Moscow's policies in Central Asia. Falling energy and minerals markets have cut demand for oil and gas the world over, curbing the strength of Russia's energy companies that once seemed unassailable. If Russia's state-controlled natural gas company, Gazprom, had succeeded in pursuing a policy in which Moscow could use natural gas as an instrument to guide relations with client countries, particularly European countries heavily dependent upon Russian gas supplies, it also implied a corresponding weakness for Russia in the context of lax demand and falling prices.

These trends put Central Asian economic and security policies in a different light. Political instability in Afghanistan, the drug trade, the specter of rising nuclear powers in South Asia and the Middle East, gathering problems of labor migration, and the continued resilience of insurgent doctrines and movements combined with economic recession to provoke new apprehensions. Uzbekistan's policy planners were particularly concerned about the region's new insecurity. From Tashkent's perspective, the region looked much less stable than a decade before and moving in yet a more threatening direction. As Uzbek strategists argue, if these trends continue, a new set of circumstances can be presaged just over the horizon in which the Afghanistan war will grind forward indecisively until Western troops leave. In such a circumstance, the Taliban will grow, the power of Kabul will crumble, Afghanistan will fragment, Iran will become more influential within Afghanistan and throughout the region, Pakistan will once again be unchecked, and Moscow will become more aggressive throughout the Central Asian region.

The present situation leaves many questions in the air, but in Central Asia a number of things are clear. Over the past two decades, the principal policy concerns throughout the Central Asian region may have focused on postcommunist transitions, managing the consequences of the Soviet collapse, and implementing systemic reform of the administrative and economic systems, but that situation is now distinctively different. The challenges of the future have overtaken the importance of the past. A backward-looking orientation in the Central Asian states has been replaced by forward-looking foreign policies addressed to the future. We may expect that Central Asian multivector foreign policies with respect to Russia will continue to play an important role in years ahead.

SUGGESTED READINGS

Collins, Kathleen. *Clan Politics and Regime Transition in Central Asia*. Cambridge: Cambridge University Press, 2006.

Jones Luong, Pauline. *Institutional Changes and Political Continuity in Post-Soviet Central Asia: Power, Perceptions, and Pacts*. Cambridge: Cambridge University Press, 2002.

Khalid, Adeeb. *Islam after Communism: Religion and Politics in Central Asia*. Berkeley: University of California Press, 2007.

Marat, Erica. *The Tulip Revolution: Kyrgyzstan One Year After, March 15, 2005–March 24, 2006*. Washington, D.C.: Jamestown Foundation, 2006.

Olcott, Martha Brill. *Central Asia's Second Chance*. New York: Carnegie Endowment for International Peace, 2005.

Promfred, Richard. *The Central Asian Economies since Independence*. Princeton, N.J.: Princeton University Press, 2006.

NOTES

1. The author wrote this chapter while on leave from the University of New Mexico, when serving at the George C. Marshall European Center for Security Studies. The views presented in this chapter do not necessarily represent the views of the U.S. Department of Defense or the George C. Marshall Center.

2. The Russian National Security Strategy was approved on January 10, 2000. The Russian Foreign Policy Strategy was approved on July 2, 2000. These are guidance documents for the Ministry of Foreign Affairs and other foreign affairs agencies, articulating the goals and objectives of Russian foreign policy. The previous doctrinal statement, often referred to as the "Kozyrev doctrine," was adopted in April 1993 during Andrei Kozyrev's tenure as minister of foreign affairs.

3. At independence, all the countries of the Central Asian region subscribed to the general principles of the international community: the sovereign equality of states; the right of noninterference in domestic affairs of the sovereign state; territorial integrity of the state; the obligation to abide by international agreements; the principle of the peaceful settlement of disputes; and the obligation to engage in international cooperation consistent with national interests.

4. See Nazarbaev's speech to the Kazak SSR Supreme Soviet, December 10, 1991, "Vybor—Tsvilizovannoe Demokratichskoe Obshchestvo," *Piat' let nezavisimosti* (Almaty: Kazakhstan, 1996), 19–24.

5. Tajikistan joined the World Bank and the IMF in 1993. Tajikistan joined the Asian Development Bank in March 1998. Turkmenistan joined the ADB in 2000.

6. Eugene Huskey, "An Economy of Authoritarianism? Askar Akaev and Presidential Leadership in Kyrgyzstan," in *Power and Change in Central Asia*, ed. Sally N. Cummings (London: Routledge, 2002), 74–96.

7. Erica Marat, *The Tulip Revolution: Kyrgyzstan One Year After, March 15, 2005–March 24, 2006* (Washington, D.C.: Jamestown Foundation, 2006).

8. *Afghanistan Opium Survey for 2006* (New York: UN Office on Drugs and Crime, 2006), iv, www.unodc.org/pdf/execsummaryafg.pdf. See Svante Cornell and

Niklas Swanström, "The Eurasian Drug Trade: A Challenge to Regional Security," *Problems of Post-Communism* 53, no. 4 (2006): 10–28. Also see Johan Engvall, "The State under Siege: The Drug Trade and Organised Crime in Tajikistan," *Europe-Asia Studies* 58, no. 6 (2006): 827–54.

9. See Luca Anceschi, "Positive Neutrality: The Role of Foreign Policy in the Consolidation of the Turkmen Regime (1992–2005)," doctoral thesis, La Trobe University, 2006.

10. Islam Karimov's justification of government policy is presented in his *Uzbekistan on the Threshold of the Twenty-first Century* (New York: St. Martin's, 1998).

11. See Shahram Akbarzadeh, *Uzbekistan and the United States: Authoritarianism, Islamism, and Washington's Security Agenda* (London: Zed Books, 2005).

12. In a specific legal sense, Uzbekistan did not "abandon the U.S. strategic partnership." The Memorandum of Understanding that established this relationship still has not been officially nullified and, consequently, continues to remain in force. On the background of U.S.-Uzbek relations, see John Daly, Kurt Meppen, Vladimir Socor, and S. Frederick Starr, *Anatomy of a Crisis: U.S.-Uzbekistan Relations, 2001–2005*, Silk Road Paper, Central Asia Caucasus Institute and Silk Road Studies Program (February 2006).

13. Materials for this discussion of Caspian Basin energy resources are drawn from the International Energy Administration of the U.S. Department of Energy and other sources. See International Energy Administration, U.S. Department of Energy, *International Energy Outlook, 2008*, www.eia.doe.gov/oiaf/ieo/index.html. Also see *Key World Energy Statistics 2008*, International Energy Agency, www.iea.org.

14. S. Frederick Starr, "Silk Road to Success," *National Interest* 78 (2004): 65–72, at 72.

15. Russia's stated objections to the agreement concern sovereignty issues, claiming that Russian sovereignty would be compromised by charter provisions regarding third-party access to pipelines and transit fees. But the unstated and more influential premise is that Russian negotiators no longer think it is in the interest of the country to enter into such constraining advance contractual obligations.

16. See http://ec.europa.eu/energy/russia/overview/index_en.htm.

17. See Michael Lelyveld, "Russia: Moscow Seeks Takeover of Latvian Oil Port," www.rferl.org.

18. See "Lithuania Seeks EU Help to Resume Oil Flow from Russia" (March 8, 2007), www.eubusiness.com.

19. Stefan Wagstyl, "Cheney Rebukes Putin on Energy 'Blackmail,'" *Financial Times*, May 4, 2006.

20. Benita Ferrero-Waldner, "Opening Address by EU Commissioner Ferrero-Waldner: Towards an EU External Energy Policy to Assure a High Level of Supply Security," at the conference in Brussels on EU External Energy Policy, November 20, 2006, www.europa-eu-un.org/articles/en/article_6500_en.htm.

21. *Kazakhstan News Bulletin*, no. 7 (September 12, 2007), http://prosites-kazakhembus.homestead.com/NB7-120907.html.

22. See the Transneft website: www.transneft.ru.

23. See the CPC website: www.cpc.ru.

Chapter Twelve

Putin, Medvedev, and the Russian Military

Dale R. Herspring

We have an army at present which has recovered from the hard times under the Yeltsin administration, and while the main problem in the army for a long time was a lack of money, the problem now has become the inability to manage money wisely.

—Ruslan Pukhov

Toward the end of his time in office, President Vladimir Putin came to the conclusion that the Russian military had to be shaken up—that it was so corrupt and hidebound, only an outsider could do the job.[1] As a result, heads are rolling and major changes are under way. If fully implemented, by 2020 the Russian military will have undergone "a revolution in military affairs," to use the late Marshal Nikolai Ogarkov's well-known phrase. The magnitude of these changes came to light in June 2008, when the chief of the General Staff, General Yuri Baluyevsky, was fired. He had consistently opposed the changes that the new civilian defense minister, Anatoli Serdiukov, was determined to introduce. That was followed by the shocking announcement that the officer corps would be cut by more than half in the near future. So far, all indications are that Serdiukov has the upper hand in spite of unhappiness on the part of many officers.

Few observers doubt the need for change in the Russian Army (the term encompasses all of the services). The military is still trying to find itself in the aftermath of the Yeltsin period, when it came close to collapse.[2] Even Russian officers admit the need for change. The problem, however, is what kind of change and how is it to be introduced? Why is that important? For the simple reason that the Russian Army, like other militaries, has its own specific culture—its way of doing business. If that culture is violated—as it

265

was under Yeltsin by his refusal to provide leadership or to show respect—
conflict intensifies.

VLADIMIR PUTIN AND THE MILITARY

The Russian Army saw a major change for the better during the Putin period. First, he provided the leadership that had been lacking. He turned the
conduct of the Chechen war over to the military, reestablished a clear chain
of command by resubordinating the General Staff to the defense minister,
and gradually forced both the defense minister (a Strategic Rocket Forces
officer) and the chief of the General Staff (a Ground Forces officer) out of
their positions, thereby removing a major source of conflict in the Ministry
of Defense (MoD). In 2001, Putin appointed one of his closest friends and
colleagues, the former KGB general Sergei Ivanov, as defense minister. In
addition to his service in the KGB, Ivanov had been intimately involved in
the Security Council's efforts to come up with a military reform plan. Many
believed that he would be the one to help the military come up with a plan
and put it back on its feet. Indeed, there was a widespread belief that a simple
increase in military spending in combination with restoring the officers' due
place in society would solve the army's problems.

There is no question that much was done. The military budget was gradually increased, efforts were made to begin training exercises anew, and an
effort (admittedly very limited) was undertaken to modernize some weapons
systems. From the generals' standpoint, the important factor was that they
were now regaining two items critical to any military: predictability and stability (*predvidenie i stabilnost*). An army cannot operate logically if the generals and admirals do not know what their budget will be—after all, under
Yeltsin, the military's budget was cut and then cut again. Then to make matters worse, the military often received only slightly more than half of what it
was promised. This seriously undermined combat readiness. The latter was
in such bad shape in 1999 that "young men who had been through four
years of training to be air force pilots were sent 'to the infantry, the armored
troops, artillery and communications.'"[3] Similarly, there were reports that
"the ground forces have at most seven combat-ready divisions."[4]

When Ivanov left office in early 2007, the military was in far better shape
than it had been in 1999. For example, the military's budget had risen from
R218.9 billion in 2001 to about R573 billion.[5] Training had also increased.
In 1999, for example, pilots were flying an average of 20–22 hours per
month.[6] By 2004, Ivanov reported that they were up to 30 hours per month,
with those in a readiness command exceeding 50 hours.[7] By the next year,
the average was up to 33 hours.[8] Furthermore, by 2006 there was a significant increase in the number of training exercises, including those involving

reservists. Even the navy, which had spent most of its time tied up at various piers, began to take part in exercises.[9]

In spite of the progress that the military appeared to be making under Ivanov's leadership, there were problems. Most notably was the issue of weapons. It was no secret that Russia's weapons inventory was in horrible shape. But Ivanov made it clear that the ministry of defense was allocating more and more money to the purchase of modern weapons. For example, in 2005 he commented that the "state defense order in 2006 will amount to $8.27 billion, up $1.88 billion for this year." According to Ivanov, that increase would permit "the spending of 70 percent of the funds on the procurement of new armaments and military hardware, or comprehensive upgrades of current hardware."[10]

However, for all the attention to the budget, little appeared in the field. One critic commented, "The weapons and material of the Russian Armed Forces are getting increasingly more obsolete and worn out, experts of the Russian Audit Chamber believe. . . . Despite the annual increase in the spending on technical re-equipment of the Armed Forces and complete implementation of everything planned in the domain, no significant improvements have been observed here." Another critic observed, "If we continue re-equipping the Armed Forces at such rates, it will take hundreds of years to achieve the goal. For instance, it will take a hundred years to re-equip combat aviation, and 200 years to rearm the Navy."[11] The situation was similar in other areas. There was a desperate need for new barracks and other infrastructure to support a professional army, just as there was a need for housing, better food, better medical care, better salaries, and so on. The key question facing the defense ministry was "why?" Why didn't the increased amount of money translate into the kind of improvements needed to put the Russian military on a level equal to NATO militaries? After all, it was expected that the new money that was largely financing this "expansion" would produce the kind of military the Kremlin needed if it was going to be seen as a world power.

FINDING THE PROBLEM

It appears that the defense procurement system essentially remained unchanged from the Soviet period because the controls previously exercised by the Main Directorate of the KGB and Communist Party of the Soviet Union (CPSU) representatives in the army were gone. That system permitted (and sometimes encouraged) officials operating within it substantial opportunities for corruption, mismanagement, and abuse of power.[12] Both Ivanov and Putin were aware of the corruption problem in the military, only neither of them appeared aware of just how serious it was.

There was a good reason Ivanov was appointed deputy prime minister in November 2005 while keeping his portfolio as defense minister. It was hoped that the added hat would give him the ability to supervise the Military-Industrial Commission, to ensure that the various ministries, agencies, and companies worked together and that the military received maximum return for its money.

But money was disappearing. As Russian journalist Pavel Felgenhauer commented, "To this day, it is unclear how the money was actually spent." It was certainly not coming out in the form of new weapons systems. According to Felgenhauer, "We are talking about very large amounts of money that are disappearing—no one knows where."[13] Unfortunately, the Duma has never been given meaningful oversight function in looking at the budget. Deputies can make recommendations, but in 2006, 44 percent of the defense budget was classified; there was no way that members of the Duma without special security clearances could pass on the budget.[14] Furthermore, even those with the required security clearance were not able to detect the problem because all they could check was the precise allocation of funds between various programs, not how the funds were actually spent.

Ivanov, having detected early on that the procurement system was the core of the problem and the hotbed of corruption, tried to change it so that opportunities for misappropriation and misuse of funds would be reduced. He attempted to do this by making an important structural modification. First, he cut back the entities within the Ministry of Defense that could purchase items for the armed forces. "When I became defense minister, 52 bodies within the Defense Ministry had the power to purchase military hardware and order research and design programs. We cut the number to 20 at first, and now it's down to only one."[15] In addition, Ivanov stated that this new Arms Procurement Agency would be staffed by civilian personnel—thereby moving military officers back a step from the actual decision to purchase weapons. It would be in charge of ordering all military supplies. It reported to the cabinet. "It is outside the Defense Ministry."[16] Ivanov hoped it would make it more difficult to misappropriate funds and would reduce corruption.[17]

Unfortunately, it was not enough. In the beginning of 2007, an article argued that corruption remained rife in the MoD: "These efforts are never crowned with success because they are essentially going after themselves. The main military secret today is that almost all generals and officers constituting the ranking nucleus of the arms of military leadership from procurement subdivisions of the MoD and the General Staff through the corresponding agencies and combat arms of the Armed Forces are members of corporate boards of directors and sit on auditing commissions and are even appointed the general managers of corporations."[18] Another source argued that there was also a serious problem with misuse of funds by civilian corporations.[19]

Recognizing the depth of the corruption problem, Ivanov privately ordered an audit of how the military budget was spent. It was becoming clear to him that just castigating individuals and making a few institutional modifications was not enough to deal with the problem. Before taking any further steps, however, it was imperative that he understand just how big the problem was. The result shocked Ivanov. On April 3, the Audit Chamber announced that over R164.1 billion had been stolen from the MoD by fraud and outright theft.[20] According to another report, the MoD "accounts for 70 percent of the budgetary resources used for purposes other than those officially confirmed." An unnamed Duma official told Interfax, "the Defense Ministry is the unchallenged leader in missing federal budget agency."[21] To his credit, Ivanov had taken this information to Putin. The Federal Security Service (FSB), in a separate report, claimed that Ivanov's reforms meant that many defense enterprises refused to accept MoD orders because they had to pay back up to 50 percent of the value of the order as a kickback.[22]

Given the enormity of the problem, and Ivanov's inability to solve it or even make headway on dealing with it, Putin decided on February 15, 2007, to elevate Ivanov to the post of first deputy premier. Then, in an effort to signal that he was making a complete break with the past, he named a hitherto unknown civilian tax official, Anatoli Serdiukov, as defense minister to deal with the military's most serious problem: corruption. One thing was certain, Putin succeeded in sending his message: almost all observers, in Russia and abroad, were shocked. It was one thing to name a noncareer military officer like Ivanov to be defense minister, but a civilian whose military experience amounted to a reserve commission as a lieutenant in the ground troops in which he served from 1984 to 1985! The appointment of Serdiukov was widely criticized. Colonel-General Leonid Ivashov, a well-known hard-liner, claimed that the military "was spat on . . . and is now in mourning." Another critic claimed that Putin "had turned the screws" on the military.[23]

However, few believed that Serdiukov's appointment meant that the MoD was in for a serious shake-up. Alexandr Golts, a well-known journalist who specializes on the Russian military, claimed that it gave a "sham impression of civilian control over the armed forces." Vladimir Dvorkin, a retired general, observed: "I think that in the situation we have today it is irrelevant who was appointed."[24]

For its part, the active duty military also did not take Serdiukov's appointment seriously. According to one columnist, "The Russian Armed Forces are in confusion. Headquarters, barracks, and military on line forums are caught up in heated debates about the newly appointed defense minister, Anatoli Serdiukov. The battles are intense. Some insist that this former 'furniture dealer' is incapable of managing Armed Forces development—backing up their arguments with jokes about Serdiukov providing new tables and chairs in all barracks."[25]

SERDIUKOV TAKES CHARGE

Serdiukov's biography is markedly unmilitary. Born on January 8, 1962, in the village of Kholmsky (Abinsky raion, Krasnodar *krai*), he graduated from the Leningrad Institute of Soviet Trade in 1984 and St. Petersburg State University in 2001. His degrees are in economics and law. He worked as a deputy section chief and then section chief at a Leningrad Furniture store from 1985 until 1991. From 1991 to 1993, he was deputy director for commercial work at Leningrad Furniture. In 1993, he moved up to become deputy director of the Furniture Market joint-stock company in St. Petersburg and then marketing director. From 1995 to 2000, he was head of the Furniture Market. In 2000, Serdiukov became deputy head of the Ministry of Taxes and Levies for St. Petersburg. In May 2001, was appointed deputy head of administration in the ministry. In November, he was promoted to head of administration. In March 2004, he was made deputy minister for taxes and levies, and on July 27, 2004, he was appointed head of the Federal Tax Service. His most famous tax victims were Mikhail Khodorkovsky and Yukos. It is no wonder that Putin picked him to straighten out spending in the MoD.

Serdiukov must have been reading the newspapers about how the military was not taking him seriously because he quickly found an opportunity to send a message to the troops. At the end of March 2007, Serdiukov made an unannounced visit to the Nakhimov Naval College in St. Petersburg. Moreover, he came in through the back door—right where the food was stored and the trash containers were located. "During his snap visit, Serdiukov discovered horribly inadequate sanitary arrangements, damp college cadets' rooms, water in the basement, fungi on the walls, and crumbling plaster." The response: the chief of the college, Rear Admiral Alexandr Bukin, was dismissed from the service.[26] Serdiukov's visit and the dismissal of Bukin sent a very clear message to the rest of the military: don't be surprised if you receive an unannounced visit—and if your command is not up to snuff, you will pay the consequences. Such an action would get the senior leadership's attention in any military.[27]

From Serdiukov's point of view, in addition to getting the troop's attention, he believed he had one primary goal and that was to straighten out the military. The question was, how to do it? Based on his subsequent actions, it is clear that his number one priority was to gain control of the MoD budget and in the process, to the maximum degree possible, stop corruption.

Serdiukov brought with him a six-person civilian team (later expanded to thirty) from the Federal Tax Service. He had no intention of relying on the MoD to supervise itself. Indeed, one of his primary goals was to take the "closed" MoD and let in some light, especially where it involved the expenditure of funds. He stated, for example, that he would focus on the "creation of a more transparent system for the rational and targeted expenditure of budget funds allocated to the Armed Forces."[28] He also made it clear that he intended to downsize the military. There were too many redundant structures. It was time to begin streamlining the MoD and make it better able to deal with the problems of the twenty-first century. In truth, no one in the military knew exactly what Serdiukov had in mind. Did he intend to go through the MoD as well as the General Staff cutting offices and organizations here and there? Were officers about to lose their jobs?

Conflict is an inevitable part of change in any bureaucracy, but it is especially prominent when one is dealing with a tightly knit, conservative group, especially one like the Russian military. By definition, it opposes the introduction of civilian outsiders. What business do civilians have meddling in military matters? They don't understand the military and involving them will only worsen matters. How can they make a decision on which airplane or tank to buy or repair? These are highly complex machines, and the military believes that only one who understands them and how they are deployed is able to make such a call. Besides, civilians are likely to get rid of structures that are indispensable when it comes to carrying out military operations. Serdiukov, however, was unfazed. He put his colleagues to work carrying out a full audit of expenses in the MoD.

Meanwhile, in an effort to quiet those who continued to point to his lack of military qualifications, Serdiukov undertook an "accelerated course at the Russian General Staff Academy."[29] The course, which reportedly occupied three mornings a week, took the form of a tutorial with primary focus on "the structure and system of administration of the Armed Forces, military policy and strategic planning, the organization of operational-tactical and combat training, and logistics and technical support for the Army and Navy and other militarized structures, as well as classes and types of combat equipment and weapons, the procedure for purchases, and collaboration with the defense industry complex."[30]

Meanwhile, Serdiukov openly recognized the inadequacy of the existing procurement and financial oversight system and promised to strengthen it by structuring "the economic-financial department on an entirely different basis." He went on to identify a number of auditing and inspection entities which will operate independently to monitor the flow of financial assets. He also attacked one of the oldest and worst sources of corruption: the assignment of military procurement representatives to factories. At present, he stated, "military representatives have essentially turned into employees of these enterprises."[31] One way of separating these officers from the enterprises was to return them to their parent units, and they would not be assigned to work with any single factory for more than two years.

In mid-September 2007, Viktor Zubkov was named prime minister. Because Zubkov is Serdiukov's father-in-law, the latter submitted his resignation in accordance with Russian law, which prohibits relatives working together. Putin, however, refused to accept Serdiukov's resignation and reappointed him defense minister, which strengthened Serdiukov's hand in dealing with the generals. As 2007 drew to a close, Serdiukov could point to some significant structural changes aimed at streamlining the procurement process and cutting corruption at the same time.

> Reorganization of the Defense Ministry's central staff was carried out during the year 2007. This was done to ensure a clearer division of functions performed by the bodies of military command, as well as to eliminate their duplication. For example, the post of deputy defense minister was introduced to increase the level of coordination and efficiency of work in developing information technology and communications. The main legal directorate was created to increase the level of legal provision for the Defense Ministry's work. The organization-inspection directorate was set up to control the implementation of all the instructions and legal acts. The directorate for exercising the property ownership rights of the Defense Ministry organizations and the Defense Ministry's inspectorate for personnel were also created.[32]

Serdiukov continued to get rid of officers who failed to perform up to his expectations. For example, he fired the commander in chief of the Air Force, General Vladimir Mikhailov, and his deputy, Air Force Chief of Staff General Boris Cheltsov. In November, he fired three more generals: General Igor Bykov, chief of the Main Medical Directorate; General Anatoli Greceniuk, who was in charge of the construction of medical facilities; and Colonel-General Vladislav Polonsky. But much remained to be done.

In early 2008, the National Strategy Institute issued a research report entitled "The Crisis of the Russian Army." It looked at both the army and the defense-industrial complex and concluded that "contrary to official information, the Russian Armed Forces are in a very deep crisis, and the unfavorable trends in the development of the military sphere have assumed an irreversible nature." The bottom line of this report was that Russian weapons were far too old. The navy had launched only three ships since the fall of the USSR, and all of them were based on 1980s technology. The command and control systems dated back to World War II. With the exception of a few aircraft, the SS300/400, a new sub, and the Topol/Bulava ICBM missiles, almost everything had to be developed anew—and there were problems in the systems noted above. For example, the new Yuri Dolgoruky class submarine was to go to sea without its Bulava missiles, which were still being tested with mixed results.[33]

It was obvious to Serdiukov that just fighting corruption would *not* do the job. Some very basic changes had to be made in streamlining the Russian military if it was ever going to measure up—in other words, some *radical* surgery was in order.

MILITARY OPPOSITION EMERGES

At the end of March 2008, a number of reports in the Russian press suggested that the chief of the General Staff, General Baluyevsky, had submitted his resignation out of frustration over his inability to work with Serdiukov. Apparently the battle between Serdiukov and Baluyevsky had been going on for some time. According to one report, Baluyevsky publicly rejoiced when Serdiukov resigned after his father-in-law became prime minister.[34] Baluyevsky offered his resignation as early as November 2007, when an outsider, Oleg Eskin, a reserve major-general in the FSB and a well-known communications specialist, was given a new deputy minister post. He was put in charge of developing automated control systems and communications—functions that were previously the responsibility of the General Staff. On January 9, 2008, Baluyevsky submitted his resignation for the second time, and at the end of February he submitted his resignation for the third time. During the Russian-U.S. summit held in Moscow on March 17–19, 2008, Baluyevsky was conspicuous by his absence. When asked by the American side where Baluyevsky was, the official explanation was that "he was on leave."[35]

Despite official denials of Baluyevsky's resignation,[36] it appears that he did attempt to resign for a second time. It was not only widely reported in the media,[37] but there are reports that Serdiukov accepted Baluyevsky's resignation and wrote on it the words "I do not object." The letter was then sent to the Kremlin for Putin's approval. It appears that Putin intervened and convinced Baluyevsky to stay, while Serdiukov agreed to continue to work with him. He apparently took part in a meeting of the Military-Industrial Commission on March 26—the same day that reports hit the media concerning his retirement.[38]

Why the battle between Baluyevsky and Serdiukov? One major thesis is that it resulted from Serdiukov's decision to bring a cadre of civilians with him. Much like the American military's response to Secretary of Defense Robert McNamara and his "whiz kids" in the late 1960s, individuals like Baluyevsky resented Serdiukov's *single focus* on saving money—dealing in an area he knew little about. To quote one source:

> The conflict between Chief of Staff General Baluyevsky and Defense Minister Serdiukov rose directly on the grounds that the civilian specialists who came with the former head of the Tax Service to the military department as advisors—and there were more than 30 of them—started to work on military-strategic problems along with financial economic issues. . . . Apparently the ambitious incompetence of some of these advisors, who are for some reason a-priori supported by the new minister, provoked Baluyevsky's decisive protest, which he expressed in the form of his resignation.[39]

It is now appropriate to assess the reform measures that Serdiukov has been implementing.[40] One of the ironies is that, according to sources in the General Staff, the directive for change "was prepared by the previous chief of the Ministry of Defense Sergei Ivanov, and that the current chief—Anatoli Serdiukov—and his staff associates and advisors have come up with the idea of implementing his predecessor's plan in order to strengthen the ministry's civilian component."[41] There are probably some differences in emphasis between Ivanov's plans and those proposed by Serdiukov. What is notable is that Serdiukov is the one who has forced the generals to deal with the reforms (with Putin's and Medvedev's support).

Moving Navy Headquarters to St. Petersburg

Moving Navy Headquarters to St. Petersburg was one of the first issues to hit the public media. The issue rose in January 2008 when, in response to a question from a member of the Academy of Military Sciences, Baluyevsky "publicly expressed his disagreement with the transfer of the Navy Staff to St. Petersburg."[42] In particular, he stated that "there was no necessity for it,"[43] an unusual action for the chief of the General Staff to take publicly toward a policy proposed by the minister of defense. Meanwhile, the civilian analysts argued that locating navy headquarters near the operating fleet would save money.

From the military standpoint, there were a number of problems with the proposal. First, as anyone who has worked in a bureaucracy knows, proximity is power. By moving the headquarters to St. Petersburg, the navy would often find itself "out of the action." The only way to deal with such matters would be to fly top navy officers to Moscow on almost a daily basis. But even then, the officers would lose the opportunity to lobby for pet projects via the many informal gatherings in Moscow. It is important to keep in mind in this context that the Russian Navy is the worst funded of the services and has to fight for every ruble it gets. Putting it in St. Petersburg would make its fight for funds even more difficult.

Second was the impact such a move would have on command and control. This is particularly important given the role the navy plays in Russia's nuclear strategy. The admirals argued that the main components of command and control are in Moscow. Moving to St. Petersburg without careful advance planning could make communications difficult in a crisis.

One of the more surprising aspects of this issue was the very strong reaction on the part of the commander of the Russian Navy, Admiral Vladimir Vysotsky. In early April 2008 he commented: "No one signed such orders. There were only oral instructions to work on the issue." Saying that debate about a move to St. Petersburg was "senseless," he noted: "We are developing a new promising fleet command system. No one will make any hasty steps. Such decisions will be taken only after a detailed examination and with available financial resources."[44] Such a firm statement from a uniformed officer in the apparent face of the minister of defense's order—even if it was verbal—is unusual in any military.

Selling Off Military Assets

The Russian military is the second largest real estate owner in Russia after the Department of Presidential Affairs, and the value of the army's real estate has been estimated at 300 billion rubles (more than $10 billion). Needless to say, when some camps were sold off in order to provide apartments for members of the military, many in the officer corps were not pleased. The action was particularly opposed by Baluyevsky and others on the General Staff. However, given the desperate need for infrastructure improvements—and especially the need to provide officers and professional soldiers (*kontraktniki*) with housing, schooling, hospitals, and other services for them and their families—it was a difficult idea to resist. After all, as of January 1, 2008, "there were 122,400 servicemen's families on the waiting list for housing (more than 65,500 of these needed permanent housing)."[45] Furthermore, the Russian Army still maintained equipment, weapons, and real estate left over from the Soviet era (even from World War I in some cases), and Serdiukov believed it was silly to keep spending money to maintain them. They were obviously irrelevant in a modern war—so why keep them? If land was not being used to sustain the Russian Army, why keep it?

In May 2008, the MoD announced that it planned to sell as many as fifty unused military sites that had become redundant.[46] At the first public auction, the ministry sold its excess real estate on Moscow's elite Rublevskoe Shosse for R2,606 billion.[47] Turning to weapons and equipment, the MoD announced that it intended "to sell off through an auction about 140 helicopters and planes, as well as six sea vessels this year. The ministry will offer 138 aircraft produced between 1963 and 1987, including Mil Mi-8 and Mi-9 helicopters and Antonov An-2, An-12, An22, and An-26, L-39, Ilyushin Il-22 and Il-76 and Tupolev Tu-134 planes. . . . The ministry also wants to sell off six vessels, including the Shuia passenger ship, an oil and garbage disposal ship, a barge, a tanker and two towboats."[48]

The biggest area where Serdiukov intended to make changes—and the one most hotly disputed by the uniformed military—concerned the transfer of military positions to civilian employees. Most important from Serdiukov's position, it would cut expenditures.

Cutting Back Military Personnel

In late March 2008, reports in the media suggested that Serdiukov wanted to downsize the officer corps. Many considered it bloated, primarily because

Russia used junior officers the way the United States used noncommissioned officers.[49] Officers make up 40 percent of armed forces personnel. In particular, one directive "discussed the possible replacement with civilian specialists of a number of military positions, which do not directly affect the troops' combat readiness." In discussing physicians, for example, the chief of the Main Combat Training Directorate noted: "It is one thing if he is a military doctor, who is directly in the troop echelon or is part of an alert shift, or is a member of a submarine team, and quite another thing if he is a doctor who is at a military hospital, military outpatient clinic or military sanatorium. Civilian doctors can very well do the latter."[50]

Not surprisingly, there was a strong and negative reaction by those who thought Serdiukov and his civilian advisors were out to get the military: "It is difficult to imagine a civilian doctor who makes a parachute jump along with the airborne troops. It is even more difficult to imagine that he volunteers to go to a garrison on Novaia Zemlia or to some other exotic, unpopulated spot."[51] And in an area such as surgery in the field, what civilian would know how to do it?

The directive also included officers working in justice, journalism, the finance service, and rear services. All or most of them would be "civilianized." This meant about 200,000 officers would be "de-officered." There were even rumors that the warrant officers, the technical specialists that Marshal Nikolai Ogarkov had created, would be abolished.[52] It was quickly denied by the MoD.[53] There were also suggestions that military intelligence (the GRU) would be cut by more than 40 percent, and those structures that dealt with "inter-nationality problems" would be cut by 70 percent.[54] Regardless of what happened, it was clear to the officer corps that Serdiukov was deadly serious about change and that he was prepared to toss a good number of officers out of the army.

Liubov Kudelina, a civilian who had been elevated to the post of deputy minister of defense and chief of the Economics and Finance Service, was fully aware of the officers' concerns and argued that the administration had no intention of firing officers in the areas noted above. In terms of the officer-civilian ratio, she argued that 20 percent of the military positions would be retained in the central apparatus of the finance service. But when it involved military units, all of the financial positions would go to officers. All in all, she maintained, in the rear services "60–80 percent of the military positions will remain, the rest will be civilians."[55] To the degree there was a plan for cutting officers, primary emphasis was placed on colonels and lieutenant colonels "who have completed their term of service."[56] In many cases, the army would use these retired officers as civilians, thereby civilianizing them while at the same time continuing to use their special skills.

In the meantime, Serdiukov ordered the commanders of all military branches, districts, and fleets to submit proposals for transferring officer posts to civilians. The overall goal was to maintain a ratio of 60/80 percent military officer to 40/20 percent civilians.[57] Needless to say, some very difficult decisions would have to be made by those in charge, decisions that would impact the lives and careers of thousands of their colleagues. A smaller officer corps also meant fewer chances for promotion.

On July 12, 2008, came the astonishing announcement that the Kremlin would be undertaking a major purge of the officer corps. "The defense minister has stated that as a result of the cuts . . . [the army] will be left with 150,000 officers. At present we have between 350,000 and 380,000 serving officers."[58] There were also reports that Serdiukov intended to cut "the central apparatus of the General Staff by 40 percent. In all instances, primary emphasis will be on officers who are eligible for retirement, who will be re-hired in a civilian capacity." The army would disband reduced-strength units "which are brought up to full strength only in the event of war." According to Russian sources, these are the units where most of the crimes are committed. "The plan is to retain only permanent-readiness troop units. These currently consist of 81 brigades and divisions."[59]

Civilians would also take the place of enlisted personnel in a number of areas. They would be the ones working in enlisted mess halls and involved in the upkeep of military posts. In addition, the army planned "to make maximum use of technical equipment and VOKhR (paramilitary security) subunits in the facilities. This world practice is within the channel for moving forward toward compact, professional Armed Forces."[60]

Another change Serdiukov introduced was the idea of physical fitness tests for all officers. From his perspective, the generals in particular were overweight and setting a bad example for the rest of their troops. The officers had to run a kilometer, swim at least 100 meters, and pull themselves up on gym bars. "A quarter of generals and other senior officers failed to meet the requirements for their age group and rank, while 30 percent were classed as overweight." According to Aleksandr Kolmakov, a first deputy defense minister, the testing requirements would be tightened up over a seven-year period beginning in 2009.[61]

Baluyevsky Is Fired

On June 3, 2008, it was announced that Chief of the General Staff General Yuri Baluyevsky was retiring but would become a deputy chair of the Security Council, technically a promotion. However, three weeks later, it was announced that he was being replaced on the Security Council by the chief of the General Staff.[62] If nothing else, the fact that Baluyevsky left after Putin granted him a waiver and an extension until 2009 because of his age, together with his short-lived presence on the Security Council, made it clear that there was major friction between him and Serdiukov. Indeed, there is little doubt that their relationship must have been a very rocky one. In the past, Baluyevsky had worked well with a number of difficult personalities: General Vladislav Achalov, a member of the State of Emergency Committee; General Anatoli Kvashnin, who was considered especially difficult to work with; and Sergei Ivanov throughout his five years as defense minister. Under Putin, defense ministers or chiefs of the General Staff were removed when their time in office expired. However, relations between Serdiukov and Baluyevsky must have deteriorated to the point where one or the other had to go. In this case, Serdiukov was doing what Putin and Medvedev wanted him to do—shaking up the army. If anything, by firing Baluyevsky, Medvedev strengthened Serdiukov's hand in dealing with the military. Clearly, Serdiukov had the president's full support.

A Purge of the Upper Ranks

Baluyevsky was replaced by General Nikolai Makarov, who is reportedly close to Serdiukov. He went up the career ladder holding the normal types of jobs—from platoon commander to commander of the Siberian Military District and was the chief of armaments. One analyst said he is "viewed by many who have worked with him as one of Russia's best generals."[63] His appointment clearly represents a break with the past. "Formerly, chiefs of the General Staff were nominated from among combined-arms commanders."[64] However, Makarov's experience as the chief of armaments gives him special expertise in an area of critical importance to the defense minister as he tries to not only reform the military but modernize it as well.

When he took over, Serdiukov fired a number of generals and admirals, some apparently because of corruption, others for what Serdiukov considered incompetence.[65] According to one source, since February 2007, "over 500 military officials, 16 of them holding general's ranks, were held criminally liable" for corruption.[66] In addition to Baluyevsky's firing, there have been a number of other moves involving generals on the General Staff. Also fired, for example, were the chief of the Main Operational Directorate, Aleksandr Rushing; the chair of the General Staff Military Committee, Colonel General Aleksandr Skvortsov; and the chief of Armed Forces Communication, Evgeni Karpov.[67] What was stunning about this action was, as one observer put it, "this is the first cadre purge in modern Russian history to affect what is the holy of holies of any country—the General Staff. Even Khrushchev, when cutting his generals, tried to avoid the General Staff, being aware of that body's great significance for the country's state security."[68] If nothing else, Serdiukov's willingness to take on the General Staff indicated that he was serious about making major changes in spite of what the generals thought. Rumors suggested that these men were close to Baluyevsky and were strongly opposed to the changes Serdiukov was instituting. Rumors also suggested that more generals were to be "retired" in the near future.

Meanwhile, the Kremlin finalized the process that Ivanov had begun: to isolate the uniformed military from involvement in the weapons and arms procurement process. The MoD was ordered to transfer to Rosoboronpostavka (Federal Agency for the Supply of Armaments, Military, and Special Equipment of Material) the placing of orders for weapons and equipment. "We will form orders, we will tell them what we need—what types, categories and models—while they will handle money matters," according to Makarov.[69]

The importance of the step noted above is significant. The Kremlin has separated the military from the procurement process. Based on the arrangement finally worked out, the military would "determine the order and say what we need—what kinds, types and models," but the new civilian procurement agency (Rosoboronpostavka) "will handle the money." This means, as one commentator put it, "Anatoli Serdiukov will be deprived of control over more than R300 billion in resources."[70] Unfortunately, corruption continues to be a major problem. In early November 2008, Chief Military Prosecutor Sergei Fridinsky stated that "the number of corruption cases in regards to the organization of the armed forces has risen by almost a third since the beginning of 2008." Furthermore, "the overall cost of corruption in the Armed Forces in the year 2008 amounted to 1.6 billion rubles." That meant that "over nine months of this year, the growth in the number of registered corruption-related crimes was 35.4 percent."[71]

Unfortunately, the problems facing Makarov go far beyond corruption. They are enormous. On February 8, 2008, addressing the State Council, Putin called for the creation of an "Innovation Army," and noted that "new types of weapons equal and sometimes superior to the weapons of other countries must be developed in Russia in the next few years."[72] Makarov promised that the innovation army would be a reality by 2020. The problem is that Russia is far behind in the development of modern weapons. One analyst observed that there is nothing to be gained by developing a fifth-generation fighter plane. "We're already 20 years behind the Americans, and when we do develop this 'super plane,' we'll discover that we've fallen even further behind."[73] To make matters worse, Moscow has yet to decide what kind of an army it wants, and it has still not developed a military doctrine—which in the Russian system determines what kind of weapons the country will purchase and use. As another writer observed, "it is impossible to plan and create a new face for the Armed Forces without a clear idea of the missions for which they must be 'sharpened.' First they must have a doctrine, only then the reforms, not the other way around."[74]

In the meantime, with an eye toward the "innovative army," Serdiukov announced on June 23, 2008, that every year 30,000 officers, especially those dealing with high-tech weapons and equipment (he singled out the Strategic Missile Troops, strategic aviation, submariners, and Space Troops), will be given bonuses of varying amounts as an incentive in the performance of their duties. Serdiukov promised that while the current plan includes only 30,000 officers, the program will be expanded from R25 billon in 2009, to 31 billon in 2010, and 42 billon in 2011.[75]

These steps represent just the beginning. Almost every aspect of Russian Army life will have to be turned upside down. That has already begun, for example, in training. In June 2008, it was announced that Lieutenant General Vladimir Shamanov had been called out of what he said was a "forced retirement" and appointed chief of the General Staff's Main Combat Training and Troop Service Directorate. Based on an interview with him, it is clear that he is planning to make major changes in the way Russian soldiers are trained. He is including the experiences of Afghanistan and Chechnya into the training plan, and "at least 50 percent of professional training must take place on simulators, and for pilots at least 60 percent."[76] He added that if decent-quality simulators cannot be found in Russia or if they are too expensive, the General Staff is prepared to purchase them from abroad. Shamanov plans far-reaching changes, not only to the type of training, but training grounds as well.

Finally, it is important to note that President Medvedev has blessed Serdiukov's reform plans. On September 29, he provided five principles that are to guide military reform: (1) improve the organizational structure and deployment of troops; (2) have greater efficiency in command and control; (3) improve and modernize military education; (4) make procurement of the most modern weapons a high priority; (5) increase pay and living conditions for members of the armed forces.[77]

On October 14, 2008, after a meeting at the Ministry of Defense, Serdiukov outlined the specific changes he planned to introduce. First, the ratio of officers will be reduced until there is one officer for every fifteen enlisted personnel. Second, the structure of the Armed Forces will be radically changed. Instead of the four-level organization (military district, army, division, and regiment), the Russian Army will go to a three-level system of military district, operational command, and brigade. Third, a noncommissioned officers corps, much like what exists in the West, will be created. Most warrant officers will either be released or become noncommissioned officers. Fourth, all units of the Ground Forces will become permanent readiness units (from 1,980 to a total of 172). Closely connected with the creation of these new units, the cadre units will be disbanded. Fifth, the General Staff and the MoD will be cut from the current level of 22,000 to a total of 8,500. Sixth, the number of military educational institutions will be cut from the current level of 65 institutions to a total of 10.[78]

CONCLUSION

One of the unanswered questions about Russian military policy is why, if Sergei Ivanov designed these measures, did he not put them through on his watch? It may have had to do with Putin's leadership style. If there was one thing that characterized Putin's time in office, it was a dedication to evolutionary change. He tried to avoid confrontations and conflict. He made some hard decisions that impacted the military, but he tried to do it in a gradual fashion. Given the extent of military resistance to the changes noted above, one must ask, would Putin have supported such a contentious action like taking on the generals and admirals? Getting rid of this or that general is one thing; however, taking on the General Staff of one of the most conservative military forces in the world is something else.

What appears to have happened is that when Ivanov confronted Putin with evidence of the extensive corruption in the military, he decided he had to find an accountant to be defense minister, if for no other reason than to get control over the armed forces and streamline it. And thus far he has been successful, but at a price. Serdiukov has alienated part of the officer corps. While it is impossible to determine the extent of opposition, it is clear that many are unhappy. As one source put it, "Dissent is growing among the highest orders of Russia's Ministry of Defense," and "military officers are dissatisfied with the performance of Anatoli Serdiukov."[79]

This situation is made worse by Serdiukov's leadership style. One source claimed that he ignores senior military officers and has little interest in their views. Another source called Serdiukov a "punishing sword," a title a lot of officers would probably agree with.[80] Furthermore, when confronted by comments that more than a dozen generals had resigned, he responded, "Nobody tenders their resignation," but "many quit when reaching retirement age. Generals also resign mostly for the same reasons. Perhaps, some media outlets, citing so-called 'high-placed sources,' are fueling various rumors and speculations."[81] Serdiukov gave the impression that he did not care if generals left the military in protest. The more who left, the easier his job would be.

Serdiukov clearly understands that his task is to bring about change. Given what we know at present of the extent of corruption and the backwardness of the Russian military when it comes to weapons and equipment, a person like Serdiukov may have been a necessity. In view of the nature of the changes, he has avoided the leadership style of a Robert McNamara or a Donald Rumsfeld, that he and his "whiz kids" know best. However, in his mind, it is the military's task to follow orders, not to tell the defense minister what to do or how to do it.

Given the nature of the changes he has instituted, many senior officers appear to think that he and his civilian colleagues "view the military as just another business venture."[82] Furthermore, Serdiukov has admitted that he does not have a "plan." As he stated on one occasion, "There is no reform, and no need to use the word. . . . We are not going to break anything up and rebuild it. We are simply restoring order in everything. . . . Years and decades passed during which nothing was done. . . . So let's deal with it."[83] It is not surprising that a veteran officer like Baluyevsky found it impossible to work with him. From Baluyevsky's standpoint, Serdiukov was destroying what remained of the military in a chaotic and irrational fashion. Baluyevsky had presented Ivanov with plans for a reorganization of the military in March 2006.[84] Why not incorporate his plan into Serdiukov's austerity measures? Doesn't the defense minister understand that the two should go together? There was no sense that these changes fit into a bigger picture, one that took the Russian Army's ability to fight a war into account. Where was the evidence to show that Serdiukov's changes could be sustained and would not undercut combat readiness?[85]

While many military officers would agree with the need to fight corruption and use money wisely, they wanted to see how it related to their ability to fight a future war. From their perspective, Serdiukov failed to answer the main question—which war does he expect them to fight? Given how important a long-term national military doctrine is to the Russian military, they cannot but be confused as to where Serdiukov is taking the armed forces. Besides, the idea of delegating authority, which is inherent in his plan to give more responsibility to NCOs, goes against the mind-set of many officers.[86]

The outlook for Russian civil-military relations is unclear. One suspects that Nikolai Ogarkov, one of the most visionary chiefs of the General Staff following World War II, would have disagreed with Serdiukov in a number of areas but would have agreed with the direction in which Serdiukov is pushing the military. Ogarkov constantly berated his uniformed colleagues, telling them to stop fighting the last war—focus on the next one. That is a major part of what Serdiukov is doing.

The best hope for reforming the Russian armed forces rests on General Makarov's shoulders. He is a different kind of officer, and perhaps in the situation the Russian military finds itself, he may be exactly what the doctor ordered. Time will tell. Serdiukov, however, may be a transitional figure. He is defense minister for one reason: to rationalize structure and spending and fight corruption. There is no doubt that his expertise is needed in that area. At some point, however, the Kremlin will have to appoint a person who has a much broader interest in and knowledge of military matters. The problems confronting the Russian armed forces go far beyond spending and streamlining issues, and the Kremlin will need the support of officers like Makarov to take military reform to the next level. Not only is the Russian Army in a desperate position when it comes to modern weapons systems, but the personnel system (especially the situation with *kontraknikis*, housing, and other types of infrastructure) needs serious help. The same is true of the military educational system. General Shamanov is right, it is time for the Russian military to pay less attention to the battles of World War II and more to the kind of substate conflicts they faced in Afghanistan and Chechnya. One of the reasons for the disastrous first campaign in Chechnya was the failure of the generals to take into account the Soviet Army's Afghanistan experience. The list goes on and on. In the meantime, Serdiukov could improve matters by reaching out to the generals. A famous American political scientist, Richard Neustadt, in referring to the American presidency, once observed that the "power of the president is the power of persuasion,"[87] which, unfortunately, is not a part of Russian political culture at present.

There are important differences between the role played by the executive in the United States and Russia. However, when it comes to civil-military relations, there is one very important similarity. Any senior civilian official can issue orders, and the military will obey. But leadership almost always involves persuasion. There is more to be gained if a person in Serdiukov's position is able to persuade the generals and admirals that he respects them and is interested in working with them.

This does not mean that Serdiukov should become the generals' captive. However, the more they support what the defense minister is trying to accomplish, the more the rest of the military will join in. It will be much easier for Serdiukov to accomplish his goals if the generals and admirals work with him, not against him. This will not be easy. With widespread corruption among many generals and admirals, and opposition to many of the changes he is introducing, it will be difficult to build support for his efforts to fight that scourge. However, gaining the support of officers who do *not* have their hands in the till and want reform will make his job easier. Makarov's appointment gives him an opening to do exactly that. However, the ball is in his court.

SUGGESTED READINGS

Betz, David J. *Civil-Military Relations in Russia and Eastern Europe*. London: Routledge, 2004.

Colton, Timothy J. *Yeltsin: His Life*. New York: Basic Books, 2008.

Daniels, Bruce. *Living with Stalin's Ghost: A Fulbright Memoir of Moscow and the New Russia*. New Haven: Connecticut Academy of Arts and Sciences, 2008.

Herspring, Dale R. *The Kremlin and the High Command: Presidential Impact on the Russian Military from Gorbachev to Putin*. Lawrence: University Press of Kansas, 2006.

Karklins, Rsama. *The System Made Me Do It: Corruption in Post-Communist Societies*. Armonk, N.Y.: M. E. Sharpe, 2005.

Lebed, Alexander. *My Life and My Country*. Washington, D.C.: Regnery, 1997.

Matlock, Jack. *Autopsy of an Empire: The American Ambassador's Account of the Collapse of the Soviet Union.* New York: Random House, 1993.
Zoltan, Barany. *Democratic Breakdown and the Decline of the Russian Military.* Princeton, N.J.: Princeton University Press, 2007.

NOTES

1. This chapter was previously published as "Russian Military Reform and Anatoly Serdyukov," *Problems of Post-Communism* 55, no. 6 (2008): 20–32. Copyright © 2008 by M. E. Sharpe, Inc. Reprinted with permission.

2. The evolution of the Russian military up to the middle of 2006 is treated in Dale R. Herspring, *The Kremlin and the High Command: Presidential Impact on the Russian Military from Gorbachev to Putin* (Lawrence: University Press of Kansas, 2006), esp. chaps. 3–6.

3. "March of 'Dropped' Lieutenants Airmen Will Be Re-trained as Infantrymen," *Moskovskii Komsomolets*, March 3, 1999, in World News Connection (March 4, 1999).

4. "Russia Needs More Soldiers to Balance NATO Commander," *ITAR-TASS*, March 12, 1999.

5. Herspring, *The Kremlin and the High Command*, 174; See also, "National Defense Reception," *Nezavisimaia gazeta*, January 9, 2006, in WNC (January 10, 2006).

6. "Russian Air Force Command Worried by Aging of Aircraft," *ITAR-TASS*, March 26, 2003, in WNC (March 29, 2003).

7. "Military Pilots Averaged 30 Flying Hours in 2003, Highest Since mid-90s," *Rossiiskaia gazeta*, January 29, 2004, in WNC (February 4, 2008).

8. "Average Flight Time for Russian Pilots Tops 30 Hours," *Agentstvo Voennykh Novostei*," November 7, 2005, in WNC (November 8, 2008).

9. "Russian Navy Commander to Monitor Northern Fleet Exercise," *Agentstvo Voennykh Novostei*, July 18, 2006, in WNC (July 19, 2006).

10. "Minister Pledges Boost in New Weapons Spending," *RFE/RL Daily Report*, December 16, 2005.

11. "Russian Experts Say Army Equipment Increasingly Aging," *Interfax*, May 22, 2006, in WNC (May 23, 2008).

12. In this chapter, "corruption" is used in the widest sense possible and includes not only "performance of an official's duties for an unlawful fee" but also all other personal enrichment schemes usually defined as "white-collar crime."

13. "Moscow Raises Spending for Defense, Police, Secret Services," *Johnson's Russia List*, August 24, 2004.

14. "Military-Fiscal Secrets Are Multiplying: The Number of Classified Items in the 2007 Ministry of Defense Budget Has Increased Substantially," *Nezavisimoe Voennoe Obozrenie*, October 27, 2006, in WNC (October 28, 2006).

15. "Ivanov: We Need at Least One Million Military Personnel," *Izvestiia*, February 22, 2005, in *Johnson's Russia List*, February 22, 2005.

16. "Interview by Andrei Zolotov," June 2, 2007, *Russia Profile*. Putin signed the law on February 5, 2007.

17. *The State of Law and Order in the Russian Federation in 2002*, a report by the General Prosecutor's Office to the president of the Russian Federation (Moscow: Publishing House of the State Duma of the Russian Federation, 2002). See also, "General Olenikov's Case," 2003, as reported in *Kommersant*, March 23, 2003.

18. "Defense Ministry Officials Are Firmly Ensconced on the Boards of Directors of Various Companies," *Nezavisimoe Voennoe Obozrenie*, March 9, 2007, in WNC (March 12, 2008).

19. E-mail of June 17, 2008, to the author from a colleague in Moscow who requested anonymity.

20. E-mail of April 4, 2008, to the author from a colleague in Moscow who requested anonymity. Another source claimed that 30 percent of the budget is being lost due to corruption. The same source noted that in 2007, "224 officers were criminally prosecuted, while hundreds of officers were dismissed from their posts and faced administrative proceedings. Of them, 16 generals and 180 colonels were criminally prosecuted. A total of 565 officials were convicted last year." See "Russian Official Says 30 Percent of Military Budget Lost through Corruption." *Agentstvo Voennykh Novostei*, July 2, 2008, in WNC (July 3, 2008).

21. "Defense Ministry Will Shed Excess Equipment," *RFE/RL Daily Report*, April 3, 2008.

22. E-mail of June 9, 2008, to the author from a colleague in Moscow who requested anonymity.

23. "Bloggers Ridicule New Defense Minister Serdiukov," *Russia—OSC Report*, February 16, 2007, in WNC (February 17, 2007).

24. "Russian Radio Pundit Sees Sham Civilian Control of Ground Forces," *Ekho Moskvy*, February 24, 2007, in *Johnson's Russia List*, March 1, 2007.

25. "Russia's Generals Don't Believe That the New Defense Minister Can Help the Military," *Versiy*, no. 8, February 26, 2007, in *Johnson's Russia List*, March 1, 2007. See also, "Faceless Defense Minister: From Civilian Face to Political Face—Or to Political Facelessness?" *Nezavisimaia gazeta*, March 5, 2007, in WNC (March 7, 2007).

26. "Nakhimov Naval College Chief Dismissed," *Agentstvo Voennykh Novostei*, March 28, 2007, in WNC (March 29, 2007).

27. This was a policy he continued. For example, in mid-May he carried out a surprise inspection of the Baikal region. Instead of waiting for programmed answers to his questions, he went to the dormitories, where "tight rooms, freshly-whitened bruises on the ceilings, and other 'charms' of any army communal living—judging by all did not at all suit the minister." "Serdiukov Is an Army Outside of a Parade Formation," *Rossiiskaia gazeta*, May 14, 2007, in WNC (May 15, 2007).

28. "Serdiukov Streamlines Defense: Financier and Inspecting General Will Be Main Levers at Current Stage of Russian Army Reform," *Nezavisimaia gazeta*, April 15, 2007.

29. "Russian Defense Minister to Undertake Accelerated Training Course at General Staff Academy," *Agentstvo Voennykh Novosetii*, March 30, 2007, in WNC (March 1, 2007). Lest the reader take this action as purely cosmetic, which it no doubt was

in large measure, there were many times when a new U.S. secretary of defense would have benefited from such a course.

30. "Defense Minister Sits at School Desk," *Nezavisimoe Voennoe Obozrenie*, April 26, 2007 in WNC (April 27, 2007).

31. "Targeted Financing: Anatoly Serdiukov Tightens Up Financial Monitoring of the Military and Plans to Build Accessible Officer Housing," *Rossiiskaia gazeta*, June 8, 2007, in WNC (June 11, 2007).

32. "Russian Defense Minister Sums Up Results of 2007," *ITAR-TASS*, December 25, 2007, in WNC (December 28, 2007). See also, Kudelina's interview in June 2008, "The Defense Ministry Is Accelerating the Movement of Money: But Expenditures for Combat Equipment Still Make Up Less than Half of the Military Budget," *Nezavisimoe Voennoe Obozrenie*, June 8, 2008, in WNC (June 9, 2008).

33. "In Thrall to a Myth: The Russian Army; Revival or Degradation," *Vremia Novostei*, February 22, 2008; "Eight Years of Falling Behind and Weakening," *Nezavisimaia gazeta*, February 13, 2008, in *Johnson's Russia List*, February 14, 2008; "The Computer Is Not Joining with Armor," *Nezavisimoe Voennoe Obozrenie*, February 26, 2008, in WNC (February 27, 2008); "Russia to Possibly Write Off 90 Percent of Military Transport Planes by 2015," *ITAR-TASS*, February 27, 2008, in WNC (Febraury 28, 2008); "India Rejects the 'Admiral Gorshkov'—Russian Fighters Don't Suit Them Either," *Trud*, February 29, 2008, in WNC (March 12, 2008). In 2008, Algeria announced that it would be returning 15 MiG-29 fighters to Russia; a year earlier, a billion-dollar contract signed in 2005 fell through for the delivery of 38 Il-76 and Il-78 aircraft to China.

34. "Kremlin Mouthpiece to Leave General Staff," *Eurasia Daily Monitor*, March 31, 2008.

35. "General Affront," *Nezavisimoe Voennoe Obozrenie*, March 30, 2008, in WNC (March 31, 2008).

36. "Russian Defense Ministry Refutes Reports of Disagreements over Its Reform," *RIA-Novosti*, March 26, 2008, in WNC (February 28, 2008); "Defense Ministry Denies Reports of Rifts in Leadership," *Agentstvo Voennykh Novostei*, March 26, 2008, in WNC (March 28, 2008). Baluyevsky claimed publicly that he did not offer his resignation, stating, "I cannot imagine myself in retirement. It would be silly to leave without seeing the results of what we would like to implement in Russia." "Chief of Russian General Staff Denies Reports of His Resignation," *RIA-Novosti*, April 10, 2008, in WNC (April 11, 2008).

37. "Frustrated Baluyevsky Offers His Resignation," *Moscow Times*, March 25, 2008, in *Johnson's Russia List*, March 26, 2008; "Russia Resignation Signals Trouble within Defense Ministry," *Radio Free Europe/Radio Liberty*, March 27, 2008; "Russian Military Chief Quits after Row with Defense Minister," *Times of India*, March 26, 2008.

38. "Russia's Top Military Official Back at Work Despite Reports of Resignation," *Agentstvo Voennykh Novostei*, March 26, 2008, in WNC (March 28, 2008).

39. "General Affront."

40. Rather than a formal plan, the proposed changes take the form of individual steps aimed at rationalizing the military by saving money and ensuring that what is spent is paid for in the most efficient way possible.

41. "De-officering: A Third of the Officer Corps Converted to Civilian Status," *Nezavisimoe Voennoe Obozrenie*, April 9, 2008, in WNC (April 9, 2008).

42. "Anatoli Eduardovich the Quietest," *Nezavisimaia gazeta*, April 7, 2008, in WNC (April 8, 2008). Another source claimed that officers made up 30 percent of the Russian Army but 15 percent in most other militaries. "Defense Will Shed Excess Equipment," *RFE/RL Daily Report*, April 3, 2008.

43. "General Affront."

44. "Navy General Staff Not to Move to St. Petersburg," *ITAR-TASS*, April 4, 2008, in WNC (April 5, 2008).

45. "Training Grounds Will Be Auctioned Off: Defense Ministry Begins Selling Off Entire Camps so as to Give Servicemen Apartments," *Izvestiia*, March 13, 2008, in WNC (March 14, 2008); "General Purge: Mass Reduction of Top Command Personnel Awaits Our Army," *Nasha Versiia*, July 28, 2008, in WNC (July 29, 2008).

46. "Russian Defense Ministry Plans to Sell 20 to 50 Unused Sites," *ITAR-TASS*, May 27, 2008, in WNC (May 28, 2008).

47. "Defense Ministry Fetches 2.606 Billion Rubles in Sale of Prime Real Estate on Rublevskoye Shosse," *Agentstvo Voennykh Novostei*, May 27, 2008, in WNC (May 28, 2008).

48. "Russian Defense Ministry to Auction 140 Aircraft, Six Ships," *Agentstvo Voennykh Novostei*, April 24, 2008, in WNC (April 27, 2008).

49. There has been an ongoing effort to produce professional noncommissioned officers in the Russian military—the *kontraktniki*—but there have been numerous problems, especially in trying to find the money to make the position attractive, and to convince officers to delegate authority to enlisted personnel. For a discussion of the problem, see Herspring, *The Kremlin and the High Command*, chap. 6.

50. "The Directive Wars: Reserve Lieutenant Serdiukov Has Taken a Stand against the Generals," *Izvestiia*, March 27, 2008, in WNC (March 28, 2008).

51. "De-officering."

52. "The Ownerless Nuclear Football," *Nezavisimaia gazeta*, April 4, 2008, in WNC (April 5, 2008).

53. "Into Barracks with a Diploma: Russian Army Is Banking on College Graduates," *Nezavisimoe Voennoe Obozrenie*, April 9, 2008, in WNC (April 9, 2008).

54. "The Ownerless Nuclear Football."

55. "Russian Military Doctors Not to Be Stripped of Ranks," *Interfax*, April 23, 2008, in WNC (April 24, 2008).

56. "Into Barracks with a Diploma."

57. "Russian Defense Ministry to Replace Some Military Officials with Civilians in June," *Agentstvo Voennykh Novostei*, April 4, 2008, in WNC (April 5, 2008).

58. "The Army Needs to be Protected from Dilettantes," Utro.ru., October 22, 2008, in WNC (October 23, 2008).

59. "Staff Awareness: Yuriy Baluyevsky's Former Deputies Dismissed," *Gazeta*, July 23, 2008, in WNC (July 24, 2008).

60. "Armed Forces and Society: The Training and Look of the Armed Forces Will Change," *Krasnaia zvezda*, June 24, 2008, in WNC (June 25, 2008).

61. "Russian Military Battles Overweight Soldiers," *Times*, April 11, 2008, http://www.timesonline.co.uk. As anyone who has spent much time around senior

Russian officers can testify, this was a reform long overdue. Another Russian source stated that 50 percent of Russian generals were overweight and that 30 percent failed to pass the test. E-mail of April 9, 2008, from a Russian colleague who requested anonymity. The problem even exists among junior officers. One report stated that 26 percent of the officers who graduated in 2007 failed to pass the fitness test. "Russian Defense Ministry Introduces Stricter Fitness Requirements," *Agentstvo Voennykh Novostei*, June 24, 2008, in WNC (June 25, 2008).

62. "Markov Replaces Baluyevsky on Russia's Security Council," *Agentstvo Voennykh Novostei*, June 27, 2008, in WNC (June 28, 2008).

63. Nikolai Makarov—The Many to Reform Russia's Military?" *Siberian Light*, http://www.siberianlight.net/2008/06/10/nikolai-makarov-russian-army -general/.

64. "Military Reform: Professionalism Is Highly Valued, but Expensive," *Slovo*, June 11, 2008, in WNC (November 11, 2008).

65. Steve Blank lists a whole series of changes that occurred during 2007. See Stephen Blank, "Russia's Serdiukov and His Generals," *Eurasia Daily Monitor*, December 13, 2007. Most notable was his promotion of Airborne Commander Colonel General Aleksandr Komakov to first deputy minister.

66. "Over 500 Military Officials Arrested for Corruption in Last 18 Months," *Agentstvo Voennykh Novostei*, July 15, 2008, in WNC (July 16, 2008).

67. Pavel Felgenhauer, "Russian Tanks Will Be Equipped with French IR TV," *Eurasia Daily Monitor*, July 10, 2008.

68. "General Purge."

69. "Russian Ministry to Cede Its Role as Ordering Customer by End of 2008," *Agentstvo Voennykh Novostei*, June 17, 2008, in WNC (June 18, 2008). One could argue that this simply transferred the corruption to the civilian sector, but that was not Serdiukov's concern. It was to clean up the military. Serdiukov will leave the larger job of gaining control over corruption to Medvedev.

70. "Ministry Stranded: Control of the Army Budget Is Being Given Away to Someone Else," *Rossiiskie Vesti*, July 22, 2008, in WNC (July 23, 2008).

71. "Corruption Threatens Officers with Civilians," Gazeata.ru, November 7, 2008, in WNC (November 8, 2008). This increase is probably due in large part to the more energetic role the Military Prosecutor's Office is playing. Senior officers are being especially hit hard. The head of the Ministry of Defense's Main Directorate for the Equipping of Troops, Lieutenant General Dvuluehansky, was fired from his post because of corruption.

72. "'The Innovation Army': What Is It?" *Nezavisimoe Voennoe Obozrenie*, June 17, 2008, in WNC (June 18, 2008).

73. "Russia Will Have Innovative Army by 2020," *Agentstvo Voennykh Novostei*, June 23, 2008, in WNC (June 24, 2008).

74. "Reforms Not for the Sake of Reforms," *Nezavisimoe Voennoe Obozrenie*, June 23, 2008, in WNC (June 24, 2008).

75. "Russian Defense Minister Gives More Details of Proposed Bonuses for Officers," *Interfax*, June 23, 2008, in WNC (June 24, 2008).

76. "Armed Forces and Society: The Training and Look of the Armed Forces Will Change," *Krasnaia zvezda*, June 24, 2008, in WNC (June 26, 2008).

77. "Dmitri Medvedev Outlined Five Challenges for Development of the Russian Armed Forces," *IA Regnum*, September 29, 2008, in WNC (September 30, 2008).

78. "Dismissed! Russian Army to Be Smaller and Ever Ready," *Rossiiskaia gazeta*, October 26, 2008, in WNC (October 17, 2008); "Reform of the Combat Spirit," *Kommersant-Vlast*, October 21, 2008; "Endless Reform: The MoD Is Planning to Abolish the Rank of Warrant Officer—He Will Be Replaced by a Professional NCO Corps," *Vedomosti*, October 28, 2008, in WNC (October 29, 2008).

79. "Russian Military Quitting in Protest of Reforms," *The Other Russia*, May 19, 2008.

80. "'Anatoly Serdiukov' Reserve Lieutenant and Marshal of Financial Skirmishes," *Nezavisimoe Voennoe Oborzrenie*, March 14, 2007, in WNC (March 15, 2007).

81. "Russia to Have 1 Million Troops by 2016," *ITAR-TASS*, April 3, 2008, in WNC (April 4, 2008).

82. "Military Denies Reports of 'Revolt' over Cuts," *RFE/RL Daily Report*, March 27, 2008.

83. "Russian Defense Minister Says He Is Restoring Order; Not Reforming Forces," *Agentstvo Voennykh Novostei*, April 16, 2008, in WNC (April 17, 2008).

84. "The Generals of Cutbacks Have Taken Charge of Military Reform," *Nezavisimoe Voennoe Obozrenie*, March 22, 2006, in WNC (March 23, 2006).

85. "The Directive Wars: Reserve Lieutenant Serdiukov Has Taken a Stand Against the Generals," *Izvestiia*, March 27, 2008, in WNC (March 28, 2008).

86. As one example, some years ago, this writer was involved in several U.S.-Russian ship visits. One of the most difficult things for senior officers to understand was the degree to which the United States delegates responsibility to NCOs. "I don't understand," one admiral told this author. "You have a 21-year-old petty officer in charge of that missile mount. In the Russian Navy, we have two officers do that job!"

87. Richard E. Neustadt, *Presidential Power and the Modern Presidents: The Politics of Leadership from Roosevelt to Reagan* (New York: Free Press, 1990), 11.

Conclusion

Whither Putinism?

Stephen K. Wegren and Dale R. Herspring

The key question for Russia going forward is how much of a departure from Putinism may be expected during the Medvedev presidency. To understand the prospects for significant change under Medvedev, we first need an understanding of Putinism. Thus we begin with the question: what was "Putinism"?

In the political sphere, several characteristics defined Putinism. Putin created a more centralized and authoritarian state than was the case under Yeltsin. The media were not as free as under Yeltsin, and they became increasingly less so as time went on. Political opposition was suppressed, both of individual leaders (Kasparov, Kasianov, Khodorkovsky, Nemtsov) and at the mass level, as popular demonstrations often did not receive permission to gather and were forcibly broken up if they did. Center-periphery relations were redefined, with a shift of power to the center at the cost of regional autonomy. Political parties were brought under control, and a "party of power" was constructed that dominated elected institutions at federal and regional levels. As a result, elections at every level became less competitive and offered voters limited choice.[1] The court system, judges, and courts became less independent as they increasingly backed the position of the Kremlin. Physical force, violence, and arbitrary applications of the law defined the relationship between the governed and those governing. This particularly pertained to individuals who spoke out against the regime or Putin himself. While the term "thug state," which has appeared in some Western papers, may be too strong a description, certain behaviors suggested movement in that direction, such as the beating of journalists, the use of force to break up demonstrations, and what appeared to be political assassinations.

To Putin, the state was just a larger form of the bureaucracy he once served in. During his time in the KGB, Putin was part of an organization in which meritocracy, discipline, and order were paramount. If he was given an order, he was expected to carry it out, and for many years he did just that. This is the paradigm he imposed on the country he governed. As a consequence, most analysts agree that Russia was much less free at the end of Putin's second term than when he took power in 2000, although we hasten to add that Russia was freer than during the communist period.

On the positive side of politics, the rise of a pro-Kremlin electoral majority in the State Duma and making the Federation Council more compliant meant that Putin worked with, not against, the legislative branch, and executive-legislation relations were much less acerbic than during Yeltsin's presidency.

In the economic sphere, growth was welcomed by the population after nearly a decade of depression.[2] By the time Putin left office, Russians had a much more optimistic view of their future than they did in 1999. And to a large degree, Putin's presidency was the reason. "There is a totally different mood in this country from what we had six years ago," said Russian scholar Vyacheslav Nikonov toward the end of Putin's first term. "Everyone was sunk in depression after all the disasters and humiliations of the 1990s. Today there is optimism. The country is moving ahead, and we have things to be proud of again."[3]

But economic growth was not necessarily an inherent characteristic of Putinism. Putin's presidency benefited enormously from the fortuitous rise in the price of oil, especially after 2003. Instead, the characteristics of Putinism in the economy were a mix of enlightened and unenlightened policies. On the enlightened side, one saw an attempt to modernize the Russian economy through integration and trade, particularly with the West and the European Union (EU) in particular. Trade and economic cooperation reached unprecedented levels. Due to increasing oil prices, Russia's economy experienced several years of high growth, even without structural reform. Large cities, such as Moscow, became boomtowns with a growing and affluent middle class.

On the unenlightened side, Russia remained suspicious of too much dependence on foreign trade—witness the rise of the political slogan "food security," which argued that Russia was dangerously dependent on foreign food imports and that protectionist measures were necessary. Russia introduced or maintained protectionist measures in agriculture, banking, insurance, and automobiles. Moreover, there was a definite trend whereby the state became more interventionist and regulatory. Certain sectors of the economy were defined as "strategic" and off-limits to foreigners. And the state muscled its way into controlling interests in the largest oil and gas companies, from which point energy policy became intertwined with foreign policy.[4]

In foreign policy, Putinism was characterized by dualism. On the one hand, the events of September 11, 2001, impelled Putin to move Russia closer to the West and to increase cooperation on issues of shared common interests (nuclear proliferation, terrorism, drug trade). On the other hand, Putinism was defined by more assertive international behavior by Russia, a rejection of what Putin called the "unipolar model," and a drive to increase the international prestige and influence of Moscow.[5]

Having defined some of the core characteristics of Putinism, the question is: to what extent may Medvedev be expected to continue along the basic lines indicated above? We would argue that the probability for continuity is very high, partly for reasons indicated in the Introduction to this book (shared common values and worldviews, and lack of political independence by Medvedev). During the first year of Medvedev's presidency, it would be hard to identify policy areas where Medvedev acted significantly differently than would have Putin.

In addition to policy arenas, there is mind-set. Putin and Medvedev appear to share a mind-set that encompasses domestic politics and foreign policy. Western analysts who expect a softer, more malleable, more "liberal" Russian president are likely to be surprised and disappointed. Indeed, a notable Russian political commentator has written that under Medvedev, "it would be extremely naïve to expect any so-called liberalization or thaw. Dmitri Anatolevich Medvedev's character is much harsher (zhestkii) than that of Vladimir Vladimirovich Putin. Over time the people will, with sadness and warmth, remember Putin in comparison with the strict rule of Medvedev."[6] We explore the argument in more detail below.

When talking about leaders' mind-set we do not necessarily have in mind a coherent ideology; in fact, it may be argued that Putin as president was distinctly nonideological. But mind-set does define an approach to society and toward those who are governed. The mind-set that defines Putinism consists of four main elements: a feeling of insecurity among the top political elite; a distrust of genuine democracy by that elite; a fear of a "color revolution" in Russia; and the threat of domestic instability, whether from domestic terrorism or domestic political opposition. These four elements are mutually reinforcing and explain the incomplete democratization in Russia. In his famous 1946 essay "The Long Telegram," George Kennan reminded U.S. policy makers about Russia's insecurity vis-à-vis the outside world, which predated Soviet rule.[7] Today, that insecurity is no less important and pertains not only to the outside world but also to the leadership's legitimacy to rule Russia. Today, Russia's leaders fear that their legitimacy is thin and they may be replaced if real democracy and democratic processes are allowed. A recognition of the existing mind-set helps us to understand the political actions taken by Putin as president, and the mind-set of Putinism continues under Medvedev today.

For contemporary visitors, Russia does not necessarily look or feel like an authoritarian state. There are numerous bars, cafes, and casinos where Russians and foreigners may interact. Internet cafes abound which provide access to outside information. Russians may purchase or rent foreign DVDs and can subscribe to satellite dish TV to receive BBC news or CNN International.

Cell phones and iPods are common sights on the street and in the metro. There are possibilities for foreign travel for Russians who have the money. Yet, beyond superficiality of consumer affluence, the Medvedev regime is no less undemocratic than was Putin's. That is not to say that the regime is incapable of reform or changing. In the United States, for example, party bosses dominated political parties in the 1950s and essentially controlled the outcomes of national conventions that selected the party's presidential candidate. Today, top-down political domination by party bosses is unimaginable in America; witness the inability of the Democratic Party establishment to get their favorite, Hillary Clinton, nominated, even when it looked as if superdelegates would play the deciding role.[8] Thus, political systems evolve, functions and powers shift, and political change is possible. Medvedev noted in an interview that Russia's democracy is "young" and would change and mature over the next 30–50 years.[9]

In Russia, the forces for democratic change—ushering in real democratization—were not only emasculated under Putin, but Medvedev continues to repress them, perhaps going even further. It is easy for Westerners to forget, or to underestimate, the impact of the 2004 Rose Revolution in Georgia and Orange Revolution in Ukraine on Russia's leaders. These revolutions, which occurred right on Russia's borders, originated from below and led to a change in the political leadership even though authoritarian means were used (not very effectively) to keep political order. Those color revolutions terrified Russia's political elite and appear to have shaped their subsequent behavior.[10] Particularly troubling from the Kremlin's perspective was the Orange Revolution that brought down a semiauthoritarian regime, one backed overtly and covertly by Putin.[11] The fear that the same social forces from below that brought down Presidents Kuchma and Shevardnadze could also topple the leaders in the Kremlin reinforced the preexisting distrust of democracy and the perception that the West preferred a weak and compliant Russia. Because Russian leaders are insecure and must have doubts about the depth of their legitimacy among the population, they tend to see threats and enemies everywhere, both internally and abroad.

Thus, based on a desire for law and order, and due to innate feelings of insecurity, Putin created a regime that may be characterized as "soft authoritarianism" (or, as Richard Sakwa called it, a soft Thermidor).[12] Under Putin, elections and electoral outcomes became managed and foreordained. United Russia as the dominant party—the party of power—was an extension of the Kremlin. Many interest groups became coopted by the government. Opposition parties were marginalized. Opposition leaders were disqualified and removed from electoral ballots. In other words, the common person lost his or her political voice by any meaningful measure. And although means of mass repression were not used, selective repression was used against certain individuals.

Under Medvedev, innate political insecurity, the distrust of democracy, and the fear of domestic political instability have gone farther. Instruments for mass repression are being put in place that may be employed against not just individuals but large numbers of people. The leadership fears that the economic and financial crisis will erode their main tenet of legitimacy— relative prosperity—and translate to political dissent, and that from there, it is a short step to overt mass political opposition. The specter of a revolution is never far from the leaders' minds. Similar to the early Putin, the early Medvedev has spoken out against corruption and stressed the need for a rule of law and the development of democracy. The reality of Putin and Putinism, in contrast to his rhetoric, was that he took the country in quite different directions. It remains to be seen what will happen during Medvedev's tenure, but the early prognosis is not particularly good if one expects Medvedev to live up to his word.

In the political sphere, instruments for mass repression were already quite numerous by the end of the first calendar year that Medvedev was in office. In December 2008, a police crackdown occurred on protests in the Far East over government-imposed protectionist measures against used foreign cars. In mid-December 2008, the government submitted to the State Duma a bill that widened the definition of treason and espionage. Treason would include endangering Russia's constitutional order, sovereignty, and territorial integrity. Espionage would include revealing state secrets to foreign nongovernmental organizations (NGOs).[13] This legislation was backed by Putin and the dominant party in the Duma, the pro-Kremlin United Russia. Human rights advocates criticized the bill as restoring Stalinist norms and labeled the bill as "in the spirit of Stalin and Hitler."[14] The logic of the bill would allow that virtually anyone who has spoken to a foreigner could be declared a traitor. Taken to its extreme, any form of dissent could be considered treason. Moreover, a bill proposed by Medvedev and backed by Putin stipulated that for persons charged with treason or espionage, jury trials would be eliminated and the case would be heard by a panel of three judges, although past experience—for example the Yukos affair—suggests that judges are easily "influenced" by the wishes of the Kremlin and are less than objective arbiters.[15] Moreover, the bill stipulated that if necessary the three-judge panel can be dismissed and replaced by a Special Conference, trying the case in the defendants' absence and barring the right of appeal and any further correspondence.[16] It is easy to see this bill's enormous potential for abuse. After significant criticism arose over its content, Medvedev withdrew the bill on espionage and treason and asked for it to be revised. At the time of this writing, it is not known what those revisions will entail.

Generally speaking, what is remarkable is how former KGB personnel and other leaders with a KGB mind-set—a deep mistrust of democracy, combined with a persecution complex whereby the outside world and particularly the West are inherently hostile to Russia—were successful in lying dormant during the Yeltsin years but were awakened and reenergized when Putin, a former KGB man, came to power. Not so much in Moscow, but in the outlying regions, the KGB mind-set is stronger than ever, and the FSB (Federal Security Service) is more active than in the 1990s. Foreigners who study Russia are considered dangerous and enemies of Russia, as are Russians who have contacts with foreigners. A fear of the West once again pervades the mind-set of Russian leaders.[17] Strong-armed tactics reminiscent of the Soviet-era KGB are still practiced today. Files on foreigners are opened and actively maintained, acquaintances and friends are pressured to become informants, and threats are made against Russians and their families who refuse to cooperate. Any information that is derogatory—or merely revealing—about Russia is considered harmful to national interests. The expression of this mind-set was evident at the end of December 2008 when Aleksandr Bragin was arrested by the Interior Ministry for publishing information that tarnished the region's image. His crime: posting on a website facts about the socioeconomic situation in Ulyanovsk, a city some 900 kilometers east of Moscow on the Volga. His article contained open-source information about unemployment, wage arrears, and inflation.[18]

In the economic sphere, there are also few signs of liberalism. In 2008, Medvedev and Putin (the prime minister is responsible for the economy) introduced additional protectionist measures. For foreign automobiles, new higher tariffs were introduced. In agriculture, quotas for imported meat were reduced in a December 2008 agreement with the United States, dropping from 900,000 tons to about 750,000 tons, thereby modifying downward the meat quota plan for 2009 that had been originally established in 2005.

In late December 2008, a disagreement between Russia and Ukraine reoccurred over price, payment of Ukrainian debt for theft that Russia claimed occurred in the transit process through Ukraine, and transit prices. As a result, in early January 2009 Russia cut off natural gas deliveries to Ukraine.[19] Because several pipelines which deliver gas to the rest of Europe traverse Ukraine, downstream users suffered. Hundreds of thousands of people in Europe were without gas for two weeks, and in Poland, where temperatures dropped to -13 Fahrenheit, ten people froze to death during the first week. Eventually, the EU brokered a deal in which monitors would check the amount of gas entering and leaving Ukraine, although it took several days for Ukraine to sign and for Russia to resume deliveries due to further politicking.[20] Even if Russia had legitimate arguments, the manner in which they dealt with the problem was heavy handed and once again set off concerns over Russia's reliability as an energy supplier to Europe (and in this respect, it remains all the more curious why the European Union has not adopted a common energy policy or a common Russia policy, the absence of which allows Russia to play individual countries off each other).

Russia continued its take-it-or-leave-it position toward accession to the World Trade Organization, an attitude that increased in the wake of the Georgian crisis when "linkage" reappeared in the Western vocabulary that would tie Russian accession to its international behavior. Although Russia had previously met most of the requirements that were set for it, changed its laws, and cracked down on piracy, Medvedev continued the stance that Russia does not need the WTO, and if the WTO wants Russia it will have to be on terms that are favorable to Russia, a continuation of the position Russia adopted in Putin's second term. Joining the WTO was not seen as inherently good in its own right, which is quite a different stance than the one espoused by Putin in 2001.

The economic crisis in Russia created pressures for liberal economics to be "given a temporary holiday." In September 2008, Medvedev spoke in support of a market economy and stated, "We do not need the militarization of the economy or a statist economy."[21] However, in 2008 the Russian stock market dropped 75 percent and tens of billions of dollars of foreign investments exited Russia. The government drew from its reserve funds and expended more than $200 billion in bailout funds by the end of November 2008, but with little beneficial effect. Moreover, the government lost more than $150 billion in its attempt to support the ruble.[22] In the first week of December 2008, Russia became the first G8 country to have its credit rating downgraded, dropping from BBB+ to BBB. In the last week of December 2008, the government expanded the accepted trading range for the ruble (in effect letting it fall against the dollar and euro) in order to stop the hemorrhaging from the government's reserves. Russia was also expected to run a current account deficit in 2009 of about 2.6 percent of GDP for the first time since 1997.[23] These events created pressures to revive the economy. The government accepted collateral in the form of shares from companies receiving bailout loans, in effect temporarily "nationalizing" those companies.[24] If the loans are not repaid, the government becomes the owner, thereby representing movement toward the "statist economy" that Medvedev said he wanted to avoid.

In foreign policy, provoked by Georgia's actions in the disputed regions of South Ossetia and Abkhazia in August 2008, Medvedev ordered the invasion of Georgia and proudly defended Russia's actions.[25] In his state of the nation speech in November 2008, Medvedev referred to Georgia's "barbarous aggression against South Ossetia" and argued that "Georgia's attack on Russian peacekeepers spelt tragedy for many thousands of people."[26] Medvedev again defended his actions in a national interview on December 28 on Russian TV, stating that he "did not hesitate one moment to defend the lives of Russian citizens" living in South Ossetia. Nor did Medvedev show any inclination to back down in his recognition of independence from Georgia for South Ossetia and Abkhazia, even though by the end of 2008 only Belarus and Nicaragua joined Russia in this recognition. Although Washington overreacted to the Georgian crisis, Russia's behavior in Georgia is troubling because it suggests that Russia may have decided "muscular intervention" is a legitimate course of action. Thus, under Putin, commentators noted that Russia was "turning revisionist."[27] But already in the first year of Medvedev's presidency, it appeared that Russia had little faith in existing multilateral institutions because they are perceived to mainly promote the interests of the United States and its European allies.[28] Therefore, Russia seems to have concluded that hard power is the real currency for international relations in the early twenty-first century, and in the future it may act outside of the institutional structures that govern international relations.

During his 2008 tour of Latin America, Medvedev stopped in Cuba and met with Raul Castro, discussing joint projects such as searching for oil in the Gulf of Mexico. Castro termed the relationship with Russia "excellent," and both leaders expressed a willingness to meet in Moscow in early 2009.[29] In late 2008, Russian warships visited Cuba for the first time since the 1991 collapse of communism in Russia.[30] During 2008, Medvedev also met with Hugo Chavez of Venezuela—a notable critic of the United States—and Daniel Ortega of Nicaragua, thereby signaling that it too could play in the backyard of a superpower. Medvedev's actions suggested a desire to broaden ties in Latin America at a time when U.S. policy toward the region seemed adrift.

Thus, in the political, economic, and foreign policy spheres, there was substantial evidence to put to rest any notion that Medvedev was a liberal, closet or otherwise. There was an evident disconnect between Medvedev's political rhetoric, which gave hope to some that he was in fact a democratic reformer, and his actual behavior. Instead, previously dormant Stalinists have reawoken and a Stalinist mind-set has reemerged among political elites—at a time when Russia is not threatened from abroad, and when Russia is more secure and more prosperous than at any time in the past fifty years. The threats that are perceived to exist are largely illusory or self-made.

But what about all the "good" things Medvedev has said that suggest he may be more dedicated to democracy and wants to liberalize society? For example, he has spoken out about the need to combat corruption, to fight against legal nihilism and create a society based on the rule of law, and to advance democratization and political accountability. Each is discussed in turn below.

CORRUPTION

In his November 2008 state of the nation speech, Medvedev repeated a common theme that corruption needs to be eliminated from Russian society.

Stating that "corruption is the number one enemy for a free, democratic and just society," he indicated that a package of reforms was under consideration for the bureaucracy at the federal and regional levels, in the courts, and in municipal governments. These reforms would include a declaration of income and its sources by state and municipal employees, including their families. The accuracy of the information supplied by bureaucrats will be "thoroughly" checked through the use of "intelligence and investigation capabilities." State and municipal employees are expected to "abide by the rules of behavior established at work." Failure to do so "should lead to disciplinary and, if necessary, administrative or criminal liability."[31]

On the one hand, this position is logical and fits within Medvedev's broad goal to modernize the Russian economy and make it more internationally competitive. Endemic corruption is both inefficient and turns away foreign investors, who can take their money elsewhere where registration, licensing, and the operation of a business is less burdensome. On the other hand, many aspects embedded within the structure of Russian society are susceptible to corruption, aspects that affect everyday lives. As the state has increased intervention in the economy and erected additional bureaucratic hoops for individuals and businesses to jump through, the opportunity for corruption has grown. Thus, it is not just low incomes that "cause" bureaucratic officials to accept bribes—as is commonly asserted by top government officials—but also the omnipresent opportunities for corruption and the fact that corruption (bribes) offer a way to circumvent a cumbersome and unresponsive bureaucracy.

For example, when a land plot is to be bought or sold, the local government has the right of first refusal. But there is ample anecdotal evidence that a buyer or seller can bribe the relevant land official in order to receive a more favorable price or to obtain a desired piece of land. Or take the example of a young couple that wants land or a housing allocation in a rural village. The state's social program is designed to keep young people in the countryside by providing housing, although demand for housing exceeds supply. It used to be that a couple would apply for land for housing, and the application would be fulfilled in the order that the application was received. However, the housing code was amended a few years ago and now allocates village land according to auction. Young couples often do not have sufficient monetary resources to win in an open auction, and thus their choices are to "influence" the outcome of the auction, continue to live with relatives, or leave for another location. Anecdotal evidence suggests that often the "winners" of auctions are the children of local officials; common people are disenfranchised.

Corruption and the size of the state bureaucracy go hand in hand. Unless the state bureaucracy is substantially reduced, and opportunities reduced, it is hard to see how Medvedev's words will be anything more than political rhetoric. The main point is that unless a top-to-bottom reform of existing laws and practices were to occur—leading to a significant reduction of the bureaucracy from economic regulation and oversight—the battle against corruption is doomed from the start. And what are the prospects for such a top-to-bottom overhaul? Remote at best.

RULE OF LAW

In a March 2008 interview, the first after his election, Medvedev offered his thoughts on a society based on the rule of law and the elimination of what he called legal nihilism. He stated: "Russia is a country where people don't like to observe the law. It is, as they say, a country of legal nihilism." Medvedev's goal is to embed the rule of law in Russian society, and he offered a three-point plan. First is the need to assert the law's supremacy over executive power and individual actions. Second is the need to create "a new attitude toward the law." As Medvedev argued, "We need to make sure that every citizen understands . . . the necessity and desirability of observing the law." Third is the need to "create an effective courts system, above all by assuring independence of the judiciary."[32] This latter point supported an earlier statement made at the beginning of December 2008 about the need to make courts more independent, including steps to protect judges from outside pressure and give them better training.[33]

If realized, these steps would represent a significant departure from Putin's "dictatorship of laws," which emphasized more of the former and less of the latter, or so argue critics. But while Medvedev is surely correct that a law-based system is needed for the "normal development" of the state and society, one wonders what his real priorities are. His emphasis is on compliance by citizens with state laws, but with the political trends described above—for example the new bill on treason and espionage—questions arise as to whether Medvedev has in mind a truly democratic society or merely a compliant one. If the laws restrict freedoms that some believe are inherent to democracy, for instance the right to demonstrate and protest (freedom of speech), are people bound to obey? His comments about an independent court system likewise seem anomalous, given the bill he sponsored that allows for the removal of judges and use of a state-appointed Special Conference in cases involving treason and espionage. Further, Medvedev appears disingenuous when he rejects reviewing the case against Khodorkovsky or pardoning him on the grounds that "no one should interfere" with the courts.[34] Thus, even though Medvedev gives lip-service to limited executive powers through law, it is fair to ask how much is political rhetoric and how much is reality.[35]

DEVELOPMENT OF DEMOCRACY

Medvedev has expressed support for the development of democracy and for a system with more political accountability in Russia. In his December 2008 interview, he stated: "I am a supporter of the values of democracy in the form that humanity has developed them over the last few centuries. My definition of democracy as the power of the people is in no way different from classical definitions that exist in all countries."[36] He also expressed confidence that Russia could develop along the lines of other countries that have chosen "the democratic path."

In this regard, it is useful to differentiate his words from action. There is little behavioral evidence to suggest that Medvedev does not support or does not adhere to the basic conception of democracy that existed in Putinism. And Putin, it should be remembered, at one time commented that Russia "will decide for itself how to ensure that the principles of freedom and democracy are implemented, *taking into account its historical, geographical and other characteristics.*"[37] In short, Putin docs *not* believe Russia should import a Western-style democratic system. Indeed, Putin openly expressed his doubts about the applicability of the Western experience in Russia in his millennium speech in January 2000:

> It will not happen soon, if it ever happens at all, that Russia will become the second edition of say, the U.S. or Britain in which liberal values have deep historic traditions. Our state and its institutions have always played an exceptionally important role in the life of the country and its people. For Russians a strong state is not an anomaly that should be gotten rid of. Quite the contrary, they see it as a source and guarantor of order and the initiator and main driving force of any change.[38]

Rhetoric aside, Medvedev's actions are highly suggestive of his real conception of democracy. Medvedev not only participated in, but also did not speak out against, the sham presidential election in March 2008 that was in essence a transfer of power by appointment. In this election, which was a clear expression of managed democracy, the opposition candidates had no chance to win and in certain instances were overtly repressed (e.g., Kasparov). The Kremlin stage-managed the electoral process and mobilized the population to validate the outcome. As one Moscow journalist, Sergei Strokan, remarked, "Putin could have nominated his dog, and it would be duly elected and inaugurated as president."[39] In other words, Medvedev directly benefited from the faux democracy that characterizes Russia's electoral politics.

Medvedev appears to be no less a law and order man than was Putin, and he sees the role of the population to be compliant and law abiding, no matter what the content of the law. Medvedev talks about political accountability of the executive to the legislature, but this is empty rhetoric when the legislature is dominated and controlled by a pro-Kremlin party. And in the case of the upper house, the Kremlin has significant influence over the selection process and composition. Finally, as noted above, the aforementioned bill on treason and espionage backed by Medvedev is perhaps the strongest insight into the mind-set of Medvedev as leader and his values. In this regard, he appears to be no less insecure and no less distrustful of real democratic processes than was his predecessor, and as equally fearful of domestic instability.

Which leaves us with the question: how stable is Russia? What is its political future? There is no absolute answer because Russia remains a country of contradictions, and predicting Russia's future is always a tricky proposition. But what can be said is the following. On the one hand, a number of elements augur for stability. (1) The Russian population is patient and unlikely to revolt over economic problems or reductions in their standard of living. After all, they endured a depression in the 1990s without political upheaval. (2) Political opposition does not have nationally recognized leadership; political opposition has been marginalized, is fragmented, lacks a compelling and coherent ideology, and has been effectively repressed. (3) There is no evidence by the ruling leadership of a loss of will to rule or use repression, as was seen among communist leaders in Eastern Europe in 1989–1990; the Medvedev-Putin regime appears able to self-perpetuate. (4) Although Russia's rate of economic growth will decline, overall Russia should continue to experience positive economic growth, and sooner or later the price of oil will rebound as the world economy recovers, which will lead to renewed revenue flows for the Russian government. (5) The Russian people are not restive, and there is little to suggest that Russia is ripe for a color revolution or collapse.

On the other hand, various elements augur for instability. (1) The bulwark of stability and regime legitimacy under Putin was economic growth, and with reduced growth or even contraction in the short-term future, it is unknown how the people will react. (2) The innate insecurity of the leadership and its fear of a revolution may lead it to overreact to a future situation that in turn will mobilize and galvanize political opposition. (3) The political leadership is increasingly out of touch with the population, and the population is increasingly alienated from the leadership.[40] In addition, political parties do not fulfill the normal functions played by parties, which may exacerbate frustrated expectations and disenchantment with the regime. (4) The political system remains characterized by massive corruption; income stratification continues to widen at a time when an increasing number of people are concerned with rising unemployment and fear for their job security. (5) Although largely apolitical, the population is less accepting of censorship, whereas the regime increasingly stifles the right to know, has more suspicion of knowledge, and has a predisposition to suppress information about Russia that may be embarrassing. (6) The political system remains largely dependent on one person, but as Lilia Shevtsova argues, Russia is too big, and one person cannot possibly do everything.[41] In a system that is leader-dependent, if leadership falters for whatever reason, Russia becomes rudderless.

What then does the future hold? Based on the essays in this book and the argument presented here, it is clear that Russia's recent past has been imperfect, and its future is uncertain.

NOTES

1. Ian McAllister and Stephen White, "'It's the Economy, Comrade!' Parties and Voters in the 2007 Russian Duma Election," *Europe-Asia Studies* 60, no. 6 (2008): 931–57.

2. See Pekka Sutela, "Economic Growth Remains Surprisingly High," *Russian Analytical Digest*, no. 38 (April 2, 2008): 2–6, plus accompanying statistical tables, in particular macroeconomic indicators on 6. And in the same issue, see Philip Hanson, "How Sustainable is Russia's Energy Power?" 8–12.

3. Vitali Tretyakov as quoted in "Why Russians Look to Putin," *Christian Science Monitor*, February 20, 2004.

4. Marshall I. Goldman, *Petrostate: Putin, Power, and the New Russia* (Oxford: Oxford University Press, 2008).

5. On the rejection of the unipolar model—by which Putin was indicting U.S. hegemony—see his speech in Munich on February 10, 2007, "Speech at the Munich Conference on Security Policy," *Johnson's Russia List*, no. 33 (February 11, 2007).

6. Vladim Solov'ev, *Putin: Putevoditel' dlia neravnodushnykh*, 2nd ed. (Moscow: Eksmo, 2008), 401.

7. See Kenneth M. Jensen, ed., *Origins of the Cold War: The Novikov, Kennan, and Roberts 'Long Telegrams' of 1946* (Washington, D.C.: U.S. Institute of Peace, 1991), 17–31.

8. See Gil Troy, "Bury the Hatchet," *Wilson Quarterly* 32, no. 4 (2008): 64.

9. Nikolai Svanidze and Marina Svanidze, *Medvedev* (St. Petersburg: Amfora, 2008), 19.

10. See Mikhail Deliagin, *Rossiia posle Putina: Neizbezhna li Rossii 'oranzhevo-zelenaia' revoliutsiia?* (Moscow: Veche, 2005).

11. See Anders Aslund and Michael McFaul, *Revolution in Orange: The Origins of Ukraine's Democratic Breakthrough* (Washington, D.C.: Carnegie Endowment for Peace, 2006).

12. Some may disagree that Putin's authoritarianism was indeed soft. But there is no doubt that only an insecure regime would emasculate the political voice of the people and adopt repressive tactics against internal "enemies" who in fact did little more than represent peaceful political opposition.

13. "Betraying the Motherland," *Radio Free Europe/Radio Liberty* (*RFE/RL*), December 16, 2008, www.rferl.org.

14. "Rights-Watchers Say New Russian Treason Legislation Harkens Back to the '30s Terror," *RFE/RL*, December 18, 2008, www.rferl.org.

15. On the lack of judges' independence, see Solov'ev, *Putin*, 402–11. The types of cases that would not be heard by a jury include terrorism, hostage taking, the organization of illegal armed forces, mass disturbances, treason, espionage, sedition, armed rebellion, and sabotage.

16. See "Russia's Judicial Counter-Reformation," *RFE/RL*, January 7, 2009, www.rferl.org.

17. See the chapter by Andrei P. Tsygankov in this book.

18. "Russian Opposition Figure Detained over Crisis Article," *RFE/RL*, December 30, 2008, www.rferl.org.

19. Russia also cut off gas supplies to Ukraine in the winter of 2005–2006 and winter of 2006–2007. This time it was different because the cutoff was ordered by Prime Minister Putin, not the head of Gazprom, which suggested that the cutoff may have been motivated by foreign policy goals—to further weaken Ukraine as it struggled through its own financial and economic crisis and to punish it for its pro-Western orientation.

20. It is interesting to note that the Russian portrayal of the situation differed significantly from the version published in the West. Russia accused Ukraine of imposing a "gas blockade" against Russian deliveries to Europe, in effect refusing to allow transit of Russian gas through Ukraine. See ITAR-TASS, January 10, 2009, www.itar-tass.com. See also the coverage in *Johnson's Russia List*, no. 7 (January 12, 2009), and no. 8 (January 13, 2009). Medvedev suggested that Ukraine's actions to block Russian gas from reaching Europe may be orchestrated by outside forces, implicitly suggesting involvement by the United States.

21. *Financial Times*, November 26, 2008, 3.

22. *Financial Times*, November 29–30, 2008, 17.

23. *Financial Times*, December 9, 2008, 1.

24. *Financial Times*, November 26, 2008, 3.

25. Much is not clear about the August 2008 events. While early world opinion put the onus on Russia, as time went on it became clear that Georgian President Saakashvili struck first and badly miscalculated the Russian response. The significant fact is that Russia responded by invading—it sent troops into Georgia and subsequently kept its troops there in the disputed regions of South Ossetia and Abkhazia after recognizing their independence. Russia was unhappy with the pro-Western regime in Georgia and its movement toward NATO membership, but that did not instigate the introduction of Russian troops into Georgia. See Stephen Sestanovich, "What Has Moscow Done?" *Foreign Affairs* 87, no. 6 (2008): 12–28.

26. "Russian President Medvedev's First Annual Address to Parliament," *Johnson's Russia List*, no. 202 (November 6, 2008).

27. Dmitri Trenin, "Russia's Strategic Choices," *Carnegie Endowment for International Peace Policy Brief*, no. 50 (May 2007): 1.

28. See Charles King, "The Five Day War," *Foreign Affairs* 87, no. 6 (2008): 2–11.

29. *Financial Times*, December 1, 2008, 7.

30. *Moscow News Weekly*, December 19–25, 2008, 2.

31. "Russian President Medvedev's First Annual Address to Parliament."

32. "Laying Down the Law: Medvedev Vows War on Russia's 'Legal Nihilism,'" *Johnson's Russia List*, no. 233 (December 26, 2008).

33. "Laying Down the Law."

34. "Laying Down the Law."

35. For example, Medvedev stated: "The only way that Russia can count on having the supremacy of the law is in a situation where the powers-that-be respect the independence of courts and judges." "Laying Down the Law."

36. "Laying Down the Law."

37. See Putin's state of the nation speech in *Johnson's Russia List*, no. 9130 (April 25, 2005).

38. Vladimir Putin, "Russia at the Turn of the Millennium," government.gov.ru/english/statVP_engl_1.html.

39. "In These Times," *Johnson's Russia List*, no. 82 (April 28, 2008).

40. "Signs of a Kremlin Fearful of Unrest," *Moscow Times*, December 12, 2008, www.themoscowtimes.com.

41. Lilia Shevtsova, *Putin's Russia* (Washington, D.C.: Carnegie Endowment for Peace, 2003), chap. 9.

Index

Note: Page numbers in *italics* indicate a figure or table.

About the Contributors

Gregory Gleason, professor of political science at the University of New Mexico, has taught international relations since joining the university in 1988. Gleason is the author of *Federalism and Nationalism* (1991), *Central Asian States* (1997), and *Markets and Politics in Central Asia* (2003), as well as many scholarly articles. He has served as a consultant to Lawrence Livermore National Laboratory, Sandia National Laboratories, the Asian Development Bank, and the U.S. Agency for International Development. His research has been sponsored by the National Science Foundation and the National Academy of Sciences as well as other public and private foundations. While on leave from the University of New Mexico, Gleason served at the George C. Marshall European Center for Security Studies, where he authored the contribution for this book.

Timothy Heleniak is in the Department of Geography at the University of Maryland. He has researched and written extensively on demographic trends, migration, and regional development in Russia and the other countries of the former Soviet Union. He previously worked at the U.S. Census Bureau, the World Bank, and UNICEF and is currently researching migration and regional development in Russia's Arctic and northern regions with support from a National Science Foundation grant.

Kathryn Hendley is the William Voss-Bascom Professor of Law and Political Science at the University of Wisconsin, Madison. Her research focuses on legal and economic reform in the former Soviet Union and on how law is actually experienced and used by economic actors in Russia. Her research has been supported by grants from the National Science Foundation, the Social Science Research Council, the National Council for Eurasian and East European Research, and the International Research and Exchanges Board. She has been a visiting fellow at the Woodrow Wilson Center and the Kellogg Institute for International Affairs at Notre Dame University. She has published widely in journals such as *Post-Soviet Affairs*, *Law and Social Inquiry*, and the *American Journal of Comparative Law*.

Dale R. Herspring, University Distinguished Professor of Political Science at Kansas State University, is a member of the Council on Foreign Relations. He is the author of twelve books and more than eighty articles dealing with Russian/Soviet, U.S., German, and Polish national security affairs. His most recent books include *The Kremlin and the High Command: Presidential Impact on the Russian Military from Gorbachev to Putin* (2006) and *Rumsfeld's Wars: The Arrogance of Power* (2008).

Maria Lipman is the editor of *Pro et Contra*, a policy journal published by Carnegie Moscow Center. She has also been a deputy editor of two Russian newsweekly magazines and was a co-founder and deputy editor of *Itogi*, the first news weekly magazine in Russia. *Itogi*, published in cooperation with *Newsweek*, was part of Russia's first privately owned media group Media-Most, destroyed by the Russian government in 2001. Lipman co-founded the newsweekly *Ezhenedel'ny Zhurnal*, which had the same editor as *Itogi* and mostly the same team of journalists. Since 2001, Lipman has written an op-ed column on Russian politics, media, and society for the *Washington Post*. She also has contributed to several Russian and U.S. publications and has been featured as an expert on a range of international broadcast media. She holds an M.A. from Moscow State University.

Michael McFaul is professor of political science at Stanford University, a Peter and Helen Bing Senior Fellow at the Hoover Institution, and a senior associate at the Carnegie Endowment for Peace. He has written extensively on political reform, democratization, federalism, elections, and other topics regarding post-Soviet Russia. He is the author of *Between Dictatorship and Democracy: Russian Post-Communist Political Reform* (2004), with Nikolai Petrov and Andrei Ryabov; *Power and Purpose: American Policy toward Russia after the Cold War* (2003), with James Goldgeier; and *Popular Choice and Managed Democracy: The Russian Elections of 1999 and 2000* (2003), with Timothy Colton.

Nikolai Petrov is a scholar in residence at the Carnegie Moscow Center, where he directs the Society and Regions project. He also heads the Center for Political-Geographic Research. Petrov is a columnist for the *Moscow Times*, a member of the Program on New Approaches to Russian Security (PONARS), and a member of the scientific board of the *Journal of Power Institutions in Post-Soviet Societies*. During 1990–1995, he served as an advisor to the Russian parliament, government, and presidential administration. He is the author or editor of numerous publications dealing with analysis of Russia's political regime, post-Soviet transformation, socioeconomic and political development of Russia's regions, democratization, federalism, and elections, among other topics. His works include the three-volume *1997 Political Almanac of Russia* and the annual supplements to it. He is the co-author of *Between Dictatorship and Democracy: Russian Post-communist Political Reform* (2004) and *The Dynamics of Russian Politics: Putin's Reform of Federal-Regional Relations* in two volumes (2004, 2005).

Thomas F. Remington is the Goodrich C. White Professor of Political Science at Emory University. He is the author of numerous books and articles on Russian legislative institutions and legislative-executive relations. His books include *The Russian Parliament: Institutional Evolution in a Transitional Regime, 1989–1999* (2001) and, with Steven S. Smith, *The Politics of Institutional Choice: Formation of the Russian State Duma* (2001).

Peter Rutland is the Colin and Nancy Campbell Professor in Global Issues and Democratic Thought at Wesleyan University in Middletown, Connecticut, and an associate of the Davis Center for Russian and Eurasian Studies at Harvard University. He is the author of *The Myth of the Plan* (1984) and *The Politics of Economic Stagnation in the Soviet Union* (1992), and editor of half a dozen books, including *Business and the State in Russia* (2001). He has been a visiting professor at the European University of St. Petersburg and Sophia University in Tokyo.

Richard Sakwa, professor of Russian and European politics at the University of Kent at Canterbury, has published widely on Soviet, Russian, and post-communist affairs. Recent books include *Postcommunism* (1999); *Contextualising Secession: Normative Aspects of Secession Struggles* (2003), co-edited with Bruno Coppieters; the edited volume *Chechnya: From Past to Future* (2005); *Russian Politics and Society* (2008); and *Putin: Russia's Choice* (2008). His most recent book is *The Quality of Freedom: Khodorkovsky, Putin, and the Yukos Affair* (2009).

Louise Shelley is professor at the School of Public Policy and the founder and director of the Terrorism, Transnational Crime, and Corruption Center. She is presently completing a book on human smuggling and trafficking that is under contract with Cambridge University Press. She has written *Policing Soviet Society* (1996), *Lawyers in Soviet Worklife* (1984), and *Crime and Modernization* (1981), as well as numerous articles and book chapters on all aspects of transnational crime and corruption. Shelley has collaborated with Russian scholars for more than a dozen years on issues of organized crime through centers that she has helped to establish and support throughout Russia.

Darrell Slider is professor of government and international affairs at the University of South Florida. He has received numerous awards and authored more than thirty-five articles, primarily concerning regional and local politics in Russia and other countries of the former Soviet Union.

Andrei P. Tsygankov is professor in the Department of Political Science and International Relations at San Francisco State University. A native Russian, he is the author of *Russia's Foreign Policy: Change and Continuity in National Identity* (2006) and *Whose World Order? Russia's Perception of American Ideas after the Cold War* (2004). His latest book is *Russophobia: The Anti-Russian Lobby and American Foreign Policy* (2009).

Stephen K. Wegren, professor of political science at Southern Methodist University, is the author or co-author of several books and more than one hundred articles and book chapters on the political economy of rural reform in postcommunist nations. His work has been supported by the Social Science Research Council, the National Council for Eurasian and East European Research, the Ford Foundation, and the International Research and Exchanges Board. His most recent book is *Land Reform in Russia: Institutional Design and Behavioral Responses* (2009).